MW01248783

ALI(

THE COLOR PURPLE

DIALOGUE
5

Edited by

Michael J. Meyer

ALICE WALKER'S
THE COLOR PURPLE

Edited by
Kheven LaGrone

Amsterdam - New York, NY 2009

Cover Design: Pier Post

Cover art: Renata E. Gray
Model: TaSin Sabir
Photography: Kheven LaGrone

The paper on which this book is printed meets the requirements of "ISO 9706:1994, Information and documentation - Paper for documents - Requirements for permanence".

ISBN: 978-90-420-2544-8
©Editions Rodopi B.V., Amsterdam - New York, NY 2009
Printed in the Netherlands

Table of Contents

General Editor's Preface

The original concept for Rodopi's new series entitled *Dialogue* grew out of two very personal experiences of the general editor. In 1985, having just finished my dissertation on John Steinbeck and attained my doctoral degree, I was surprised to receive an invitation from Steinbeck biographer, Jackson J. Benson, to submit an essay for a book he was working on. I was unpublished at the time and was unsure and hesitant about my writing talent, but I realized that I had nothing to lose. It was truly the "opportunity of a lifetime." I revised and shortened a chapter of my dissertation on Steinbeck's *The Pearl* and sent it off to California. Two months later, I was pleasantly surprised to find out that my essay had been accepted and would appear in Duke University Press's *The Short Novels of John Steinbeck* (1990).

Surprisingly, my good fortune continued when several months after the book appeared, Tetsumaro Hayashi, a renowned Steinbeck scholar, asked me to serve as one of the three assistant editors of *The Steinbeck Quarterly,* then being published at Ball State University. Quite naïve at the time about publishing, I did not realize how fortunate I had been to have such opportunities present themselves without any struggle on my part to attain them. After finding my writing voice and editing several volumes on my own, I discovered in 2002 that despite my positive experiences, there was a real prejudice against newer "emerging" scholars when it came to inclusion in collections or acceptance in journals.

As the designated editor of a Steinbeck centenary collection, I found myself roundly questioned about the essays I had chosen for inclusion in the book. Specifically, I was asked why I had not selected several prestigious names whose recognition power would have spurred the book's success on the market. My choices of lesser-known but quality essays seemed unacceptable to those who ran the conference which produced the potential entries in the book. New voices were unwelcome; it was the tried and true that were greeted with open arms. Yet these experienced scholars had no need for further publications and often offered few original insights into the Steinbeck canon. Sadly, the originality of the lesser-known essayists met with hostility; the doors were closed, perhaps even locked tight, against their innovative approaches and readings that took issue with scholars whose authority and expertise had long been unquestioned.

Angered, I withdrew as editor of the volume, and began to think of ways to rectify what I considered a serious flaw in académe. My goal was to open discussions between experienced scholars and those who were just beginning their academic careers and had not yet broken through the publication barriers. Dialogue would be fostered rather than discouraged.

Having previously served as an editor for several volumes in Rodopi's Perspective of Modern Literature series under the general editorship of David Bevan, I sent a proposal to Fred Van der Zee advocating a new series that would be entitled Dialogue, one that would examine the controversies within classic canonical texts and would emphasize an interchange between established voices and those whose ideas had never reached the academic community because their names were unknown. Happily, the press was willing to give the concept a try and gave me a wide scope in determining not only the texts to be covered but also in deciding who would edit the individual volumes.

When Kheven LaGrone proposed a volume on Alice Walker's *The Color Purple,* I encouraged him to pursue a call for papers. The resulting essays address many of the issues that caused the novel to be such a controversial text; the abrupt change in narrative voice, the frank addressing of lesbian desire and sexual abuse, the blunt criticism of the insensitive black males all were features that made its selection for the 1983 Pulitzer Prize a very unpopular choice. In this volume's pages, such issues are not avoided but are addressed skillfully by authors with a variety of publication histories, some experienced, some neophytes. All are committed to a discussion of what earlier reviewers had determined were pluses and minuses of *The Color Purple*'s characters and plot and to addressing elements in Walker's stylistics and themes that were seen as flaws. As you will see, some of authors break fertile new ground in the process, and offer approaches that will help readers see the novel from several new angles.

This volume on *The Color Purple* will soon be followed by a volume on Laura Esquivel's *Like Water For Chocolate,* and one on

Sandra Cisneros' *Woman Hollering Creek*. It is my hope that as each title appears, the Dialogue series will foster not only renewed interest in each of the chosen works but that each will bring forth fresh interpretations and will open doors to heretofore silenced voices. In this atmosphere, a healthy interchange of criticism can develop, one that will allow even dissent and opposite viewpoints to be expressed without fear that such stances may be seen as negative or counter-productive.

My thanks to Rodopi and its editorial board for its support of this "radical" concept. May you, the reader, discover much to value in these new approaches to issues that have fascinated readers for decades and to books that have long stimulated our imaginations and our critical discourse.

Michael J. Meyer
2009

Introduction:
To Follow the Hero's Journey

Kheven LaGrone

Over twenty years ago, when I first read Alice Walker's Pulitzer Prize-winning novel, *The Color Purple,* I thought it was a wonderful story about personal transformation and empowerment. Celie was at the "bottom" of America's social caste: She was ugly, not pretty; she was black, not white; she was female, not male; she was poor, not rich; she was bisexual/lesbian, not heterosexual; she was dark-skinned, not light-skinned; she was uneducated, not educated. Her story illustrated how being passive about a negative condition creates victimhood. Her example showed that by fighting back against adversity, one can simultaneously examine identity, discover selfhood, and free the spirit from the bondage of oppressive. The book became my anthem and my inspiration.

Unfortunately, some called the story maudlin. It seems that they felt the controversial topics, like rape, incest and lesbianism, were mere titillation for an otherwise empty story. Some said the story was poorly crafted and that Celie's victimhood was too extreme and taken too far, that her transformation was too fantastical to be believed. Others felt the ending was unrealistic and that the story required too much "willingness to suspend disbelief" in order to make it readable. Black women and men alike were offended by the imagery of monstrous black masculinity—especially since the story received so much international attention.

Media and literary attacks on Alice Walker and *The Color Purple* became personal. In her autobiography, *The Same River Twice: Honoring the Difficult*, Alice Walker wrote that many critics of *The Color Purple* accused her of hating Black men and of attacking the Black family—accusations she denounced and rejected in her autobiography (22).

Despite these objections, on April 18, 1983, Alice Walker became the first Black woman to win a Pulitzer Prize in fiction, and a short time later *The Color Purple* also won the 1983 American Book Award in Fiction.

* * *

Even though Alice Walker wrote in her autobiography that she was bisexual and Celie was a lesbian (35), Celie's story was in direct contrast to the many white gay male coming out stories that mourned the loss of white male entitlement and privilege. For example, in his autobiography *Straight from the Heart: A Love Story*, white gay model and bodybuilder Rod Jackson wrote:

> "I had people convinced that I was this all-American kid, yet I was always afraid that somebody was going to discover who I really was.
>
> "If I'd been non-gay and born into my family looking the way I look, I would have been your typical arrogant high school jock." (p. 63)

Jackson testified that since he grew up as a white male, his inherently comfortable place on America's social ladder was never questioned. Even though he secretly felt "different," his society only saw him as "all-American." As a white male, this was his entitlement. Additionally, he realized that his good looks privileged arrogance and fostered condescension. Clearly, his homosexual preference made him keenly aware of the entitlements he had taken for granted all his life.

Yet Jackson didn't name his whiteness or the white skinned privilege. He saw his whiteness as the norm, the desirable, the all-American. Part of the power of whiteness in America is not naming itself and assuming it is the norm—even claiming to be the "universal" or "colorblind." It decides what racial issues and whose "victimhood" are to be discussed and which ones are to be downplayed. Unfortunately, whiteness, and its position in the American hierarchy, is not critiqued or interrogated. Thus, much of the controversy over *The Color Purple* focused on the abuse of Celie by black men. Consequently, the white American racism that segregated her and separated her from "their" world was overshadowed by the critical emphasis on black male abuse. For example, little attention was given to the white male mayor's physical attack of Sofia and even less attention has been given to continual spiritual rape and emotional abuse of Sofia by the mayor's wife (a white woman). Before the attack, Sofia had been proud and empowered—an unchallenged entitlement. The mayor's actions changed that; his assault affected Sofia both physically and spiritually, and later his wife continued the abuse. Further indication of critical misdirection is the fact that few of the debates around *The Color Purple* focused on the emotional rape and abuse of Sofia's children by watching this occur. Critics ignored the fact that they would learn disempowerment and discover "their" low places on America's social ladder by watching their mother's inability to win in a white society. In contrast to Rod Jackson, these black children would never be good-looking white men anxious about falling off their high place on America's social ladder.

* * *

Some of the controversy caused by *The Color Purple* reflected a time less enlightened than today. For example, in a letter to the editor, writer Ishmael Reed wrote that the novel "promotes the point of view, embraced by a minority within the feminist movement, that lesbian love is a panacea for . . . what they feel to be the inevitable unhappiness caused by heterosexual relationships." Later in the letter, Reed wrote:

> Perhaps Ms. Walker's bleak view of heterosexual relationships stems from her contention that black men are 'evil,' a term applied to this class of persons in a letter Ms. Walker wrote to *The New York Times Magazine* section, following the publication of an interview of Ms. Walker by writer David Bradley.

Later in the letter, Reed deplored:

> Ms. Walker's shrill attempt to boycott black male writers whose female characters don't adhere to her notion of what an ideal female character should be [. . .] presumably a tortured, neurotic, unhappy, hateful person, full of hostility towards people whose only crime is that they were born male.

Mr. Reed's letter showed his ignorance of homosexuality and demonstrated a misreading of the role of homosexuality in the story. Since Celie was sexually aroused when she first saw Shug (*The Color Purple* 49), one must consider that Celie's lack of sexual interest in her husband might have also been because, repressed or not, she craved sex with another woman. As a heterosexual male writer in the 1980s, Mr. Reed unfortunately seems to be unaware of the fact that lesbian sexual feelings may not simply be a reaction to men. One wonders if he would read the story differently today.[1]

However, some of the criticism of Walker's Black male bashing may have been well-founded. Some Black men who read the novel did feel vilified. For example, in the *New York Times* interview referred to by Mr. Reed, David Bradley, who had met Walker and had spent time with her, wrote that her writings were troubling because they suggested that the author had "a high level of enmity toward black men" (34). He also wrote:

> [S]ome of the "hurtful" criticism is demonstrably true: Black men in Alice Walker's fiction and poetry seem capable of goodness only when they become old like Grange Copeland, or paralyzed and feminized, like Truman Head. If they are not thus rendered symbolically impotent, they are figures of malevolence. (34)

Later, in the article, Bradley quotes Walker's writing that her brothers and father had failed to "give me male models I could respect" (34).

Obviously, each of us brings our personal experiences into our reading of a novel. After reading the accusations that *The Color Purple* bashed Black men, I discussed those accusations with a friend back in the early 80s. Since I had never known a physically abusive male-female relationship while growing up, I (perhaps naively) argued *The Color Purple* was just fiction and did not reflect Walker's perspective on reality. My friend disagreed. He argued that the Black men in the book reflected the men that he had grown up with. He said that he liked the book because, to him, it told the truth.

Similarly, white feminist Gloria Steinem, in her profile of Alice Walker, described *The Color Purple* as "dead-honest" (89). Yet I wonder if Ms. Walker's rendering of Black masculinity/Black fatherhood reflects most Black women artists? While serving as the curator/founder for the show "BABA: Black Artists' Expressions of Father" in 2006 in San Francisco and in 2007 for the International Fatherhood Conference and in New York City in 2008, I noticed that there were subthemes—the strongest being Black women artists who had been "daddy's girls" and adored their fathers. They were happy to be in the show as a tribute to their fathers. To them, fathers were loving and protective. For these Black women artists, fatherhood was love and protection. Women eagerly participated in the show because they said that they wanted to create positive images of Black men to counter the negative images in the media. They too, resented seeing Black men being vilified. Doll maker Karen Henderson said, "I'm excited about being in the show because this is the first opportunity

I've had to do a piece on what father means to me. I want to show my appreciation to all fathers. I am touched by this experience."

Clearly, Celie was no daddy's girl. Based on her description of her father, Walker was not one either. But I began to question how much of the popularity of *The Color Purple* was due to the vilification of black masculinity? And I wondered if *The Color Purple*—with its controversial themes of rape, illiteracy, poverty, physical abuse, pure victimhood, etc.—had not been based on an African American, would it have been so well-received? I concluded that the significance of *The Color Purple* in Western literature should be discussed using Nobel Prize-winning writer, Toni Morrison's theory on the African American presence in American literature. In her book *Playing in the Dark: Whiteness and the Literary Imagination,* she wrote:

> As a disabling virus within literary discourse, Africanism has become, in the Eurocentric tradition that American education favors, both a way of talking about and a way of policing matters of class, sexual license, and repression, formations and exercises of power, and meditations on ethics and accountability [. . .] It provides a way of contemplating chaos and civilization, desire and fear, and a mechanism for testing the problems and blessings of freedom. (7)

                                       * * *

Clearly, the story of *The Color Purple* continues the African American presence in American entertainment. In a September 2000 essay titled, "From Minstrelsy to Gangsta Rap: The Nigger as Commodity for Popular American Entertainment," I argued that throughout American history, the violent nigger has been the most popular commodity in American entertainment. The nigger theme of minstrel shows is a tradition which continues in today's "gangsta rap." Not surprisingly, the nigger in American entertainment must have its female counterpart to demean. Therefore, in "gangsta rap," the black woman was rendered as the bitch and ho. Ironically, the poor, unattractive African American women of today's rap music seem to mirror the Celie that Alice Walker was defending and giving voice to in *The Color Purple* just a few years earlier. Walker, like gangsta rappers, sold the "nigger" or violent Black male. However, Walker, in *The Color Purple,* reversed the emphases on black and white conflict; instead the victim of the violent black male and hero is a Black woman.

"Pioneering" gangsta rappers Niggas With Attitude (N. W. A.) argued that their work was meant to heal their "people" or "community"—not to antagonize or belittle them. Within two weeks

of its release and with no commercial radio play, N. W. A's album
NIGGAZ4LIFE, was the fastest-selling album in the country
("Number One With a Bullet"). The liner notes of their 1996 *N. W.
A's Greatest Hits* CD read:

> [. . .] the group changed the face of hip-hop. While many might
> accuse them of being responsible for half the violent sentiments
> and misogyny expressed in rap nowadays, they liberated the art
> form by showing that a black artist could express any viewpoint,
> even if the government worked against it, and still reach the
> people in black and white communities around the world. If
> anything, songs like "Fuck Tha Police," and "Gangsta Gangsta"
> were the Hardcore Hip-Hop Nation's Declaration of
> Independence and Bill of Rights . . . at a time when young black
> urban males didn't have a voice that could express their anger and
> frustration with a system that clearly didn't give a damn about
> them.

Walker also has argued that she had a similar intent to use her
art to liberate. She wrote in the preface of her autobiography:

> I belong to a people so wounded by betrayal, so hurt by
> misplacing their trust, that to offer us a gift of love is often to risk
> one's life, certainly one's name and reputation . . .
>   I belong to a people, heart and mind, who do not trust
> mirrors. Not those, in any case, in which we ourselves appear.
> The empty mirror, the one that reflects noses and hair unlike or
> own, and a prosperity and harmony we may never have known,
> gives us peace. Our shame is deep. For shame is the result of
> soul injury. Mirrors, however, are sacred, not only because they
> permit us to witness the body we are fortunate this time around to
> be in, but because they permit us to ascertain the condition of the
> eternal that rests behind the body, the soul. As an ancient
> Japanese proverb states: when the mirror is dim, the soul is not
> pure.
>   Art is the mirror, perhaps the only one, in which we can
> see our true collective face. We must honor its sacred function.
> We must let art help us.

Thus, both Walker and N.W.A. argued that constructing the
violent black male and his misogyny could benefit Black America and
did not reflect negativity and pessimism about black males.

                                    * * *

Looking back, I have to ask if *The Color Purple* really revolutionized
the discussion of race and misogyny in America? In the decade
following the novel's literary acclaim, "gangsta rap," with its strong

misogyny, was to become the most popular form of entertainment in America. The victims of its misogyny were assumedly Black women since the rappers were rapping about the women they encountered in their Black communities. A commodity sells successfully when it fulfills a demand or need; gangsta rap fulfilled America's demand/need for Black misogyny. The success of gangsta rap in America (and around the world) proved that, in reality, its audience was white America. In 1994, The National Political Congress of Black Women and other Black women groups urged the start of a national crusade to persuade the music industry to clean up violent "gangsta rap" lyrics that the groups said demeaned and threatened [Black] women ("Black Women Crusade Against "Gangsta Rap"). Later that year, when white conservative politicians pressured Time Warner executives to stop selling records containing controversial lyrics by rap artists (that also offended white teen females), several Black leaders, including Rev. Jesse Jackson and Reverend Al Sharpton ironically came to the music's defense—protesting the censorship and championing the right to free speech ("Black Leaders Weighing In On Rape Debate").

America was caught in another controversy regarding the demeaning of Black women in 2007 when Donald Imus, a white shock jock, referred to an innocent group of Black women college basketball players as "nappy-headed ho's." This time Reverends Jackson and Sharpton reacted in quite an opposite way, leading the crusade to have the shock jock fired. Yet one rapper did not feel that the shock jock's demeaning of Black womanhood was the same as his lyrics. Rapper Snoop Dogg, one of the worst offenders, told the media: "we ain't no old-ass white men that sit up on MSNBC going hard on black girls. We are rappers that have these songs coming from our minds and our souls that are relevant to what we feel. I will not let them mutha—as say we in the same league as him." ("Snoop Says Rappers and Imus Are 'Two Separate Things'")

Snoop reminds us that the "bitch/ho" is a construction that rappers created and rendered believable. It is an American commodity that rappers created to portray the bottom of the American social ladder, the most devalued group in America. Snoop, speaking for other rappers, claimed ownership of the "bitch/ho." He was possessive of his "product." Snoop also reminded America that the women being demeaned were the [Black] women he knew—not white or Asian women. Thus, the "bitch" and "ho" of rap music is the new Celie.

Considering the American minstrel tradition, *The Color Purple* could be called the "elder sister" of gangsta rap since both Walker and Snoop argue that the negative people in their worlds inspired their body of work. White feminist Gloria Steinem's cheering of the novel (89-90) parallels the popularity of gangsta rap amongst white suburban teens.

* * *

Still, I first read the story of *The Color Purple* as one hero's journey of triumph and transformation. Yugoslavia-born theater director and historian of Arts and Ideas, Slobodan Dan Paich, theorizes that stories personify abstractions or things. He writes:

> Just like the physical body continuously works to keep body fluids moving, temperature almost constant, the stomach acid at manageable levels, etc., so does the psychological self produce compensating, relieving images and nonverbal scenarios, or *proto-stories*² to help us deal with life's complexities.

In addition, Paich theorizes that story-seeking may give us a sense of belonging and that individuals may find relief in "joining the established flow of existing stories and well-known myths." I grouped the essays in Rodopi's *Dialogue: Alice Walker's The Color Purple* based on Paich's theory.

The essays in "Rendering the Womanist Hero" explore victimhood and personal disempowerment and personification of the hero's journey to selfhood and personal empowerment through *The Color Purple*. Gloria Steinem, who called Celie "the downest and outest of women" (89), wrote that one of the pleasures of *The Color Purple*:

> is watching people redeem themselves and grow, or wither and turn inward, according to the ways they do or don't work out the moral themes in their lives. In the hands of this author, morality is not an external dictate. It doesn't matter if you love the wrong people, or have children with more than one of them, or whether you have money, go to church, or obey the laws. What matters is cruelty, violence, keeping the truth from others who need it, suppressing someone's will or talent, taking more than you need from people or nature, and failing to choose for yourself. It's the internal morality of dignity, autonomy, and balance.
>
> What also matters is the knowledge that everybody, no matter how poor or passive on the outside has, these possibilities inside. (89)

In the section titled "The Theology of Liberation," the writers discuss the re-creation/redesign of religion through Celie. What true journey of personal empowerment or transformation can take place without a discussion of faith and religion? Religion can uplift; religion can repress. Obviously, religion has been used to keep African Americans enslaved and homosexuals unhappy; yet people continued to turn to faith and prayer during hard times. Celie must transform her religion in order to begin her own transformation. She must look critically at her religion in order to find its true purpose. Prussian philosopher and revolutionary Karl Marx wrote in 1843:

> [. . .] the criticism of religion is the prerequisite of all criticism. [. . .] Man makes religion, religion does not make man. [. . .]
>
> The abolition of religion as the *illusory* happiness of the people is the demand for their *real* happiness. To call on them to give up their illusions about their condition is to call on them to *give up a condition that requires illusions*. [. . .]
>
> The criticism of religion disillusions man, so that he will think, act, and fashion his reality like a man who has discarded his illusions and regained his senses, so that he will move around himself as his own true Sun. Religion is only the illusory Sun which evolves around man as long as he does not revolve around himself. ("Works of Karl Marx")

After transforming herself, Celie begins a journey to transform her present community or to find a new community that is supportive. In her first letters, a timid Celie reaches out only to God; in the last letter, an empowered Celie reaches out to God, "peoples" and everything (*The Color Purple* 285). The essays in "Dear God . . . Dear Peoples . . . Dear Everything," examine this aspect of Celie's journey.

Finally, place is central in Paich's theory primarily because personification happens in a place. As Paich theorizes:

> spirit of place—with its number of meanings ranging from the special atmosphere of a place, through human cultural responses to a place, to notions of the guardian spirit of a place—may offer a common link to the archaic layers of our socialized self . . .

He concludes that studying the place of a story may lead to greater self-knowledge and reflection. As discussed in the essays of "The Spirit of Space," Celie's newly transformed language and self need their own supporting home or space. These essays go beyond the setting of *The Color Purple*. In her discussion of *The Color Purple* in her autobiography, Walker wrote that Virginia Woolf's *A Room of One's Own* "made me happy to be a writer, an bolstered and brightened my consciousness about the role other women, often silenced or even long dead, can have in changing the world" (41). In order to become a "light and fluffy" Broadway musical, *The Color Purple* had to be adapted.

* * *

Critics of *The Color Purple* have called the novel poorly-crafted, polemic and mere titillation. Yet in *Dialogue's* section titled "The Classic Beneath the Polemic," scholars defend the novel's place amongst the classics.

Many black scholars have argued a black art aesthetic. In her 1970 essay titled "The Humanistic Tradition of Afro-American Literature," novelist and black arts and literature historian, Margaret Walker wrote:

> When we speak in the vernacular of our people, when we deal with folkways, folk beliefs, folk sayings; when we revolt against form and create new rhythms, improvise as the jazz musicians do, sing the blues, or dance the limbo, then we are dealing with an idiom that is most indigenous to Black people: always natural, freely experimental, always humanistic, most of all authentic of what is most real in the Black experience, then we are following an ancient tradition that is definitely not Anglo-Saxon. (123, 124)

Scholars of African American arts and literature have also argued that polemics can be an important and definitive aesthetic element of African American arts and literature. In her 1976 essay "Some Aspects of the Black Aesthetic," Margaret Walker wrote about "art for art's sake":

> This, to me, seems a direct contradiction of all the humanistic traditions of Afro-American art and literature. The gospel of social justice, freedom, peace, and human dignity has been preached in all the art of Afro-America from its beginnings to the present. The slogan "Art for the People" is not a new nor radically different tag from what it has always been among Black people. African art from its ancient beginnings has always been functional in its highest spiritual sense. (115)

Besides, how would a novelist define a Negro hero in a story that is based in the early twentieth century America without being polemic? In his 1944 book titled *An American Dilemma: The Negro*

Problem and Modern Democracy, Swedish social economist Gunnar Myrdal wrote "The definition of the 'Negro race' is thus a social and conventional, not a biological concept. The social definition and not the biological facts actually determine the status of an individual and his place in interracial relations" (115). He later proceeds to compare "American caste system" in the mid-twentieth century to those of India and America's ante-bellum South (668).

Even Myrdal's definition of the Negro was controversial. In his review of *An American Delimma*, writer Ralph Ellison argued:

> In our society it is not unusual for a Negro to experience a sensation that he does not exist in the real world at all. He seems, rather, to exist in the nightmarish fantasy of the white American mind as a phantom that the white mind seeks unceasingly, by means both crude and subtle, to lay to rest. (328)

Later Ellison wrote:

> [. . .] Are American Negroes simply the creation of white men, or have they at least helped to create themselves out of what they found around them? Men have made a way of life in caves and upon cliffs; why cannot Negroes have made a life upon the horns of the white man's dilemma?
> Myrdal sees Negro culture and personality simply as the product of a "social pathology." Thus he assumes that 'it is to the advantage of American Negroes as individuals and as a group to become assimilated into American culture . . .' (339)

Hence, the essays in "The Classic Beneath the Polemic" value the polemics of *The Color Purple* and offer fresh dialogues on the black and non-black aesthetic.

*   *   *

America has changed since *The Color Purple* first roiled the international literary world. Today, an African American woman is one of the richest and most powerful people in the media. Additionally, African Americans now run major American corporations, and African American women have been crowned Miss America. Same-sex marriage has been included in national political debates. Black gay and lesbian communities are celebrated throughout the country; Black gay men have been the subject of New York Times bestsellers. In 2008, a white woman and a Black man have run for president of the United States of America—and now a black man has been elected president of the United States. The First Lady of the United States is a brown-skinned African American woman.

Twenty-five years after it won the Pulitzer Prize, is *The Color Purple* still relevant or subversive? Did time prove that the book was truly worthy of the Pulitzer Prize? How could letters written by a simple, timid Negro girl roil controversy? How could her letters receive international acclaim? How would today's thinkers and writers read *The Color Purple*? These questions are explored in *Dialogue: Alice Walker's The Color Purple.*

Notes

[1] It should be noted that Mr. Reed was invited to contribute to this project on "The Color Purple," but he declined.
[2] Dan Paich defines proto-story as a thought, idea, dream, fantasy, etc. before it has been made into a tell-able story.

Works Cited

"Black Women Crusade Against 'Gangsta Rap'," *Jet* (10 January 1994): 15.

Bradley, David. "Telling the Black Woman's Story." *The New York Times Magazine* (8 January 1984): 34.

Braxton, Greg and Jerry Crowe. "Black Leaders Weighing in On Rape Debate." *Los Angeles Times* 14 June 1995: F8.

Ellison, Ralph. "*An American Dilemma*: A Review" in *The Collected Essays of Ralph Ellison.* ed. John F. Callahan. New York: Modern Library, 1995.

Jackson-Paris, Rod and Bob. *Straight from the Heart: A Love Story.* New York: Warner Books, 1994.

LaGrone, Kheven. "From Minstrelsy to Gangsta Rap: The Nigger as Commodity for Popular American Entertainment" *Journal of African American Studies* 5.2 (September 2000): 117-131.

Morrison, Toni. *Playing in the Dark: Whiteness and the Literary Imagination.* New York: Vintage, 1992.

Myrdal, Gunnar. *The American Dilemma.* New York: Harper & Row. 1944.

"Number One With A Bullet." *Newsweek* (1 July 1991): 63.

Paich, Slobodan Dan. "Scenography and *Genus Loci*—Re-Investing Public Space with Mytho-Sculptural Elements for Performance." Paper presented at the *Research Conference on Transliteracy—The History and Theory of Scenography: Interdisciplinary Making and Reading of Images in Entertainment Environments* (Scenography International Prague Quadrenniale, 23-25 June 2007).

Reed, Ishmael. *"The Color Purple." The Oakland Tribune* 2 July 1984: Letter-to-the-Editor, B-6.

"Snoop Says Rappers and Imus Are 'Two Separate Things'." On line at: http://www.mtv.com/news/articles/1556803/20070410/snoop_dogg.jhtml (consulted 28 July 2008).

Steinem, Gloria. "Do You Know This Woman? She Knows You: A Profile of Alice Walker." *Ms. Magazine* (June 1982): 89-90.

Walker, Alice. *The Color Purple*. New York: Harcourt Books, 1982.

—.*The Same River Twice: Honoring the Difficult*. New York: Scribners, 1986.

Walker, Margaret. "Some Aspects of the Black Aesthetics" in *How I Wrote Jubilee and Other Essays on Life and Literature*. ed. Maryemma Graham. New York: The Feminist Press at City University of New York, 1990. (115)

—. "The Humanistic Tradition of Afro-American Literature" in *How I Wrote Jubilee and Other Essays on Life and Literature*. ed. Maryemma Graham. New York: The Feminist Press at City University of New York, 1990. (123 - 124)

'Works of Karl Marx 1843: Introduction to A Contribution to the Critique of Hegel's Philosophy of Right.' On line at: http://www.marxists.org/archive/marx/works/1843/critique-hpr/intro.htm (consulted July 29, 2008).

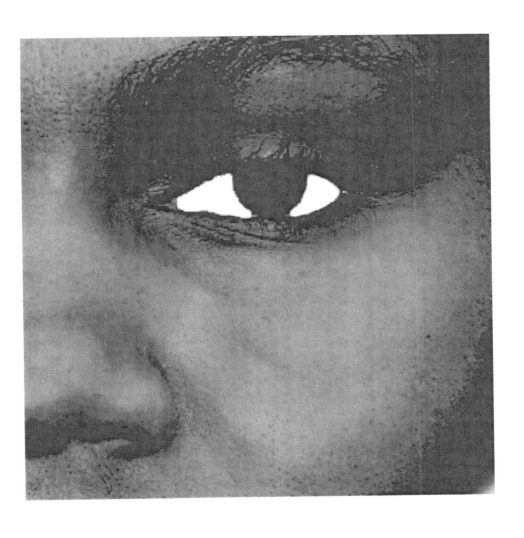

Rendering the (Womanist) Hero

We Need a Hero: African American Female *Bildungsromane* and Celie's Journey to Heroic Female Selfhood in Alice Walker's *The Color Purple*

Brenda R. Smith

> When I first read [*The Color Purple*], my life felt like Celie's story.[...] the fact that the first letter is about, 'Dear God, I'm 14 years old'—I've been right there. [...]I remember closing the book and weeping, because my God, this is my story. This is my story. Somebody knows how I felt. And at the time I read *The Color Purple* I had not told anybody that I'd been sexually abused [. . . .] So, to see it written and to have the feelings on the page that were also my feelings was—the earth moved for me [. . .] because you say, 'Somebody knows. Somebody else knows what this is like.' [. . .] And it is because of The Color Purple that I made the decision [. . .] never again will I ever be told what I can and cannot do. So, it was life changing in, oh so many ways.
> (Oprah Winfrey, "Oprah Comes Full Circle")

> I relate to Miss Celie. She went through a lot of things I went through, but she came out a strong woman. And so did I.
> (Fantasia Barrino, "Fantasia Rehearses *The Color Purple*")

The Color Purple[1] has been the subject of much scholarly analysis and the object of considerable literary controversy. The novel has been approached as social history, psychoanalytic case study, love story, and fairy tale. At the center of all of these critical approaches is a consensus that *The Color Purple* is a pivotal text in the tradition of literature by black women writers who have taken as their theme a young black woman's journey from silence to voice and "authentic female selfhood" (Eysturoy 85)—an autonomous identity that reflects the female protagonist's agency and her authority over her own life and her own story. While African American men and women have been silenced historically because of race and class, African American women's silencing is compounded, both within and without the black community, by gender. *The Color Purple* is Walker's response to this history of silencing and oppression. The novel fulfills African American women's need for a "female hero," an African American "everywoman" whose condition speaks to that of many other African American women and who ultimately masters her world and claims her place within it as an autonomous, courageous and creative self. With *The Color Purple*, Walker sets forth a modern myth of empowerment for African American women, one that liberates them from their history of oppression, subordination and silence. In creating a hero for African American women, Walker created a hero for others as well.

Modern Culture's Need for Myth

In order to chart the effectiveness of Walker's myth-making, it is helpful to understand the need for and the function of myth in modern culture. As mythologist Joseph Campbell explains:

> There is a [. . .] function of myth, and this is the one that I think everyone must try today to relate to—and that is the pedagogical function, of how to live a human lifetime under any circumstances. Myth can teach you that. . . .The threat to our lives that we all face today [is,] . . . is the system going to flatten you out and deny you your humanity, or are you going to be able to make use of the system to the attainment of human purposes? . . . Myths inspire the realization of the possibility of your perfection [and] the fullness of your strength [. . . .] Myths grab you somewhere down inside [. . . . They] are infinite in their revelation. (*Power* 39, 175, 183)

As Campbell indicates, myths are relevant and necessary to modern culture. However, modern times require modern myths. If members of modern culture are to benefit from the revelatory and transformational powers of myth, they need narratives that are archetypal in nature but grounded in the situations, problems, and concerns of living in the modern world. They need heroes who model ways to triumph over challenges and circumstances similar to their own, characters whose transformations of consciousness lead them to ultimately discover or accomplish something "beyond the normal range of achievement and existence" (Campbell, *Power* 151). In crafting her narrative, Walker demonstrates keen insight into the function and the power of modern myth.

Walker's Myth-Making

The Color Purple is, in keeping with the conventions of modern myth, a syncretization of realism and fabulation.[2] While Walker positions her female protagonist Celie—the victim of physical, sexual and verbal abuse, rendered a virtual non-entity within her community—at the extreme end of the spectrum of women's subordination and oppression within the male-dominated social order, she grounds her novel in a culture and a collective experience that the female reader recognizes and inhabits. Within this historical framework, Walker proceeds to craft a narrative that ultimately transcends and transforms the socio-cultural pathologies and existential "dead-ends" that distinguish the black female experience.

Integral to Walker's creation of myth is her womanist ideology, a visionary and archetypal doctrine of African American feminism that privileges the following: sororal bonds; the possibility of sexual intimacy between women and the acceptance of sexual and non-sexual love for men; the preference for women's culture; the acknowledgement and affirmation of women's strength; a commitment to the survival and wholeness of black people, male and female; and a woman's love of the Spirit, love, the Folk and herself, regardless of the forces that seek to distort or destroy that love (*In Search of Our Mothers' Gardens* xi-xii). Through the reification of her womanist doctrine, Walker challenges and subverts the predominant myths and stereotypes that perpetuate the condition and treatment of women, in general, and black women, in particular, within the patriarchy. She dislocates the existing archetypal and stereotypical patterns of the black female socio-cultural experience, loosening and, in some instances, removing the constraints under which black women exist. The result is a mythic narrative that deliberately and unapologetically flies in the face of what is expected and accepted as historically and culturally plausible for poor, oppressed black women, offering an alternate path from subordination and victimization to "heroic female selfhood."

Heroic female selfhood is a subjectivity derived from the female hero quest paradigm set forth by literary scholars Carol Pearson and Katherine Pope. Pearson and Pope's paradigm delineates three stages of the traditional female *Bildungsroman*:(1) The Call to Adventure/Departure; (2) The Journey/Initiation; and (3) The Return. Pearson and Pope note that the quest is not always linear; the stages do not always occur in the same order. Many times, the stages are not separate—they may occur simultaneously within the course of one event; one stage may occur over a long period of time, constituting a journey in itself. Regardless of how the quest is structured, each stage of the quest is comprised of "trials" or obstacles that may thwart the successful completion of the female protagonist's quest (viii, 77). In this analysis of *The Color Purple*, special emphasis is placed on two specific trials within the protagonist's quest, the mastery of which is deemed imperative to the achievement of "heroic" selfhood: Heroic female selfhood is achieved when the protagonist successfully subverts those conventions of the established social order that oppress and subordinate her. She creates an identity that embodies her unique perceptions of self and privileges her individual experiences within the social order. Most definitively, the female protagonist achieves heroic status when she discovers or creates a "community of equals" (Pearson and Pope 22) that sustains or promises the survival of her newly-created self.

Through her use of these strategies, Walker succeeds in writing her female protagonist Celie from tragic heroine to female hero, an empowered and empowering subjectivity that resonates for black women, for the black community, and for others. It is a subjectivity that reflects Walker's recognition of the culture's need for an African American female hero, as reflected in Oprah Winfrey's and Fantasia's opening quotes.

Celie's *Bildung* Begins

Celie is fourteen years old at the onset of her journey to selfhood, reflecting a later beginning of *Bildung* that is characteristic of African American female protagonists.[3] The impetus for her journey conforms to the first stage of the female hero quest paradigm, where the female protagonist is compelled by catastrophe, alienation, disillusionment, or anger to embark on her quest and to leave behind those people upon whom she has been dependent, but who she now sees as perpetuating the very conventions that oppress and subordinate her (Pearson and Pope 92).

Celie's *Bildung* is set in motion by a warning from the man whom she believes is her father: "You better never tell nobody but God. It'd kill your mammy" (1). This admonition restricts Celie to silence about the fact that Pa has continually raped her and that she has had two children by him, both of whom he has taken away at birth. Celie's victimization by Pa, one of the very people from whom she should be able to expect guidance and protection, disconnects her from the familial and moral dynamics on which she has previously depended and fragments her developing sense of self. Her external reality is immediately set in opposition to her inner self or central consciousness. This inside/outside dichotomy is characteristic of female *Bildungsromane*, reflecting the reality that although the female protagonist's *Bildung* may include a physical journey, it typically begins—and may persist—as a psychological or spiritual one. Carole Boyce Davis, African American literature scholar, states: "because of the restrictions placed on the black heroine's physical movement, she must conduct her quest within close boundaries [. . .] Her journey is an internal one" (131).

Prohibited from articulating her experiences to the outside world, Celie begins writing letters to God, sharing with him the unspeakable circumstances of her life and asking for "a sign" (1) that will help her to understand what is happening to her. Celie's first letter has two-fold significance. It indicates her awareness, if only on a fundamental level, of power dynamics within her environment: If Pa, a man, has the power to unsettle the world as she knows it then only a more powerful entity, God, has the potential to set it right. Her letter also indicates her confusion about what has happened to her and the extent to which it has fragmented her sense of self. In her letter, Celie states with certainty, "I am fourteen years old" (1), a fact that no one can dispute. However, her next statement is less certain, "~~I am~~ I have always been a good girl" (1) and reflects the inner struggle between her desire to hold on to her individual perception of self and her internalization of society's negative judgments about her self-worth.

Some literary scholars view Celie as the quintessential victim and find the path she takes on her journey to voice and selfhood, and the outcome of her journey, implausible (Harris 197; Blount 122). Celie is raped and impregnated by Pa; her children are taken away from her; her formal education is terminated against her will; she is married off to Mr.____, who is more concerned with the cow that serves as Celie's dowry than he is with her; and she endures abuse at the hands of both her husband and his children. From outward appearances, Celie represents the tragic heroine, whose journey to authentic selfhood is traditionally thwarted, leaving her proscribed by societal expectations of female passivity and submissiveness.

However, Celie's heroic potential and the strength of her central consciousness are apparent from her first letter to God. Her act

of writing reflects both obedience and subversion. She literally
follows Pa's edict to tell "nobody but God" (1); however, her letters
indicate her awareness that all is not right in her world. The letters
reveal the sheer force of her survival instinct and her resistance to
internalizing a definition of self that is imposed on her. Her inner
strength is also indicated by three actions: her decision to use herself
as a diversion so that Pa will not abuse her sister Nettie; her desire to
take Nettie and run away; and clandestine learning sessions with
Nettie, during which Nettie teaches her everything that she has
learned in school.

Celie has been beaten down, but she is not wholly broken.
What she lacks at the beginning of her *Bildung* are alternative options
for her "being" and her "becoming." Her experiences have been
limited to the trauma that she has suffered at the hands of the men in
her life, and she is unable, at this point, to imagine any other
possibilities for herself. Nettie and Mr. ____'s sister, Kate, tell Celie
to "fight" (17, 21). However, Celie's focus is survival; she states: 'I
don't know how to fight. All I know how to do is to stay alive" (17).
Before Celie can fight, she needs to understand more fully what she is
fighting against, and what she is ultimately fighting for. This is no
small feat, given her circumstances. However, if, as literary scholar
and poet Lynette Seator states, "language is a way of becoming" (32),
then the potential for Celie's successful *Bildung* is seen in her
appropriation of language, in her becoming the narrator of her own
text. Although she has been forbidden to voice her experiences to the
outside world, her letters are an affirmation of her being and of her
refusal to have her story told by anyone other than herself.

Like Celie's letters, sororal or sisterhood bonds, which are
integral to Walker's womanist ideology and to the successful *Bildung*
of the female protagonist, also pose a direct challenge to patriarchal
proscriptions of the female self. Women friends often serve as guides
and rescuers for the protagonist. They model the attributes and
provide the emotional support that the protagonist needs to persevere
and succeed in her quest (Pearson and Pope 188). As Celie embarks
on her journey to voice and selfhood, she encounters several women
who model alternate ways of being female within her environment.
Nettie is the first woman to serve as guide for Celie. She provides
Celie much needed emotional support and serves as her teacher,
providing Celie the basic tools necessary to process her environment
and the people in it. However, Nettie has yet to embark on her own

Bildung and lacks the life experience necessary to serve as an effective model of female resistance.

It is Sofia, Harpo's wife, who sets Celie firmly on the path of *Bildung*. Sofia is the first woman to model active resistance in a way that captures Celie's attention. Sofia possesses a physical presence—Celie describes her as being "Solid. Like if she sit down on something, it be mash" (34). Sofia also possesses a strong inner resolve. She directly confronts and challenges any and all attempts to force her into passivity and submission; she doggedly defends her right to freely exist. Celie is initially so envious of Sofia's defiance that when Harpo asks her advice on how to make Sofia obey him, Celie tells him to beat her.

However, this advice lies so heavy on Celie's conscience that she has trouble sleeping. When Sofia confronts Celie, Celie admits that she is jealous of Sophia because, as she states, "You do what I can't [. . .] Fight" (40). The conversation that ensues between the two women forges bonds of sisterhood on which both women eventually draw. Sofia tells Celie about her family, in particular about her mother, whose situation is very similar to Celie's: "My mamma [. . .] under my daddy foot. Anything he says goes. She never say nothing back" (41). Although Celie remains silent about her victimization by Pa and merely laughs at the sheer audacity of Sofia's advice to "bash Mr.____ head open" (42), Celie shares, for the first time, a connection with someone other than Nettie and receives, in return, a new perspective on her situation. Sofia sows the seed of possibilities in Celie's consciousness; her voice is the first voice to penetrate the shell of Celie's repressed emotions.

Celie's Journey

While Sofia sets Celie on the path of *Bildung*, it is Shug Avery, a blues singer, Mr.____'s mistress and mother of three of his children, who facilitates Celie's journey to heroic selfhood. In this second stage of her quest, Celie's relationship with Shug provides her the means through which to confront, challenge and transform the stereotypical myths of female selfhood and to ultimately integrate the outer and inner aspects of her self.

Celie hears about and sees a picture of Shug before her marriage to Mr.____ and before she meets Shug in the flesh. The picture provides Celie an image of womanhood that she has not previously seen; she states, "Shug Avery was a woman. The most beautiful woman I ever saw" (6). Celie knows instinctively that Shug exists beyond the limitations and constraints under which she struggles. However, she also perceives that Shug has dealt with her own suffering: "Her eyes serious tho. Sad some" (6); and the perception of common suffering forges an immediate bond with Shug in Celie's growing consciousness.

When word reaches the community that Shug is sick, and the minister "take[s] her condition for his text" (43), Celie defends Shug as she wishes someone had defended her. When Mr.____ brings a sick Shug into his and Celie's home, Shug's illness, and the temporary dependency it imposes on her, facilitates a mutual bond between the women. Celie nurses and nurtures Shug back to health, as she wishes her mother had been there to nurture her and as she wishes she had been able to care for her own children. Shug, in return, brings the outside world—magazines, cigarettes, makeup, and eventually the life of the juke joint and the blues circuit—into Celie's closed-off environment and broadens Celie's horizons.

As guide and rescue figure, Shug nurtures and protects Celie and teaches Celie a new language through which she is able to create an alternate context for her developing self. Most significantly, Shug and Celie begin a sexual relationship, through which Shug guides Celie into a new perception of her sexuality. For Shug, virginity is defined not in terms of biology, but in terms of pleasure; since Celie has never enjoyed sex, has never had an orgasm, she is still a virgin. Through Shug's definition of virginity, Celie moves from a perception of herself as sexual object to an understanding and appreciation of herself as sexual subject. From a broader perspective, Celie's intimate relationship with a woman subverts the myths of virginity and romantic (heterosexual) love and moves Celie's *Bildung* beyond the constraints of conventional marriage.

To accomplish this goal, Walker situates Celie and Shug's sexual relationship within the context of her womanist ideology— "Womanist . . . A woman who loves women, sexually and/or nonsexually. Appreciates and prefers women's culture" (*In Search of Our Mothers' Gardens* xi)—casting the relationship as the ultimate expression of sisterhood; as Celie records in her letters to God, she and Shug eventually interact "like sisters" (146). By privileging sororal love as the primary emotional bond in the novel, Walker subverts marriage as the *telos* of the female protagonist's quest and facilitates the success of Celie's journey to heroic selfhood.

As Celie is increasingly able to reclaim and affirm essential aspects of herself, she is finally able to give voice to the traumatic experiences to which she has been subjected. She tells Shug about her rape. As Celie expresses and allows herself to feel the pain of this experience, she moves beyond the need to "make [her]self wood" (22) in order to survive; she reconnects with her emotions and learns to channel them in service to her successful *Bildung*. When she and Shug discover that Nettie has been writing to Celie for years and that Mr.____ has been intercepting and hiding Nettie's letters, Celie has such a rush of emotion that her instinct is to slit Mr.____'s throat. Shug literally and figuratively takes the razor out of Celie's hand. She helps Celie to realize that revenge is the ultimate capitulation to patriarchal codes of behavior; giving in to her violent impulses will only chain Celie to the very social order from which she is struggling to free herself. Through Shug's guidance, Celie replaces the razor with a sewing needle, diverting her destructive impulses into creative ones.

Sewing is as integral to Celie's *Bildung* as writing. Not only does it serve as a catalyst for Celie's economic and emotional independence, but it is—as is writing—a vehicle for Celie's self-expression and for her creation of an alternate socio-cultural context within which to exist. Celie decides that she will sew unisex pants, a decision which directly challenges gender-role stereotypes and furthers Walker's womanist ideology and Celie's *Bildung*. Also, in that Celie creates pants for the people in her life that reflect their unique personalities and life choices, she re-humanizes the community, demonstrating personal insight and artistic creativity that is self-affirming.

As Celie proceeds through her *Bildung*, she creates not only a communal context, but a historical/cross-cultural context for her developing heroic self. The vehicle for this aspect of her transformation is Nettie's letters. Some scholars and critics have criticized Nettie's letters as "really extraneous to the central concerns of the novel" (Harris 157), contending that "Netti's [sic] letters [. . .] appearing as they do, after Celie's intensely subjective voice has been established [. . .] seem lackluster and intrusive" (Watkins, *Some Letters*). However, when viewed from the perspective of Walker's re-casting of the archetypal patterns of African American female life, the letters take on a new significance. Nettie's letters describe and draw parallels between the culture and customs of the Olinka tribe and those of African-Americans in the American South; they establish parallels between colonialism and Jim Crow, African and African-American. The letters also serve to place Celie's quest for heroic selfhood within a larger context of black and female oppression and resistance. Through Nettie's letters, Celie is able to construct selfhood within a female tradition that reaches all the way back to the "Motherland."

Nettie's letters are also important because they ultimately lead Celie to a new level of spiritual awareness. When Celie reads the letter in which Nettie reveals the truth about their family history, Celie loses confidence in the God to which she has been writing for years. In her final letter to God, she writes:

> 'My daddy lynch. My mama crazy. All my little half-brothers and sisters no kin to me. My children not my sister and brother. Pa not pa.
> You must be sleep.' (177)

Celie believes that any God that would allow such circumstances to exist:

> '[. . .] is a man. And act just like all the other mens I know. Trifling, forgitful and lowdown.' (192)

As she situates Christianity within the context of those cultural forces that function to oppress her, Celie opens herself to re-envision God in a form that exists outside of these forces. Again, Shug serves as Celie's guide:

> 'God ain't a he or a she, but a It [. . .]
> God is everything [. . .] Everything that is or ever was or ever will be. And when you feel that, and be happy to feel that, you've found it.' (195)

Celie's ability to "git man off [her] eyeball" (197) allows her to open her consciousness and to develop a new perspective of being that incorporates "everything."

As is customary in the female hero quest paradigm, Celie has experienced all of the challenges that typically comprise the first and second stages of quest before she embarks on her physical journey. She has named and validated her experiences as well as her own perspectives; she has confronted and successfully challenged those societal conventions that function to oppress and subordinate her; and she has come to a new understanding of herself and her relationship to her community and to the universe. She is poised to "enter into the Creation" (199); and as she prepares to embark on her physical journey, she comes into full voice. When she announces to her family that she is leaving to live with Shug in Memphis, Mr.____ attempts to re-impose all of the degrading definitions of self that Celie has overcome during her *Bildung*: "You black, you pore, you ugly, you a woman. . . . you nothing at all" (206). Celie now has the language and the self-possession that enable her to fight, and she directs at Mr.____ all of the anger and resentment that she has repressed over the years. She "curses" him (206), wishing that he will suffer all of the pain to which he has previously subjected her; and in the ultimate act of self-affirmation, she tells him, "I'm pore, I'm black, I may be ugly and can't cook . . . But *I'm here*" (207). With her response to Mr. ____'s diatribe, Celie reclaims the "I am" she was forced to amend at the beginning of the novel. With this affirmation of self, Celie asserts her heroic selfhood.

As Celie comes to full voice, affirms her heroic self and embarks on her physical journey, it would seem that her *Bildung* is complete. However, the most important aspect of the female hero's quest is The Return, which comprises the final sections of *The Color Purple*. There are several lessons that Celie has yet to learn before she can claim the ultimate "reward" that results from having achieved heroic selfhood. One of these is to confront the "seducer," a character who promises to rescue the female hero but usually turns out to threaten her with another form of confinement (Pearson and Pope 143). In Celie's case, Shug is both rescuer and seducer. Like Janie's feeling for Tea Cake in Zora Neale Hurston's *Their Eyes Were Watching God* (1937), Celie's love for Shug is "self-crushing" (Hurston 122). Throughout her *Bildung*, Celie's sense of self has been inextricably connected to Shug's feelings for her. It is no wonder then that Shug's affair with a young musician in her band threatens to emotionally destroy Celie. However, rather than attempt to repress the pain as she did at the beginning of her *Bildung*, she acknowledges her ability to feel and express that pain as a sign of her vitality. She writes to Nettie, "My heart broke" (247); but in a later letter she says, "My heart must be young and fresh though, it feel like blooming blood" (259). Through her separation from Shug, Celie ultimately comes to an awareness of herself as an autonomous being. When Shug writes to tell Celie that she is coming home, Celie's response is, "If she come, I be happy. If she don't, I be content [. . .] I figure this the lesson I was suppose to learn" (283).

The female hero must also confront death—not only physical, but spiritual and/or psychological death—and affirm life (Pearson and Pope 5), which Celie does in the handling of her break with Shug, the news of Nettie's death and her reconnection with Mr.____. When Celie receives a letter telling her that the ship on which Nettie, Nettie's husband, and Celie's children are sailing home to America has sunk and they are dead, Celie's new spiritual worldview enables her to persevere. Ironically, Celie continues to write letters to her supposedly deceased sister; and in one letter she states:

> 'How can you be dead if I still feel you? Maybe, like God, you changed into something different that I'll have to speak to in a different way, but you not dead to me Nettie. And never will be.' (260)

Celie also affirms Mr. ____'s new lease on life. As a result of what Mr.____ terms "experience" (270)—his abandonment by both Celie and Shug and his acknowledgment of the pain he has caused the women in his life—he rather suddenly undergoes his own inner transformation. In Celie's letters, Mr.____, an agent of the oppressive patriarchy becomes Albert, a man who engages Celie on a more evolved, human level. In renewing her association with Albert, not only does Celie affirm his newly-formed self, but she demonstrates the full extent of and affirms her own spiritual and psychological rebirth.

Celie's Heroic Return

Finally, once the female hero has claimed the "treasure" of a whole and authentic self, she is ready to return "home," either her ancestral home or the place from which her *Bildung* began (Pearson and Pope 68). With the death of Pa, who Celie now knows is her stepfather, Celie returns to her childhood home and the place of the onset of her *Bildung* and discovers that she and Nettie are the rightful heirs of the land and of the house, built by Pa, that now replaces their childhood home. Through these circumstances, Walker provides her hero a site for the creation of a new community, which is the most important aspect and the ultimate measure of the female hero's successful quest. Having successfully overcome all of the trials in her journey to heroic selfhood, Celie's reward is a community of equals—which includes Shug, Sofia, and Albert—that values and supports her heroic qualities: autonomy, persistence, courage, intelligence and achievement.

In the salutation of Celie's final letter, she addresses "the cosmos" (Pearson and Pope 259): "Dear God. Dear Stars. Dear tress, dear sky, dear peoples. Dear everything. Dear God" (285). Her salutation is not only a legitimization of self but also an affirmation of unity with all of creation.[4] At the successful completion of her *Bildung*, Celie has "love, work, money, friends . . . time" (215) and a house of her own in which she can gather her newly created community, all of the members of whom have been transformed by and through her heroic transformation. Eventually, Celie's *Bildung* comes full circle when she and Nettie are reunited. When the sisters face each other for the first time in over twenty-five years, they regress to infantile behavior. They "totter toward one another like . . . babies" (286); they sit down on the porch with their family members towering above them and intone each other's names as infants just learning to speak. The sisters re-establish the sororal bonds that initially sustained Celie. Celie's final words, "I think this is the youngest us ever felt" (288), are emblematic of rejuvenation or rebirth, the emergence of a revised history and a new legacy of empowerment for black women and ultimately for the black community.

Some literary scholars have criticized what they perceive as the novel's fantastical, "'happily ever after' ending" (Harris 160) and have argued that the novel's ending "leaves the precincts of realistic fiction" (Boesenberg 216). Perhaps these criticisms are prompted by the fact that very few female *Bildungsromane* achieve this level of successful *Bildung* for the female protagonist. It is significant that the shift in narrative pattern corresponds with the end of Celie's *Bildung*. Women writers of female *Bildungsromane* appear to have no shortage of narrative strategies at their disposal to facilitate their female protagonists' successful navigation through the first two stages of the female quest paradigm. However, it is The Return—the final stage of the paradigm and the stage which is essential to the female protagonist's achievement of "heroic" selfhood—that traditionally poses the biggest challenge to women writers of *Bildungsromane*; the female protagonist's journey is often thwarted by the writer's inability to create or derive narrative strategies that facilitate its successful completion. Pearson and Pope state:

> The author may portray a heroic woman, demonstrate the problems she encounters by virtue of being unconventionally heroic and female, and still be unable to imagine a narrative framework in which to resolve the dilemma. Myths about female

behavior, moreover, make it difficult for authors to find suitable
plots for the exploration of female heroism. (11)

There are, admittedly, several events that occur at the end of
The Color Purple that can be interpreted as pushing the limits of
realism. However, as with any myth, the reader must suspend
disbelief. Also, it is at the ending of the novel that Walker's crafting
of myth is most apparent. In the archetypal hero quest paradigm, the
hero is rewarded for the successful completion of his quest (Campbell
246). Within the context of this paradigm, the events that are perhaps
the most implausible—Albert's transformation, Celie and Nettie's
inheritance, Nettie's return from Africa with Celie's children—can be
interpreted as rewards for Celie's heroism. Similarly, within the
context of the female hero quest paradigm, these events make possible
Celie's creation of the new community of equals through which the
culture is transformed—the ultimate measure of heroic selfhood.
Walker's appropriation of mythic paradigms "shift aspects of realism
just enough to open spaces" (Gant-Britton 60) within which her
female protagonist can actualize her full heroic potential and within
which Walker can render her myth of African American female
heroism complete.

Walker's Successful Quest

In an interview about her involvement with the film and Broadway
productions of *The Color Purple*, Oprah Winfrey stated that when she
first read the novel, she bought all of the copies that her local
bookstore had in stock and passed them out to black women on her
job, at the hair salon, and on the street ("Oprah Comes Full Circle").
She, like Alice Walker, recognized and responded to the need for
representations of heroic females in African American women's
literature and in their lives.

The relevancy of Walker's myth is evident not only in the
lives of women like Oprah and Fantasia, but in Walker's personal
"color purple experience" on the set of the film adaptation of her
novel. In her autobiography, *The Same River Twice* (1996), Walker
reveals that during the filming of "The Color Purple" she was
suffering from an illness that was so debilitating that it drained both
her physical and spiritual strength. She recounts:

> I sat under a tree [. . .] painfully conscious of my fuzzy thinking
> and blotchy-skin, my soul-deep exhaustion and an almost ever-

present nausea. I was unequal to the task of pointing out to Steven
[Spielberg, the film's director] every 'error' I saw about to be
made. [. . .] This pained me; I felt it an unexplainable and quite
personal failing [. . .]

[However,] I was moved by the way actors themselves
often saved the day. . . . I cheered inwardly to see Whoopi stand
toe to toe one day with Steven and insist that Celie would not age
the way he was envisioning her [. . .] Because Oprah reminded
me of my mother as she was when I was small, I could barely
resist sitting beside her [. . .] and putting my head in her lap. (30-
31)

Just as Celie was nurtured and empowered by her sister-friends during
her journey, the myth manifested in Walker's life as she drew strength
from the female cast members during her journey of making the film.

Of equal significance is the ability of Steven Spielberg, the
director of the film, and Menno Meyjes, the film's screenwriter—both
white men—to capture the heart of Walker's myth. While Walker
admits she was often frustrated by creative differences over details
depicted in the film (the superficial treatment of Celie and Shug's
intimate relationship; the use of voice-over to replace the actual act of
Celie's writing), Spielberg and Meyjes seemed to appreciate, and both
men strove to preserve, the archetypal qualities of Walker's story.
Spielberg drew his inspiration for the depiction of the female
characters in the film from Walker, of whom he stated:

[Alice] is otherworldly. And I mean that in the most positive
way. She is here, she is real, but she has one foot in the other
world. (qtd. in Featherston 190)

Walker, in turn, expressed her appreciation of Spielberg's "love of
and enthusiasm for my characters. His ability to see himself in them"
(*The Same River* 30). Meyjes, when asked whether he, a white male
and a Dutchman, could "really understand and empathize with the
feelings and motivations of black women living in rural Georgia half a
century ago," stated, "The book is so good, it transcends any barriers"
(qtd. in Featherston 185-86).

Despite differences over specific scenes in the film, Spielberg
and Meyjes were ultimately unwilling or unable to compromise the
success of Walker's finely-wrought myth. Walker says of the finished
product: "I loved the film [. . .] I was finally able to see *it*, and to let
go of the scenes that were *not* there" (*The Same River* 163). The
relevancy and resiliency of Walker's myth is further supported by the
film's reviews.   In his review, movie critic Colin Jacobson states:

"*The Color Purple* [. . .] seems more like a fairy tale than a believable and realistic drama. Spielberg makes the African American female characters relentlessly positive [. . .] they inevitably end up as positive role models for us" (*DVD Movie Guide*).

Responses to *The Color Purple*—across genders, across ethnicities, across genres—affirm the success of Walker's myth-making quest. Through her synthesis of realism and fabulation, the reification of her archetypal womanist doctrine and her privileging of unconventional social conventions and narrative strategies, Walker successfully crafts a mythic narrative that transcends the accepted and plausible endings of quest for black women who, like her protagonist Celie, are struggling under untenable circumstances from which there appears to be no relief or escape. The result is a relevant, relatable, life-changing myth of empowerment that liberates African American women and other individuals from their respective histories of oppression, subordination, silence and passivity and actualizes the achievement of agency in all areas of their lives—a modern myth for modern times.

Brenda R. Smith, Ph.D., Kent State University

Notes

[1] Henceforward cited in the text as "TCP."
[2] Cuddon, J. A. ed., *Dictionary of Literary Terms & Literary Theory* (London: Penguin, 1998) 44, 302. *Fabulation* is defined as "A term used to describe the *anti-novel*," fiction that "tends to be experimental and breaks with traditional story-telling methods and forms of the novel. [. . .] It establishes its own conventions and a different kind of realism [. . .]."
[3] In traditional female *Bildungsromane,* the typical age for the onset of Bildung is 10-12 years old. According to Sondra O'Neale, in her essay, "Race, Sex and Self: Aspects of Bildung in Select Novels by Black American Women," *MELUS* 9:4 (Winter II 1982): 25-36, African American female *Bildungsromane* reflects a later age for the onset of Bildung. The later beginning of *Bildung* for black female protagonists can be attributed to the aim of African American women writers "to make their fiction more compatible with actual Black female experience in this country. . . . In seeking self-discovery, heroines must struggle with issues of not only race, skin color, and sex, but of . . . often despicable expectations for Black women preordained by society. Resolutions of these and other conflicts [that are] more specifically typical of Black women's awakening come much later than the age prescribed in Western male development" (26).

[4] When the hero claims the treasure of her true identity, "the kingdom is transformed and she experiences community with herself, with others, and with the cosmos" (Pearson and Pope 259).

Works Cited

Abbandonato, Linda. "A View from 'Elsewhere': Subversive Sexuality and the Rewriting of the Heroine's Story in *The Color Purple*" *PMLA* 106:5 (Oct. 1991): 1106-1115

Blount, Marcellus. "Review: A Woman Speaks" *Callaloo* 18 (Spring-Summer 1983): 118-122.

Boesenberg, Eva. *Gender—Voice—Vernacular: The Formation of Female Subjectivity in Zora Neale Hurston, Toni Morrison and Alice Walker*. Heidelberg: Universitätsverlag C. Winter,1999. 197-218.

Campbell, Joseph. *The Hero with a Thousand Faces*. Princeton: Princeton U P, 1973.

—. *The Power of Myth*. New York: Anchor Books, 1988.

Cheung. King-Kok. "'Don't Tell': Imposed Silences in *The Color Purple* and The Woman Warrior" *PMLA* 103:2 (March 1988): 162-74.

Cuddon, J. A. ed. *Dictionary of Literary Terms & Literary Theory*. London: Penguin Books, 1998. 44, 302.

Curry, Ann. "Oprah Comes Full Circle." *Dateline NBC*. NBC. 21 May 2006. Transcript. 13 April 2008 <http://www.msnbc.msn.com/id/12821015/print/1/displaymode/1098/>.

Davies, Carole Boyce. *Black Women, Writing and Identity: Migrations of the Subject*. New York: Routledge, 1994.

Du Plessis, Rachel Blau. *Writing Beyond the Ending: Narrative Strategies of Twentieth-Century Women Writers*. Bloomington: Indiana U P, 1985.

Eysturoy, Annie O. *Daughters of Self-Creation: The Contemporary Chicana Novel*. New Mexico: U of New Mexico P, 1996. 85-111.

Featherston, Elena. "The Making of 'The Color Purple.'" *San Francisco Focus* Dec. 1985. Rpt. in *The Same River Twice: Honoring the Difficult: A Meditation on Life, Spirit, Art, and The Making of The Color Purple Ten Years Later*. Ed. Alice Walker. New York: Scribner, 1996. 182-90.

Gant-Britton, Lisabeth. *Women of Color Constructing Subjectivity Towards the Future: Toni Morrison, Octavia Butler and Cynthia Kadohata.* Diss. U of California, Los Angeles, 1997. Ann Arbor: UMI, 1998. ATT 9811511.

Harris, Trudier. "On *The Color Purple,* Stereotypes, and Silence" *Black American Literature Forum* 18:4 (Winter 1984): 155-61.

Heilbrun, Carolyn G. *Reinventing Womanhood.* New York: W. W. Norton, 1979.

Heller, Dana A. *The Feminization of Quest-Romance: Radical Departures.* Austin: U of Texas P, 1990.

Hurston, Zora Neale. *Their Eyes Were Watching God.* New York: Harper & Row. 1937.

Jacobson, Colin. Rev. of *The Color Purple.* dir. Steven Spielberg, *DVD Movie Guide* 7 Feb. 2003. 30 Apr. 2008 <http://www.dvdmg.com/colorpurplese.shtml>.

Karafilis, Maria. "Crossing the Borders of Genre: Revisions of the Bildungsroman in Sandra Cisneros's The House on Mango Street and Jamaica Kincaid's Annie John" The *Journal of the Midwest Modern Language Association* 31:2 (Winter 1998): 63-78.

LeSeur, Greta. *Ten is the Age of Darkness: The Black Bildungsroman.* Columbia: U of Missouri P, 1995.

O'Neale, Sondra. "Race, Sex and Self: Aspects of Bildung in Select Novels by Black American Women" *MELUS* 9:4 (Winter II 1982): 25-36.

Pearson, Carol and Katherine Pope. *The Female Hero in American and British Literature.* New York: R. R. Bowker, 1981.

Seator, Lynette. "*Emplumada*: Chicana Rites-of-Passage" *MELUS* (Summer 1984): 23-48.

Selzer, Linda. "Race and Domesticity in The Color Purple" *African American Review* 29:1 (1995): 67-82.

Vineyard, Jennifer. "Fantasia Rehearses 'The Color Purple.' *MTV News.* MTV. 9 Apr 2007. 13 Apr 2008 <http://www.mtv.com/news/articles/1556695/20070409/fantasia.jhtml>.

Walker, Alice. *In Search of Our Mothers' Gardens: Womanist Prose.* New York: Harcourt Brace Jovanovich, 1983. xi-xii.

—. *The Color Purple.* Orlando: Harcourt, 2003.

—. *The Same River Twice: Honoring the Difficult: A Meditation On Life, Spirit, Art and the Making of 'The Color Purple' Ten Years Later.* New York: Scribner, 1996.

Watkins, Mel. "Some Letters Went to God." Rev. of *The Color Purple. New York Times* 25 July 1982. 30 Apr. 2008. <http://query.nytimes.com/gst/fullpage.html?res=9400EEDA 1539F936A15754C0A964948260>.

Making Hurston's Heroine Her Own:
Love and Womanist Resistance in *The Color Purple*

Tracy L. Bealer

> I love the way Janie Crawford / left her husbands
> (Alice Walker, "Saving the Life That Is Your Own" 7)

The unmistakable and intense affiliation between Zora Neale Hurston's *Their Eyes Were Watching God* (1937) and Alice Walker's *The Color Purple* (1982) has attracted much comment, most notably from Walker herself.[1] In his introduction to a collection of essays addressing Walker's work, Harold Bloom frames the connection between Hurston and Walker as primarily imitative: "The authority of the male voice, and its sexism, may well be subverted by Hurston [. . .] But what has Walker subverted by imitating and so repeating a revisionist moment she has not originated? No feminist critic will admit the legitimacy of that question, but it abides and will require an answer" (4). Bloom's question can be answered by re-working the premise of the question: Walker is not merely replicating the subversive moments in Hurston, but rather rewriting Janie's heroine's journey with a politically significant twist. *The Color Purple* features another African American woman who achieves self-actualization and resists sexist oppression through romantic love, but does so by overcoming a different set of challenges than Janie faces. Celie's dark skin and homosexuality position her as a heroine particularly suited to resonate within her reformulation of the radical feminist politics of the 1980s.

    The Color Purple was written in the midst of an intense examination and critique of the precepts and assumptions of white feminism. During the decade following "A Black Feminist Statement" from the Combahee River collective (1977), many writers took up the statement's challenge to explore the "interlocking" systems of "racial, sexual, heterosexual, and class oppression" (*Some of Us Are Brave* 13). The 1980s consequently saw an explosion of fiction and nonfiction that addressed the marginalization of poor women, women of color, and lesbians in feminist politics. Collections like *This Bridge Called My Back* (1981) and *All the Women Are White, All the Blacks Are Men, But Some of Us Are Brave* (1982) articulated the frustration many women felt with a movement they argued was white dominated, classist, homophobic, and willfully ignorant of the cultural differences that shaped women of color. Walker's landmark collection of essays, *In Search of Our Mothers' Gardens: Womanist Prose* (1983), coined the term "womanist" as one theoretical framework for distinguishing social goals specific to African American women and presented sexual, sororal and maternal love between black women as a political tool for radical social change

Walker opens *Mothers' Gardens* with four numbered definitions of a womanist (xi-ii). The first entry explains that the word is appropriated from the Black folk expression "womanish," connoting maturity and authority in an African American woman. The second and third definitions Walker assigns to womanist—the heart of her explanation of the term—are directly concerned with how and whom a womanist loves. Whereas the third entry reads as an epic catalogue of aesthetic and self-love, the second entry specifies the interpersonal erotics of womanism: "A woman who loves other women, sexually and/or nonsexually. Appreciates and prefers women's culture, women's emotional flexibility. *Sometimes* loves individual men, sexually and/or nonsexually" [emphasis added]. A womanist's first erotic loyalty is to other women, whether that love is expressed sexually or platonically. Whereas love for men is allowed for within womanism, the "sometimes" is telling. Walker explicitly privileges the love women have for each other as a means to the womanist precept of "[a]cting grown up. Being grown up." Walker conflates the ability and willingness to love other women either sexually or nonsexually with growth as a human being. The fourth definition compares womanism to feminism by way of color: "Womanist is to feminist as purple is to lavender" (xii). This analogy implies not only that womanists are literally darker in hue than (white) feminists, but also that womanism is richer and less diluted than feminism.

Additionally, as Janet Montelaro convincingly suggests, the invocation of "purple" can hardly be accidental. She argues that the fourth definition is "a fitting prelude to *The Color Purple*" (14). The novel invokes both its title and its author's definition of womanism in a speech from Shug Avery who argues that "it pisses God off if you walk by the color purple in a field somewhere and don't notice it" (197). The color's metonymic relationship to both nobility and spirituality, coupled with the beauty of the natural world that demands to be noticed and appreciated, makes purple a fitting symbol for Walker's commitment to recovering Black female artists from historical neglect, and celebrating the ennobling and self-actualizing love between African American women both past and present. By rhetorically linking her novel to her definition, Walker implies that *The Color Purple* is a fictional representation of what womanism would look like as a lived experience.

Though the collection was published after *The Color Purple*, the essays themselves were written before and while Walker was composing her novel and therefore serve as a glimpse into how she sought to unite her political commitments with her artistic process. As the titular essay, "In Search of Our Mothers' Gardens," reveals, one of the prerogatives of Walker's womanism is a communal recovery of African American foremothers both biological and conceptual (the "mothers" of the title is plural), and within the collection, Walker addresses her artistic debt to and familial affection for Hurston in several places. One of these tributes, "Saving the Life That Is Your Own," relates Walker's serendipitous discovery of Hurston when she was researching a short story. Walker needed source material on voodoo, but found much more in Hurston's oeuvre: "a golden key to a storehouse of varied treasures" (12). According to Walker, Hurston's life and work as an African American woman of letters literally enabled the younger author's ability to create: "I would not have written the story [. . .] had I not known that Zora had already done a thorough job of preparing the ground over which I was then moving" (13). Taken together, the key and the trailblazer metaphors from "Saving the Life That Is Your Own" illuminate the relationship between the two novels. *Their Eyes Were Watching God* gives Walker an African American, female perspective on the socio-historical milieu of Eatonville, Florida, in the 1930s—a world where Black folk culture was not marginalized but dominant. Within this textual space, Hurston revises the traditional hero narrative by privileging the experience of a poor African American woman whose successful quest achieves knowledge of self by and through an equitable and sensually satisfying love relationship.

Of course, one of the reasons (along with residual racism affecting academic "canons") Walker had to "discover" Hurston rather than already enjoying a familiarity with the earlier writer is that the very ground that Hurston covered was, in her historical moment, intra-racially controversial. The very elements that Walker "needed" to create a womanist heroine overcoming classist, racist, and misogynist oppression—folk speech and cultural practice—were the very parts of Hurston's novel that were attacked by, among others, Richard Wright and Alain Locke upon its publication (Hemenway 241).

Her inclusion of folklore and focus on rural African Americans who were, in large part, isolated from white people was criticized by proponents of social fiction as "counter-revolutionary." Ironically, Walker's novel, though it was awarded the Pulitzer Prize and enjoyed a wide critical and popular readership, was similarly critiqued for being politically unsavvy but on different grounds. The rigorous exploration and critique of intra-racial gender relations and Black female sexuality that Walker includes in *The Color Purple* brought her vocal and persistent criticism for being anti-Black male.[2]

Both Hurston and Walker were criticized for their willingness to fictionally represent aspects of the experience of some Black women that were often ignored or marginalized by white and African American authors. In so doing, they complicated reductionist definitions of "the Black community" or "feminism," and thereby, contrary to the charges of their detractors, demonstrated a profoundly progressive political consciousness. Cherríe Moraga argues that only by confronting marginalized human beings can people come to terms with their complicity in oppression: "When we do rub up against this person, *there* then is the challenge. *There* then is the opportunity to look at the nightmare within us. But we usually shrink from such a challenge" ("La Güera" 33). By revising Janie the way she does in *The Color Purple*, Walker forces her readership to confront their own classist, colorist, and heterosexist prejudices.

The most obvious way *The Color Purple* follows Hurston's path is by creating another Black female heroine in the Jim Crow South, Celie, who also resists masculinist misogyny and achieves self-actualization through sexual love. Because this path has been cleared by Hurston, Walker has the freedom to more fully explore and complicate the terrain of Black female oppression and resistance in fiction. As Walker articulates in her poetic tribute to *Their Eyes Were Watching God*, what she loves about Janie Crawford is her refusal to settle for men who do not offer her the type of love that will enable and appreciate her humanity and independence. Janie's rejection of both "the one who wanted to change her / into a mule / and the other who tried to interest her / in being a queen" (Walker 7) allow her to eventually find an equitable and sensually satisfying (though temporary) love from her third husband, Tea Cake.

However, in order to achieve this relationship, Janie must undergo a literal and psychic journey that both reflects and revises comparative mythology scholar Joseph Campbell's paradigmatic hero narrative. In *The Hero With a Thousand Faces,* Campbell identifies "the difficult, dangerous task of self-discovery and self-development" (23) as the mythological hero's most important work. Campbell's language of self-actualization can be easily applied to Hurston's novel. Janie experiences her body's sexual awakening as a teenager in the safe space of her grandmother's yard in West Florida. She reaches an orgasmic state alone, surrounded by the sensory stimulation of the natural world. Because of this utopian experience, Janie understands sexual fulfillment as the most reliable indicator of heterosexual love and searches for a man who can provide her with the same sensual satisfaction she enjoyed under the blooming pear tree. Janie's physical movement matches her erotic transition from husband to husband and replicates the development of her own psychic conception of what she values in life, from other people, and herself.

The specific revisions Walker makes to Hurston's heroine — her color and her sexuality—indicate the novel's relationship to Walker's womanism. Janie's light skin conforms to European standards of beauty, and, because of the importation of this racist definition of female attractiveness into the Black community, she is thereby made susceptible to men who appropriate her body to bolster their own aspirations to white definitions of power. Joe Starks is the novel's most extensive treatment of this problematic and is the husband who wants to make Janie a "queen" in Walker's poem. In the essay "If the Present Looks Like the Past, What does the Future Look Like?" (published the same year as her novel and collected in *Mothers' Gardens*), Walker identifies "colorism" as one intra-racial obstacle to liberation for Black people. In the essay, Walker recasts the "mulatto privileges" Janie presumably acquires with her Euro-American features as vulnerabilities in a sexist, colorist society. Walker reads the devastating scene where Tea Cake beats Janie as a symptom of the otherwise ideal man's internalization of white standards of beauty: "One reason TeaCake [sic] is jealous is because it is so unusual for a woman as light and well-to-do as Janie to be with a man as poor and black as he is. Not because all the light-skinned women chase after and propose to light-skinned men, but because both light- and dark-skinned men chase after and propose to light-skinned women" (304).

Walker here connects disparagement of black(er) skin with a type of racial self-loathing that is imported from a white culture that disparages blackness and becomes an impediment to realizing a more hopeful future for African Americans: "to me, the black black woman is our essential mother—the blacker she is the more us she is—and to see the hatred that is turned on her is enough to make me despair, almost entirely, of our future as a people" (291). Making Celie and Shug "black black" women is a way for Walker to rehabilitate the Black foremother as a powerful and relevant force for change.

Additionally, Celie's sexual identity subverts the hetero-normative paradigm rigorously challenged by lesbian feminists during the novel's cultural moment. Cherríe Moraga, in the preface to *This Bridge Called My Back* challenges radical feminists of color to "develop a movement that can live with the fact of the loves and lives of these women in [*This Bridge*]" who experience sexism and heterosexism. Janie's relationship with her "kissin'-friend" of twenty years, Pheoby, which frames the novel's central narrative and is by all accounts deeply intimate and mutually satisfying, is not an exact replication of Janie's ideal love paradigm because it lacks the explicitly sexual pleasure Janie initially experienced under the pear tree and later recreated with Tea Cake. However, Walker imagines what would be possible for another Southern Black heroine, the novel's narrator, Celie, if an intimate relationship with another woman *did* in fact provide both sexual gratification and equitable partnership. Celie experiences her sexual awakening because her lesbian desires lead her to Shug, a woman uniquely suited to help her combat and defeat the masculinist oppression preventing her liberation. Janie, who is heterosexual, does not have the desire for a sexual partner other than men, who Hurston suggests often express their racial anxiety as sexist domination. Walker casts lesbian desire as a privilege rather than an obstacle. The novel demonstrates that Celie's love for and with a Black woman is literally and conceptually capable of healing physical abuse and undoing the previous oppression.

Walker argues throughout *The Color Purple* that sexual dissatisfaction in women is the logical consequence of the kind of masculinist misogyny that expresses itself through physical abuse and dominative sex. In the novel, these three concepts—hierarchical gender organization and both its violent manifestations—are in fact inseparable. Men instill and ensure subservience in women's minds by and through dominating women's bodies. Celie's first heterosexual encounter teaches her that sexual touch is a physical expression and reinforcement of the violent masculinist domination that pervades all aspects of her domestic space. Whereas Janie's experience under the pear tree enacts a model of non-dominative sex that she can use as a basis for comparison with later lovers, Celie's first sexual encounter is a profoundly devastating violation from the man she believes to be her biological father, Alphonso.

In the novel, Celie is radically alienated from her body's capacity to engage with the world sensuously. She describes herself at the beginning of her story as numb and incapable of interpersonal connection because she refuses to touch or be touched intimately by other people, in both the physical and emotional connotations of the word (23). Celie's lack of emotional connection is both because she is being abused and because she has not yet met a woman with whom her authentic desire could be satisfied. However, Walker is committed to demonstrating that the causes and the manifestations of masculinist domination are not an inextricable part of being human (or of being Black or poor) but are socially produced and therefore capable of improvement through equitable and satisfying love. For Celie, that experience of love can only come from another woman.

For Celie, sex with Mr. ___ is consistent with his model of dominative masculinity, and highlights her internalization of Alphonso's imperative to be silent and compliant in the face of violation. Mr. ___ organizes all his relationships (with the exception of his love for Shug Avery) in terms of paternalistic power. He ranks his family with himself at the head and subjects his wife and children to his will. As he tells his son Harpo, "Wives is like children. You have to let 'em know who got the upper hand. Nothing can do that better than a good sound beating" (36). Mr. ___ further stabilizes the unjust domestic hierarchy he has created with violence that is perversely termed "good" and "sound" expressions of intrafamilial touch. When Celie describes sex with Mr. ___ to Shug, Celie articulates how their sexual contact is always infected by his dominative impulses (78). She explains "he git up on you, heist your nightgown round your waist, plunge in."

The sex, though semi-consensual (mainly because Alphonso's rapes have rendered Celie unable to conceive of sex as something she can refuse), replicates her stepfather's violation. Mr. ___'s penetrative "plunge" into her body echoes Alphonso's "push." Mr. ___'s "heist" of her nightgown, though a Black folk English rendering of "hoist," also neatly echoes the etymology of rape: a theft of Celie's capacity to enjoy intimate contact. She figures Mr. ___ "git[ing] up on" her as if he was climbing on a horse or a piece of furniture. His physical position during sex, above Celie, also enacts and enforces his degradation and objectification of her. Celie's sexual relationship with Shug will similarly enact and enforce the equitable and mutually pleasurable dynamic of their relationship, because Shug is an appropriate love object for Celie both because she is a woman, and she is a sensitive and empowered model for Celie to emulate for escaping Mr. ___'s oppression.

Before Celie is ready to make a definitive break from Mr. ____, she must acquire the capacity to love other Black women. Celie's suggestion to her stepson Harpo that he beat his wife, Sofia (37), suggests that Celie, in experiencing masculinist domination, has to some degree normalized it, thereby preventing the formation of a loving friendship with the independent and headstrong woman. Celie's conversation with Sofia after she has discovered Celie's complicity in Harpo's abuse is a preview of the emotional and physical work Celie must undergo in order to liberate herself from excusing abuse and open herself up to friendship with other Black women (39-42). The guilt Celie feels after betraying Sofia is counterintuitively the first hopeful sign that her capacity for human feeling is being reawakened. Celie's confrontation with Sofia leads to a realization that she wants to "fight," but lacks the emotional and physical strength to do so (40). Celie's admission of jealousy and shame effectively disarms Sofia's justified anger and opens a space for a constructive conversation between the two women. Sofia, "sad now" at realizing the depth of Celie's vulnerability, tells Celie her own story of domestic strife and how she was able to overcome the "family of men" that threatened her safety (40).

Sofia, in stark contrast to Celie, is a physically powerful and emotionally headstrong woman, and her response to masculinist abuse is markedly different than Celie's emotional shutdown: Sofia fights back. Her strong body, described as soldier-like (31) and Amazonian (68) in the text, matches and overwhelms Harpo's attempts to physically dominate her. Sofia's emotional fortitude is expressed by and through her muscular body. However, Walker does not suggest resistance to masculinist domination is only possible through physical strength. Rather, Sofia's powerful body is a textual marker for the familial support system that makes resistance possible.

Sofia's sisters are an example in *The Color Purple* of the necessary material and emotional support women need in order to escape domestic domination. Mr. ___'s original rejection of Harpo's intention to marry the pregnant Sofia is not disastrous for her because "She say, Naw. I ain't living in the street. I'm living with my sister and her husband. They say I can live with them for the rest of my life. She stand up, big, strong, healthy girl, and she say, Well, nice visiting. I'm going home" (32). The safe home "for the rest of [her] life" enables Sofia's "big, strong, healthy" femininity. Her sister's protection facilitates Sofia's financial and emotional independence from Harpo. When his abuse becomes intolerable, she takes their children (thereby interrupting the transmission of toxic masculinity to their son[3]) to her sister's house, where they remain for the majority of the novel. Walker suggests that Sofia is lucky. She was born into a family of six girls "all big and strong like [her]" who "stick together" when her father and brothers threatened them (40-41). However, the novel does not conclude that Black women without such a biological support system are doomed to inescapable suffering.

Throughout the novel, Celie, whose own beloved sister was banished by Mr. ___ when she refused his sexual advances, is depicted as an individual who has to learn to create and sustain a circle of sisters whose emotional and physical love culminates in her relationship with Shug, and that educative process begins with the conversation with Sofia about her sisters (39-42). Celie, who begins the letter identifying her guilt, ends the missive by relating her delight. Sofia's directive to "bash Mr. ___ head open" and "[t]hink bout heaven later" is not one that she is at this moment equipped to perform, but the laughter that follows, both because Celie feels amusement and because the feeling is shared with Sofia, is a necessary step towards being able to resist Mr. ___'s later domination in a more definitive way. Honest and open conversation between the two women thaws Celie's emotional numbness and creates an ally against her abusive husband. By placing the letter describing Shug's arrival immediately after this exchange, Walker suggests that Celie needed to learn how to be emotionally available to an independent and supportive woman before she would be able to receive the more intense and intimate love offered by Shug.

Because Shug is not confined by societal mandates (like paternalist misogyny or compulsive heterosexuality) that distort or forbid expressions of love, she is the character capable of reactivating Celie's capacity for emotional and physical intimacy. After Celie successfully negotiates Shug's initial hostility about being cared for by her lover's wife, the two create a connection based in physical pleasure that enables Celie to reclaim many of the feminine love relationships that Alphonso and Mr. ____ denied her: "I work on [Shug] like she a doll or like she Olivia [Celie's lost daughter]—or like she mama. I comb and pat, comb and pat. First she say, hurry up and git finish. Then she melt down a little and lean back gainst my knees. That feel just right, she say. That feel like mama used to do" (53). By and through touching Shug, Celie gets to experience the roles of a young girl, a mother, and a daughter—precisely the relationships that Alphonso's rapes and Mr. ____'s abuse preclude. In turn, Shug, living up to her nickname, "melt[s]" onto Celie's body and into a trusting and loving child. This emotional and sensual awakening (and its rewards) intensifies as the two women's relationship becomes explicitly sexual.

Just as sex with a dominative man reflects and reinforces that domination, Walker figures the best, most liberating kind of sex as a physical expression of emotional intimacy and respect between two people. Though there is something of the familial in Celie's love for Shug (they "sleep like sisters" [146] and "are each other's peoples" [184]), Walker figures Celie's attraction to Shug as above all erotic. Celie admires Shug's beauty in a photograph before they meet, worries that she's "turned into a man" because of the intensity of her attraction at seeing Shug's naked body (49), and feels an overwhelming desire to "tast[e] [Shug's] fingers in [her] mouth" (51). Shug is the first person (other than God) that Celie tells about Alphonso's rapes and therefore enables Celie's first active refusal of her stepfather's command to "shut up" and "git used to it."

The sexual contact between the two that follows from Celie's revelation of her past trauma is figured as coextensive with both emotional intimacy and resistance to masculinist oppression:

> 'Oh, Miss Celie, she say. And put her arms round me. They black and smooth and kind of glowy from the lamplight.
>
> I start to cry too. I cry and cry and cry. Seem like it all come back to me, laying there in Shug's arms. How it hurt and how much I was surprise. How it stung while I finish trimming his hair. How the blood drip down my leg and mess up my stocking. How he don't never look at me straight after that. And Nettie.
>
> Don't cry, Celie, Shug say. Don't cry. She start kissing the water as it come down side my face.
>
> [. . . .] She say, I love you Miss Celie. And then she haul off and kiss me on the mouth.
>
> *Um*, she say, like she surprise. I kiss her back, say, *um*, too. Us kiss and kiss till us can't hardly kiss no more. Then us touch each other.
>
> I don't know nothing bout it, I say to Shug.
>
> I don't know much, she say.
>
> Then I feels something real soft and wet on my breast, feel like one of my little lost babies mouth.
>
> Way after while, I act like a little lost baby too.' (112-113)

Shug's audible expression of compassion and her embrace create the physical and psychic space Celie requires to process the horror of the abuse. Rather than imaginatively absenting herself from the memory (a strategy of negation that extends to her sexual relationship with Mr. ___), Celie experiences fully, possibly for the first time, the pain and shame Alphonso's violation provoked. Shug's response literalizes empathy by incorporating Celie's tears into her body. This intimacy is expressed verbally ("I love you") and physically (with a "kiss . . . on the mouth"). The kisses and erotic touching that follow are textually marked by their innocence—both through the comparison with infancy and in the sense of inexperience with or ignorance of lesbian sex. This episode is the exact inverse of Alphonso's rapes and Mr. ___'s domination. Rather than physical pain, emotional oppression, and loss, sex with Shug is likened to plenitude—being fed by and feeding the beloved. The physical and emotional relationship Celie creates and sustains with Shug directly leads her to a rediscovery of the sisterhood that both Alphonso and Mr. ___ thwarted.

The novel conceptually affirms the power of erotic pleasure to enable loving relationships by making Celie's emotional reconnection with Nettie and her acquisition of the truth about her family's history textually dependent upon her reclamation of her sexuality. Walker uses her novel to show how a radical reawakening of the body's capacity for pleasure can translate into political progress. Herbert Marcuse, an interpreter of Freud, makes a similar argument in *Eros and Civilization* (1955). He suggests that a liberated social system will follow from a liberated body. Walker's plot reinforces that theory by making Celie's discovery of her sister's survival follow directly from her sexual relationship with Shug. "One night in bed" Shug asks Celie for details about Nettie and realizes that the letters with "funny stamps" she sees when accompanying Mr. ___ to the mailbox must be from Celie's lost sister (120). She then surreptitiously acquires one by flirting with him (121) and also devises a plan for allowing Celie to read all the letters Mr. ___ has been hiding without him realizing the missives have been discovered (126). The bed, the place of sexual and emotional intimacy, transforms into a space for reclaiming (biological as well as metaphorical) sisterhood and defying Mr. ___'s cruelly imposed isolation. Significantly, it is after Celie and Shug have created an open and intimate love relationship that Celie is rewarded with her sister's stolen letters and their enclosed revelations: Celie's children are alive and well and living with Nettie and their adoptive family, and Celie's biological father is not the dreadful Alphonso, but an honest and loving man who was the victim of lynching. If Celie had remained "wood" (23), unable to open herself physically or emotionally to Shug, she most likely would never have learned about Nettie's survival, and her life as a missionary in Africa. Also, as scholar Maria Lauret points out in *Alice Walker*, Shug's successful singing career provides Celie with the material support and domestic shelter she needs when she finally breaks from Mr. ___, and enables her to replicate the role that Sofia's sisters play (93).

bell hooks, in an attentive and provocative reading of the novel's lesbian politics, poses serious questions about the efficacy of Walker's treatment of Celie and Shug's sexual relationship in the novel as liberating. hooks affirms that "Walker makes the powerful suggestion that sexual desire can disrupt and subvert oppressive social structure because it does not necessarily conform to social prescription," but this realization is undermined by the refusal to acknowledge it as threatening—dangerous" ("Writing the Subject"

217). Specifically, hooks objects both to the lack of judgmental derision from a homophobic community to Celie and Shug's sexual affair and to Celie's eventual loss of Shug as a sexual partner, when sexuality is so crucial to her liberation. The first claim overstates the knowledge and interest of the small circle of friends and family that would be in a position to judge Celie and Shug when they initiate their sexual relationship at Mr. ___'s farm and understates the anonymity the couple would have enjoyed while Celie was ensconced at Shug's Memphis mansion.[4]

hooks's second claim is more troubling. If Celie's "life is presented in reference to her sexual history" (217), then what is the significance of Shug's dalliance with another lover and the ambiguous nature of Celie and Shug's relationship when they are reunited near the conclusion of the novel? Even if Celie and Shug do not resume their sexual life together, the emotional and physical intimacy of which sex is a culmination, but not the sole expression, remains and does its liberating work. Walker has demonstrated that the physical pleasure available through sexual touch has little to do with the sex itself, but is an extension of emotional receptivity to and trust in another human being. If sex alone were the *only* "subversive transformative force, one that enables folk to break radically with convention" (hooks 217), then Celie's possible celibacy at the end of the novel would be a devastating flaw. However, the emotional and physical reawakening Celie acquired through sex with Shug—an ability to open herself to the sensual pleasure of loving other people and the natural world—is the "transformative" force that Walker ultimately wants to endorse, and it finds its expression through a liberatory love that encompasses, but is not reducible to, sexuality. As poet and essayist Cheryl Clarke argues in "Lesbianism: an Act of Resistance," the very fact of loving other women sexually, "no matter how a woman lives out her lesbianism," is by its nature a "passion [that] will ultimately reverse the heterosexual imperialism of male culture" (128).

Walker figures familial love in the novel as so powerful that the mere knowledge that Nettie is still alive, that her children are safe, and that her biological father cared for her enables Celie to boldly resist and ultimately defy what literary critic Linda Abbandonato terms the "unholy trinity" (302) of masculinist domination that has subjugated her. Celie, more so than Janie, *progressively* acquires voice, independence, and strength through the course of the novel.

Carla Kaplan, in her chapter on *Their Eyes Were Watching God* in her book *The Erotics of Talk*, calls into question previous readings that understand the novel as a fictional account of a black woman's acquisition of voice, arguing quite convincingly that Janie already has the self-possession to argue with her Nanny and stand up to her first husband (103). This reading makes her second husband's suppression of Janie's strong sense of self even more upsetting. Celie, however, begins *The Color Purple* as profoundly fearful of speaking or resisting men due to Alphonso's abuse, and evolves markedly after befriending Sofia, loving Shug, and reading Nettie's letters. Celie writes, "Now I know Nettie alive I begin to strut a little bit. Think, When she come home us leave here. Her and me and our two children" (148).

After Celie reads the letter that details the tragic story of her and Nettie's father's death and their mother's resultant insanity (explaining, if not excusing, her failure to defend Celie from Alphonso's abuse), Celie begins to write to Nettie rather than to God, definitively abrogating Alphonso's command to not talk to anyone but God about her misfortunes. In fact, she qualitatively rejects the Christian conception of deity altogether in this letter, arguing that "the God I been praying to is a man. And act just like all the other mens I know. Trifling, forgitful and lowdown" (193). The letter immediately following describes Celie's audacious and self-possessed rebuke of Mr. ___ and his treatment of her over the past decades, informing him that she is leaving him for good: "You a lowdown dog is what's wrong, I say. It's time to leave you and enter into the Creation. And your dead body is just the welcome mat I need" (202).

Indeed it appears that Celie's knowledge of and love for Nettie and her children are factors that directly enable her to verbally and physically[5] challenge Mr. ___'s domination. She threatens him with a beating from the combined physical force of Nettie and her restored children (202). Celie has finally acquired the strength, confidence, and support she needs to threaten Mr. ___ with the beating Sofia recommended during their conversation about his abuse. Though Celie never physically strikes Mr. ___, she does lay a curse on him that dooms his attempts to live alone until he atones for his abusive treatment, and becomes a man more similar to the one Shug fell in love with.

Shug and Celie's physical, emotional, and sexual intimacy enable Celie to claim independence from Mr. ___ and both conceptual and literal sisterhood. In fact, the novel argues that autonomy is only possible through relationships with others. One could argue that Celie's reunion with her lost sister and children at the conclusion of *The Color Purple* is a naively utopian moment in a novel otherwise committed to candid honesty about the harsh lives of poor, Black women. Critic Martha J. Cutter, in an essay investigating the intersection of sexuality and voice in the novel, also reads *The Color Purple* as about a woman who is able to successfully resist the "violent patriarchal inscription of male will onto a silent female body" (163). Whereas Cutter locates this resistance only in the realm of discourse, Celie's bodily resistance (through reacquisition of sensory pleasure) is equally crucial to her success.

However, the restitution of Celie's family can also be understood as a literalization of Celie's journey as a whole. Nettie would have done her best to return to Celie whether she had discovered and read her letters or not. However, Celie would not have been the open, loving, and engaging woman that Nettie finds on the steps of their family home; one can imagine a wildly different future for Celie if she had not been able to become intimate with Shug and learn that her sister and children were alive. She might have been so emotionally and physically destroyed by Mr. ___'s domination that she might have died or gone mad, as her mother did. However, because Celie creates a family by opening herself physically and emotionally to other people, she is able to welcome Nettie as a whole person who has learned how to love and be loved. The women Celie gathers around her enable her to value herself as a person worthy of happiness, facilitate knowledge of her past and present biological family and give her material and emotional support to leave Mr. ___.

In both Hurston's and Walker's novels, the heroines achieve self-actualization and independence by and through repairing the damage wrought on their minds and bodies by masculinist misogyny, thereby achieving what Campbell in his cross-cultural mythological study terms the "effect of the successful adventure of the hero . . . the unlocking and release again of the flow of life into the body of the world" (40). In *Their Eyes Were Watching God*, this unlocking is represented in Janie's final act of gathering "her horizon like a great fish-net . . . over her shoulder" and marveling at "so much of life in its meshes" (184). However, Janie ends her narrative not completely reintegrated into her community, with no living family, and without the romantic love she has sought and only briefly enjoyed throughout the novel. *The Color Purple*, though, concludes with Celie surrounded by her restored family and living with the woman she loved most in her life. Why did Walker reward her heroine with such a happy ending?

   In "Beyond the Peacock: The Reconstruction of Flannery O'Connor," an essay in the collection inspired by another Southern literary ancestress, Walker figures writing as a cross-temporal and trans-spatial collaboration: "I believe that the truth about any subject only comes when all sides of the story are put together, and all their different meanings make one new one. Each writer writes the missing parts to the other writer's story." *The Color Purple*'s embrace of Hurston's chosen time period and problematic of how to love in a racist and sexist world affirms the continued relevance of *Their Eyes Were Watching God* nearly fifty years after its original publication and establishes a direct line of literary inheritance. The critical task then becomes understanding the terms of the imaginative collaboration: What does Walker contribute to Hurston's portrait of oppressed but audacious Black femininity in the Jim Crow South? What, in Walker's terminology, "missing parts" is she composing, and what is the resultant "whole story"? Walker's definition of womanism provides one way of answering. The manifestation of Celie's biological family at the end of the book (a reunion that is celebrated, significantly, on Independence Day[6]) rewrites the "missing parts" of Hurston's portrayal of a woman's quest for subjectivity by revising the terms of autonomy and liberty. Walker counter-intuitively suggests that interpersonal connection and communal support, not stoic individualism, makes personal freedom possible and, in so doing, employs a womanist philosophy to offer a radical revision of the paradigmatic solitary American hero.

   Whereas *Their Eyes Were Watching God* loosely replicates the hero's journey of excursion and return, concluding with Janie alone and reflective in her bedroom, the conclusion of *The Color Purple* conceives of a different way to tell a story of Black, female, American independence. Walker's novel can be placed into productive dialogue with classic narratives of American heroism typified by Cooper and Melville, skillfully nuanced by Ralph Ellison and Richard Wright, and updated by contemporary writers like Ishmael Reed's *Flight to Canada* (1976), Cormac McCarthy in *Blood Meridian* (1992), and Ernest J. Gaines in *A Lesson Before Dying* (1993). Walker, along with other post-war Black female authors like

Toni Morrison and Gloria Naylor, question this narrative's conflation of isolation with subjectivity and independence.

However, in order to arrive at this revision, Walker had to embark on a heroine's journey of her own. Until she discovered Hurston, Walker figures herself in "Saving the Life That Is Your Own" as "wandering in the wilderness" in danger of losing the "authentic black folklore" that structured her family's history. After immersing herself in Hurston's work, Walker, much like Celie, arrives at a place where she is *"with* a great many people . . . eager to let me know, through the joy of their presence, that, indeed, I am not alone" ("Saving the Life That Is Your Own 12, 13).

Tracy L. Bealer, University of South Carolina

Notes

[1] Henry Louis Gates Jr. offers a foundational analysis of Walker's "Signifyin(g)" on Hurston's use of folk speech in *The Signifying Monkey*. Maria Lauret argues that both Hurston and Walker transform Black folk English into blues-inflected art. See also Michael Awkward's intertextual reading of Hurston and Walker's interest in the enduring spiritual strength of Black southern women, and Mel Watkins's early review of the novel.

[2] Debate over Walker's treatment of Black men has periodically waxed and waned since the novel's publication, intensifying when Steven Spielberg's film version premiered in 1985. For a good overview of the participants in and terms of the dialogue, see Jacqueline Bobo "Sifting through the Controversy: Reading *The Color Purple*" and Evelyn White's biography of Walker, 362-64.

[3] After Sofia describes her forced servitude to the white mayor's family as slavery, her oldest son, "tall and handsome" insists she was not a slave, but a "captive" (105). This politically charged reclamation of his mother's subjectivity makes Sofia "glad he hers" and alerts the reader to a different possibility for Black masculinity. Walker fully realizes this trope with Celie's son Adam's feminism.

[4] Walker includes some textual clues that Celie and Shug were "sneaking around" while at Mr. ___'s (113, 145), and though Celie did leave Georgia to move in with Shug immediately after leaving Mr. ____, so did Mary Agnes. Though Mr. ___ eventually realizes that Celie "loves" Shug the way he does (274), Walker implies that, on some fundamental level, he doesn't understand Celie's lesbianism; he proposes to live as man and wife with Celie after she has returned from living with Shug.

[5] Celie stabs him in the hand with a case knife (203).

[6] Keith Byerman writes that the ending betrays the novel's folk sensibility by seemingly transcending history and suffering ("Walker's Blues"). Lauren Berlant reads this coincidence as especially jarring in a novel that seems otherwise committed to questioning the exclusion of African Americans from dominant definitions of

American populism. However, I contend that Walker orchestrated the synchronicity as an ironic commentary on the popular fiction of the stoic, solitary American hero. Celie achieves her heroism not by isolating herself from others, but by and through fostering loving relationships.

Works Cited

Abbandonato, Linda. "Rewriting the Heroine's Story in *The Color Purple.*" *Alice Walker: Critical Perspectives Past and Present.* Ed. Henry Louis Gates Jr. and K.A. Appiah. Amistad Literary Ser. New York: Amistad, 1993. (296-308)

Awkward, Michael. *Inspiriting Influences: Tradition, Revision and Afro-American Women's Novels.* New York: Columbia UP, 1989.

Berlant, Lauren. "Race, Gender, and Nation in *The Color Purple.*" *Alice Walker: Critical Perspectives Past and Present.* Ed. Henry Louis Gates Jr. and K.A. Appiah. Amistad Literary Ser. New York: Amistad, 1993. (211-38)

Bloom, Harold. Introduction. *Modern Critical Views: Alice Walker.* Ed. Harold Bloom. Modern Critical Views. New York: Chelsea House, 1989. (1-4)

Bobo, Jacqueline. "Sifting through the Controversy: Reading *The Color Purple.*" *Callaloo* 12.2 (Spring 1989): 332-42.

Byerman, Keith. "Walker's Blues." From *Fingering the Jagged Grain.* Athens: U of Georgia P, 1985. [Rpt. in *Modern Critical Views: Alice Walker.* Ed. Harold Bloom. Modern Critical Views. New York: Chelsea House, 1989. (59-66)]

Campbell, Joseph. *The Hero With a Thousand Faces.* New York: MJF Books, 1949.

Clarke, Cheryl. "Lesbianism: an Act of Resistance." *This Bridge Called My Back: Writings By Radical Women of Color.* Ed. Cherríe Moraga and Gloria Anzaldúa. Watertown, MA: Persephone Press, 1981. (128-37)

Combahee River Collective. "A Black Feminist Statement." *All The Women Are White, All the Blacks Are Men, But Some of Us Are Brave: Black Women's Studies.* Ed. Gloria T. Hull, Patricia Bell Scott, and Barbara Smith. Old Westbury, NY: The Feminist Press, 1982. (13-22)

Cutter, Martha J. "Philomela Speaks: Alice Walker's Revisioning of Rape Archetypes in *The Color Purple*." *MELUS* 25.3/4 (Fall/Winter 2000): 161-80.

Gates Jr., Henry Louis. *The Signifying Monkey: A Theory of African-American Literary Criticism*. New York: Oxford UP, 1988.

Hemenway, Robert E. *Zora Neale Hurston: A Literary Biography*. Urbana: U Illinois P, 1977.

hooks, bell. "Writing the Subject: Reading *The Color Purple*." *Modern Critical Views: Alice Walker*. Ed. Harold Bloom. Modern Critical Views. New York: Chelsea House, 1989. (215-28). [Also published as "Reading and Resistance: *The Color Purple*." *Reading Black, Reading Feminist: A Critical Anthology*. Ed. Henry Louis Gates Jr. New York: Penguin, 1990. (454-71) and *Alice Walker: Critical Perspectives Past and Present*. Ed. Henry Louis Gates Jr and K.A. Appiah. Amistad Literary Ser. New York: Amistad, 1993. (284-95).]

Hurston, Zora Neale. *Their Eyes Were Watching God*. 1937. New York: Harper & Row, 1990.

Kaplan, Carla. *The Erotics of Talk: Women's Writing and Feminist Paradigms*. New York: Oxford UP, 1996.

Lauret, Maria. *Modern Novelists: Alice Walker*. Modern Novelists. New York: St. Martin's, 2000.

Marcuse, Herbert. *Eros and Civilization: A Philosophical Inquiry into Freud*. 1955. Boston: Beacon P, 1966.

Montelaro, Janet J. *Producing a Womanist Text: The Maternal as Signifier in Alice Walker's* The Color Purple. ELS Monograph Ser. 70. Victoria, B.C., U of Victoria (Canada), 1996.

Moraga, Cherríe. "La Güera." *This Bridge Called My Back: Writings By Radical Women of Color*. Ed. Cherríe Moraga and Gloria Anzaldúa. Watertown, MA: Persephone Press, 1981. (27-34)

—. Preface. *This Bridge Called My Back: Writings By Radical Women of Color*. Ed. Cherríe Moraga and Gloria Anzaldúa. Watertown, MA: Persephone Press, 1981. (xiii-xix)

Sadoff, Dianne F. "Black Matrilineage: The Case of Alice Walker and Zora Neale Hurston." *Signs: Journal of Women in Culture and Society* 11.1 (Autumn 1985). [Rpt. in *Modern Critical Views: Alice Walker*. Ed. Harold Bloom. Modern Critical Views. New York: Chelsea House Publishers, 1989. (115-34)]

Walker, Alice. *The Color Purple*. 1982. Orlando: Harcourt, 2003.

—. *The Same River Twice: Honoring the Difficult, A Meditation on Life, Spirit, Art, and the Making of the Film* The Color Purple *Ten Years Later*. New York: Scribner, 1996.

—. *In Search of Our Mothers' Gardens: Womanist Prose*. San Diego: Harvest-Harcourt Brace Jovanovich, 1983.

—. "Beyond the Peacock: The Reconstruction of Flannery O'Connor" in *In Search of Our Mothers' Gardens* (1983).

—. "Saving the Life That Is Your Own" in *In Search of Our Mothers' Gardens* (1983).

Watkins, Mel. "*The Color Purple*." The *New York Times Book Review*. 25 July 1982. [Rpt. in *Alice Walker: Critical Perspectives Past and Present*. Ed. Henry Louis Gates Jr. and K.A. Appiah. Amistad Literary Ser. New York: Amistad, 1993. (16-18)]

White, Evelyn C. *Alice Walker: A Life*. New York: W.W. Norton & Co., 2004.

Alice Walker's *The Color Purple*: Womanist Folk Tale and Capitalist Fairy Tale

Raphaël Lambert

Alice Walker's *The Color Purple* (1982) tells the story of Celie, a poor, downtrodden African American girl from rural Georgia who, in the early twentieth century, breaks free from her abusive husband and achieves material, spiritual, and emotional independence. This reflection argues that behind the provocative tone and reformist spirit foregrounded in *The Color Purple* lies the myth of the self-made (wo)man. Following in the steps both of old folk tales and feminist stories, *The Color Purple* forcefully restores the dignity of the female character. Many critics feel that it does so, however, to the detriment of male characters, which undermines Walker's principles of gender tolerance and forgiveness. I would contend that *The Color Purple* bears a remarkable likeness to many traditional fairy tales, which appeared in the sixteenth and seventeenth centuries and corresponded to the written, bourgeoisified versions of earlier oral folk tales. Duplicating the new creed of free-market economy and adjoined Calvinist values that once informed fairy tales, the story of Celie becomes a capitalist fantasy very much at odds with Walker's initial project. In fact, the exceptional destiny of Celie, this reflection concludes, may be seen as negative reflection on the African American community rather than as indicator of its conquering spirit.

Womanism, Folk Tales, Feminist Tales, and Masculinity

In her essay collection *In Search of Our Mothers' Gardens* (1983), Alice Walker defined the term womanism, a concept whose principles already permeated *The Color Purple*. By her definition, womanism is a response to the predominantly white feminist movement, and intends to bear witness to the black experience in every domain. A womanist, Walker explains, is "a black feminist or a feminist of color." It is also "a woman who loves other women sexually and/or non-sexually. Appreciates and prefers women's culture, women's emotional flexibility, and women's strength. Sometimes loves individual men sexually and/or non-sexually [...] Traditionally universalist [...] traditionally capable [...]" A womanist, Walker continues, "Loves music. Loves dance. Loves the moon. *Loves* the spirits. Loves love and food and roundness. Loves struggle. Loves the Folk. Loves herself [...]" Womanism, Walker concludes, "is to feminism as purple to lavender" (xii). Walker's definition clearly extols animism, sapphism, and universalism, all of which are essential components of the novel. Indeed, the ending of The Color Purple features an ideal social state, a sort of blissful matriarchal phalanstery where reformed males are accepted, indeed welcome into the fold. It is only a Utopian vision but it fosters the hope of a better future for an ethnic minority. Through Celie's wondrous transformation, African American women—past, present, and future—can envision a better world in which to live.

The ideal universe Walker creates in *The Color Purple* is reminiscent of the universe typifying oral folk tales of the past. As folklore scholar Jack Zipes explains in *Breaking the Magic Spell* (1979), folk tales were addressed to the community at large and played a crucial role in society: "Not only did the tales serve to unite the people of the community and help bridge a gap in their understanding of social problems in a language and narrative made familiar to the listeners' experiences, but this aura illuminated the possible fulfillment of Utopian longings and wishes which did not preclude social integration" (4). In this sense, folk tales reflected the community and its psychology. They also provided the hope for self-transformation, and "they sought to celebrate humankind's capacity to transform the mundane into the Utopian as part of a communal project" (*Breaking* xi). There is no doubt that *The Color Purple* shares with these folk tales a capacity to satisfy unconscious desires and fantasies. It is wish fulfillment—a chimerical inverted world where the poor become the powerful where the oppressors are punished and the oppressed find freedom.

In another study, *Fairy Tales and the Art of Subversion* (1983), Zipes argues that folk tales stemmed from matriarchal societies and depicted men as brutes or beasts who needed to be domesticated—a point that enhances the correspondence between folk tales and Walker's novel. Philosopher Heide Göttner-Abendroth comments on these tales of yore:

> In the eyes of the matriarchal woman, who created a cultivated environment for herself, [man] has never developed beyond the condition of predatory animal that roams the woods. He is

still covered by fur or feathers, while she wears human clothes
which she herself has made. (qtd. in *Fairy Tales* 33)

Fur and feathers aside, the parallel with the character Mr. in
Walker's novel is unmistakable. Before his conversion at the very
end of the story, Mr.____ *is* a brute mostly driven by violence and
sexual urges. After Celie leaves him, his life deteriorates and a
comment by Sofia suggests that Mr.____ has reverted to a sort of
infantile, primitive state:

> 'Mr.____ live like a pig. Shut up in the house so much it stunk.
> Wouldn't let nobody in until finally Harpo force his way in.
> Clean the house. Got food. Give his daddy a bath.' (224)

The Celie character also falls into the pattern of these old stories:
upon leaving the cruel Mr.____, Celie not only creates a better
enviorment for herself; she also wears clothes she "herself has
made," and even ends up clothing other people as she becomes a
successful tailor.

In "Things Walt Disney ever Told Us," folklorist Kay
Stone reports that tales with worthy heroines have been excised
from modern collections: "The popularized heroines of the Grimms
and Disney are not only passive and pretty, but also unusually
patient, obedient, industrious, and quiet" (44). In other words, fairy
tale heroines do not need o be invented but re-discovered.
According to Stone, in the two hundred and ten original Grimm
tales, only twenty percent of female characters were unassertive
and compliant. Significantly, only a bit more than ten percent of the
Grimms' stories have been selected and translated by Anglo-Saxon
editors, and their choices seem to have clearly been informed by a
sexist mentality since whimsy, apathetic female characters now
represent seventy five percent of all stories. In the late 1970s and
early 1980s, feminist writers such as Anne Sexton (e.g.,
Transformations, 1971), Olga Broumas (e.g., *Beginning with O*,
1976), and Joy Williams (e.g., *The Changelling*, 1978) sought to
redress such imbalance in gender representation by ridding pre-
adolescent literature of female stereotypes. These liberating tales
often borrowed well-known patterns and totally reversed them. *The
Color Purple* follows the same path: in contrast to the typically
cute, submissive, and often witless fairytale heroine, Walker's
protagonist Celie takes her destiny in her own hands and becomes
the architect of a successful life without Prince Charming and
without idealized heterosexual love.

Stone also notices that in the fairy tales to which mass-mediated culture has conditioned us, female sexuality is not dealt with. At puberty, Stone notes, females in many stories are locked up or put to sleep, only to reappear when it is time to marry or procreate. *The Color Purple* disrupts this pattern: not only is Celie raped at age thirteen, but the institution of marriage, along with the church and family, is depicted as inhuman and coercive while female homosexuality is openly set forth. Analyzing motherhood in fairy tales, folklorist Steven Swann Jones remarks that, "in some fairy tales [...] the heroine is being replaced after she is married, frequently after her child is born" (65). Swann Jones states further that it is not uncommon to see the heroine given to a new husband like a piece of chattel (70), which is reminiscent of the fate of Celie whom Pa, her purported father and the father of her two children, gives to Mr.____. Once the heroine is expelled, Swann Jones observes, "the quest undertaken by the heroine is to find a new home and rebuild her life. In some versions of the tales that depict this calumniation of the heroine, she is taken in by fairies who magically care for her" (26). Walker also subverts this traditional pattern as Celie, rather than being expelled, frees herself from the state of bondage in which Mr.____ has held her. Walker retains, however, the paradigm of the fairy through the Shug character even if Shug is not a traditional fairy or godmother.

Shug is first presented as a depraved, kinky, and obnoxious blues singer. The first time Shug meets Celie, she behaves like a witch, and what she tells her is one of the most memorable utterances in the novel: "You sure *is* ugly" (46). Shug, however, will mend her ways and help Celie "find a home" both denotatively and connotatively. In his third work on fairy tales, *Don't Bet on the Prince* (1986), Jack Zipes offers an interpretation of folk and fairy tale characters that helps explain the atmosphere surrounding Shug and Celie:

> As we know, witches, werewolves, and wolves were once revered in archaic societies as the mediators between the wilderness and society. They provided contact with the other world, or sacred divine and forbidden world. And this contact was necessary if the civilized world were to rejuvenate itself. So, the witch [...] lives on the outskirts of society [...] and represents the true healer of society, one who will be used and abused until "civilized" peoples learn to live in harmony with nature again, which also means living in harmony with our own bodies. The rearrangement of bodies demands a political

experiencing of a different mode of child rearing and sex roles
in which exploitation of nature no longer takes place. (25)

The resemblance of this description of the witches' environs and
the world of Shug is striking as are some of the key events that
occur in the novel. Shug is not a witch, but her way of life is
marginal. She is an independent woman, a blues singer on the road
who worships nature and advocates pantheism as a panacea to the
evils of society. Like witches and werewolves of bygone times,
Shug brings Celie out of her torpor, rejuvenates her, and teaches
her how to create a world where she can live in harmony with
others. More than a lover and confidante, Shug becomes a nurturer
and a spiritual guide to Celie. Specifically, Shug shows nihilistic
Celie that she fits in the natural order of the universe: "God is
inside you and inside everybody else. You come into the world
with God. But only them that search for it inside find it" (195). As
feminist scholar Stacie Lynn Hankinson points out, God, in Shug's
cosmogony, is not "He" any longer (324). The male connotation
has been removed. God is *it*; God, Shug contends, "is everything"
(195). Shug concludes her speech by telling Celie that God as Celie
knows it is an invention, and she teaches her how to find the real
God:

> 'Man corrupts everything [...] He on your box of grits, in your
> head [...] He try to make you think he everywhere. Soon as
> you think he everywhere, you think he God. But he ain't.
> Whenever you trying to pray, and man plop himself on the
> other hand of it, tell him to git lost [...] Conjure up flowers,
> wind, water, a big rock.' (197)

Celie is quick to embrace Shug's new creed; perhaps
because Shug is "the most beautiful woman I ever saw [...] more
pretty than my mama [and] bout ten thousand times more pretty
than me" (6). In short, Celie considers Shug as a princess and she is
fascinated by her. Not surprisingly, as in a fairy tale, this princess
who makes Celie turn "into a man" (49) ends up sleeping with
Celie. This is the completion of Celie's spiritual conversion and
rejuvenation. In a womanist/Walkerian tour de force, Shug
reconciles sex and religion[1]. Shug tells Celie God approves of
pleasure, even masturbation, and continues:

> 'God love all them feelings. That's some of the best stuff God
> did. And when you know God loves 'em you enjoys em a lot
> more.' (196)

Armed with her new faith (a combination of libertinage and animism) and buoyed by the discovery of her sister Nettie's letters, Celie is going to gather the strength required to confront and leave Mr.____.

Celie's metamorphosis is one of several occurrences whereby Walker's *The Color Purple* successfully challenges the widespread, degrading model of female behavior displayed in fairy tales. However, as scholar Ruth Mac Donald warns, feminist fairy tale writers always incur the risk of turning a tale demeaning to females into a male-bashing tale, yet again writing a sexist narrative. Although African American males are rather unflatteringly portrayed in *The Color Purple*, the end of the story appears to rehabilitate them as the brutal, almost bestial Mr.____ has become the soft-spoken, gentle, caring Albert who gladly helps his ex-wife to prosper and be happy. But Albert's transformation is so radical that it seems overdone. In short, Walker's depiction of male characters tends to affect her overall womanist agenda (which emphasizes open-mindedness, tolerance, and forgiveness) as it reveals Walker's own difficulties when grappling with gender issues.

By the end of the novel, men who are accepted in Celie's world have undergone a significant transformation that implies, if not their feminization, at least the renunciation of male prerogatives and traditional roles of dominance. This male transformation happens to be contemporaneous with the new male image of the 1980s. This new man does the dishes, the laundry, or changes the diapers. He willingly embraces tasks formerly ascribed to housewives and is not ashamed to acknowledge the feminine side of his personality. Anachronistically, Walker created Harpo, a character who, in early twentieth century rural Dixie, behaves like the idealized, urban modern male of her age. Harpo, more than his father Mr.____, is a model of new masculinity. On discussing Harpo's chronic gluttony with his wife Sofia, Celie ventures that Harpo licks all the dishes instead of doing them because, like his father, he hates to do the dishes—a statement Sofia immediately refutes:

> 'You reckon [...] He seems so much to love it. To tell you the truth, he love that part of housekeeping a heap more 'en me. I rather be out in the fields or fooling with the animals. Even chopping wood. But he love cooking and cleaning and doing little things round the house.' (59)

The fact that Harpo loves domestic chores and displays, more than Sofia, uxorial qualities, seems to partake of Walker's intention to present an alternative model of male behavior. Yet, Walker's reformist endeavor is immediately obstructed when the text emphasizes Harpo's immaturity. In Celie's following letter, Harpo snivels because, as he tells Celie between two sobs, he is unable to have the upper hand over his wife Sofia as his daddy does over Celie. Harpo, the text implies, does not behave like a responsible adult because he is not the one calling the shots at home (62).

The same impression prevails when it comes to Mr.____.
Walker tries to rationalize Mr.____'s feminization by having Shug report that he used to be a cross-dresser:

> 'I used to put on Albert's pants when we was courting. And he
> one time put on my dress [...] But he loved to see me in pants.
> It was like a red flag to a bull.' (147)

The very masculine Mr.____ is sexually aroused when his girl friend dresses like a man. This twist whereby Walker ascribes to Mr.____ a seemingly deviant behavior is a rather contrived way of justifying Mr.——'s transformation from a diehard misogynist to a new man who, late in his life, finally assumes his feminine side.

Some have interpreted Walker's treatment of female homosexuality as equally expedient as Celie's homosexuality comes across as resulting from men's cruelty. Sapphic love is arguably Celie's only way of experiencing love, which has led some to argue that lesbianism in *The Color Purple* is purely adventitious: men are brutes; therefore women become lesbians[2].

Fairy Tales, Free Market Economy, and Calvinism

"I am so happy. I got love, I got work, I got money, friends and time" (*Color Purple* 215). This is the introductory line of a letter from Celie to Nettie. Celie has been living in Memphis, Tennessee, under Shug's roof for a little while. She is free from Mr.____'s oppression, she has discovered love in her relationship with Shug, and she has started a pants making business that is rather successful and makes her financially autonomous. This new stage in Celie's life is an intentional contrast to her sordid existence at the beginning of the novel. There has been a revolution in Celie's life and what made it all possible is the miracle of free enterprise. The tale of Celie the pants maker is a celebration of capitalist values.

While *The Color Purple* shares characteristics both with oral folk tales and feminist tales, it is also indebted to the world of

fairy tales. In *Fairy Tales and the Art of Subversion*, Jack Zipes
underscores the ideological agenda of such tales: "The fairy tales
were cultivated to assure that young people would be properly
groomed for their social functions" (14). As distilled, genteel
versions of oral tales, fairy tales not only catered to the taste of the
dominant classes but also ambitioned to disseminate their values.
These tales adhered to the kind of bourgeois, patriarchal principles
Alice Walker endeavors to subvert in her novel, but they emerged
concomitantly with the metamorphosis of Europe from a pre-
industrialist society to a mercantile economy and carried in them
the new ethics of a nascent capitalism—ethics that are also
promoted, intentionally or not, in *The Color Purple*.

    According to Zipes, pre-capitalist folk tales focused on
"class struggle and competition for power among the aristocrats
themselves and between the peasantry and aristocracy" (*Breaking*
29). The central theme of all folk tales, Zipes argues, was "might
makes right":

> He who has power can exercise his will, right wrongs, become
> ennobled, amass money and land, win women as prizes. This is
> why the people were the carriers of these tales: The *Märchen*
> catered for their aspirations and allowed them to believe that
> anyone could become a knight in shining armour or a lovely
> princess, and they also presented the stark realities of power
> politics without disguising the violence and brutality of
> everyday life. (29)

Although these oral tales featured a "reversed" world, they did not
subvert the values of the dominant classes; rather, these tales would
create situations in which downtrodden people appropriated what
the ruling class possessed. But such reversals of fortune did not
imply questioning or transforming the existing social system. In
this sense, folk tales were not subversive because they took the
system of birthright for granted.

    In many respects, fairy tales are not that different from folk
tales as they present a world where those who feel inferior can
project and fulfill their dreams. Yet while folk tales are
fundamentally escapist, fairy tales, as they typify the new
mercantile creed, are more pragmatic and progressive in that they
foster a hope for change in social relations and class structure. I
believe that *The Color Purple* oscillates between the chimerical
world of folk tales and the more down-to-earth world of fairy tales.
One of the harshest criticisms leveled at Walker is her tendency to
confuse historical reality with fantasy[3]. Walker did not deny that

The Color Purple is the realization of a private fantasy. She rewrote the life of her grandmother on whom the character Celie is based: "I liberated her from her own history. I wanted her to be happy" (qtd. in Colton 40). By taking license with history and conjuring up a better destiny for her ancestor, Walker openly indulged in wishful thinking[4]. At the same time, the idea that change is possible is central to Walker's viewpoint: "I believe in change: change personal, and change in society" (*In Search* 252). It is this desire for change that Walker staged in *The Color Purple*, and it is not so coincidental that in her attempt to cover up her fantasized version of the past under a veneer of reality, Walker resorted to situations and values that define both the modern capitalist world she lives in and the world of fairy tales, for these worlds are intimately connected.

While the "might-makes-right" tenet of folk tales also permeated fairy tales, wealth and power now had to be gained according to a set of rules suitable to the new values: modesty, frugality, and work ethic, as opposed to birthright alone. In fairy tales, the pursuit of freedom and happiness was an opportunity for any citizen to seize. Success resulted from each and every individual's will and choice. Folk tales focused on social groups; fairy tales focused on the individual. As such, it encouraged private fantasy, and *The Color Purple*, by focusing on Celie's personal success, honors this tradition of the fairy tale. In spite of its claim to communality, Walker's novel is, above all, the story of Celie— not the story of her people.

These new principles pervading fairy tales found a practical application in daily life, implemented as they were by the new emerging mercantile class and encouraged by the Reformation. John Calvin's *Institutes of the Christian Religion* (1534-36) was a denial of "might makes right" within the clergy since it rejected the authority of the Pope and reaffirmed an individual's capacity to cultivate an absolute faith in God. This affirmation of the importance of the average man, as well as the confidence placed in individualistic deeds, not only fit the mercantile mentality but also traveled through space and time to form the founding values of the United States of America. From Benjamin Franklin's *Poor Richard's Almanack* in the eighteenth century, to Horatio Alger's juvenile fiction in the nineteenth, to *The Color Purple* in the twentieth, the same strive-and-succeed philosophy is at work. The success of Celie with American readers is due to the duplication of the defining paradigm of social mobility and the self-made (wo)man. *The Color Purple*, especially in its first half, is unconventional as it focuses on African American women at the dawn of the twentieth century and describes, without compromise, life in its rawness. Nevertheless, it is far from being a revolutionary work since the story clearly conforms to the established pattern of the American success story, in no way challenging the social status quo.

In "The Enchanted World of *The Color Purple*," scholar Margaret Walsh compares Celie to Cinderella, claiming that they both exemplify the rags to riches pattern of fairy tales. Indeed, Celie has a lot to do with Cinderella and other abased fairy tale heroines: "Celie [...] is an ideal fairy tale heroine, pitilessly victimized, simple, passive, defenseless, good—and in need of a fairy godmother" (94). Of course, Walker's protagonist is not a typical Cinderella in that she does not wait for a Prince Charming to find her and make her rich and happy. Instead, Celie learns to discover her inborn qualities and optimizes them. In "Beyong Morphology: Lévi-Strauss and the Analysis of Folktales," historian David Pace compares the story of Cinderella to the myth of social mobility. In the Cinderella myth, Pace argues,

> this theme of mobility through maturation is combined with an adult myth that it is possible to move from the scullery to the palace, provided one is patient and understanding. Behind both notions of social mobility lies the belief that there is an innate justice within the social system and that wrongs will eventually be righted. (254)

The virtues of patience and humility ascribed to the chosen woman are connected to patriarchal values, and the notion of innate justice echoes the Calvinist theory of predestination. This doctrine of (female) predestination as understood in popular thinking (be beautiful, compliant, and patient) is transformed in *The Color Purple* when Celie the simpleton turns out to be a smart, resourceful person. Celie's intelligence, the novel implies, is her sense of business. After all, Celie is the audacious entrepreneur who first invented unisex sportswear in the world. Additionally, with her racially integrated dry goods store, she is an innovator who is several decades ahead of her time. Celie does not succeed because she is docile and comely, but because she reveals herself as a natural-born entrepreneur; and this is where the Calvinist doctrine of predestination, as adulterated by Capitalist ideology, enters the novel.

In the Protestant ethic, as it is observed today in the United Sates, hard work is regarded as the key virtue to securing one's place in Heaven. In the Calvinist doctrine, as the first New

Englanders practiced it, God chose the Elect, regardless of their deeds on earth. More than a story from rags to riches, Celie's is a story of riches recovered. Shug does not help Celie to *dis*cover, but to *re*cover her gift as a businesswoman. As we remember, Pa is not Celie's real father and happens to be a property stealer. It is Nettie who reveals this secret to Celie. The news is so big and so hard to swallow for Celie (and for the reader) that Nettie decides to narrate the circumstances as she would a fairy tale:

> *Once upon a time*, there was a well-to-do farmer who owned his own property near town. Our town, Celie. And as he did so well farming and everything he turned his hand to prospered, he decided to open a store, and try his luck selling dry goods as well. Well, his store did so well that he talked two of his brothers into helping him run it, and, as the month went by, they were doing better and better. Then the white merchants began to get together and complain that this store was taking all the black business away from them, and the man's blacksmith shop that he set up behind the store, was taking some of the white. This would not do. And so, one night, the man's store was burned down, his smithy destroyed, and the man and his two brothers dragged out of their homes in the middle of the night and hanged. (174) (Emphasis mine)

By lynching Celie's father and his siblings, the white merchants violated the basic rules of free-market economy. They prevented the so-called "invisible hand" from regulating the market by carrying out, as it were, an extreme form of protectionism. As it has been the case since the dawn of capitalism, the market is free so long as the dominant group wants it to be free. The murder of Celie's father exposes the fallacy of a "free" market inviting all to compete on equal terms, and it is a reminder that the prime value at the heart of capitalism is, as in folktales, "might makes right." What the cruel Alphonso, a.k.a. Pa, understood is the shrewd, albeit self-debasing, accommodationist attitude. As he tells Celie:

> I know how [white folk] is. The key to all of 'em is money.
> The trouble with our people is as soon as they got out of
> slavery they didn't want to give the white man nothing else.
> But the fact is, you got to give 'em something. Either your
> money, your land, your woman or your ass. So what I did was
> just right off offer to give 'em money. Before I planted a seed,
> I made sure this one and that one knowed one seed out of three
> was planted for *him*. Before I ground a grain of wheat, the
> same thing. And when I opened up your daddy's old store in
> town, I bought me my own white boy to run it. And what make
> it so good, he say, I bought him with white folks' money.
> (182)

When Alphonso dies, Celie inherits, or more exactly
retrieves, a fabulous fortune. On top of her pants making business,
Celie is now at the head of an estate comprising a mansion, land,
and a dry goods store. Earlier in the story, when Celie pays a visit
to Pa in order to clarify their kinship—or lack thereof—she notices
how "Pa's land is warm and ready to go [...] It all so different from
the rest of the country [...] even the sun seemed to stand a little
longer over our heads" (178-79). Even Pa himself looks very
young. Pa's youth and the fertility of his land are the result of the
magic that surrounds him, and this magic is prosperity and money.
In *The Color Purple* money, more than anything else, bestows
grace and happiness. The elect are those who make money. Celie
the simpleton has become rich, and in such a world, to be rich is a
sign of intelligence and signifies future successful endeavors.

Celie's story does not so much resemble "Cinderella" as it
does Hans Christian Andersen's "The Ugly Duckling." The ugly
duckling is in fact a swan but the other lower-class animals of the
hen yard cannot discern its beauty, i.e., its noble identity. Like
Celie, the duckling is convinced of his inferiority and only comes
to realize his majesty after many ordeals. Again like Celie, the
swan is saved and restored to his true status. Andersen concludes
the tale thus: "it does not matter that one has been born in the hen
yard as long as one has lain in a swan's egg" (qtd. in *Fairy Tales*
88). The ugly duckling tale, Jack Zipes argues, makes a very
ambiguous statement as it embraces the bourgeois notion of the
self-made-man but also betrays admiration for the upper classes,
implying that upper class people are innately superior. The same
ideology is at work in *The Color Purple*: Celie is endowed with a
gift and is naturally restored to her rank of successful merchant.

Beyond the well-intentioned tale of Celie looms a more
maligned yet widespread mentality that progressives have long

been battling in America: those who do not "make it" have only themselves to blame. They are responsible for their failure. Considering that social success in America is still strongly contingent on racial background and being a part of a majority, it is not hard to foresee the dangers of such an ideology. The womanist Utopia featured in *The Color Purple* is as much the fruit of sisterhood as it is of Calvinist capitalism. *The Color Purple* is telling us that even the most oppressed people can make it in America. Nevertheless, any attempt to reconcile the values of free market economy (competitiveness, will to dominate, exacerbated individualism) with ideals of communal life implying sharing, nurturing and working for a more equal society, is inherently paradoxical. This confusion between two incompatible concepts has even greater repercussions in *The Color Purple*. Willingly or not, Walker's story awakes in the reader's imagination the inchoate idea that if African Americans did not succeed in America to this day, it is their fault. Behind Celie's incredible, but personal success, lurks the failure of her community and the notion that the members of this community should blame themselves. Celie's happiness, based in great part on her money and material possessions, seems to exculpate America from the sordid conditions of living in which most of Celie's community is still imprisoned. Thus, Celie, with her phenomenal success, seems to be merely an apology for the pitiful downfall of her community.

Raphaël Lambert, University of Tsukuba

Notes

[1] Shug is Alice Walker's spokesperson in the novel. The parallel between author and character is obvious in the following statement by Walker in 1983: "Certainly I don't believe there is a God beyond nature. The world is God. Man is God. So is a leaf or a snake" (*In Search* 265). A few years later, Walker is even more explicit about Shug as the vehicle for her womanist message as she underlines "Shug's completely unapologetic self-acceptance as outlaw, renegade, rebel, and pagan; her zest in loving both women and men, younger and older" (*Same River* 35). And Walker concludes: "When Shug says [...] 'I believe God is everything that is, ever was, or ever will be,' she is saying what I [Alice Walker] too believe" (35).
[2] These lines are in reference to the fierce controversy surrounding Walker's treatment of both sexual preferences and African American male characters in *The Color Purple*. In a letter-to-the editor for the *Oakland Tribune* in 1984, African American novelist Ishmael Reed spoke for many when he criticized Walker's book for "promot[ing] the point of view [...] that lesbian love is a panacea for [...] the inevitable unhappiness caused by heterosexual relationships" (B6); and

56 _Raphaël Lambert_

Reed linked this interpretation of lesbianism to Walker's "shrill attempt to boycott black male writers whose female characters don't adhere to her notion of what an ideal female character should be" (B6), i.e., a female character whose tribulations are caused by men.

[3] Many critics, such as bell hooks, have raised an eyebrow at Walker's treatment of history: "Relying on historical referents only in so far as they land an aura of credibility to that which is improbable [...] Walker mocks the notion of historical truth, suggesting that it is subordinate to myth, that the mythic has far more impact on consciousness" (291-92).

[4] History, for Alice Walker, is as contingent on mystical inspiration as it is on sheer recording of facts. Thus, she once declared she had experienced "transference of energy" when reading Arna Bontemps (_In Search_ 258) or that she had been visited by her characters—Celie, Shug, Albert, Sofia, or Harpo—for advice or bantering conversation while writing the novel (Ibid. 357-58).

Works Cited

Colton Catherine A. "Alice Walker's Womanist Magic: The Conjure Woman as Rhetor" in _Critical Essays on Alice Walker_. Ikenna Dieke, ed. Westport, CT: Greenwood, 1999. (33-44)

Hankinson, Stacie Lynn. "From Monotheism to Pantheism: Liberation from Patriarchy in Alice Walker's _The Color Purple_" in _Midwest Quarterly_ 38:3 (Spring 1997): 320-328.

hooks, bell. "Reading and Resistance: _The Color Purple_" in _Alice Walker: Critical Perspectives, Past and Present_. Henry Louis Gates, Jr. and K.A. Appiah, eds. New York: Amistad, 1993. (284-295)

MacDonald, Ruth. "The Tale Retold: Feminist Fairy Tales" in _Children's Literature Association Quarterly_ 7 (Summer 1982): 18-20.

Pace, David. "Beyond Morphology: Lévi-Strauss and the Analysis of Folktales" in _Cinderella: A Casebook_. Alan Dundes, ed. New York: Wildman, 1983. (245-258)

Reed, Ishmael. "The Color Purple" in _The Oakland Tribune_ (2 July 1984): Sec. B6.

Stone, Kay. "Things Walt Disney Never Told Us" in _Woman and Folklore_. Claire R. Farrer, ed. Austin: U. of Texas, 1975. (42-50)

Swann Jones, Steven. _The Fairy Tale: The Magic Mirror of Imagination_. New York: Twayne, 1995.

Walker, Alice. _In Search of Our Mothers' Gardens_. New York: Harcourt Brace Jovanovich, 1983.

—._The Color Purple_. 1982. New York: Harcourt, 2003.

—.*The Same River Twice: Honoring the Difficult*. New York: Scribner, 1996.

Walsh, Margaret. "The Enchanted World of *The Color Purple*" in *The Southern Quarterly* 25 (1987): 89-101.

Zipes, Jack. *Breaking the Magic Spell: Radical Theories of Folk and Fairy Tales*. London: Heinemann, 1979.

—. *Fairy Tales and the Art of Subversion: The Classical Genre for Children and the Process of Civilization*. New York: Wildman, 1983.

—. *Don't Bet on the Prince: Contemporary Feminist Fairy Tales in North America and England*. New York: Methuen, 1986.

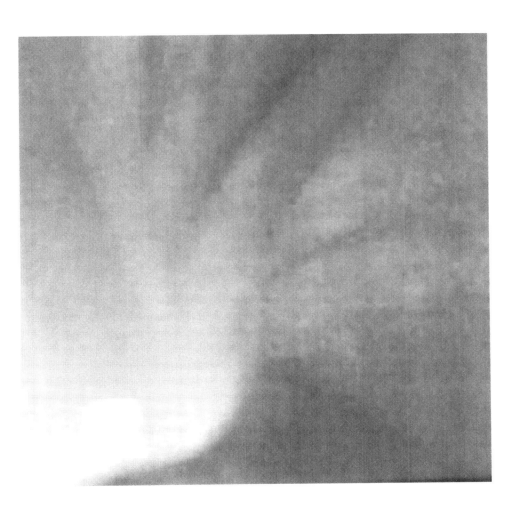

Theology of Liberation

Rendering the African-American Woman's God through *The Color Purple*

Patricia Andujo

The historical development of the African-American woman can be traced within the African-American literary tradition while locating religion as a central influence of her strength, character, and dedication to her family and community. Alice Walker's *The Color Purple* demonstrates how African-American women have redefined religion (traditional Christianity) to empower themselves beyond their double minority status in America. It is undeniable that religion, specifically Christianity, has traditionally been conceived of, by some, as a sexist and delimiting institution for women. Biblical scriptures such as I Corinthians 14:34-35 and I Timothy 2:11-12 appear to place women in subjection to men and suggest that it is advisable for women to keep silent, especially in the church. Celie, the protagonist of Walker's novel, spends the majority of her life engaging in a peculiar monologue with a male God who renders her neither empowerment, voice, nor self-esteem, yet appears to sustain Celie through one-way conversations.

In light of the women's suffrage movement during the 1880s and the women's liberation movement in the 1960s, American women found it difficult to reconcile their interest in religion with their desire to obtain equality and liberation. Within the American cultural context, African-American women have had to struggle with the double bind of racial and gender inequity. They have had to create a separate voice that speaks to their unique position in American culture. Furthermore, during the nineteenth century, African-American women were the only women forced to conciliate the supposed legitimization of slavery in the Bible (Ephesians 6:5-6) with a position that granted them a mere three-fifths percentage of a full human being (United States Constitution, article 1, section 2, paragraph 3).

Alice Walker's novel serves as commentary on the survival and transformation of religion in the lives of African-American females as they are forced to renegotiate previously established religious discourse. Celie, Nettie, Sofia, and Shug must rethink the way they feel about God, gender, and religion if they hope to triumph over their double minority status. This transformation is most evident in the protagonist, Celie. Once she takes individual ownership of God, she becomes empowered through her new understanding of religion. Celie's eyes are finally opened, and though she "feels like a fool," she also feels liberated. Throughout the course of time, Celie becomes empowered through a God that eventually "change[s] into something different that [she has] to speak to in a different way" (*The Color Purple* 260). God is no longer sleeping as she supposed Him to be earlier in the novel. What results is an awakening of Celie's sexuality, self-esteem, independence, and ultimate liberation.

To understand the rhetorical strategy used by Walker, readers must journey back nearly 150 years to visit the inception of a religious discourse that rendered African-American women a sense of empowerment through the inspiration of a divine power. In early autobiographies by women such as Jarena Lee (*The Life and Religious Experience of Jarena Lee*, 1836), Julia Foote (*A Brand Plucked From the Fire*, 1879), Maria Stewart (*Productions of Mrs. Maria W. Stewart. Spiritual Narratives*, 1879), and Sojourner Truth (*Narrative of Sojourner Truth; A Bondswoman of Olden Time, With a History of Her Labors and Correspondence Drawn from Her "Book of Life,"* 1878), we find women who have had to consistently reorder the structure and scope of their spirituality as a way of gaining power and control over their lives, an action which implies that institutionalized religion (Christianity) was incapable or unwilling to accommodate their spiritual needs. None of these authors wanted to completely forsake Christianity to gain voice; however, they were all willing to rebel against the African-American church for the sake of their calling. Their actions can be called "divinely inspired resistance" since they all claimed that is was God who wanted them to preach. To prove this, Jarena Lee nearly died trying to avoid her call to the ministry until she was absolutely certain that it was God, and not herself, who wanted to preach (*Life and Religious Experience* 14). Julia Foote opposed female preachers until she, herself, was called to preach. After two months of failing health, which Foote attributed to her disobedience to God's call, she finally relented and accepted God's will (*Brand Plucked* 55). Maria Stewart was willing to be a martyr in obedience to her call (*Productions* 18). Sojourner Truth endured verbal abuse and discrimination, believing that she was carrying out God's mission (*Narrative* 33). So their resistance to the church, they believed, was legitimized by a deity more powerful than man. Ultimately, they faced their "triple indictment" (being an African-American, a female, and a preacher) with a spirit of boldness as they became confident in their call to the ministry. The reality of their triple-minority status was confirmed by their resistance. They would have never had to usurp the authority of the church had their stations in life been something other than "African-American-female-preacher." Out of their resistance emerged a new voice, a new character, a new strength, and a new power that African-American women had never experienced before. These were groundbreaking females whose voices would be needed to fuel the efforts of more African-American female leaders to come. The implication of their act is that religion leaves room for everyone to embrace, adopt, and adapt their own understanding of God and power. It is man who places limitations on religion. Important to note is the fact that their efforts were always unequivocally inclusive. They never excluded those who were unlike them (males, Whites, non-Christians, laymen, etc.). In all of their divinely inspired power, they always remained humble enough to welcome anyone who was willing to come into their fold. As such, they were womanists—that is, women who believed in the power of the female without excluding others for the sake of their work. As Alice Walker said, "committed to survival and wholeness of entire people, male *and* female" (xi). The fact that they were at the lowest rung of the ladder made them sensitive to others and careful not to discriminate. For example, Jarena Lee and Julia Foote prayed for, and later with, the very men who fought their ministry. Maria Stewart was never too much of a leader that she couldn't help her poor uneducated people. Sojourner Truth aligned herself with White women because she believed in their fight for gender equality. If the male leaders of the African-American church would have had the same disposition, the possibilities are infinite as to what the combined efforts of African-American male and female leaders could have produced for the African-American church. We understand that upon gaining their freedom, African-American ex-slave males had a single focus of establishing the power that was ascribed to their gender. Including African-American women in their fight for power and leadership in America was not an immediate concern. In his essay "Press Your Teeth Together and Learn to Hush," Chester Fontenot, chair of the English department at Mercer University, states:

> African American male religious leaders have appropriated the patriarchal discourse that resides within the linguistic constructs of Christian churches. While this dialogical borrowing, so to speak, served to empower them against a religious-based system that attempted to negate their voices as men, it likewise rendered African American women silent within the male-structured hierarchies of historical African American independent churches and denominations. (1)

Lee, Foote, Stewart, and Truth understood the necessity of reconfiguring a spiritual language that would grant them access and entrance into a male dominated religious discourse. These nineteenth century females are the foremothers of twentieth century African-American womanists. In search of their mothers' gardens, twentieth century African-American female writers like Alice Walker find the legacy of Lee, Foote, Stewart, and Truth's divinely inspired resistance, and though the daughters may not require divine inspiration for their resistance, they nonetheless, tap into that same rhetoric that asks "ain't I a woman?" The connection between the foremothers and the daughters is their continuous battle with race and gender discrimination in America and literary discourse. They face the same struggle for voice in a society that attempts to renders them powerless and insignificant. They have had to persistently defend their competency and value as leaders. With regard to religion, the daughters face the same struggle that the foremothers faced. They have to restructure and recreate their own perception of religion and how it fits into their lives. What Alice Walker struggles with is the "maleness" of God and how the perpetuation of this maleness influences her characters' liberty and power as females. Moreover, she searches to redefine God beyond gender. Yet we see that her language and discourse is one of liberation and power, the same as her foremothers.

Alice Walker's *The Color Purple* is an epistolary novel in which female protagonist, Celie, goes through tumultuous relationships with the male counterparts in her life: her step-father, her husband, and even her God. With each encounter, Celie is victimized and dehumanized, yet she understands that her relationship with God is the key to salvaging her dignity and self-worth. She says that as long as she can spell "G-O-D" she has someone by her side. Ironically, what Celie failed to realize is that this relationship and understanding of God has stifled her growth and livelihood as an independent African-American woman. Feminist theology scholar, Delores S. Williams, suggests that one of the main reasons why Celie is unable to establish a meaningful relationship with God is because her understanding of God is derived from a man, her Pa (275). It is Pa who initially forges a relationship between Celie and God when he tells her "You better not never tell nobody but God.   It'd kill your mammy" (TCP 1). So God becomes a non-responsive confidant and keeper of secrets instead of a friend and protector.

Walker establishes, in Celie's first letter, the unfortunate reality that the God Celie speaks to is incapable of or unwilling to speak back. Celie asks God to "give [her] a sign letting [her] know what is happening to [her]" (1). However, this God not only fails to give her a sign, He is a God that "just sit up there glorying in being deef" (193). The silence of God here suggests that in writing letters to the deity, Celie is engaging in hegemonic discourse which places her in the delimiting role of the passive, abused female who is waiting hopefully for the external divine intervention of God, who is characterized as male. Moreover, since the written prayer tradition is foreign to the African-American religious tradition, Celie not only appeals to a God who is distant and male, but she also tries to appropriate sacred discourse for which a trope does not exist within her cultural tradition. Keith Byerman, professor of English and Women's Studies at Indiana State University, says, "Celie writes herself into humanity and thereby contradicts the stipulation that she be a mere cipher. She gives herself an inner life and a concrete history and thus an otherness that the patriarchal order denies her" (qtd. in Wilson 60).

For Celie, there are very few distinctions between a male and God. She visualizes God as a man who is "big and old and tall and greybearded and white" with bluish-grey eyes (194). Thus, one can argue that her victimization by her stepfather and husband is validated by the God that she serves. In her essay, "Theology and Androgyny: The Role of Religion in *The Color Purple*," Lori Duin Kelly concurs that "to Celie, raped at fourteen by her step father and trapped in a loveless marriage and a cycle of domestic abuse as was her mother, male means power, and so it is no wonder that she characterizes God as a 'he'" (8). When Celie's mother asks her about her child's paternity, she says that God is the child's father and that God took the child while she was sleep. God is even responsible for her subsequent infertility. Pa tells Mr.____:

> But she ain't no stranger to hard work. And she clean. And God don fixed her. You can do everything just like you want to and she ain't gonna make you feed it or clothe it. (8)

Readers can define Celie's infertility as a curse or as a blessing. She doesn't have to bare anymore children out of rape, but she'll never experience the maternal joy of raising a child. Just as her stepfather physically rapes her, God also rapes her spiritually and emotionally through His denial of compassion and protection. Williams observes that "oppression and violation render Celie emotionally numb" (97). Thus, the will to do more than merely stay alive is obliterated. Nevertheless, Celie's letters to God serve a need to communicate her feelings—feelings that she is unable to share with anyone else. Celie's sister, Nettie, says to her:

> I remember one time you said your life made you feel so ashamed you couldn't even talk about it to God, you had to write it… Well, now I know what you meant. And whether God will read letters or not, I know you will go on writing them. (130)

Celie's letter writing is life-sustaining as she has yet to engage in real dialogue with God.

Williams writes, "For Celie, the practice of addressing God simply reaffirms her solitude; she is essentially writing to herself. *The Color Purple* is thus an example of an epistolary novel with close affinities to the journal, diary, or autobiographical confession" (277). Williams' comparison of *TCP* to other genres magnifies the gravity of it actually being an epistolary novel. With a journal, diary, or autobiography, there is no expected return correspondence. The letter, however, anticipates a return correspondence which Celie never receives. Even though Nettie sends Celie letters, Celie is never aware that she is dialoguing with her sister, and as a result, Celie is forced into seclusion.

For the majority of Celie's adulthood, she is dependent upon the mercy of men and an unresponsive God to survive. When Mr.____'s children begin to misbehave, Nettie tells her, "you got to let them know who got the upper hand." Celie responds, "They got it." "You got to fight. You got to fight" Nettie insists. "But I don't know how to fight. All I know how to do is stay alive" Celie says (17). Celie's attitude is reminiscent of Christian belief that God should serve as man's warrior. "For the battle is not yours, but Gods" (II Chronicles 20:15). Celie's obvious problem is that God refuses to fight for her. Later, when Celie thinks that Nettie is dead, her fear of fighting back is reinforced:

> I think bout Nettie, dead. She fight, she run away. What good it do? I don't fight, I stay where I'm told. But I'm alive. (21)

Celie has come to accept her weakness as an inevitable part of life for women's survival. Nevertheless, as Williams notes, "Writing—as opposed to speech—seems safe, seems even the sign of ongoing life. Within this context, epistolary itself must be seen to present both the resignation of Celie's silence and its implicit strength: her silent refusal to lose her identity, despite her isolation" (276).

For Celie, to assert herself as a human being capable of feeling, wanting, and thinking would be disturbing God's structure for mankind. When Sofia usurps Harpo's role as head of the household, Celie advises Harpo to beat Sofia to make her "mind." Yet, Celie envies Sofia's ability to fight back. Celie's understanding of male-female relationships stems from her concept of God's relationship with African-American women. She says, "if [God] ever listened to poor colored women the world would be a different place" (192). This statement is similar in kind to the characterization of African-American women as "mules of the world" as explained by the character, Nanny, in Zora Neale Hurston's *Their Eyes Were Watching God*. In both instances, black women are commodified, delimited, and subject to physical abuse while hoping for divine intervention.

Other than Nettie, Sofia is Celie's first real example of an assertive woman who is unwilling to accept the conventional role of an abused voiceless woman. Sofia lives to chop wood and hunt, and is not afraid to fight anyone, even Whites. She says, "All my life I had to fight. I had to fight my daddy. I had to fight my brothers... But I never thought I'd have to fight in my own house... I loves Harpo... God knows I do. But "I'll kill him dead before I let him beat me" (40). Sofia is also the first to challenge Celie's concept of God. Celie tells Sofia, "well, sometimes Mr.___ git on me pretty hard. I have to talk to Old Maker. But he my husband... This life soon be over, I say.

Heaven last all ways" (42). But, Old Maker is no protector of women; he is an ally of men. Shrugging her shoulders, Celie realizes that it is useless to take her problems to God.

Sofia offers her a window of escape when she says, "you ought to bash Mr.___ head open [...] Think bout heaven later" (42). For Sofia, religion is only relevant when it is useful—should it stand in the way of one's empowerment, it must be discarded. Sofia's personality and language radically oppose Celie's. Sofia is assertive, aggressive, and described in masculine terms; Celie is passive, weak, and described in sympathetic, and somewhat feminine, terms (17, 37). Sofia's unwillingness to rely upon an outside deity to resolve human, female problems suggests that she rejects Celie's embrace of her delimiting condition and, instead, offers a perspective which is empowering. Celie does not feel such empowerment until she learns to reconsider her understanding of God.

Walker's appropriation of God's vastness is a prevalent theme throughout the novel, which is essential to Shug's survival, and thus, Celie's survival. Had Walker limited Shug's scope of God to conventional Christianity, Celie's conversion would have been subject to the boundaries of a male dominating institution. In her essay, "Right on Time: History and Religion in Alice Walker's *The Color Purple*," Kimberly R. Chambers notes that

> Walker is careful to qualify her religious beliefs, claiming she needs 'a wider recognition of the universe' than she finds in formal religion. As she says, 'I am trying to rid my consciousness and my unconsciousness of the notion of God as a white-haired British man with big feet and a beard' ... *The Color Purple* is steeped in the religious element that, however unconventional in its expression, seems to flow directly from the piety of church-going Southern blacks, a piety with roots in the folklore tradition which Alice Walker respects and defends. (52, 57)

Indeed, Walker leaves room for both, Christianity and a broader concept of spirituality, in *TCP*. She dedicates *TCP* "To the Spirit," careful not to attach herself to any particular form of religion. When Celie decides to not to write God, she is essentially rejecting institutionalized religion because it's not working for her. The "maleness" of God precipitates her rejection. She says, "the God I been praying and writing to is a man. And act just like all the other mens I know" (192). Celie's refusal to pray (and write) to God is similar to Zora Neale Hurston's decision not to pray (*Dust Tracks* 26).

They both come to the conclusion that there is no power in prayer, instead power comes from within.

Celie's sister, Nettie, is also instrumental in transforming Celie's thoughts about God. She tells Celie that:

> God is different to us now, after all these years in Africa. More spirit than ever before, and more internal. Most people think he has to look like something or someone—a roofleaf—or Christ—but he don't. And not being tied to what God looks like, frees us. (257)

Nettie realizes that one's perception of God is influenced by one's culture. In America, one might see a blond-haired blue-eyed Jesus. In Africa, one might envision a roofleaf. Nettie understands what Celie later accepts as a new form of spirituality—God is not something apart from humanity, but something that is inseparable from man. Such an understanding forces one to tap into one's inner strength rather than rely upon external support. Celie's education of African customs helps her gain a sense of self-worth and pride. Though Africa, for Celie, is a distant unrecognizable spot on a map, it is, nonetheless, a source of pride. She even boasts that her children are being raised in Africa, learning different languages. The cultural connection is more empowering than her spiritual connection to God. As such, Celie becomes receptive to other interpretations, such as the one offered by Shug, of God.

Celie's initial infatuation and eventual love for Shug enables Shug to win her trust and direct her to a broader understanding of God. Williams suggests that "the awakening of Celie's sexuality begins the process of replacing God with the sister as addressee" (278). Notice how Celie associates her sexual experience to a religious experience. "I wash her body, it feel like I'm praying" (49). However, as Williams notes, Celie's sexual experience with Shug serves a greater purpose than prayer does. There is no response to her prayers, however, she gains a friend, lover, protector, and confidant from her sexual partner, Shug. Shug further challenges Celie's concept of God when she tells Celie that "God ain't a he or a she, but a It" (195). The ability to accept and internalize this understanding of God is crucial to Celie's metamorphosis.

This form of theology negates the presence of gender in one's conceptualization of God. It's the same idea that Nettie was trying to convey to Celie. Shug opens up Celie's understanding to an entirely different God—a God that loves women, sinners, and good times. Although Celie temporarily stops writing God, she doesn't forsake God all together, only the male-God. She still adopts Shug's "inclusive" God and learns to see God differently. The transformation is a difficult one; Celie says, "this hard work, let me tell you. [The image of a male God] been there so long, he don't want to budge. He threaten lightening, floods and earthquakes. Us fight. I hardly pray at all. Every time I conjure up a rock, I throw it" (197).

To disassociate herself with a male God means that she has to rethink cultural norms. Even in this statement, she still refers to God as "He." Shug understands that Celie's understanding of God has been influenced by a patriarchal culture. Shug has to make a number of revealing statements before Celie receives revelation:

> 'Ain't no way to read the bible and not think God white, she say. Then she sigh. When I found out I thought God was white, and a man, I lost interest... Here's the thing, say Shug. The thing I believe. God is inside you and inside everybody else. You come into the world with God. But only them that search for it inside find it. And sometimes it just manifest itself even if you not looking, or don't know what you looking for.' (195)

> 'I laughed and I cried and I run all around the house. I knew just what it was. In fact, when it happen, you an't miss it. It sort of like you know what, she say, grinning and rubbing high up on my thigh. *Shug!* I say. Oh, she say. God love all them feelings. That's some of the best stuff God did. And when you know God loves 'em you enjoys 'em a lot more. You can just relax, go with everything that's going, and praise God by liking what you like.' (196)

> 'Man corrupt everything, say Shug. He on your box of grits, in your head, and all over the radio. He try to make you think he everywhere. Soon as you think he everywhere, you think he God. But he ain't . Whenever you trying to pray, and man plop himself on the other end of it, tell him to git lost, say Shug. Conjure up flowers, wind, water, a big rock.' (197)

Though she feels foolish about her traditional understanding of a male God, Celie accepts her spiritual awakening and rejoices in her new-found liberation. Celie's new God is one who grants her self-esteem, voice, independence, and sexuality; this God is one who actually listens and cares about Celie. Kelly points out that Celie become strong enough to

Challenge and defy the conventional definitions of male-female behavior that underlie and, in a sense, justify such treatment of women. Celie does this by appropriating elements that are traditionally the exclusive domain of the male: in fashion – she wears pants; in career – she runs a successful business; and in romance – she loves another woman, Shug. Celie does this, moreover, without the surrendering of the more traditional female characteristics of being empathetic and nurturing. (8)

Shug and Celie's relationship develops into a physical intimacy that Celie is unable to experience with a man. Shug informs Celie that Celie is still a virgin since she had never experienced the erotic pleasures of sex. For Shug and Celie, sex between two unmarried females is natural, not a shameful sin. As Shug says, "God loves all them [sexual] feelings" (196). Celie comes to understand that worshipping God consists of more than cleaning the church and praying. Worship involves appreciating the beautiful things in nature like the color purple and communion with everything that God created. She knew that "if [she] cut a tree, [her] arm would bleed" (196). Shug's spiritual awakening did not occur at church, but rather when she was able to free herself from the white male image of God and embrace the God that was inside her. Shug's spiritual awakening was almost sexual just as Celie's spiritual and sexual awakening occurs simultaneously. Shug teaches Celie to love and explore her body as a form of self-realization. In his article, "A Fairy-Tale Life: The Making of Celie in Alice Walker's *The Color Purple*," Daniel W. Ross asserts that "respect and appreciation for the body are necessary for self-esteem and, ultimately, for life. In Celie's case, the repossession of her body is even necessary for the development of meaningful speech" (160). Celie later associates God with love making. She says, "I smoke when I want to talk to God. I smoke when I want to make love. Lately I feel like me and God make love just fine anyhow" (220). Celie realizes that she is, in fact, blessed to be able to explore her sexuality without feelings of guilt or shame.

Celie's new found self-esteem enables her to demand respect from Mr.___ and to love herself. At one point, she is even willing to kill Mr.___ for withholding Nettie's letters over the years, but when she finally confronts Mr.___, she conjures God's help. She says, "I give it to him straight, just like it come to me. And it seem to come to me from the trees" (206). Since God is a part of everything in nature, the tree is merely a fraction of God. Even the dust of the earth empowers Celie as it speaks through her to curse Mr.___. Celie says, "a dust devil flew up on the porch between us, fill my mouth with dirt. The dirt say, Anything you do to me, already done to you" (207). But previously, the invoking of God for strength and courage had never been an option for Celie before she learned to free God from the limitations of a man.

Now, however, Celie knows that in order to please God, she must learn to love herself since God created her. Loving herself also means leaving Mr. ___, accepting the house that she inherited from her mother, and enjoying everything that life has to offer. She says, "I am so happy. I got love, I got work, I got money, friends and time" (215). God has finally smiled upon her, and she feels Its presence in everything that she encounters. Celie even tries to impart a dose of self-assertiveness to Squeak, Harpo's new girlfriend. She tells Squeak to make Harpo call her by her name, Mary Agnes, if she wants him to start respecting her. Celie realizes that the only way for African-American women to gain respect is to demand it. Williams points out that "Celie also learns another important lesson. Females must affirm each other as they struggle to free themselves from male domination and abuse" (98).

Leaving Mr.___ and his male dominance is central to Celie's new found independence. With the help of Shug, Celie enhances her creative sewing skills so well that she is able to become self-sufficient by selling her popular pants. With independence comes the understanding that love is a free agent that is not subject to man's limitations. When Shug falls in love with a younger man, Celie learns that love has no boundaries. She tries to convince herself that "just cause I love her don't take away none of her rights… Who am I to tell her who to love? My job just to love her good and true myself" (269).

Shug is the last person that Celie is dependent upon for love, support, and happiness. Once she breaks her dependency, Celie is no longer bound to anyone or anything, but nature, and nature is God. When Shug promises to come back home, Celie thinks, "if she come, I be happy. If she don't, I be content. And then I figure this the lesson I was suppose to learn" (283). Celie learns that inner contentment is the key to a happy life. If she is happy, then God is happy, and she is once again in tune with God's plan for humanity.

Celie's transformation extends beyond her own redemption. Through their love for Shug, Mr.___ and Celie eventually develop a relationship of mutual respect and compassion. Mr.___ also gains a sense of self awareness. He says, "I'm satisfied this the first time I ever lived on Earth as a natural man" (260). Celie recognizes that Mr.___ even "appreciated some of the things God was playful enough to make" (260). Mr.___, consciously or not, is starting to adopt Celie and Shug's God. Scholar Emma Dawson states that "the contact with Mr.__ and his perception of her as family ultimately provide Celie a necessary context and a direction. Through them, she sees the way to continue the re-creation of her own self, her true identity" (80).

Celie's spiritual rebirth comes full circle in her last letter. The letter reveals a reordered perspective toward God, who is no longer a depersonalized male deity, but a personalized God who reveals divinity through nature. Chambers observes that "instead of diaries of suffering, [Celie's letters] become records of growth" (59). Celie says, "Dear God.   Dear stars, dear trees, dear sky, dear peoples. Dear Everything. Dear God" (285). It is clear that Celie no longer views God as the once "trifling, forgitful, and lowdown" man that once yielded her little, if any, reason to live (199). By the end of Celie's transformation, she has become a triumphant, independent, happy, lively woman. She is no longer the victim of men; she depends only on God for emotional stability; she understands that the only thing that God requires of people is the appreciation of everything "It" creates, and in return, God and humanity become inseparable; her livelihood stems from inner strength and determination.

Chambers points out that Celie's new God is "a God best described by the words of an old spiritual: 'He may not come when you want Him, but He's right on time'" (55). Though a middle-aged woman, Celie feels younger than she has ever felt in her entire life. She has truly been born again. Celie manages to emerge as a "womanist" in her own right. She fits one of Walker's definitions of a womanist:

> a woman who loves other women, sexually and/or nonsexually. Appreciates and prefers women's culture, women's emotional flexibility (values tears as natural counter-balance of laughter), and women's strength. Sometimes loves individual men, sexually and/or nonsexually. Committed to survival and wholeness of entire people, male and female. (*In Search of Our Mother's Gardens* xi)

Alice Walker presents Celie, Sofia, Nettie, and Shug's appropriation of a gender-neutral God, who understands the trials of women, as an empowering and coping mechanism that ultimately renders them a "true" sense of freedom—free of victimization, silence, and unhappiness. All of the women become more complete by the end of the novel. When Walker introduces Mr.___ into this new fold, she taps into that all-inclusive womanist ideology, which suggests that perhaps African-American women are not the only ones in need of a new perception of God. Walker's reworking and rethinking about God reaches far beyond gender concerns; these are human concerns.

Alice Walker has responded to the call of her foremothers in her own way. While she has apparently chosen to abandon traditional Christianity to a large degree, she still honors the legacy of Christianity in African American culture. She pays homage to Lee, Foote, Stewart, and Truth by continuing to adapt religion (or spirituality) as an empowering agent. Wilson observes that "Walker never lose[s] sight of this world; [she] look[s] not for an externally imposed God or religion but at a divinity arising from interaction with nature, community, and self.   Such an earth-rooted vision characterizes the spirituality of... Alice Walker" (68). Perhaps one reason why Walker chooses to focus so heavily on earth elements is for the sake of balance. She never goes so far as to make herself higher than God; she always maintains a respectable equilibrium between woman/man and God, which emphasizes a consistent need for a higher power. The foremothers realized the same thing; while they rejected the higher authority of the African-American church, they maintain a reverence for God.

In conclusion, by early writers like Lee, Foote, Stewart, and Truth developing a discourse that encourages liberation, we must question whether or not they created an environment in which African-American females are finally free. Alice Walker evidently was not content with, although respectful of, the efforts of her foremothers. The inadequacies of Christianity result from cultural and human interference, as Shug says (195). It is interesting that the Christian God that Walker rejects is the same God that empowers her foremothers. This is an indication, not that God has changed, but that women have evolved into even more independent people. The connection between the written discourse of the foremothers and the daughters is one of creative power. Lee, Foote, Stewart, and Truth's creative task was to rework the language of the Bible and the Holy Spirit so that they become inclusive of the authority that the church reserved for men. Walker utilizes and redirects their creativity through the genre of the novel. She speaks spiritual "truths" that empower her protagonist, but more importantly her readers.

Patricia Andujo, Ph.D., Azusa Pacific University

Works Cited

Chambers, Kimberly R.   "Right on Time: History and Religion in Alice Walker's The Color Purple." *College Language Association Journal* 31:1 (1987): 44-62.

Dawson, Emma.   "Redemption Through Redemption of the Self in *Their Eyes Were Watching God* and *The Color Purple*." *Alice Walker and Zora Neale Hurston: The Common Bond*.   Ed. Lillie P. Howard. Connecticut: Greenwood Press, 1993.   69-82.

Fontenot, Chester.   "Press Your Teeth Together and Learn to Hush: The Silencing of Women in the Ministry by African-American Male Religious Discourse, 1789-1903." *Women and Religious Discourse: Proceedings of the 27th LAUD Symposium*.   Ed. John Ries and Benjamin Biebuyck. Frankfurt: Peter Lang, 2002. 1-40.

Foote, Julia A. J.   *A Brand Plucked From the Fire: An Autobiographical Sketch by Mrs. Julia A. J. Foote*.   Ohio: Lauer & Yost, 1879.

Howard, Lillie P. ed.   *Alice Walker and Zora Neale Hurston: The Common Bond*.   Connecticut: Greenwood Press, 1993.

Hurston, Zora Neale.   *Their Eyes Were Watching God*.   New York: Harper & Row, 1937.

—. *Dust Tracks on a Road: An Autobiography*.   Ed. and Introduction by Robert Hemenway.   Urbana: University of Illinois Press, 1984.

Kelly, Lori Duin. "Theology and Androgyny: The Role of Religion in *The Color Purple*." *Notes on Contemporary Literature* 18:2 (1988): 7-8.

Lee, Jarena.   *The Life and Religious Experience of Jarena Lee, A Coloured Lady, Giving an Account of Her Call to Preach the Gospel*.   *Sisters of the Spirit: Three Black Women's Autobiographies of the Nineteenth Century*.   Ed. William Andrews. Bloomington: Indiana University Press, 1986.

Ross, Daniel W. "A Fairy-Tale Life: The Making of Celie in Alice Walker's *The Color Purple.*" *Teaching American Ethnic Literatures: Nineteen Essays.* Ed. John R. Maitino. Albuquerque: University of Mexico Press, 1996.

Stewart, Maria. *Productions of Mrs. Maria W. Stewart. Spiritual Narratives*: The Schomburg Library of Nineteenth-Century Black Women Writers, introduction by Susan Houchins. Oxford University Press: New York, 1988.

Truth, Sojourner. *Narrative of Sojourner Truth: A Bondswoman of Olden Times, With a History of Her Labors and Correspondence Drawn From Her "Book of Life."* The Schomburg Library of Nineteenth-Century Black Women Writers, introduction by Jeffrey C. Stewart. Oxford University Press: New York, 1991.

United States Constitution. Article I, section 2, paragraph 3.

Walker, Alice. *The Color Purple.* Orlando: Harcourt, 1982.

—. *In Search of Our Mothers' Gardens.* New York: Harcourt Brace Jovanovich, 1983.

Williams, Carolyn. "'Trying to Do Without God': The Revision of Epistolary Address in *The Color Purple.*" *Writing the Female Voice.* Ed. Elizabeth C. Goldsmith. Boston: Northeastern University Press, 1989. 273-286.

Williams, Delores S. "Black Women's Literature and the Task of Feminist Theology." *Immaculate and Powerful: The Female in Sacred Image and Social Reality.* Ed. Clarissa W. Atkinson. Boston: Beacon, 1985. 88-107.

Wilson, Mary Ann. "That Which the Soul Lives By: Spirituality in the Works of Zora Neale Hurston and Alice Walker." *Alice Walker and Zora Neale Hurston: The Common Bond.* Ed. Lillie P. Howard. Connecticut: Greenwood Press, 1993. 57-68.

God is (a) Pussy: The Pleasure Principle and Homo-Spirituality in Shug's Blueswoman Theology

Marlon Rachquel Moore

> Preach the Blues, sing them Blues, they certainly sound good to me
> Moan them Blues, holler them Blues, let me convert your soul
> —Bessie Smith, "Preachin' the Blues"[1]

> When black women relate to our bodies, our sexuality, in ways that place erotic recognition, desire, pleasure, and fulfillment at the center of our efforts to create radical black female subjectivity, we can make new and different representations of ourselves as sexual subjects. (bell hooks, "Selling Hot Pussy")

Shug Avery is many things to many people in the novel *The Color Purple*. To Albert, she is the love of his life, an unfinished story to which he returns again and again. To the men and women who are threatened by her sexual independence, Shug is a "nasty" woman, a whore. For the jook-joint crowd, she is a sexy songstress, beloved for her soul stirring renditions of popular Blues ballads. The most intriguing role, however, is as a priestess in her relationship with Celie, a function I describe as "Blueswoman evangelist." The phrase "Blueswoman evangelist" unifies the multi-layered, intersectional relationships between Shug's private/community life, the public "ministry" of the blues music she performs, and her influence as Celie's spiritual guide. Shug's ways of seeing and being in the world—blues artist, black woman and evangelist—should be understood as nonhierarchical, for each aspect of her personhood informs and reinforces the others. Shug's "Blueswoman theology" is a spiritual model that facilitates Celie's sexual discovery. Celie's spiritual growth is also examined for the ways it reveals the foundation of Shug's bodily-based theology: that a woman who recognizes her own sexual pleasure as sacred is a woman intimate with God.

Blues Consciousness and Transgressive Black Womanhood

In Blues Legacies and Black Feminism, Angela Davis reminds us that
there were three areas of African American life that were transformed
dramatically in the post-Emancipation experience: the possibility to
travel, opportunity for individual education and the freedom to choose
sexual partners. Because of these profound changes in the life of the
black masses, travel and sexuality were ubiquitous themes in early
blues lyrics. These themes form a worldview, a "blues consciousness"
that was shaped by and gave expression to this social transformation.
The blues genre was formed out of the same social and musical fabric
that the spirituals issued from, but with blues the social emphasis
becomes more personal (Jones 63). That is to say, because the blues
was (and is) an aesthetic of the psycho-emotional life and—composed
of moans, hollers and a "churchy" tone—it is considered the secular
counterpoint to spirituals, or "secular spirituals" (Cone qtd in Davis
8).

    According to this logic, if the spirituals are "God's music,"
then classic blues, its musical twin, belong to the Devil. In broad
terms, the Devil's music is a site of diverse, unsanitized expressions
of black experiences. In women's blues particularly, the lyrics speak
of women's frustration with cheating men, the loneliness and jealousy
of being the other woman, good and bad lovers, domestic violence,
homosexuality, suicide, violent revenge, drunkenness, incarceration
and poverty. They often speak of romantic love but not in the
idealized terms of mainstream love songs. Whether or not they
authored the songs they sang, blueswomen represented versions of
romance and sexuality that "often blatantly contradicted mainstream
ideological assumptions regarding women and being in love" (Davis
8-11). As a blueswoman then, Shug Avery represents unchaste,
unholy, 'nasty' womanhood.

    Alice Walker situates Shug in the blues tradition by linking
her to Bessie Smith, the first real superstar in African American
popular culture. Smith's first recording, *Down-Hearted Blues*,
established her as the most successful black performing artist of her
time. "Her broad phrasing, fine intonation, blue-note inflections, and
wide, expressive range made hers the measure of jazz-blues singing in
the 1920s" ("Bessie Smith"). "First Shug sing a song by somebody
name Bessie Smith," Celie writes, "She say Bessie somebody she
know. Old friend" (TCP 72). The evocation of Smith's legacy is key

to understanding Shug's position among the other women in the story. Smith is known in African American folklore for her indiscreet romances with women and men, her high tolerance for alcohol, and her fearless fighting attitude (Davis 37-39). The samples of her lyrics below illustrate the extralegal and what some critics consider the unsavory lifestyle her blues music represent:

"Tain't Nobody's Business"
Well I'd rather my man would hit me,
than to jump right up and quit me
'Tain't nobody's bizness if I do, do, do do
I swear I won't call no copper
If I'm beat up by my papa
'Tain't nobody's bizness if I do, if I do

"Jailhouse Blues"
Lord, this house is goin' to get raided, yes, sir!
Thirty days in jail, with my back turned to the wall, to the wall
Thirty days in jail, with my back turned to the wall
Look here, mister jail keeper, put another gal in my stall
I don't mind being in jail, but I got to stay there so long, so long

"Me And My Gin"
Stay away from me 'cause I'm in my sin.
If this place gets raided, it's just me and my gin.
Don't try me nobody, oh, you will never win.
Don't try me nobody, 'cause you will never win.
I'll fight the army, navy just me and my gin.

"You've Got To Give Me Some"
Loving is the thing I crave
For your love I'll be your slave
You gotta give me some, yes give me some
Can't you hear me pleading, you gotta give me some
Said mister Jones to old butcher Pete,
I want a piece of your good old meat
You gotta give me some, oh give me some
I crave your round steak, you gotta give me some

These expressions of unabashed sexual desire and normalized violence, as well as the unapologetic indulgence in "sinful" intoxication are themes that mark the blues genre as unrespectable and lacking "class." These same characterizations were also the white supremacist, elitist perspectives of African American folk culture. This is a culture that blends real world experiences with belief in the supernatural, magic and a dynamic ancestor presence. Toni Morrison describes this worldview as an always already "discredited knowledge." This is so, according to Morrison, "...because black people were discredited [,] therefore [,] what they *knew* was 'discredited'" (2288). Bessie Smith's renditions of familiar situations and this way of knowing, as Richard Wright poetically illustrates, placed her on the highest pedestal among African American consumers:

> Bessie Smith might have been a "Blues queen" to the society at large, but within the tighter Negro community where the Blues were a total way of life, and major expression of an attitude toward life, she was a priestess, a celebrant who affirmed the values of the group and man's ability to deal with chaos. (qtd. in Crockett 321)

Smith's "priestess" appeal is that her songs "exposed the stereotypes and explored the contradictions" of black sexual politics (Davis 41). Consistent with Smith's Blueswoman aesthetic, Shug revels in the street life of a traveling musician and shrugs off other "respectable" modes of black womanhood.

Although she does marry Grady and shares a home with Celie for years, Shug maintains her autonomy and rejects idealized notions of femininity. For example, she challenges the presumption of a natural maternal instinct that is assumed of all women who give birth. "My kids with they grandma..." Shug confesses, "She could stand the kids, I had to go" (50). This stance places her even beyond the realm of Strong Black Woman figure who works for financial sustenance, but whose passions are gratified by motherhood and service. Like many successful men, Shug does not allow her parental status to hinder her pursuit of the goals that satisfy her need for self-expression and individual identity. These factors contribute to her mobility and independence. They also supply the black community's moral leader, the church pastor, with fodder for his sermon. He holds Shug up as the antithesis of Christian womanhood:

> 'Even the preacher got his mouth on Shug Avery... He don't call no name, but he don't have to. Everybody know who he mean. He talk bout a strumpet in short skirts, smoking cigarettes, drinking gin. Singing for money and taking other women mens. Talk bout slut, hussy, heifer and streetcleaner.' (44)

His laundry list hits upon every aspect of Shug's gender transgressions. Her violation is not the act of singing, but that she does not do it in service of the church. Religion and church membership were highly regarded indicators of civility in the African

American culture at the turn of the century. Leroi Jones documents
this prominent attitude in *Blues People*, where he traces the African
American musical heritage. "In the post-bellum Negro society..."
Jones confirms, "The black woman had to belong to the Church, even
if she was one of the chief vestals of the most mysterious cult of
Shango, or be thought 'a bad woman'" (Jones 92). Shug is also
immoral because she flaunts her sexuality. Her revealing clothes and
multiple partners make her a "slut." Similarly, her generally careless
attitude toward the rules of "proper" (hetero) sexuality and femininity
marks her as "loose."

    Beyond his perception of her as immoral, the preacher's
dislike of Shug is also related to the competition for an audience that
Shug represents for the church. As alluded to by Wright and discussed
more directly by Davis, blueswomen in the early 20th-century were
bestowed with a secular priesthood. This is because "preaching" in
black vernacular was also a metaphor for blunt truth-telling and, as
mentioned above, the blues was a site of candid sadness, pain, desire,
love, regret and redemption expressed in narratives many people
could identify as reflective of real life situations.[2] Bessie Smith—and
Shug by extension—"preached the blues" in a manner that contested
the church's moral authority. The church embraces absolutes, and has
limited definitions of good/evil behaviors while the blues
consciousness allows for messy gray areas. Davis puts this tension in
historical context:

> The Blues were part of a cultural continuum that disputed the
> binary constructions associated with Christianity. In this sense,
> they blatantly defied the Christian imperative to relegate sexual
> conduct to the realm of sin. ... But precisely because they offer
> enlightenment on love and sexuality, *Blues singers often have
> been treated as secular counterparts to Christian ministers,
> recognized by their constituencies as no less important authorities
> in their respective realms.* However, from the vantage point of
> devout Christians, Blues singers are unmitigated sinners and the
> creativity they demonstrate and the worldview they advocate are
> in flagrant defiance of the community's prevailing religious
> beliefs. (123-24, emphases added)

In other words, blues ideology, as it relates to sex and sexuality,
contests Christian views. In blues doctrine, sexual relationships are
not separated into right/wrong or good/bad—lovers are. Blues reflects
back to the audience, non-judgmentally, to the listeners' assorted
painful and pleasurable realities. In contrast, Christianity seeks to
tame and tidy up certain sexualities, while completely demonizing

others. If blues promotes any worldview, it is that the line between pleasure and pain is a blurred one.

The Pleasure Principle

The preacher's sermon at Celie's church reflects a Christian code of morality which privileges spiritual pursuits over the body's desires, a splitting of the self conveyed best in the Bible verse, "Watch and pray, that ye enter not into temptation: the spirit indeed is willing, but the flesh is weak" (Matthew 26:41 King James Version). Shug, the symbol of blues discourse, promotes a different value system. While the preacher sermonizes against her, Shug struts about in short skirts, smokes, drinks, and has multiple sex partners; she still considers herself a sacred being in a state of holy communion with the Creator at all times. It is her view that "God love all them feelings." It is this version of freedom that she impresses upon Celie in their discussion about God, sex, the universe and all of Creation.

Full appreciation of sensual pleasures is the foundational principle of Shug's construction of humanity's relationship to God. This is the distinction she draws between her blueswoman theology and the preacher's orthodoxy. The difference, as Shug bluntly states, is that the blues performance puts "singing and dancing and fucking together. That's the reason they call what us sing the devil's music. Devils love to fuck" (115). In her assertion that devils "fuck," she connotes the wildness of the jook-joint atmosphere and identifies those women who frequent them as sexually indulgent. "Devils" are those "loose" or nasty" women who bask in the sexual energy—they represent unfettered and reckless expressions of desire and gratification. While Shug accepts this distinction, her statement actually begs the question of whether this assessment of difference is accurate. There is only a *perceived* difference in the energetic current that flows through the sanctioned sensuality in the church space and the fluid energy in the club atmosphere. When analyzed closely, it is revealed that the church and the jook-joint share an identical erotic dimension.

Theologian Dwight Hopkins argues that eroticism includes sex but also situates sex within a broader framework. "Eroticism works itself from the inside out," he explains, "The inside consists of a transcendent life force, an integrated spirituality clinging sensuously to the flesh" (189). In other words, the erotic experience is simultaneously and necessarily spiritual and physical. Beneath the surface of Shug's claim about devils is the implication that church cultures deny their erotic potential by limiting worshipful sensuality to singing and dancing. Actually, Shug's assumptions about Holy Roller cultures (Holiness/Pentecostal sects in which spirit possession is an encouraged part of the worship experience) are inaccurate. The erotic dimension that one can experience while dancing and singing in church may be an unacknowledged dimension, but it is not absent.

When one visualizes the two scenes of charismatic, communal jubilation side-by-side, the jook-joint atmosphere can mirror the emotionalism and physical release present in the church service. The wildness is similar in that flamboyantly dressed women, some in heavy make-up (looking their "Sunday best"), are inclined to flail about uncontrollably, as they shout and dance in the name of the Lord. Some people fall to the floor in a trance-like state and speak in "tongues." Others twitch spasmodically until they are physically spent. In many churches, these scenes can begin during the "praise and worship" portion of the program in which the locus of activity is the music. The progression moves thusly: singing leads to dancing, which then leads to the ecstasy of being "touched" by God and then, ultimately, the entranced person submits to the holy "bridegroom,"[3] as evidenced by uncontrollable crying or fainting. To the naked eye, this not a very far stretch from putting, as Shug says, "dancing and singing and fucking together." The difference lies in the discourse—the erotic energy in church is not recognized as such, while the spirituality of sexual energy is presumed in the blues. "In the Blues, physicality and spirituality exist as a dynamic quilting of the life force among Black folk" (Hopkins 189). The same quilting exists in religious fervor as well. Angels and devils are twin spirits, exerting identical powers over their believers.

The preacher and the Blueswoman evangelist, with their conflicting messages, are also connected by their shared audience. That is why Celie can say with confidence that without the preacher mentioning Shug's return to town, "everybody know who he mean." This is because secular and religious black music cultures are in constant dialogue. For example, the influence of blues stars Ma Rainey and Bessie Smith's performance styles turn up time and again in the memoirs and biographies of gospel-turned-secular artists. Notably, Mahalia Jackson, who famously refused to perform jazz or blues on the grounds of her Christian convictions, cites Ma Rainey as an irresistible "indecency" she secretly indulged in when she could (Sheftel). It is from this context that Shug's theological perspective is formulated. Shug embodies a blues consciousness which enables her to locate a sacred plane within corporeal pleasure.

Celie's religious upbringing has taught her to think of the world as a temporary but inevitable state of suffering, and that peace or meeting God are things one can only look forward to in the everlasting afterlife. "This life be over soon" she consoles herself, but "heaven last all ways" (42). Shug insists on the sacredness the Here and Now and God's presence in the physical world:

> 'Here's the thing, say Shug. The thing I believe, God is inside you and inside everybody else. You come into the world with God. ... Don't look like nothing, she say. It ain't a picture show. It ain't something you can look at apart from anything else, including yourself. I believe God is everything, say Shug. Everything that is or ever was or ever will be. And when you can feel that, and be happy to feel that, you've found It.' (195)

This pronouncement brings Heaven down from the skies into Celie's immediate surroundings. Celie's past, present and future potential are all suddenly in the realm of the godly. If God is everything, then God is no longer The Father in Heaven, but a force, an energy that moves through and around her.

This idea is expounded upon in Walker's *The Temple of My Familiar*, the sequel to *Color Purple*, where Shug publishes her version of the Beatitudes (also known as Jesus' "sermon on the mount" in *Matthew* 5). In "The Gospel According To Shug" she teaches: "Helped are those who *love the entire cosmos* rather than their own tiny country, city, or farm, for to them they will be shown *the unbroken web of life* and the meaning of infinity" (*Temple* 288, emphasis mine). So life, death and love are cyclical, self-perpetuating and nonhierarchical. If Celie can imagine a god that is not spatially above her or separate from her, she can rely on her spiritual power to become an agent of change in her own life. This type of intervention is exemplified when Celie describes the God of her imagination as "tall and graybearded and white," and Shug insists that she must "git man off [her] eyeball before [she] can see anything a'tall" (*Purple* 197). She gives Celie permission to abandon that image for a more inclusive and affirming one. In this spiritual model God is all bodies and, simultaneously, disembodied and inanimate; prayers can be directed toward rocks, trees, flowers and enacted through sex. This gesture not only de-genders God, it also releases Celie from the doctrinal pressures to please God through ritualized acts like attending church and finding "salvation." In effect, God is as present as one's awareness of It. God is because she is. In Shug's gospel, derived from her blues consciousness, the sin/salvation and body/soul binaries do not necessarily exist. The absence of Christianity's overarching narratives of restraint and guilt creates space for the exploration, affirmation even, of Celie's burgeoning lesbian identity.

Shug also reconfigures the Creator as an It rather than a male figure. In doing so, she discursively evaporates the patriarchal justification for women's bodies and loyalties to always be under control of men, whether those men are their husbands, fathers, or the masculine Holy Trinity. "Men and their religions have tended to make love for anything and anybody other than themselves and their Gods an objectionable thing, a shame" Walker writes in *The Same River Twice*, "But that is not the message of Nature, the Universe, the Earth or of the unindoctrinated [sic] Human Heart, where everything is profusion, chaos, multiplicity, but also creativity, containment and care" (171-2). It is Walker's "message of Nature [and] the Universe" that Shug brings to Celie in a way that equates sexual ecstasy with spiritual ecstasy, a message that includes homoerotic and masturbatory experiences.

God Is (a) Pussy and Other Homo-Spiritual Concepts

Shug testifies that when she found It, it was on a day when she "was sitting quiet and feeling like a motherless child, which I was, [and] it come to me: that feeling of being part of everything..." (195). This sentiment is a testimony of emotional development. The confession of being a "motherless child" underscores Shug's state of disconnection: she is "motherless" metaphorically because of her "nasty woman" outsider status in the community. That she was "sitting quiet" suggests a meditative or prayerful state during which her connection to and clearer understanding of her inextricable link the Universe descended upon her. Shug laughed, cried, and "run all around the house" (196), behavior that evokes the religious ecstatic moment described above, in which a person "catches the spirit" and runs down aisles, shouts, or burst into "tongues."

Next, Shug echoes her "singing and dancing and fucking" association by insisting that the spiritual breakthrough, to find It inside and around oneself, feels "sort of like *you know what*... [as she is] grinning and rubbing high up on [Celie's] thigh" (196, emphases mine). For Celie, this description enables a particularly lesbian interpretation of God's presence. This becomes clear when one

considers *where* Shug's hand presumably points to as she caresses the
thigh, and, equally important, *how* Celie knows what the "what" is. To
be clear, Shug's sexual identity is not being argued here. It is
established early in the novel that she has sexual-erotic connections
with men as well. Shug's analogy of spiritual ecstasy and orgasm in
this moment with Celie can only be labeled lesbian in that it refers
directly to an exclusively woman-to-woman emotional/erotic
experience (Rich 239). Remarkably, Shug's inability to report this
poignant moment in her life with straightforward detail is akin to
ethnographer Glenn Hinson's findings in a study of transcendent
encounters in Sanctified (Holiness) church programs. "The saints of
the African American sanctified community say that soul is the
domain not of body or mind, but of spirit," Hinson expounds, "And
when [God's] Spirit touches [human] spirit, the soul rejoices in an
epiphany of truth and knowledge" (2). Even though several 'saints'
testified of being touched by the Spirit they could not describe it
beyond clichés such as "getting happy" or "blessed by the Spirit"
Eventually, Hinson explains this "issue of tellability" as the limitation
of language:

> In my quest for phenomenological understanding, I ws asking for
> no less than a description of ecstasy. And that, my friends in the
> church patiently explained, entailed describing an encounter with
> the divine. Which is impossible. Human language can no more
> capture the essence of holy experience than the mind can
> understand the mysteries of God. Again and again, I was told that
> the words simply don't exist. Hence all one can do is talk *around*
> the experience, struggling to convey meaning through metaphor
> and connotation. (17, original emphasis)

As Hinson's subjects were unexpressive, Shug, too, is at a
loss for precise descriptors of her transcendent experience. So her
gateway to Celie's spiritual consciousness is Celie's knowledge of
clitoral orgasm—pleasure that can only emanate from the pussy.
Shug's theology insists that to "enter into Creation," that is, to fully
access one's power in the cosmological scheme of the Universe, a
woman must be able to appreciate all of life's pleasures. Yet she
identifies her deepest spiritual release, "the feeling of being part of
everything" (195) as an unmistakable, yet indefinable dimension of
knowledge, one she can only name through its similarity to the erotic
heights one can reach between Celie's thighs. So for Celie to truly
conceive of Shug's testimony of submission to the Spirit, she must

recall her own submission to "you know what." For Celie, God is (a) pussy.

The linguistic relationship between "you know what" and sex is drawn in an earlier scene in which Shug introduces Celie to the prospect of clitoral orgasm:

> Listen, she say, right down there in your pussy is a little button that gits real hot when you do *you know what* with somebody. It git hotter and hotter and then it melt. That the good part. But other parts good too, she say. Lots of sucking go on, here and there, she say. Lot of finger and tongue work. (77)

This conversation marks the beginning of Celie's journey into claiming her body for her own sexual pleasure. The homoerotic connection (from Celie's perspective) is already established by this point. She has documented a few occasions upon which her body responds to Shug's beauty or scent. Celie consistently couches her language in religious terminology, beginning with the scene in which she bathes Shug, where she "thought [she] had turned into a man" (49). "[When] I wash her body," she recalls, "it feel like I'm praying. My hands tremble and my breath short" (49). Later, she becomes aroused while watching Shug perform. "All the men got they eyes glued to Shug's bosom" Celie observes, "I got my eyes glued there too. I feel my nipples harden under my dress. My little button sort of perk up too. Shug, I say to her in my mind, Girl, you looks like a real good time, the Good Lord knows you do" (81). With Shug's aid, Celie has had a glimpse of what a "real good time" can look like between women and, after their first night together, she says that sleeping with Shug "feel like Heaven" (114).

Significantly, there is lesbian potential in Shug's description of orgasm. The omission of gendered pronouns in this definition creates imaginary space for Celie to insert Shug as the "somebody" to do the "finger and tongue work" in her pussy. Yet, Celie will be the first to actually touch herself there. Later that night, Celie tearfully masturbates while listening to Shug and Albert make love (79). The first time the women actually engage in sex, the details are left out. Celie simply says they kiss and "touch" each other (113). So, for Celie, the only logical reference to "you know what" when Shug rubs her thigh is the "little button" at the tip of Shug's fingers. In this way Shug constructs a sexualized spirituality in which the fire of the Holy Ghost melts the "little button" during orgasm. For Celie, the ecstasy of knowing God can be found through her familiarity with her pussy.

Finally, Shug's sermon about God and pleasure is homo-spiritual in that it elevates lesbian sex into the realm of praise and worship. In light of their lesbian relationship, Shug's assertion that "you have to git man off your eyeball to see anything a'tall" takes on dual meanings. On one level, she is suggesting to Celie that her feelings of alienation and abandonment by God are related to her views of God as an anthropomorphic, white paternal figure. Because of the brutal racism she's witnessed and her traumatic experiences with male domination, this is a god with whom Celie cannot truly identify. Shug's blues ministry molds the universe to include her black, female and her sexual selves in order to find peace in the world around her. But this introspective "getting man off the eyeball" doctrine could also be perceived as reclaiming female sexuality from the male gaze. "It is both the breaking of taboo and the rejection of a compulsory [heterosexual] way of life. It is an attack on male right of access to women, a form of naysaying [sic] to patriarchy, an act of resistance" (Rich 239). Once Celie understands her life and her body as always already blessed by God, and when she can dis-articulate her sexuality from her past with men, she is free to settle into a spirituality that allows her to "praise god by being liking what [she] likes" (196).

In this way, Shug's blues ministry constructs praise and worship as a seemingly selfish indulgence. This is a stark contradiction to the Christian dictum to "deny yourself" in exchange for sanctification and happiness in the afterlife, a doctrine based directly on Mark's recitation of Jesus' proselytizing rhetoric:

> Then he called the crowd to him along with his disciples and said: If anyone would come after me, he must deny himself and take up his cross and follow me. For whoever wants to save his life will lose it, but whoever loses his life for me and for the gospel will save it. What good is it for a man to gain the whole world, yet forfeit his soul? Or what can a man give in exchange for his soul? (Mark 8:34-38 NIV)

One religious website explains the meaning of such bodily denial in great detail:

> Denying self means that we repudiate our natural feelings about ourselves, i.e., our right to ourselves, our right to run our own lives. We are to deny that we own ourselves. We do not have the final right to decide what we are going to do, or where we are going to go. When it is stated in those terms, people sense immediately that Jesus is saying something very fundamental. It strikes right at the heart of our very existence, because the one

thing that we, as human beings, value and covet and protect above
anything else is the right to make ultimate decisions for ourselves.
We refuse to be under anything or anybody, but reserve the right
to make the final decisions of our lives. This is what Jesus is
talking about. He is not talking about giving up this or that, but
about giving up our selves. [...] If you are going to follow Jesus,
you no longer own yourself. [...]—deny our self-trust, deny our
self-sufficiency, deny our feeling that we are able to handle life
by ourselves and run everything to suit ourselves. ("Deny")

In light of this common interpretation of body/soul-splitting
spirituality, we can see how Shug's theology operates as a struggle to
undo antagonisms between bodily pleasure and spiritual strivings. In
fact, her "praise God by liking what you like" doctrine allows full
ownership and integration of one's body and one's soul. This image
of sexuality is of the sort bell hooks calls for in the citation at the
beginning of this essay. In "Selling Hot Pussy," hooks explores the
perpetual eroticisation of black women's bodies for white and male
consumers in US popular culture. A radical aesthetic, she argues,
would be an image of black female sexual subjectivity as self-
affirming and transgressive of conventional erotic iconography. Shug
represents such a woman, one in a relationship with her body that
"flaunts a rich sensual erotic energy that is not directed outward
[purely for consumption], it is not there to allure or entrap; [but] is a
powerful declaration of black female sexual subjectivity" (hooks 76).
Shug's Blueswoman theology liberates black female sexuality as it
reconciles the body to the soul, and it expands the spiritual
possibilities of all who seek God within themselves.

Marlon Rachquel Moore, University of Florida

Notes

[1] Quoted in Angela Davis's *Blues Legacies and Black Feminism,* p. 130. See Works
Cited for full citation.
[2] The use of past tense is not to suggest that the blues tradition and its artists are no
longer characterized this way. While the blues is no longer the most popular black
music genre in the US, the tradition is still very much alive and continues to be a site
of secular preachin'.
[3] Among the titles of Christ, The Bridegroom is closely associated with human life
and also rich in spiritual significance. It is a familiar description in Scripture and is
used some 14 times in the New Testament. It represents the expressiveness of His
covenantal relationship with His people. The Church is depicted as the bride of Christ

and as a Bride is spiritually united with Christ. Some verses: Matthew 9:14-15, Revelation 21 and 22, Ephesians 5:22-33. (www.tne.net.au/~abdaacts/bgroom.html)

Works Cited

"Bessie Smith." http://www.pbs.org/jazz/biography/ artist_id_smith_bessie.htm. Accessed 11/12/07.

Crockett, Kennette. "Bessie Smith: One of the First Divas." In *The Greatest Taboo: Homosexuality in Black Communities.* Edited by Delroy Constantine-Simms, Ed. Los Angeles and New York: Alyson Books, 2000. pg 321-326

Davis, Angela Y. *Blues Legacies and Black Feminism: Gertrude "Ma" Rainey, Bessie Smith and Billie Holiday.* New York: Random House, 1998.

"Deny Yourself of Sin's Pleasures." 7777777 Ministries: *Reaching The World & Changing Lives.* http://www.7777777.org/iii__deny_yourself_of_sins_pleasures.htm. Accessed 11/12/07.

Hinson, Glenn. *Fire in My Bones: Transcendence and the Holy Spirit in African American Gospel.* Philadelphia: University of Pennsylvania Press, 2000.

hooks, bell. "Selling Hot Pussy." In *Black Looks: Race and Representation.* Boston: South End Press, 1992.

Hopkins, Dwight N. "The Construction of the Black Male Body." *Loving the Body: Black Religious Studies and the Erotic.* Edited by Dwight Hopkins and Anthony Pinn. New York: Palgrave Macmillan, 2004.

Jones, Leroi (Amiri Baraka). *Blues People: Negro Music in White America.* New York: HarperCollins Publishers, 2002.

Lorde, Audre. *Zami: A New Spelling of My Name.* Freedom (CA): The Crossing Press, 1982.

Morrison, Toni. "Rootedness: The Ancestor as Foundation" In *The Norton Anthology of African American Literature 2nd Edition.* Edited by Henry Louis Gates, Jr. and Nellie Y. Mckay, New York and London: W.W. Norton, 2004.

Rich, Adrienne. "Compulsory Heterosexuality and Lesbian Existence." In *The Lesbian and Gay Studies Reader.* New York and London: Routledge, 1993.

Ryan, Judylin. S. *Spirituality as Ideology in Black Women's Film and Literature*. Charlottesville and London: University of Virginia Press, 2005.

Sheftel, Jeff. *Mahalia Jackson—The Power and the Glory: The Life and Music of the World's Greatest Gospel Singer*. DVD-Video. Xenon Studios, 2003.

Walker, Alice. *The Color Purple*. First Harvest Edition. Orlando: Harcourt Inc., 2003.

—. *The Same River Twice: Honoring the Difficult: A Meditation on Life, Spirit, Art, and the Making of the film* The Color Purple *Ten Years Later*. New York and London: Scribner, 1996.

—. *Temple of My Familiar*. New York: Harcourt Brace Javonavich, Inc., 1989.

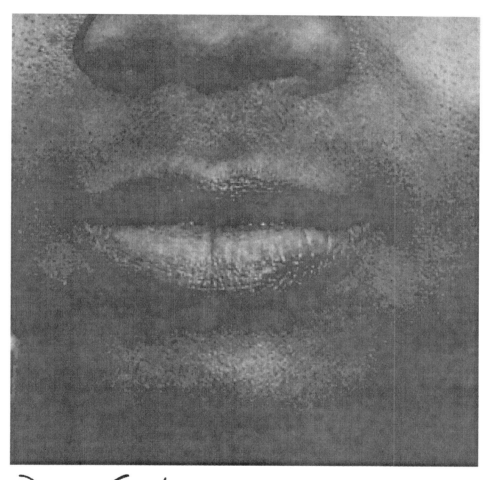

Dear God . . .
        Dear Peoples . . .
                Dear Everything

Witnessing and Testifying: Transformed Language and Selves in *The Color Purple*

R. Erin Huskey

With *The Color Purple*, Alice Walker appropriates both the theme of the *bildungsroman*, or the novel of education, and the form of the *epistolary novel*, a novel comprised of letters, to challenge the racially and culturally determined relationships between individuals and language. In what Linda Abbandonato calls a "conscious rewriting of canonical male texts," Walker writes views "from elsewhere" (296-8). What Walker offers is an intensely personal and individualized engagement with the revitalization of language and form—both literary and bodily—to signal that alternatives for community start with individual growth and commitment to the self. Throughout her career, Walker has written extensively about the relationship between writing and survival and growth, for both the author and the reader. Some of her most poignant comments on this conclude her essay, "Saving the Life That Is Your Own":

> It is, in the end, the saving of lives that we writers are about. [. . .] It is simply in our power to do this. We do it because we care. We care because we know this: *the life we save is our own*. (14)

What is clear by the end of this essay is that as a writer, Walker understands that saving herself is dependent on saving others by telling them—through her novels, stories, essays, and poems—about how she has made it through her pain.

In *The Color Purple*, Walker shows her characters living through their painful pasts rather than just showing them *dealing* with their painful pasts in the present. The novel is a textual act of testifying and witnessing to inspire the reader to transform his/her life and the terms in which he/she thinks about the self. While both "testifying" and "witnessing" have strong connections to the Christian act of public profession of faith, they do not rely on Christianity for definition. Rather, these acts can be defined as "affirming something from experience" and "seeing something happen" (Encarta Dictionary). As Janie tells Pheoby at the end of *Their Eyes Were Watching God*, we see Walker's characters "go there" and witness them learn to "know there."

Feminist Gloria Steinem, Walker's former colleague and close friend, praises Walker for this ability to know her readers and help them transform their lives through her books. Steinem's review—originally published in *Ms.* magazine and reprinted in a collection of her essays—cites the claims of an "angry young [male] novelist" as evidence: "'I've been a much better person [. . .] since I've been under the care and feeding of Alice Walker's writing'" (283). Then Steinem elaborates on how she has witnessed this effect on many readers over the years. *The Color Purple*, she notes, is particularly transformative because the "pleasure [in it] is watching people redeem themselves and grow [. . .] It's an organic morality of dignity, autonomy, nurturing, and balance" (290).

Not all feminists and critics agree with Steinem's praise, however. For in allowing her characters to experience transformation, Alice Walker has been criticized for creating a form and a vision that is utopian and disingenuous because, though the novel ends "happily ever after," for Celie, she has done nothing to make her world a better place for African Americans. The novel made a significant impact on the feminist movement, sparking scathing criticism from Trudier Harris, Camille Paglia, and bell hooks. Trudier Harris, a most vocal critic of Steinem's endorsement, charges that the novel "silences [criticism] by its dominance," (155) "gives validity to all the white racist's notions of pathology in the black community," (157) and that the novel's "fairy-tale structure" affirms only passivity (160). Camille Paglia categorizes the novel as a "sociological soap opera" that became a "token text for liberal literature textures aiming for quick and easy racial diversification of their class reading lists" and snidely suggests that the novel's success could in part be attributed to Walker's association with Steinem ("The Phallic Guns of July").

bell hooks is perhaps the most stringent critic of Walker's vision:

> [W]alker creates a fiction wherein an oppressed black woman can
> experience self-recovery without a dialectical process; without

> collective political effort; without radical change in society. [...]
> It is a brand of false consciousness that keeps everyone in place
> and oppressive structures intact. (295)

Whereas the aforementioned critics focus on public reception of the
novel and what it does and does not do in the context of the culture
wars of the 1980's, hooks situates the novel in a tradition of personal
and social transformation. In connecting African American women's
texts to the history of American social transformation, Melissa Walker
offers a further perspective on the significance of attention to the
personal form in *The Color Purple*. A portion of the novel is set in the
1930's, a time, Melissa Walker explains, of disparate viewpoints on
the goals and progress of civil rights for the African American
community. Furthermore, many did not even know that a change was
possible:

> For African Americans who had little evidence that life could be
> different, the concept of progress had little meaning. [...]
> Progress in *The Color Purple,* however, is entirely in the private
> domain, as characters relinquish destructive behaviors, develop
> satisfactory personal relationships, and construct economically
> viable lives in the midst of a hostile, oppressive, and essentially
> unchanged society. (50)

The first portion of Melissa Walker's commentary is certainly true.
However, Alice Walker clearly indicates that her characters contribute
to a spirit of change and personal transformation in the individual and
communal lives of society members as well. Yes, their society is still
hostile and oppressive.

But to declare that it is "essentially unchanged" denies the
power of the individual changes that promote transformation in the
lives of others. Furthermore, it subtly reinforces an ideology that
suggests African Americans are unable to control or shape their
communities while it robs both individuals and communities of voice.
Perhaps what these critics miss is that change begins on a very
personal level. Walker demonstrates this through both the form and
the content of the novel. As an author, she transforms historically
oppressive dominant literary forms and asserts her voice as
represented by the tangible object of the novel. This is an object or
text that symbolizes Walker's personal transformation and envisions
the possibility of transformation in the reader. This latter
transformation is dependent on the internalization of the novel's

message: neither Celie nor any other character can help anyone in the community until they first figure out how to help themselves.

And helping one's self is inextricably linked to the language one uses in self-reflection, in internal monologue, in dialogue, and in communal exchanges. If one does not know how to make new meaning for language, forms, and constructs and wrest them from their ability to oppress entire groups of people and suppress individual voice, one cannot effect lasting and meaningful social change. Because language, both oral and corporeal, enables communication, it is the foundation of society. Changes in the autonomous and the relational self begin with language. When we communicate with this transformed language—whether it is by writing a text, reading a text that in turn inspires transformation, or by telling others about our transformation—we are contributing to change in society.

In the African American women's oral and literary traditions, there is a history of rhetorical and formal experimentation that has at its roots an ideology that affirms positive transformation, something I term "gospel ideology." The gospel ideology is a cultural paradigm that is most readily identified with the Christian concept of witnessing, or giving a public testimony of one's personal beliefs. Most importantly, this is a phenomenon that takes place in a community context. When a congregant testifies, he or she shares trials, triumphs, tests, and acts of faith with a community of like-minded believers as an act of public expression. Testimony can also be used to edify the downtrodden, create a sense of belonging for the friendless, serve as a cautionary tale for the potential sinner, and inspire non-believers. It is not that this ideology carries any specific beliefs about a religious doctrine or sect: at the most basic level of definition, *gospel* is the good story. Essentially, this is a set of beliefs about the abilities of language and bodily expression to enact personal and social change.

Translated to literature, the gospel ideology functions where there is a testifier, an auditor, and a witness. Testifying is achieved through narration, a character's act of writing, direct discourse, free indirect discourse, and physical action. Thus, testimony is oral, written, and physical. An auditor can be another character in the text—a deity such as the Judeo-Christian God addressed through varieties of prayer and praise, and who is always the reader. Auditory and reading acts do not always ensure that there will be a witness. To be a witness does not merely entail listening, watching, or reading.

Witnessing here is not merely a passive act of reading the text and reacting to it; rather, witnessing in the gospel ideology calls for the subsequent act of testimony in word and deed. An auditor listens or reads the testimony, but an auditor does not always become a witness. To clarify, to be a witness, an auditor must be inspired or moved to transformation by the testimony he or she has heard and then return to the community to testify about this transformation.

This term *gospel ideology* is comprised of a number of influences, including the cultural and literary theories of Ralph Ellison and Craig Werner, in addition to the cultural connotations connected with the concept of gospel. In *Higher Ground*, Craig Werner expands Ralph Ellison's concepts of blues, jazz, and gospel impulses. Werner characterizes the *gospel impulse* as something that encourages the development of relational selves committed to individual and community transformation:

> The gospel impulse helps people experience themselves in relation to others rather than on their own. [. . .] There is a bigger energy than yourself [. . .] it breaks down the difference between personal salvation and communal liberation. [. . .] Whereas blues celebrates survival, gospel seeks redemption—it reconnects individuals with powers and communities larger than themselves. (7)

Thus, the gospel impulse is not strictly a religious phenomenon. Rather, one of its few "requirements" is a community context. Werner's description of the *gospel impulse* informs the use of the *gospel ideology* as a cultural and psychological experience that shapes literary production and reception.

In the literary realm, personal beliefs can be shaped as a result of the reading act. In order for the reader to be transformed by the reading act, it cannot simply be about interpreting the text based on one's experience or reading community. Rather, it must be about the impulse to interpret and rewrite one's life based on the text. In turn, the witness testifies about his or her transformation so that the community can also be transformed. This ideology provides the impetus and the rhetorical and bodily strategies for one to take the language and re-make it, to define one's self and to name the terms of one's text. For the authors, signifying on and revising literary forms associated with the dominant culture function as testimony to the possibility of reclaiming and reshaping language.

One way that African American authors have traditionally reclaimed and reshaped language while representing the black voice is by *Signifyin(g)*. In *The Signifying Monkey*, scholar Henry Louis Gates, Jr. contextualizes and defines the term *Signifyin(g)*. According to Gates, in Standard English the definition of the verb "signify" is to mean something or to be a symbol of something. When a speaker or writer *Signifies*, he or she engages in a complex language act that both redefines the original term "signify" at the same time it symbolizes that transformative language act by using the same term:

> By supplanting the received term's associated concept, the black vernacular tradition created a homonymic pun of the profoundest sort, thereby marking its sense of difference from the rest of the English community of speakers. Their complex act of language Signifies upon both formal language use and its conventions, conventions established, at least officially, by middle-class white people. (47)

Ultimately, Gates sums up the definition of the African American vernacular term "Signifyin(g)" as a category that covers an array of transformative linguistic and cultural interactions : "To Signify, in other words, is to engage in certain rhetorical games" (48). African American authors *Signify* by paying homage to the vernacular and literary traditions, by transforming subgenres and forms of the dominant literary tradition, and by representing black voice in dialogue and interior monologue, in addition to many other ways. Signifyin(g) to Gates is a trope of tropes; in keeping with his concept, "Signifyin(g)" and "signifying" will be used as Gates defines them in order to denote the difference in these homonyms.

Walker *Signifies* through her revisions of the *epistolary novel* and the *bildungsroman*. She demonstrates that Celie comprehends multiple varieties of Southern American English because Celie writes her letters in African American Vernacular English, but she also clearly comprehends her sister Nettie's letters and the dialects used by various members of the white community (e.g. Miss Millie, the shopkeeper, etc.). As the author, Walker *Signifies* through Celie's interactions with multiple dialects: Celie clearly understands several, but her oral and written utterances are deliberately in African American Vernacular English.

Again, Henry Louis Gates, Jr. has written extensively on the ways in which Walker pays homage to Hurston and Celie's use of and comprehension of various dialects of English as forms of *Signifyin(g)*.

Gates discusses the history of the politics of the textual representation of black voice and characterizes the theme of the black voice as a metaphor:

> For just over two hundred years, the concern to depict the quest of the black speaking subject to find his or her voice has been a repeated topos [traditional theme] of the black tradition, and perhaps has been its most central trope. . . . the representation of characters and texts finding a voice has functioned as a sign both of the formal unity of the Afro-American literary tradition and of the integrity of the black subjects depicted in this literature. (239)

Gates characterizes Hurston's narrative voice as the "authority of the black vernacular tradition [. . .] a nameless, selfless tradition, at once collective and compelling, true somehow to the unwritten text of common blackness" (183). Significantly, Gates identifies Hurston's "search for a telling form of language" as a search that coincides with the search for self. In turn, he demonstrates how Walker *Signifies* on the history of devising a black literary voice:

> [W]alker's text points to a bold new model for a self-defined, or internally defined, notion of tradition, one black and female. The first step toward such an end, she tells us, was to eliminate the 'white man' to whom we turn for 'teaching' and the 'giving [of] understanding. (258)

Celie represents a similar notion both in her transformed concept of God and through her commentary on a Memphis friend's—Darlene— efforts to teach her how to talk. While Darlene contends that the way Celie talks marks her as a "hick" to whitefolks and that Shug must be ashamed of the way she talks, Celie reads the primers Darlene brings her merely to appease her. In her letter, however, Celie writes that these storybooks with "whitefolks . . . talking about apples and dogs" are far removed from her experience of life, and, when Darlene attempts to correct the way she talks, Celie feels like she cannot think: "Look like to me only a fool would want you to talk in a way that feel peculiar to your mind" (216). Clearly, Celie can read and understand the Standard English primers as well as Nettie's letters, but when she talks and writes about her own life, it must be in her voice.

Furthermore, the *epistolary novel* is a vehicle that can give its fictional writer dominion over form, content, and the body through articulation of the self. Walker makes her revisions of the *bildungsroman* and the *epistolary novel* intersect at Celie's assertion of self and rejection of her initial self-abnegation. Whereas Celie begins her first letter to God by striking out the phrase "I am" and replaces it with "I have always been," she begins the conclusion of her last letter to Nettie with the phrase "*I be so calm*" (283). Walker makes significant use of Celie's dialectal variety of African American Vernacular English in the tenses of the verb "to be." "I am" indicates that Celie believes she is currently something. "I have always been," indicates that Celie believes that she had always been something up until a certain point or event; she is no longer that something. And finally, "I be," indicates that presently Celie believes she is calm and will remain in that state. Most significant is the fact that Celie is asserting her existence in the present moment. As Walker has Celie write herself into an understanding of self, it is witnessed by a community of willing auditors, both characters and readers. In short, Walker's heroine writes an understanding of the self, witnessed by a community . . . readers.

In order to understand the significance of the transformation from "I have always been" to "I be" as a rejection of the oppression of language invoked through authority figures and as a claim to transformative political power, we must look at the italicized command to Celie that precedes her first letter. Though the command is unattributed, it is clearly uttered by Alphonso, and it is significantly one of two italicized utterances in the text. In word and deed, Alphonso succeeds in convincing Celie she is a nonentity, merely a receptacle through which he can fulfill his sexual desires. He transgresses the boundaries of a parent/child relationship. Even though he is not her biological father, Celie is not aware of this significant fact.

Furthermore, he bestows upon himself an authority likened to that of God, an authority that Celie certainly will not disobey. In *The Wayward Preacher in the Literature of African American Women,* James Robert Saunders discusses the danger of self-definition through religion. Certain African American authors, he claims, "are warning against capitulation to religious functionaries who insist that the self must be virtually obliterated in order for salvation to be attained" (7). Theologian Theophus Smith underscores the significance of defining a deity in African American culture: "To designate a deity is also to image or reimagine the self" (312). While Alphonso is not a "religious functionary," Celie's identification of him with God imbues him with a similar authority and promise of retribution for transgressing his edicts. Celie's only auditor—God—then is incapable of witnessing. And she immediately disembodies her voice both through writing rather than speaking and by striking out the phrase "I am."

Here Walker *Signifies* on the tradition of the disembodied voice. While the connection between transformed language and personal transformation is evident in the earliest extant African American texts, for women authors in particular, the call and authority to do so was often attributed to a God that required an erasure of the self from the literary act. Given the politics of literary production and reception, a brief look at the evolution of this connection leading up to Walker's novel in particular is helpful.

The black person's—and particularly the black woman's—foray into the literary world was complicated by both whites and blacks as a direct result of the blackness of the body. Slavery, segregation, sexual abuse, and injustices of all kind were rationalized and justified on the purported difference found in the black female body. Black women in a public role were thus faced with the challenge of fulfilling their mission at the risk of losing their femaleness and respectability merely for placing their bodies in the public eye. Black women were taught that their role was service; they were to be neither seen nor heard. What resulted, particularly in the literary arts, were conventional rhetorical strategies calculated to replace the body with an empowered voice.

Inspired by David Walker's *Appeal* and a conversion experience, essayist and lecturer Maria Stewart began to write inspiring and edifying religious tracts for African Americans and became heavily involved in the antislavery movement in the early 1830's. But Stewart attributes her transformation to God's grace, while at the same time she discounts her "elegance [and] taste in composition" (251) And in 1861, Harriet Jacobs wrote about her escape from the "patriarchal institution" of slavery to "arouse the women of the North to a realizing sense of the condition of two millions of women at the South, still in bondage, suffering what I suffered, and most of them far worse" (281). Significantly, Jacobs does not reveal her true identity. Rather, she apologizes for her incompetency and lack of education while crediting Bishop Daniel A. Payne as the authority who compelled her to write her story for the sake of those still enslaved.

The disembodied voice is also present in early autobiographical writings by Zilpha Elaw, Julia Foote, and Jarena

Lee, as well as in postbellum and Progressive era literature by Francis
E.W. Harper and Charlotte Forten. These women all cite a calling that
is an apologia of sorts for placing themselves in the public sphere, and
there is a fascinating relationship here between the body and the
creator of the linguistic act. Carla Peterson locates the origin of this
phenomenon in the Judeo-Christian tradition:

> [G]od authorizes man to divest himself of his body and seek
> power through the making of material artifacts, including
> language; in Christian interpretations of death, finally, the
> resurrection of the soul privileges the verbal category over the
> material by endowing man with an immortal voice. (387)

These women relied on specific rhetorical forms of the church to
nearly obliterate their presence in bodily form. They all claim
inspiration by and authority endowed by God while at the same time
they apologize for their incompetency as mortal women. But this was
not done as an act of passive submission to the ideology; rather, these
women sought to call attention away from their bodies as linguistic
creators and focus attention on altering the ideology.

Peterson claims that this "self-marginalization" was done in
the effort to both challenge and gain entry into the institutions that had
barred black women. The black women writers of this era had been
conditioned to believe that the body was a problem, that it in fact
hindered their work, and that the only way to overcome it and the
stereotypes on which race difference had been constructed was to
prove to the dominant culture and black patriarchal leaders that black
women could be respectable.

In the way Alice Walker has Alphonso use "God," she indicts
those who have reinforced rather than remade structures designed to
oppress and control. Part of Celie's image of this God comes from the
Bible, a book that gives her a code that makes her deny her feelings
and right to enjoy her life:

> I used to git mad at my mammy cause she put a lot of work on
> me. Then I see how sick she is. Couldn't stay mad at her.
> Couldn't be mad at my daddy cause he my daddy. Bible say,
> Honor father and mother no matter what. Then after while every
> time I got mad, or start to feel mad, I got sick. Felt like throwing
> up. Terrible feeling. Then I start to feel nothing at all. [. . .] This
> life soon be over, I say. Heaven last all ways. (41-42)

It is this code, in part, that makes her vulnerable to victimization, oppression, and self-denial. Quite simply, Celie can only unburden herself to a being who cannot repeat any of her secrets or "sins." Her auditor is thus limited to an ethereal, spiritual being that Celie believes has a close resemblance to the white man on a cereal box. This is a concept of a God who has traditionally either ignored or not defended the oppressed voices of African Americans. Rather, he is a white God, designed by white people to protect and promote their self-interests. And he has often been invoked to harm and exploit African Americans. Very quickly, Celie associates this concept of God with what she knows of Alphonso. If it is not made clear in her references to God being the father of her children as well as the person who took them away from her, then Walker further clarifies Celie's conceptualization by typographically referring to both God and Alphonso with the capitalized pronoun "He."

In contrast to what detractors of the novel claim, Celie is not a mute and numb fairytale heroine whose life is transformed without any personal struggle or interaction with other members of her community. Her transformation is a long process that involves learning that she can – in fact she must – tell others about what has happened to her. Before she can do that, she has to learn about the pain that she causes others by staying in her place and maintaining oppressive structures. The most striking example of this is realizing the harm she has done Sofia in telling Harpo to beat Sofia just like Mr. _____ has beat her. Celie writes that "a little voice" revealed this to her.

Furthermore, Celie thinks about her connections to other people and records the first time she thinks about the world:

> 'What the world got to do with anything, I think. Then I see myself sitting there quilting between Shug Avery and Mr. _____. Us three set together against Tobias and his fly speck box of chocolate. For the first time in my life, I feel just right.' (60)

Celie is clearly aware of herself as a communal self, connected in some allegiance to creation. And while critic Trudier Harris asks why Celie does not make an earlier attempt to leave Mr. _____, Celie does signal the desire to move out of this oppressive structure but is unable to do it until she speaks aloud her story and confronts the voices that have silenced her own.

One of the many purposes Shug fulfills is to help Celie remake her image of God so that she may find her voice and tell her story. Shug espouses a belief in the divinity within and an animism that asserts God is everywhere, in everything:

> God is inside you and inside everybody else. You come into the world with God. But only them that search for it inside find it. And sometimes it just manifest itself even if you not looking, or don't know what you looking for. Trouble do it for most folks, I think. Sorrow, lord. Feeling like shit. [. . .] Don't look like nothing, she say. It ain't a picture show. It ain't something you can look at apart from anything else, including yourself. I believe God is everything, say Shug. Everything that is or ever was or ever will be. (195)

Shug represents a very personal relationship with divinity, a theme that is present in Walker's early novels such as *The Third Life of Grange Copeland*. Her ideas imply that the search for God inside oneself effects both personal transformation and connection to others. And by extension, when the reader frees the self from the terms by which oppression has defined and limited life, the reader then transforms the lives and selves of those other people to whom she is connected.

In Walker's work, there is a close link connecting the creative impulse to personal transformation and the identification of the divinity within the self. This link is further connected to Theophus Smith's assertion that designating a deity leads to reimagining the self. Thus, it is no surprise that Shug is not only a blues singer, but she also composes her own songs, cooks, and draws up plans for her unconventional round house and helps Celie in her process of transformation. Shug also encourages Celie's creativity in sewing her Folkspants. In addition to being an economic venture that can allow her to support herself, Celie's Folkspants, Unlimited represent her ability to creatively express her divinity and to share that with her community. Significantly, Celie experiences Shug's concept of God before Shug describes it to her. Walker subtly uses this device to reinforce the legitimacy of Shug's beliefs when the reader encounters them. Before Celie can remake her concept of God and name it so, she has to move from the private writing act to the public act of witnessing and testifying. Even though her creativity has been sparked and she understands that she needs to drive the white God out of her mind, Celie has not yet made the connection between replacing that

God with her own creation and achieving a stable sense of self. Both deficiencies are indicated by the persistence of a divided sense of self, the dependence on the image or the physical presence of Shug for a sense of security, and a preference for written over oral expression.

Walker uses the letters to create two Celies: the one she presents to her relatives and community and the one she freely reveals on paper. There are frequent discrepancies between what Celie records as her thoughts and what she records as her speech. One of the first occurrences is when Harpo comes to her for advice about marrying Sofia: "Talk to Mr.____, I say. He your daddy. Maybe he got some good advice. Maybe not. I think" (30). Clearly, Celie feels safety in writing down what she dare not say aloud.

Celie's divided sense of self is thus connected to the choices she makes in written and oral expression. On one of the last occasions of her preference for writing over speech, the three things she relies on rather than an independent sense of self—writing what she cannot say, writing the textual Celie versus acting with a sense of agency, and the physical presence of Shug – come together in a climactic moment. When Shug tells Celie that she has fallen for Germaine, Celie writes that she feels like "shit." What she *tells* Shug is that she is killing her, but even this is lost on Shug. In her letter, Celie writes, "I don't say nothing. I pray to die just so I don't never have to speak" (250). She doesn't speak; instead she writes "Shut up" to Shug. Celie's end of the conversation continues with written responses until Shug asks if she loves her. Then Celie speaks with startling clarity, "I love you, I say. Whatever happens, whatever you do, I love you. [. . .] But I can't stay here" (251). This signals yet another move out of place and away from an oppressive structure. And even though Celie is despondent, her thoughts, language, and actions are finally in alignment.

What she has discovered is that she has spent so much time trying to empty God of the notions inscribed by whites that she has not allowed herself to create her own form:

> Trying to chase that old white man out of my head. I been so busy thinking bout him I never truly notice nothing God make. [...] Whenever you trying to pray, and man plop himself on the other end of it, tell him to git lost, say Shug. Conjure up flowers, wind, water, a big rock. (197)

From the beginning of the novel when Celie nearly writes herself out of the text, Walker is emptying the form of the novel of its associated meanings. When Celie writes the pivotal comment, "Pa not Pa"(177), Walker starts accumulating new meanings for the novel, for God, and for Celie. Throughout the novel, Celie works with the ways in which other people define her and finally takes control over her own form, translating that control to transform God, self, and relationships. Celie's transformation is from one of Hurston's "mule of the world" who exists only in letters intended for no one's eyes, to a fully developed and audible presence in the story and in the hands of the reader.

Part of the transformation involves Celie and Mr. ____ witnessing and testifying to each other. Through her conversations with Mr. ____, Celie begins to be grateful for Nettie and Shug who have both fought for her and listened to her. Mr. ____'s new appreciation for the things God has made helps Celie to realize that every time she has felt like "shit," she *has* had somebody along with her, whether that person is there in body or in spirit. Together, Celie and Mr. ____ reminisce over Shug and work out their feelings for her and each other, not just attending to their individual growth but to their relationships with one another. Celie also realizes that love is not possessive and controlling: "Just cause I love her [Shug] don't take away none of her rights. [. . .] Who am I to tell her who to love? My job just to love her good and true myself" (268-269). She helps Mr. ____ to see that Shug loves him, even if that love is like the love felt for her brothers. Celie then indicates she understands the intersection of language, creation, revision, and God is found in the self: "Well, I say, we all have to start somewhere if us want to do better, and our own self is what us have to hand" (271).

Once Walker brings Celie to the realization that God is not a form outside of herself, that in fact God—as Shug says—is everything, her spirit is reunited with her body and her linguistic activity. In fact, Walker comments on this very thing in her film soundtrack liner notes for the song "Maybe God is Tryin' To Tell You Somethin,'" a song that is connected both to the "little voice" Celie hears when she has wronged Sofia, as well as to her ability to decide what that "little voice" is:

> [We] must ask who or what is this 'God' that's trying to 'tell us something.' [. . .] Is it someone or something completely outside ourselves? Or are 'God' and 'Jesus' essentially code names for the voice that speaks the truth within us and finds its echo in the mysteriousness of the perceived and imperceivable universe? For

> someone brought up in the church as I was, and who found it
> obstructionist rather than helpful in finding 'God,' labels of any
> kind attached to the inner voice and the outer spirit are distracting
> and loaded with racist, classist, sexist, ideological baggage. [. . .]
> For whatever the inner voice is called [. . .] the voices in this song
> direct us to a feeling recognition of the inner voice itself, refusing
> to let us get stuck outside ourselves struggling over and fussing
> with names. Not only are we the world, we are the universe, the
> cosmos. There is no separation between us whatsoever. Therefore
> we have only to truly *listen* to hear ourselves speak.

This has powerful implications for Celie, her society, and for the reader, for if God is everything, the moment that concept is internalized, the self is transformed. This transformation allows Celie to write to Nettie that whether or not Shug comes home, she will be content: "*I be so calm.* If she come, I be happy. If she don't, I be content. And then I figure this the lesson I was suppose to learn" (283). Walker's use of italics here demonstrates that Celie no longer needs to write to an external spirit and a divided consciousness. In writing to Nettie that she says "I be so calm" to herself, Celie is writing to a somebody who has been with her all along. Most significantly, Celie is able to write what she has said rather than what she wishes she would have said. Furthermore, there is no longer any textual evidence that Celie is the divided self of the earlier letters. Rather than writing what she formerly felt she could not say aloud, she says what she thinks and then records that in letters to someone she knows is alive. The letters are thus transformed as a means of communicating experience to someone who will read them rather than a means of recording the things that Celie dare not say or write to anyone who can hear or read. Celie then addresses her last letter to God and Everything, including herself. No longer are her thoughts and words relegated to auditors who either cannot hear her or are not likely to ever receive the letters. Instead, her sense of self comes together in oral, written, and corporeal expression.

Again, the questions of whether or not the text engenders a "brand of false consciousness" (hooks 295) and if it endorses progress only in the private domain arise. All seems good for Celie and her extended family, but what about the rest of her community, and by extension, the readers of the text? It is important to note that Celie's transformation does not take place in isolation. Rather, it is through the influence of and interaction with other characters in her family and community. Not only does Celie send a message about the fallacy of gender roles to her community through her Folkspants business venture, she engages in positive entrepreneurship when she takes over the store she inherited from her biological father, and she serves as a living example of someone who has experienced transformation. Furthermore, Shug's ministry is not limited to Celie, for Celie shares what she has learned by encouraging self-assertion and transformation in Mary Agnes, Sofia, and the reader.

Central to the definition of a gospel ideology is a concern for the community as a body, and Walker makes this concern preeminent in her novel. The evidence of such a concern is a further indication that criticisms such as those offered by bell hooks and Melissa Walker do not take into account the progression of transformed language to personal transformation to social action. This does not signal the individual's capitulation to dominant ideologies or the community's will. Rather, it is through the individual's experience in defining and asserting the self that he or she participates in community healing and building. African American Literature and Women's Studies scholar Lovalerie King makes a similar observation in commenting on this theme running through Alice Walker's fiction:

> Though Walker's process [of describing her womanist aesthetic] is supposedly de-centered, the quest for personal and communal *wholeness* is the one aspect of the process that is most apparent in all six of her novels. In this project, she employs recurring motifs of the spiritual journey or questing self, rebirth and transformation, the universality of pain and suffering, and a holistic view of life that brings her idea of connectedness into full relief. At issue is the condition of the soul, and it is not simply a matter of the individual soul. She or he who achieves wholeness, or who aspires to achieve *wholeness*, bears the responsibility for showing others the way, *for lifting as they climb.* One imagines a chain, or a continuum, of humanity with each leading the next. (239) [King's emphasis]

Community healing and building are both fictional and real necessities, and while the setting of this novel is in the first half of the twentieth century, communities are still suffering from the effects of self-loathing, both mental and corporeal. These effects are conveyed largely through the means of linguistic oppression. Among the evils that endanger community are miseducation and miscommunication, two elements Walker explores in *The Color Purple*. Although these threats begin with the individual, Walker demonstrates how, when left unchecked, they destroy families and communities. However, when individuals go through the process of redeeming the self, their words and deeds serve as testimony that this redemption is a possibility for their community and that ruptures can be healed on more than a personal level.

Walker demonstrates that when other characters experience redemption, it inspires Mr.___'s redemption, and in, turn offers possibility for the next generation. She uses Harpo's redemption to demonstrate the importance of sharing that experience; it is the thing that allows Harpo to re-educate his own father. Though their lives have been inscribed by miscommunication and miseducation, Harpo baptizes his father, allowing him to "enter into Creation." Moreover, Harpo's testimony to his father re-awakens Sofia's love for Harpo, and as a result, the relationships and futures of many other characters are redeemed. Sofia and Harpo are able to newly create a loving and nurturing environment, not only for the children they had together, but also for Henrietta and Mary Agnes. As an act of witnessing both to another individual and to her society, Celie hires Sofia to serve her African American customers in her store and to serve up a little verbal sass to the white customers who try to put her, and all other African American women by extension, in a role defined by race and gender:

> 'Plus, she scare that white man. Anybody else colored he try to call 'em auntie or something. First time he try that with Sofia she ast him which colored man his mama sister marry.'. (280-281)

Lest the conclusion of the novel sound like a fairytale, Walker reminds the reader that just because transformation has occurred, everything is not always going to be perfect. Families are reunited, relationships (both fraternal and romantic) are mended, and the community is being revitalized through Celie's entrepreneurship, but the transformations Walker writes about are true to life in that they are clearly not harbingers of "happily ever after." Despite redeemed selves, healed ruptures, and community building, if this narrative were to continue, it is clear that these characters are headed for personal and community struggle. And these are the types of struggles that readers will continue to face throughout their lives.

One such personal struggle is implied in Tashi's physical mutilation. Given the historical setting of the novel, the African American community would not have accepted Tashi's facial scars as anything other than shameful marks of Eurocentric notions of African savagery. The notions of assimilation to Euro-American standards of beauty and decency and the rejection of anything African were still very much a part of the message of racial uplift. While Walker explicitly deals with this issue in her subsequent novel *Possessing the Secret of Joy*, she foreshadows it with Tashi's concerns that Americans will think she is ugly and that Adam will forsake her for

women who embody the Euro-American aesthetic. Rather than exploring the origins of such tribal traditions or the reception of such obvious physical markers of Africa in this novel, Walker chooses instead to focus on the meaning of the rituals and comparing their acceptance to the way in which cyclical oppression and violence threaten African American families. Tashi is deluded into thinking that participation in these rituals will strengthen community through the preservation of them. Tradition has perpetrated on these Olinkan women the idea that mutilating their bodies, and thereby denying their rights to sexual pleasure, is in the best interest of their community. Walker calls blind obedience to ritual into question here, subtly paralleling this situation with Harpo's confusion of traditional gendered behaviors with masculinity. These characters are faced with the difficult consequences of adhering to customs and traditions for which the meaning has been lost.

Community struggle is also indicated by Sofia's relationship with Eleanor Jane, the mayor's daughter. While Sofia has some affection for her, she refuses to be relegated to the role of the Southern black mammy who relinquishes a relationship with her own children in favor of that of one with her oppressor's offspring. This problematic relationship is characterized by Sofia's response to Eleanor Jane's insistence that Sofia express love for Reynolds Stanley:

> Did I ast him to come? Do I care whether he sweet or not? Will it make any difference in the way he grow up to treat me what I think? [. . .] I don't feel nothing about him at all. I don't love him, I don't hate him. I just wish he couldn't run loose all the time messing up folks stuff. [. . .] I feel like he been here forever. [. . .] I love children [. . .] But all the colored women that say they love yours is lying. [. . .] Some colored people so scared of whitefolks they claim to love the cotton gin. [. . .] I got my own troubles, say Sofia, and when Reynolds Stanley grow up, he's gon be one of them. [. .] I'm telling you *I* won't be able to love your own son. You can love him just as much as you want to. But be ready to suffer the consequences. That's how the colored live. (264-266)

While healing has occurred for individuals and relationships in Sofia's African American community, she understands that not enough has changed in the relationship between the black and white communities for her to truly love this white baby boy. She knows that he will, in all likelihood, grow up to take advantage of African Americans and uphold the practices and attitudes that keep oppressive structures in place. Whereas Eleanor Jane sees Sofia as the only person who has truly loved her, taking care of her was accomplished at the expense of Sofia's not being able to take care of her own children.

Their relationship is eventually mended, indicating that while prejudice and racism is far from over, individual understanding is the first step in eradicating oppression. Because Sofia has had a major role in raising Eleanor Jane, and because Eleanor Jane feels an abiding love for Sofia, she takes Sofia's words to heart and decides to take care of Henrietta while Sofia is working in Celie's store. In discussing the arrangement with Harpo and Celie, Sofia responds to the call for the necessity of individual transformation: "It not my salvation she working for. And if she don't learn she got to face judgment for herself, she won't even have live" (281). This passage suggests that each person is responsible to that God who is within the individual and everywhere else at the same time. Eleanor Jane became a witness after Sofia told her the true story of how Sofia came to work for Miss Millie. While her subsequent actions and change in attitude are significant, some critics might argue that Eleanor Jane is only one white person among many in this text. But then again, change begins with one willing witness.

Walker has commented extensively and written about how writing as an act of testifying and witnessing is a transformative experience for her. Before writing *The Color Purple*, she wrote of her experiences growing up in the segregated South, her self-loathing, and her three-day ordeal wrestling with the choices of abortion or suicide in *From an Interview*. The reason she relates these experiences, she writes, is that they made her a survivor, and she firmly believes she is meant to share them with other women. Elsewhere in this essay, she describes her mission as a writer: "Writing poems is my way of celebrating with the world that I have not committed suicide the evening before" (249), "I am preoccupied with the spiritual survival, the survival *whole* of my people," (250), "The white women writers that I admire [. . .] are well aware of their own oppression and search incessantly for a kind of salvation. Their characters can always envision a solution, an evolution to higher consciousness on the part of society, even when society itself cannot" (251), "I believe in change: change personal, and change in society" (252), and finally "I believe in listening [. . .] especially to young black women whose rocky road I am still traveling" (272). If we consider these statements in conjunction Walker's commentary on the song "Maybe God is Tryin' to Tell You Somethin'," Walker's philosophy about the translation of personal transformation to social action becomes clear: listening to others gives rise to your own voice, and speaking or writing can change the lives of whoever is listening.

In "Writing *The Color Purple*," Walker writes that she carried the "germ" of the novel with her through "all kinds of heartaches and revelations," as the novel tried to form (356). She is adamant that the characters contacted her to serve as their mouthpiece. In fact, she dedicates the novel "*To the Spirit*" and closes it with a thank you to everyone in the book. Additionally, she titles herself "author and medium." While at first glance, this conjures up a host of pejorative connotations that could accumulate to demean the novel and the author's testimony, these comments must be taken in the context of the novel functioning within a tradition that insists upon call and response, individual and communal selves, and personal transformation translated to political power.

For this much is clear, that the germ of a story that Walker had was a true anecdote, and while the consolation and the desire to know the rest of the story Walker drew from it got her through her bad times, that story was begging to be told. In that sense, then, Walker functions like Hurston's Phoeby whom Janie charges with the task of telling her story to the rest of the community.

In order to tell that story, though, Walker had to experience it. She was unable to write this story in her beloved New York City, for this was not a place where she could truly listen to these characters: "As long as there was any question about whether I could support them in the fashion they desired (basically in undisturbed silence) they declined to come out" (357). Walker had to be able to hear their stories so she could repeat them; she had to move away from the structures that silenced their voices to a place of comfort for both herself and her characters. Walker's ability to sustain a connection with these characters, however, was severed by her constant travels and speaking engagements. Only when she stopped talking and started doing the daily activities her characters would have done (with the exception of grueling farm work), did Walker become a witness to their stories. And only when Walker's daughter Rebecca came to live with her were both she and her characters inspired to transform their lives:

> My characters adored her. They saw she spoke her mind in no uncertain terms and would fight back when attacked. When she came home from school one day with bruises but said, You should see the other guy, Celie [. . .] began to reappraise her own condition. Rebecca gave her courage (which she *always* gives me) [. . .] on the very day my daughter left for camp, less than a year after I started writing, I wrote the last page. And what did I do that for? It was like losing everybody I loved at once. [. . .] Mercifully my quilt [that she had made while waiting for the characters to come to her] and my lover remained. (359-360)

Walker implies many things in this last section of the essay. First, although she removes herself from the city, Walker's and Celie's transformations are achieved only in the context of community exchange. Rebecca's ability to fight back *and* talk about it transforms the character Celie and inspires courage in her mother so that she could write the story and testify to readers. After all, it was Rebecca who quite earnestly transformed the definition of Walker's damaged eye from a painful deformity to a "world in [her] eye" ("Beauty" 393). And even though there is a public record of their troubled relationship, so too are these positive and powerful acts a matter of public testimony. Most significantly, perhaps, Walker neither keeps her transformation to herself nor is she left alone: she has her novel to share with readers, the quilt she made as evidence of the transformation, and at least one witness.

Oprah Winfrey has been one very vocal witness to the transformative powers of *The Color Purple*. On the December 5 and 9, 2005 episodes of *The Oprah Winfrey Show*, Oprah spoke at length about her experiences with the novel. Because of the powerful message *The Color Purple* spoke to this African American woman who had been sexually abused, silenced, and mocked for her obesity, she claims she became "obsessed" with it. Describing it as her favorite "Let go, let God" story, Oprah says that she carried a backpack full of the novels and gave copies to people wherever she went.

The Color Purple is a testimony that inspired Oprah to transform her life. In turn, she has witnessed and testified about the novel to countless other people. Oprah has shared this testimony many times, but one truly powerful instance was on the October 3, 2005 episode of *Oprah After the Show*. She shared how the novel and auditioning for the role of Sofia in the film version both taught her to "Let go and let God" and to realize that her self-image need not be reduced to a description of her physical appearance. The importance of the self-image cannot be minimized here. For in Oprah's story, the true battle was not about winning the role; rather, it was about the ability of a victim to triumph despite how others read her personal appearance. Her epiphany was that she had to let her anxiety about the movie role go and move on, a striking parallel to Celie's "*I be so calm*." Just as she had this realization, she received the phone call awarding her the role. And while this might seem like a fairytale, especially given Oprah's present-day wealth, prominence, and influence, she makes it clear that it was the realization preceding the triumph that made the transformation in her life:

> [N]ow I live to be full of myself and my stuff and not everyone else's stuff. [. . .] After than happened, I thought 'that's how you do it.' [. . .] I learned in that moment that you do all that you can do, and when you've done everything that you know how to do, you surrender it to the power that's greater than yourself. ("Oprah on *The Color Purple*")

It is a victory like that of Celie's when she announces to Albert, "I'm pore, I'm black, I may be ugly and can't cook, a voice say to everything listening. But I'm here" and Shug witnesses, "Amen" (207). No better example of testimony and witness exists, for Oprah has since gone on to triumph over her detractors and pass this "good story" on through multiple mediums, including her numerous philanthropic efforts, to countless willing listeners.

　　Touching the life of the reader is the ultimate goal of any text informed by the gospel ideology. In *The Color Purple*, both the characters and their bodies participate in expressing their individual and communal selves. Walker combines the oral/vernacular tradition and the literary tradition, asserting that they must come together to empower and re-educate the community. After hearing the characters' stories, the reader is left with the choice of what to do with what he or she has witnessed. Like Alphonso or Old Mr.____, the reader can refuse to see the self because it is easier to blame someone else, to take another person's definition of the self, rather than go through the process of self-definition. Or like Celie, the reader can go to the source of pain, embrace the physical and spiritual body, and assert the self by telling the story. And by telling one's own story, the reader takes the first step in making Alice Walker's vision a reality.

Dr. R. Erin Huskey, Valdosta State University

Works Cited

Abbandonato, Linda. "Rewriting the Heroine's Story in *The Color Purple.*" *Alice Walker: Critical Perspectives Past and Present.* Eds. Henry Louis Gates, Jr. and K.A. Appiah. New York: Amistad, 1993.

Gates Jr., Henry Louis. *The Signifying Monkey.* New York: Oxford University Press, 1988.

Harris, Trudier. "On *The Color Purple*, Stereotypes, and Silence." *Black American Literature Forum.* Winter, 1984: 155-161.

hooks, bell. "Reading and Resistance: *The Color Purple.*" *Alice Walker: Critical Perspectives Past and Present.* Eds. Henry Louis Gates, Jr. and K.A. Appiah. New York: Amistad, 1993.

Hurston, Zora Neale. *Their Eyes Were Watching God.* New York: Perennial Classics, 1998.

Jacobs, Harriet. *Incidents in the Life of a Slave Girl. The Norton Anthology of African American Literature.* 2nd edition Eds. Henry Louis Gates, Jr. and Nellie McKay. New York: Norton, 2004.

King, Lovalerie. "African American womanism: from Zora Neale Hurston to Alice Walker." *The Cambridge Companion to the African American Novel.* Ed. Maryemma Graham. Cambridge: Cambridge University Press, 2004.

Paglia, Camille. "The Phallic Guns of July." *Salon.* Jun 1997. 29 Oct 2007. <http://www.salon.com/june97/columnists/paglia970624.html>.

Peterson, Carla L. "'Doers of the Word': Theorizing African-American Women Speakers and Writers in the Antebellum North." *African American Religious Thought.* Eds. Cornel West and Eddie S. Glaude, Jr. Louisville: Westminster John Knox Press, 2003.

Saunders, James Robert. *The Wayward Preacher in the Literature of African American Women*. Jefferson, NC: McFarland & Company Publishers, 1995.

Smith, Theophus. "Exodus." *African American Religious Thought*. Eds. Cornel West and Eddie S. Glaude, Jr. Louisville: Westminster John Knox Press, 2003.

Steinem, Gloria. "Alice Walker: Do You Know This Woman? She Knows You." *Outrageous Acts and Everyday Rebellions*. New York: Henry Holt, 1983.

Stewart, Maria. "Religion and the Pure Principles of Morality, the Sure Foundation on Which We Must Build." *The Norton Anthology of African American Literature*. 2nd edition Ed Henry Louis Gates, Jr. and Nellie McKay. New York: Norton, 2004.

"Testifying." Def. *Encarta Dictionary*. 2007.

Walker, Alice. "Beauty: When the Other Dancer Is the Self." *In Search of our Mothers' Gardens*. New York: Harvest, 1983.

—. *The Color Purple*. Orlando: Harcourt, 2003.

—. "From an Interview." *In Search of our Mothers' Gardens*. New York: Harvest, 1983.

—. "Maybe God is Tryin' to Tell You Somethin'." *The Color Purple Motion Picture Sound Track*. Quincy Jones Productions, 1986.

—. "Saving the Life That Is Your Own." *In Search of our Mothers' Gardens*. New York: Harvest, 1983.

—. "Writing *The Color Purple*." *In Search of our Mothers' Gardens*. New York: Harvest, 1983.

Walker, Melissa. *Down from the Mountaintop: Black Women's Novels in the Wake of the Civil Rights Movement 1966-1989*. New Haven: Yale University Press, 1991.

Werner, Craig Hansen. *Higher Ground*. New York: Crown Publishers, 2004.

Winfrey, Oprah. *The Oprah Winfrey Show*. 28 Dec. 2005. 30 Oct. 2007. <http://www.oprah.com/tows/pastshows/200510/tows_past_20051003.jhtml>.

Winfrey, Oprah. "Oprah on *The Color Purple*." *Oprah After the Show*. 3 Oct. 2005. 30 Oct. 2007. <http://www.oprah.com/tows/pastshows/200510/tows_past_20051003.jhtml>.

"Witnessing." Def. *Encarta Dictionary*. 2007.

"My Man Treats Me Like a Slave": The Triumph of Womanist Blues over Blues Violence in Alice Walker's *The Color Purple*

Courtney George

> [...]if Celie were singing, she would be like Mamie, Bessie, and Ma Rainey, all of whom were abused. Those women were abused by men. I always feel so deeply when I listen to them, and then I think about how people took it for granted that your man would be this way. Of course you'll be abused. And so they weren't really heard, and they got used to it, actually dancing to this. It was like a spiral that was not going up but going down. People sing about this and then expect it in relationships. It was self-perpetuating. I doubt if any of these people had relationships that nourished them. They had relationships, instead, that prompted cries of anguish that were then used to entertain. The people who were entertained modeled themselves on what they were hearing, and it was just a very bad cycle. (Alice Walker, "I Know What the Earth Says")

In the blues-filled world of *The Color Purple*, Alice Walker revisits and revises the historical era of 1920s blues singers like Mamie Smith, Bessie Smith, and Ma Rainey. Shug, Celie, Sofia, and Squeak revive the spirit of the great blues divas and their audiences but also break out of the cycle of abuse to which Walker alludes above. In these characters, Walker engenders a new type of blues lifestyle—a blues that combines her love of these historical women's songs and lives with her conception of "womanism." Walker defines womanists as feminists of color, women who love women, women who are concerned with the salvation of the *entire* race (not just women), and women who love to sing and dance. By merging these characteristics with the strengths of the first popular blues women, Walker creates a womanist blues to demonstrate how her female characters emerge as successful women who combat the violence done to them by men.

Because womanism is interested in uplifting men as well as women, Walker also uses the blues to consider how black men, who internalize violence from a racist white power structure, are caught in these same cycles of abuse when they exercise violence on their daughters, wives, and lovers. In his book *Seems Like Murder Here*, cultural and literary blues scholar Adam Gussow discusses this kind of domestic violence as it occurs in blues culture, terming it "intimate" violence. Gussow defines intimate violence as "the violence that black folk inflict on each other: the cuttings, shootings, razor slashings, beatings, and murders described—and more often than one might expect, celebrated as a locus of power and self-making—by African American blues people in both story and song" (196). In her revision of blues history, Walker suggests that the blues community's celebrations should not be imbued with violence, but instead with harmony and love. While women can also inflict intimate violence as Walker herself depicts, the intimate violence in *The Color Purple* is aligned with a dominant male perspective as readers watch Pa, Albert, and Harpo brutally try to tame their wives and children. Walker pits intimate male blues violence against an intimate female blues womanism; the latter ideology triumphs over blues violence and allows for a collective union between black men and women. In critiquing the brutality present in historical depictions of the blues, Walker twists the abuse "spiral" upwards; she creates an alternate womanist blues history that calls for unity amongst southern African Americans in order to transcend the "very bad cycle" of gender and sexual violence perpetuated by racism and sexism.

Although Walker draws from the history of blues men and women to fill the pages of the novel, she employs these historical portraits to create the fictionalized *memory* through the autobiographical letters of narrator Celie. Because Celie does not sing (like Mamie, Bessie, or Ma), she writes—letters that are first addressed to a white God and then to her sister Nettie. In the first lines of the novel, Celie's Pa forbids her to speak of his rape of her to anyone except God, which automatically signals to readers the black woman's silent plight with domestic abuse. In incorporating women's blues (a public acknowledgement of abuse) through Shug, Walker allows Celie to voice her interior struggles out loud by the novel's end. Her transition—from first addressing letters to God and later addressing them to her sister Nettie—shows how Celie moves from an object in a patriarchal society to a subject in a womanist space.

Walker tells Celie's life story in the vernacular language of a poor, uneducated black woman living in the Jim Crow South. Celie's fictional letters act as recorded memories, reclaiming the working class black woman's historical voice, which was virtually absent from southern text-book histories written by white males. As Walker submits in her essay, "Coming in from the Cold," a love of memories is what unites non-elite people:

> It is because the language of our memories is suppressed that we tend to see our struggle to retain and respect our memories as unique. And of course our language is suppressed because it reveals our cultures, cultures at variance with what the dominant white, well-to-do culture perceives to be. To permit our languages to be heard, and especially the words and speech of our old ones, is to expose the depth of the conflict between us and our oppressors and the centuries it has not at all silently raged (63).

Walker suggests that historical accounts often do not acknowledge the voices of those oppressed by a racist, sexist, and classist social structure, no matter how loudly they might be speaking. In combining Celie's vernacular language with the oral form of the blues (both the voices of "our old ones"), Walker recreates the collective memory of black southern communities and asks readers to reclaim those *unsilent* cries—particularly about abuse—voiced in blues music. Scholar Maria Lauret argues that Walker uses the blues to give a historical voice and place back to black women: "Ultimately, *The Color Purple* is a monument, not just to Bessie Smith and Zora Neale Hurston, but to the black victims and survivors of sexual abuse who historically have been silenced in white (and black male) literature, but who have expressed their pain in the vernacular of the blues. It is also, crucially, a monument in which the black English of the oral tradition is forever carved in stone" (120). Scholar Gunilla T. Kester also suggests that Celie and Shug must learn to speak to each other through the blues: "Because *The Color Purple* juxtaposes the epistolary mode (with its long standing western tradition) with the blues, it intensifies the issue of cultural voice [...] it shows that healing can only begin when women share the tradition of black cultural representation thematically inscribed as the blues" (120).

Although Walker tells her story through the individual memory of Celie, *The Color Purple* is not simply one black woman's story. As literary scholar Thadious M. Davis argues, "Despite her concentration on the brutal treatment of black women and the unmitigated abuse of children, Walker believes in the beauty and the power of the individual, and ultimately of the group" (37). In endowing her characters with blues qualities, Walker engenders a collective memory that speaks to an alternate experience of oppressed southern blacks in the Jim Crow era by celebrating black folk life and the black community's will to endure. Celie's narrative challenges white-perpetuated stereotypes of black people as somehow less than human—as happy, lazy children; primitive male brutes; and overly-sexed female seductresses. Through Celie's memorial descriptions, the readers watch the black community overcome struggles and experience growth. While Celie's memories are private, Walker uses them to recall how the publicly-performed blues influenced the social identity of black southerners as a group. As Ralph Ellison writes, the blues evoke the private sphere: "As a form, the blues is an autobiographical chronicle of personal catastrophe expressed lyrically" (79). Yet, the blues also speak for the black community and the brutal trials they faced during and after slavery. Again, according to Ellison, the blues are "thus a transcendence of those conditions created within the Negro community by the denial of social justice. As such they are one of the techniques through which Negroes have survived and kept their courage during that long period when many whites assumed, as some still do, they were afraid" (257). Although a blues singer meditates on a personal situation, when performing to an identifying audience, the blues man or woman voices collective frustrations about oppression. In Walker's novel, when Celie reflects on her private life through letters, the reading public can also identify with her situation, almost as if Celie sings just like Mamie, Bessie, or Ma in songs like "Black Eye Blues," "Sweet Rough Man," and "Outside of That"—all songs where the female protagonists try to understand why men physically abuse them.

Because the African American blues man or woman sings of an individual experience that serves as an alternative voicing of collective oppression (alternative to the idealized white literary and historical depictions of racial integration and equality in the South), this music can be linked with definitions of cultural or collective memory: an individual memory that is constructed from and thus recalls a cultural memory that challenges dominant history. Cultural critic Marita Sturken writes of collective memory:

> The collective remembering of a specific culture can often appear similar to the memory of an individual—it provides cultural

identity and gives a sense of the importance of the past. Yet the
process of cultural memory is bound up in complex political
stakes and meanings. It both defines a culture and is the means by
which its divisions and conflicting agendas are revealed. (1)

One person's memory is inevitably tied to the memories of the larger
group with which they identify—whether a racial, national, regional,
religious, gendered, sexual, class, or ethnic group (or some
combination). W. Fitzhugh Brundage explains:

> Nearly all personal memories, then, are learned, inherited, or at
> the very least, informed by a common stock of social memory
> [...] the act of remembering the past and of assigning levels of
> significance to it...is an act of interpretation. No longer can we
> presume the existence of fixed images of the past that we retrieve
> intact through acts of memory [...] Collective memories, like
> personal memory, are constructed, and not simply reproduced. (4)

Brundage draws his ideas from philosopher Maurice Halbwachs's
book *The Collective Memory*. Importantly for this study, Halbwachs
believed that musical communities in particular offered a stunning
example of collective memory because musicians often tailor
performances by audience response. Musicians do not merely play a
song from sheet music—especially in popular forms like blues or
jazz—but instead recall the audience response from a past
performance, which influences playing styles. Because Walker, as an
author of fiction, configures Celie's memory, the reader acts as an
audience member and realizes that memory is a construction and then
questions the consequences of Walker's choice to use historical traces
of the blues in Celie's constructed memory. What larger blues
community is she asking readers, as an identifying group, to
remember or revise? What resistances and agendas are revealed?

Theories from French philosopher Pierre Nora can be used to
show how blues history interacts with the collective memory
presented in Celie's letters. According to Nora, the discipline of
history attempts to represent or record the events of the past, while
memory is a living fluid representation of the past in the present. Nora
argues that, in recent years, historical accounts are informed by
individual memories that confuse or alienate past accounts of national,
regional, or social collective representation. In the wake of these
individual accounts, humans long for a connection to community, and
representations that attest to a collective history (which Nora terms

lieux de mémoire) are continuously appearing. Lieux de mémoire, as defined by Nora, are symbolic sites of collective memory such as portraits of historical figures, archives, memorials, monuments, books, and letters. Nora's study asks scholars to focus not on the facts of the historical person or event, but on why and how the cultural memory of such a person or event is portrayed (in these sites). Discussing African American memory and history, historians Robert O'Meally and Genevieve Fabre use Nora's concept of sites of memory to argue that such sites perform a crucial role in bridging personal and collective memory: "in the quest for identity and the assertion of birth right and ancestry, sites are anchors and frames…memory ultimately becomes the essential metaphor, a means to confront the troublesome past and the uncertain present" (O'Meally et. al 10). Popular music functions as lieux de mémoire: "the blues, sounding through a hundred years of the music in a variety of forms and fashions" constitute an important site for African Americans trying to reconstruct a collective memory and identity (8).

In using Nora's theory of collective memory to understand the history of the blues as represented in *The Color Purple*, the attention is turned away from the singers and their songs; the pictures of blues men and women and the written and oral recordings of their tunes are simply representations of their historical presence. Using Nora's theories to read Walker's novel challenges readers to consider what resistances Walker exposes through her memories of blues people and their blues. How and why is the history of blues people portrayed, and who gains power from what portraits? What power does Walker gain from using traces of the blues? What message is she sending forth and why? While she alludes to historical blues women, Walker includes more than just historical images, delving into what caused black people to sing the blues, what healing or harming effects these blues had on the community, and what challenges and changes the blues posited against a racist, sexist power structure, particularly about the concerns of abuse and violence in the black community. Literary critic Keith Byerman sees Walker as abandoning her blues folkways because Celie later transcends her oppressive conditions: "In *The Color Purple*, she has in effect moved to allegorical form in order to transcend history and envision the triumph of those principles she espouses. But in doing so, she has neutralized the historical conditions of the very folk life she values" (66). I argue that Walker purposefully disrupts or neutralizes those historical conditions by using memorial traces of the blues—sites that ask readers to investigate further the conflicts between southern black men and women in those blues, to search for the meanings behind and consequences of those conflicts.

While Celie's plight as a black woman is the novel's focus (it is her memory we read through letters), Walker also engenders a collective memory about the abuses that all black blues people faced—whether men or women—in the Jim Crow South; Walker tells us not just one black woman's story but the collective story of a black community affected by abusive racist oppression. As blues scholars concur, one of the main themes of the blues is violence. For black women especially, feminist scholar Angela Y. Davis argues in her 1998 study of classic blues women, *Blues Legacies and Black Feminism*, the blues offers a place to voice conflict about domestic violence, which was otherwise silenced by ideals of white womanhood:

> There is [...] a body of preserved oral culture [...] about domestic abuse in the songs of blues women like Gertrude [Ma] Rainey and Bessie Smith. Violence against women was always an appropriate topic of women's blues. (25)

Davis's overall arguments about working-class women's blues invoke the concept of collective memory to challenge the ideal of white womanhood:

> Through the blues, black women were able to autonomously work out—as audiences and performers—a working-class model of womanhood. This model of womanhood was based in part on a collective historical memory of what had been previously required of women to cope with during slavery. But more important, it revealed that black women and men, the blues audience, could respond to the vastly different circumstances of the post slavery era with notions of gender and sexuality that were, to a certain extent, ideologically independent of the middle-class cult of "true womanhood" (46).

In *Tomorrow is Another Day: The Woman Writer in the South 1859-1936*, feminist critic Anne Goodwyn Jones describes the ideal of southern white womanhood as perhaps informing roles for all American women (9). This ideal represents white upper-class women as southern culture's "idea of religious, moral, sexual, racial, and social perfection" (Jones 9). The white woman was innocent, chaste, and virtuous: "Finally, she serves others—God, husband, family, society—showing in her submissiveness the perfection of pure sacrifice" (Jones 9). While Shug and Sofia's characters more closely resemble Davis's descriptions of working-class blues women, Celie's character fits almost perfectly within the confines of white womanhood—a role ultimately unavailable to her because she is African American.

As Davis argues, in singing about the abuse they faced from their men at home—a private matter—classic blues divas brought the issue to the public, making the collective community aware of this problem. Blues men also sang about violence (what Adam Gussow terms "intimate" violence amongst the black community) in order to divulge publicly the threats they faced from whites in the Jim Crow South. Even while the blues was often marginalized as the "devil's music," this undervalued form still provided black women and men with a public space for protest. Using the guiding principles of womanism in *The Color Purple*, Walker forges connections between the blues violence that black men and women sang about by revealing how white racist, sexist, and classist hierarchies instigated the intimate and domestic violence that took place in the black community. She employs blues themes to unite separate visions of male and female black communities and to critique how blues people reacted to the threat of white violence collectively; she exposes the sometimes veiled cultural memories left to us in blues songs and proposes an end to the cycle of abuse perpetuated in the blues. Ellison suggests that the blues "at once express both the agony of life and the possibility of conquering it through sheer toughness of spirit. They fall short of tragedy only in that they provide no solution, offer no scapegoat but the self" (94). Unlike Ellison's blues, Celie's blues-inspired memories move beyond examinations of the "self" to propose a collective womanist solution to blues violence—a solution that fosters love and cooperation in a utopian black southern community; Walker moves beyond Celie's self-reflection to show how a communal womanist vision could exist outside of the mainstream violence perpetuated and informed by the racist white Jim Crow South. Walker asks readers to shift concentration from Shug's performances as a classic blues diva to how Shug's collective audience members (Celie, Albert, Sofia, Mary Agnes, Harpo) respond and remake her performances into a blues womanist ideology that exists despite white constructions of racism and sexism.

As many critics have suggested, through the fictional blues singer Shug Avery, Walker evokes the 1920s classic blues divas that first recorded and popularized the form. Critics Thomas F. Marvin and Jerry Wasserman carefully compare Shug to blues singers Ma Rainey and Bessie Smith, using blues lyrics from the era as evidence of Shug's similar characteristics. In Marvin's "Preachin' the Blues: Bessie Smith's Secular Religion and Alice Walker's *The Color Purple*," he compares the religion in Smith's lyrics and Shug's ideology, arguing that this religion stems from African religions. In "Queen Bee, King Bee: *The Color Purple* and the Blues," Wasserman more generally compares Shug to Smith, Rainey and other blues favorites, using images and song lyrics to argue that Shug blurs gender roles in her appropriation of bad bluesmen and divas.

Yet Shug combats "bad" bluesmen instead of taking on their qualities; Shug's power is in making them over, not imitating them as Sofia and Celie do. Scholar Cheryl Wall also discusses Shug's character as influenced by the 1920s female blues community. Wall argues, "Shug inspires Celie's and Albert's transformations because she is the novel's moral agent. Of course, hers is not the perceived morality; when judged by conventional standards, Shug is deemed profoundly immoral (as were Bessie Smith, Ma Rainey, Ida Cox, and others)"(149).[1] Wall reconstructs the lives of 1920s blues divas to match Shug by relying on Angela Davis and Daphne Duvall Harrison. Wall's excellent argument goes on to understand Walker's new portrayal of religion as drawn not only from African traditions (as Marvin argues) but also traditional Christian values—she views this religion as a "futuristic" merging of the two. In their well-known cultural studies of blues women, Daphne Duval Harrison, Angela Y. Davis, and Hazel V. Carby also mention Shug Avery as a literary archetype of these great singers.

In varying ways, these critics argue that, like the classic blues women, Shug remains unafraid to sing about and live her life outside the confines of society's mores and gender roles. Most works that investigate blues tropes in *The Color Purple* focus on how Shug transforms Celie's religious and sexual self. Like many of the classic blues women, Shug and Celie find an alternative to abusive heterosexual relationships by trusting in one another and remaking traditional white Christianity. Drawing from blues women's advice songs that preached the dangers of men to other female audience members (and also songs which celebrate lesbianism like Rainey's

"Prove it on Me Blues"), Walker uses Shug and Celie's sexual relationship to revise dominant heterosexism.[2] Cultural critic Maria V. Johnson's "Jelly Jelly Jellyroll: Lesbian Sexuality and Identity in Women's Blues" offers a close reading of how blues women created a female community through their songs and how, in particular, these songs often celebrated and affirmed lesbian sexualities.

Yet exploring the blues themes of violence and abuse shows how Walker engenders a womanist story that testifies to the experiences of blues women *and* men. From the beginning of the novel's reception, critics and reviewers have critically debated whether or not Walker depicts black men as stereotypical sexist brutes. Early reviewers Robert Towers and Darryl Pinckney unabashedly attacked Walker's depictions of Albert and the other male characters in the novel as overtly violent and brutal. Trudier Harris's article, "On *The Color Purple*, Stereotypes, and Silences" discusses her own love-hate relationship with the novel as well as classroom reactions to the text; she somewhat ambivalently agrees with male students' descriptions of male characters as either cruel or weak.[3] In this reading, Walker's use of blues memories does not reinforce stereotypes of black men but asks readers to uncover the formation and perpetuation of such stereotypes as embodied in white southern racist and sexist social structures.

Walker asks her readers to recognize how racist tactics were passed down to the black community in the form of oppressive gender tactics and to sympathize with the plight of black men (as well as women) under patriarchy. While Walker defines a womanist as "a woman who loves other women, sexually and/or nonsexually [and] appreciates and prefers women's culture, women's emotional flexibility (values tears as natural counterbalance of laughter), and women's strength," she makes clear that a womanist is also "committed to the survival and wholeness of entire people, male *and* female. Not a separatist, except periodically, for health. Traditionally universalist..." (*In Search* xi-xii). A womanist loves women and women's culture first and foremost, but a womanist works to save her entire race; she is universal in her love for the black folk and their ways. In promoting a blues-inspired womanist agenda in *The Color Purple*, Walker asks that readers understand how black men's struggles with racism inform black women's struggles with sexism, linking men and women's plights to reveal how the black community unites in resistance against a powerful white patriarchal South.

Shug's love for singing and dancing, her professed outrageous behavior and her love for women and men fit within Walker's prescribed definitions of womanism. In merging Shug's blues with a womanist perspective, Walker creates a blues womanist figure able to conceive of a black community free of sexist, racist, and religious constraints imposed by the elite white South. Shug's combatant attitude towards abuse no doubt reverberates with songs of the classic blues women as described by Angela Davis in *Blues Legacies and Black Feminism*. Davis recounts numerous songs detailing violence and how to fight it as sung by Rainey and Smith, concluding "Women's blues suggest emergent feminist insurgency in that they unabashedly name the problem of male violence and so usher it out of the shadows of domestic life where society had kept it hidden and beyond public or political scrutiny" (29). While Walker uses traces of the blues women of which Davis speaks in the *The Color Purple*, Walker does not simply rewrite the history of the classic blues female. Through Celie's memory of not just Shug, but also Sofia, Squeak, Pa, Albert, and Harpo, Walker creates a collective story about blues violence—a memory that displays the cultural trauma of racism and sexism and simultaneously proposes a womanist solution of cooperation and love.

Walker tackles the intimate male blues violence expressed by the male figures in the novel in order to uplift black blues people as a whole. As Angela Davis suggests, women's blues failed to consider why men beat women:

> In Ma Rainey's and especially in Bessie Smith's blues, the problem of male violence is named, and varied patterns to implied or explicit criticism and resistance are woven into the artists' performance of them. Lacking, however, is a naming or analysis of the social forces responsible for black men's propensity (and indeed the male propensity in general) to inflict violence on their female partners. (33)

In Walker's memorial revision of classic blues women's history, she investigates how black men have (perhaps unconsciously) inherited the violent ways that white plantation owners maintained power over their black subjects. Like the racist white community of the plantation and the subsequent Jim Crow South, black men sometimes use brutality to control their women and children. Walker's story can be linked to blues themes, particularly the intimate blues violence of which Adam Gussow writes in his book *Seems Like Murder Here*.

Gussow explores the seeming absence of southern blues lyrics and lifestyles that protest southern violence and lynching. His study proposes that "black southerners evolved blues as a way of speaking back to, and maintaining psychic health in the face of, an ongoing threat of lynching" (xii). Gussow understands the violence present in blues lyrics (and in the jukejoints) as one of the three main themes of blues music (along with travel and sexuality). He argues that "intimate violence"—the violence acted out between black people in jooks or sung about in the blues—"was an essential, if sometimes destructive, way in which black southern blues people articulated their somebodiness, insisted on their indelible individuality" in the face of white racism (5). In order to feel powerful (in a racist society designed to make black people feel powerless), the black community used the blues to boast about (and to mourn) the stabbings and beatings that often took place in jukejoints, at home, or in the workplace. Gussow considers blues violence as containing a sexual dimension since the blues often meditated on the beatings and mistreatings between black men and women. His reading of the blues offers new insight into the violent actions of Harpo, Albert (Mister), and Celie's step-father (Pa) as reactions to the threat of southern racism.

Gussow views Celie's history—the fact that her real father was lynched because he stood up to the white community—as engendering her blues character: "If Celie's life-journey will eventually lead, with blues singer Shug Avery's help, to sexual liberation, expressive mastery, and spiritual homecoming, her father's spectacle lynching and her mother's traumatized response is what prompts her birth as a blues subject: Celie is a true child of Jim Crow terror" (123). But before Celie ever learns of her real father's death, she faces emotional, physical, and sexual abuse from both her step-father (Pa) and her husband Albert (Mister), which are also consequences of Jim Crow era violence. At age fourteen, Celie begins an account of how her step-father rapes and impregnates her (thereby sterilizing her), sells away her children, and forces her into a marriage with Albert. As Pa barters Celie away after describing her as a sexually spoiled cow, readers see that he values women as he would livestock: for reproductive and labor power. Pa's treatment of other women is no better; when he remarries after Celie's mother dies, he simply uses his new wife as a sexual object, maid, and care-taker for his six children. When the new wife becomes sick, Celie must sacrifice herself to ward off Pa's advances toward her younger sister,

Nettie. Pa remains an unsympathetic revolting character throughout the novel; many critics view him as an example of Walker's negatively flat portrayals of men, but I argue that Walker offers some insight as to why Pa mistreats women.

When Celie discovers that Pa is her not her real father but her step-father, she and Shug visit Pa to confront him. Walker analyzes the legacy of slavery and white control as influencing Pa's attitude and infiltrating his every action. After he tells Celie that her real father was lynched for standing up to the white townspeople, Pa reveals how he manages to stay alive and sustain his lifestyle:

> 'I know how they [white people] is. The key to all of 'em is money. The trouble with our people is as soon as they got out of slavery they didn't want to give the white man nothing else. But the fact is, you got to give 'em something. Either your money, your land, your woman or your ass. So what I did was just right off offer to give 'em money. Before I planted a seed, I made sure this one and that one knowed one seed out of three was planted for *him*. Before I ground a grain of wheat, the same thing. And when I opened your daddy's old store in town, I bought me my own white boy to run it. And what makes it so good, he say, I bought him with whitefolks' money' (182).

Pa believes that he has cheated the racist white community, but Walker intimates that, because of his greed, Pa has in fact become just like the white men he wants to manipulate. Walker solidifies Pa's relationship with the town's white men when he hunts with them, and Celie dresses wild game for a week (10). Pa relies on his wives and children to maintain his lifestyle, brutally using them as slaves just as white plantation owners used the black populace. By juxtaposing the histories of Celie's step-father and real father, Walker simultaneously discloses the two consequences black men faced in a white-controlled South: the threat of becoming like the white oppressor or being lynched for fighting for freedom and individuality. The stories of Celie's father and her step-father demonstrate that neither path— rebellion nor conformity—benefits the black community. Even though Celie's real father emerges as a hero, his grave remains unmarked; his death leaves fatherless children and an unstable wife. The black community must revise their ways of life and thinking to exist outside of the white mainstream—a revision that Walker suggests relies on blues themes and womanism. Walker's subtle insertion of these men's histories illuminates the racist system under which black men and women were forced to live. In doing so, Walker explains that while

Pa's behavior and choices are despicable, his actions are compelled by the white racist world around him.

The examples of Celie's father and step-father exemplify the very limited opportunities for black males, exposing their frustrations and their misplaced blame of black women. With Albert, Walker renders these conflicts more directly in the blues. Albert's love for Shug creates a bluesman out of him—a frustrated bluesman who cannot possess the woman he loves. Because he cannot be with Shug, he beats his misery out on Celie. Like Pa, Albert views women as objects to be used and controlled. Celie describes her situation with Albert as worse than being dead: "If I was buried, I wouldn't have to work" (17). She slaves away under Albert, allowing him and his children to abuse her, and she describes her sexual encounters with Albert as if he uses the "toilet" on her (77). When Albert deprives Celie of her sister Nettie's letters, he exercises ultimate control over Celie—body and soul. Albert reveals the way he views women when Harpo asks why he beats Celie: "Cause she my wife. Plus, she stubborn. All women good for—he don't finish. He just tuck his chin over the paper like he do. Remind me of Pa" (22).

Celie's connection between Albert and her step-father might lead readers to believe that Walker suggests that all men are alike: abusive and unappreciative of women. Walker actually presents readers with not only black men's propensity for violence against women, but also a view of the white racist structures which enable and influence such mistreatment. In "Coming in from the Cold," Walker explains how the reader gains insight into Albert's (Mister) misogynist attitude by understanding his relationship with his father:

> [...] it is clear that Mister's father is part-white; this is how Mister comes by his run-down plantation house. It belonged to his grandfather, a white man and a slave owner. Mister learns how to treat women and children from his father. Who did Old Mister learn from? Well, from Old Master, his slave-owning father, who treated Old Mister's mother and Old Mister (growing up) as slaves, *which they were.* (81)

The legacy of self-loathing and powerlessness bequeathed to black men from their white slave-owning fathers induced men like Old Mister and his son (Albert) to grasp at power wherever they could. In a racial hierarchy that placed only black women and children below black men, these men often exercised control over their subjects violently—just as their racist white counterparts used lynching in the Jim Crow South.

Albert's need to possess and control women through violence relates directly to how Adam Gussow terms intimate blues violence as a need to express power and individuality through blues brutality—to show how black men have internalized white Jim Crow violence to the point of hurting each other in an attempt to regain the power denied them by an oppressive white South. Scholar Matthew B. White also connects black men's limited opportunities with their use of the blues to control women. He argues that, in the early twentieth century, "due to societal restrictions and structural constraints, black men in general were restrained—politically, socially, and economically. They were unable to assert all of their power and realize their full potential. In addition, while black men were living in a patriarchal society, they were unable to use much of the power and privileges which came with being a man in such a culture" (White 3). Albert tackles his powerlessness with Shug through his beatings of Celie. Albert's inability to marry (and so possess) Shug again stems from Old Mister's plantation-derived beliefs about women. Albert tells Celie how he mistreated his first wife, Annie Julia, because he really loved Shug: "I didn't want her [Annie Julia]. I wanted Shug. But my daddy was the boss. He give me the wife he wanted me to have" (270). Walker shows readers that black men are not immune from the cruel exclusions of patriarchy, extending her womanist focus on the entire race by exposing how both Albert and Celie's stories are informed by a paternalist southern system; both characters' fathers control their lives and choice of partners. In "Coming in From the Cold," Walker comments on Old Mister's internalization of the slave master's role when he discourages Albert from taking Shug in because she is too black and ugly; Walker describes Old Mister's words as "*a slave owner's description of a black woman*" (81). Albert is denied Shug because of his complicity in the white supremacist and sexist mentality passed down to him from the southern plantation system, and when he cannot possess Shug, he begins to mistreat the other women in his life—first Annie Julia and then Celie.

Albert's views of and violence toward women fall in line with the songs of early bluesmen. White describes how bluesmen used song to usurp control over women they described as gold diggers or unfaithful lovers:

> By reducing all women to simple stereotypes, the bluesmen are
> able to assert control over women. Stereotyping or categorizing
> women makes women manageable; by understanding the
> stereotype, the bluesmen are able to understand all women. He
> believes he knows their drives, traits and very nature. (8)

Like a frustrated blues man, Albert's comments about women (as only
sexually useful or requiring beatings like children) expose a need to
stereotype and reduce women to an inferior status. Whereas blues
women often sang about retributive violence against abusive men, as
evinced by Angela Davis's analysis, men boasted about the brutal
ways they controlled women in their blues. White discusses songs like
Blind Willie McTell's "Married Man's a Fool," where the singer
threatens to beat his wife when she disobeys, and Robert Johnson's
"32-20 Blues," where the singer threatens to slice his "unruly" wife
with a razor (10-11). Just as Old Mister passed on his misogyny to
Albert, Albert passes it on to his son, Harpo. Walker envelopes
Harpo's conflict with his wife Sofia in the blues; when Harpo's
beatings fail to control Sofia, he transforms their old home into a
jukejoint (or jook), a gathering place historically referred to as the
center of blues culture.

While Zora Neale Hurston defines the jook as "a Negro
pleasure house" (89), Adam Gussow argues that the jukejoint or jook
could also function as a hub for violence in the black community, with
the "roughest black jooks...termed 'Buckets of Blood'" (202). In
trying to gain power in a southern society based on racial and sexual
hierarchies (where white male was at the top and black woman was at
the bottom), the black blues community inflicted violence on each
other as a symbol of power and freedom learned from the oppressive
white community. As Gussow explains it, "Cutting and shooting,
literal and figurative, were ways in which black blues people, male
and female, claimed and reclaimed their own and each other's bodies
within a self-created passional economy that was none of the white
man's business" (209). Even as blues people exercised rights over
their own bodies through abuse, ironically, their power was negated as
they threatened and inflicted harm on one another—a position of
which the racist white community both influenced and approved. As
Gussow argues, because black bodies were no longer valued
economically after the abolition of slavery, the white community
looked on and condoned such violence as long as it remained within
the black community (211).

Harpo intends his jukejoint to be a place free from white restrictions and therefore open to intimate blues violence. Sofia leaves Harpo after fighting off his abuse for too long, and he starts construction on the jook as a way to gain back the control that he has lost. When Celie asks what Harpo is building way down in the woods in place of his old house, he and his friend Swain explain the nature of the jook to Celie:

> 'Jukejoint supposed to be back in the woods, say Harpo. Nobody be bothered by the loud music. The dancing. The fights.
> Swain say, the killings.
> Harpo say, and the police don't know where to look'
(Walker 69-70).

The jukejoint operates not only as a place for dancing and singing but also for fighting and killing. In Harpo's blues jook (just as Gussow describes in his study) blues people act intimately violent with one another beyond the arms of the white law. For Harpo, this freedom also relates to his (mis)treatment of women; in the jukejoint setting, Harpo gains control over women much like his father. Harpo finds a new half-white girlfriend, Squeak, who Celie describes as "a nice girl, friendly and everything, but she like me. She do anything Harpo say" (82). Harpo gives Squeak her name to solidify his ownership over her, refusing to call her by her family-given name, Mary Agnes, and thereby relegating her status to that of his child. Harpo's jook becomes not just a violent locale for the blues community, but also a place where Harpo can personally exercise control over women like Squeak. While the reader witnesses Harpo's failed attempts to "break" Sofia, in this new blues setting, Harpo finds a woman he can own just as Albert owns Celie.

Walker also uses Harpo's jukejoint to criticize how black women have internalized the brutal attitudes shown to them by black men. Readers already understand how Celie believes women should be subordinate to male authority. From the beginning of the novel, when she obeys her step-father and silences herself on the rape she endures, Celie allows herself to be abused with no hope of escaping her circumstances. When Harpo asks Celie how he can dominate Sophia, Celie tells Harpo to beat his new wife, even though Celie believes the couple to be happy as they are (36). Celie bows to a racist and sexist system, where black men (like their white slave owners and Jim Crow counterparts) flaunt their possession over black women through violence. Once married to Albert, Celie accepts her mistreatment as part of her role as his wife. She tells Sofia, "Well, sometime Mr.___ [Albert] git on me pretty hard. I have to talk with Old Maker. But he my husband. I shrug my shoulders. This life soon be over, I say. Heaven last all ways" (42). Walker critiques Celie's internalization as made worse by her belief in a white God that asks her to obey and serve her father and husband.[4]

Sofia, on the other hand, stands up to the abusers in her life—whether they are men or women. Like a female blues protagonist, Sofia retributively deals back the violence Harpo commits on her, and then finally leaves him. Similar to the classic blues divas, Sofia emerges as a dominant, independent woman of whom Celie feels jealous. While readers view Sofia as strong and capable (like Shug), Walker explains that Sofia has internalized violence as a defense mechanism because she was raised in a home where her father's word ruled (41). As Sophia tells Celie, "All my life I had to fight. I had to fight Daddy. I had to fight my brothers. I had to fight my cousins and my uncles. A girl child ain't safe in a family of men" (40). Sofia's and Celie's plights as black women under black men's authority are very similar, but Sofia's response is to fight back. While Celie and Shug suffer under sexism, Walker also uses these characters as a reflection of the choices that black men faced under racism; neither conforming (as Celie does) nor rebelling (as Sofia does) helps women gain power in the patriarchal structure that the black community has inherited from an oppressive Jim Crow South.

In a scene that takes place in Harpo's jook, Sofia risks becoming like the men she defends herself against by using violence to fight back. When Sofia visits Harpo's, Squeak feels threatened when she sees the two dancing together. Harpo tells Squeak that he has a right to dance with his wife, and Squeak responds by antagonizing Sofia and affirming that Harpo is now her possession. In two tiny words, "my man," Squeak expresses her need to control Harpo. In her vernacular language, Celie tells what happens next:

> 'Sofia don't even deal in little ladyish things such as slaps. She ball up her fist, draw back, and knock two of Squeak's side teef out. Squeak hit the floor. One toof hanging on her lip, the other one upside my cold drink glass.' (83)

Celie's words demonstrate that Sofia also becomes like the controlling male in the jook; Sofia's actions are not "ladyish" by any means.

While Celie describes the fight between the two women comically, Walker makes plain the connections between female and male violence, suggesting that brutality is not a productive way of gaining power for either sex. Squeak and Sofia take on the roles of violent bluesmen; Harpo's jook becomes not only a metaphorical setting for male blues violence, but also an actual stomping ground for the female characters who have internalized such a system of fighting for dominance by becoming like the men that abuse them. In "Women and the (Ab)use of Power in *The Color Purple*," scholar Tuzyline Jita Allen argues that Walker creates interracial and intraracial conflicts between the female characters in the novel to critique feminist ideologies that simply reinscribe patriarchy. Yet Walker is not only critiquing women's abuse of power, but also using blues metaphors to show how the underlying systems of (white) racism and sexism inform such abuse.

When Sofia practices violence outside of the jook in the larger southern community, she faces much worse consequences. In the chapter following the incident in the jook, Sofia verbally challenges the white mayor's wife Ms. Millie and subsequently fights the mayor. Walker investigates how this form of self-defense is unsustainable when pitted against a powerful white community that exercises the same oppressive tactics. Through Sophia's situation, Walker critiques the white threat of violence and the culture of fear that promoted blues violence. As Gussow describes, as long as blues violence was kept within the black community, the white Jim Crow South did not interfere: blues people *"claimed* each other's bodies through the medium of intimate violence; asserted their fragile pride with the help of guns and knives; became agents of their own fate at the cost of inflicted pain and social mayhem [...] The jooks roared on, by and large, with the white man's approval" (211). Violence practiced outside the safety of the jooks threatened the white-dominated social order, leading whites to reassert their power through lynching. When Sofia's violence emerges outside of the jook, the white police force beats her and takes her to prison. Sofia tries to act a good prisoner, but she describes how she must lower herself to do so:

> 'Good behavior ain't enough for them, say Sofia. Nothing less than sliding on your belly with your tongue on they boots can even git they attention. I dream of murder, she say, I dream of murder sleep or wake.' (Walker 89)

In Sofia's predicament, Walker blatantly critiques the larger white racist southern community. Walker extends her womanist objectives in exposing how Sofia's plight under a racist system creates violent murderous compulsions, linking Sofia with Pa, Albert, and Harpo. As with Celie's father and step-father, Sofia seemingly has two choices—to continue bowing or to fight back. Yet, Walker reveals that Sofia has no choice when it comes to preserving her sanity or dignity in the face of the Jim Crow South. When Sofia dreams of murder, Walker illustrates how the abuse Sofia endures at the hands of the white world threatens to make her like her oppressors. As critic Gina Michelle Collins writes, Sofia "does not realize that any attempt to fight the system by its own rules and on its own ground is doomed inevitably to failure. This is why it is so vitally important to oppressors that the oppressed share their values" (81). In *"The Color Purple*: What Feminism Can Learn from a Southern Tradition," Collins offers for a slightly subversive reading of the novel, which suggests that Sofia, Nettie, and even Shug are trapped within patriarchal strictures whereas Celie never identifies with patriarchy; it is Celie who teaches these characters "sharing, cooperation, and love" (84). However, Celie is, at least at first, firmly entrenched in patriarchal values, which Walker signals to her reader through Celie's undying faith in a white Christian God and the promise of heaven.

If the jook is a setting that promotes power and individuality through intimate violence (the brutal tool of the oppressor), in Walker's novel, the jook also provides a celebratory gathering spot where individual domination can be remade into collective cooperation and acceptance. Harpo's jukejoint represents not only the negative consequences of blues violence but also provides a breeding ground for a womanist blues perspective, particularly through the audience response to Shug's performances. While Walker situates the male characters on the periphery of the blues (Harpo as the jukejoint owner and Albert as Shug's lover), Walker's women—particularly Shug and Squeak—take on centralized roles as blues singers. One crucial moment in Celie's changing view of herself happens when Shug sings a public song for her at Harpo's. After Shug sings the Bessie Smith standard "A Good Man is Hard to Find" for Albert, she begins to sing an original composition, "Miss Celie's Song," inspired by Celie's warm demeanor as she nurses Shug back to health. Walker's shift from a classic blues song to an original composition signals a revision of blues themes. Walker explains how Shug's song

inspires Celie to escape from the patriarchal restrictions of the blues;
Celie describes how the song "all about some no count man doing her
wrong, again. But I don't listen to that part. I look at her and I hum
along a little with the tune. First time somebody made something and
name it after me" (73). Importantly, even while Shug's lyrics remain
within the confines of the destructive heterosexual relationship (which
so many blues women's songs are based on), Celie revises the
meaning of Shug's tune. As Celie makes her own meaning, Walker
also revises the audience response to women's blues about abuse and
no-good men.[5] Shug's song acts as a catalyst for Celie's change, but
Celie herself—as a female audience member—shrugs off the
patriarchal values and understands the song's hidden meaning as a
tribute to her individual personhood and womanhood. In this brief
moment, Walker revises the "very bad cycle" of abuse as sustained by
the blues. The jukejoint begins to represent a place where change—as
well as violence—can take place. While the blues allow Celie to
understand herself outside of male control, Walker also uses the
character of Squeak (Mary Agnes) to show how blues womanism can
triumph over blues violence.

When Sofia is jailed for her "offense" against the mayor,
Celie visits her and sees that the police continually beat the spirit out
of her. Afterwards, Harpo's blues community—normally engaged in
singing and violence—unites to combat Sofia's white oppressors,
knowing that Sofia will surely die if left to suffer in jail. Walker
implies that collectivity between black men and women can be
achieved when fighting back against the white Jim Crow South.
Squeak (Mary Agnes) reveals that she is the white warden's niece,
and Albert urges her to see him and plea for Sofia. When Squeak
visits the warden, Walker makes the threat of white violence—
particularly against black women—absolutely clear. Squeak returns
with her clothes ripped and tells how she was raped because she
looked so much like the warden: "He took my hat off, say Squeak.
Told me to undo my dress. She drop her head, put her face in her
hands [...] He say if he was my uncle he wouldn't do it to me. That be
a sin. This just a little fornication. Everybody guilty of that" (96). The
warden rapes Squeak to control her and to prove that, just because she
shares his blood and physical traits, she does not demand his respect
or equal treatment; the rape allows him to excise through violence the
familial ties he shares with a black woman. Just as in the plantation

system, the white power structure employs the rape and abuse of black women as sites of domination in the Jim Crow South.

Walker also inserts Squeak's interaction with her white uncle to relate white power abuse to black men's abuse. After Celie's transformation occurs when she hears Shug's song, she advises Squeak to make Harpo respect her by calling her Mary Agnes (84). Squeak finally understands Celie's advice when she makes the connection between her rape by a white man and Harpo's condescending treatment of her. As Harpo wraps his arms around her after the rape to reassure her that he loves her, Squeak makes a bold move and takes possession of her own body: "She stand up. My name Mary Agnes, she say" (97). Squeak literally stands up for herself; she decides to become, like Shug, a blues singer so that she can voice her individual frustrations with oppression as brought on by the white and black male communities. Harpo describes Mary Agnes's need to sing as "sudden," and Celie concurs that Mary Agnes's new career seems unfit for her: "she got the kind of voice you never think of trying to sing a song" (98). Like the 1920s classic blues women, Mary Agnes's song is brought on by the male violence—white and black—visited on her; Walker transforms her into a singer to combat male blues violence but also to remake her as a womanist figure.

Walker suggests Mary Agnes's womanist similarity with Shug when Celie tells us how, at first, Mary Agnes sings Shug's songs (98). Mary Agnes begins to make up her own songs, and in fact, the only song lyrics in the book come from Mary Agnes, suggesting that her song might be more important than "Miss Celie's Song." Mary Agnes's song clarifies her need to belong in a black sisterhood denied her because of her half-white "yellow" status: "But if yellow be my name/Why ain't black the same/Well, if I say Hey black girl/Lord, she try to ruin my game" (99). Unlike Old Mister or his son Albert, who are still trapped by their inherited white blood, Mary Agnes wants to shed her status as a part-white woman, which allows her to be abused by black men and also excludes her from the community of black women. Gussow describes the stereotypes of women in the jook as perpetuated by male blues singers. He explains the conflict between the "violent, ax-wielding 'black gal'" as a "figure for black blues culture in its rough, vulgar, unrepentantly low-down incarnation" (like Sofia or Shug) and the less-threatening "sweet-talking, sweet-loving 'yaller wife'"—like Mary Agnes (207). In her song, Mary Agnes revises these stereotypes and calls for equal treatment within the black community, regardless of color. She wants to be desired and respected as a "black" woman instead of mistreated as a near-white "yellow" girl. When she sheds her yellowness, Mary Agnes sheds her cowardice and servitude in her relationship with Harpo, whom she leaves for a blues career in Memphis. Sofia responds to Mary Agnes's call by promising to care for her daughter while she is away: "Go on sing, say Sofia, I'll look after this one till you come back" (204). Where the two women once fought over Harpo's attention in the jook, they now support each other in a non-violent way. Mary Agnes's song and transformation begin a shift towards a blues womanist consciousness that is just as important as Celie's revising of Shug's song at Harpo's. Brought together, the actions of Walker's female characters challenge intimate male blues violence and inspire changes in the male community.

As literary scholar Barbara Christian writes, "[…] Celie's attainment of freedom affects not only others of her sisters, but her brothers as well" (53). Because Walker incorporates a womanist perspective with the history of the classic blues women, Walker also illuminates how Albert and Harpo are redeemed (while Pa dies and Celie subsequently inherits his property). After Celie curses and leaves him, Albert falls into a state of misery, and Harpo finally breaks into the house to care for him. Albert and Harpo turn to each other like the women in the novel have previously done, and Harpo makes Albert send Nettie's letters to Celie. Once Sofia sees the love between the men, she and Harpo move back in together to raise their children. While Sofia says that being with Harpo is not always easy, the two are able to sustain their relationship without violence; Sofia works while Harpo tends to the house, and they learn to accept each other as equals. Albert apologizes for his treatment of Celie, and they spend time together while Shug is away with her new lover Germaine; their love for Shug brings them together. Walker uses blues womanism to foster forgiveness and communication between Celie and Albert, who chat like old friends and sew pants together. Mary Agnes retrieves her new child and leaves her new man to return to singing in Memphis full time, and Shug later leaves Germaine to return to Celie and singing at Harpo's. Finally, the entire community is restored when Nettie and Celie's children return from Africa. bell hooks has written about the novel's conclusion, "The message conveyed in the novel that relationships no matter how seriously impaired can be restored is compelling. Distinct from the promise of a happy ending, it allows for the recognition of conflict and pain, for the possibility of reconciliation" (227). hooks also criticizes the novel's ending because Celie gains power through inheritance and not political struggle:

> To make Celie happy she creates a fiction where struggle—the arduous and painful process by which the oppressed work for liberation—has no place. This fantasy of change without effort is a dangerous one for both oppressed and oppressor. It is a brand of false consciousness that keeps everyone in place and oppressive structures intact. (227)

While hooks makes a strong critique, Walker shows the propensity for struggle and change from "oppressive tactics" in the relationship between Sofia and Miss Eleanor, suggesting that, like the black community, the white community can learn to give, love, and cooperate despite the racist social structures present.

While reconciliation between men and women is overtly womanist, the recognition of pain and conflict is inherently blues-oriented; Walker combines blues and womanist themes to revise the history of abuse in the black community. Walker uses Celie's letters (like the blues) to publicly recognize private domestic abuse, while the female blues audience in the novel remakes blues violence into a womanist-inspired resolution. Notably, in the last scenes of the novel, Walker shifts the setting of a family celebration from Harpo's jook to Celie's home, signaling an ultimate break in the blues cycle of abuse; the Harpo's blues community now unites in cooperative harmony as everyone takes on a duty in preparing the July 4th feast. Harpo and Mary Agnes exchange a brief conversation over the meaning of the day, again signaling Walker's revision of the black experience in southern history:

> 'Why us always have family reunion in July 4th, say Henrietta, mouth poke out, full of complaint. It so hot.
> White people busy celebrating they independence from England July 4th, say Harpo, so most black folks don't have to work. Us can spend the day celebrating each other.
> Ah, Harpo, say Mary Agnes, sipping some lemonade, I didn't know you knowed history.' (287)

Harpo's version of history—the black folk celebrating one another—challenges the white version of history; Harpo's small statement represents the black community as subordinate to white power ("most black folk don't have to work") but also reveals his revised perspective on the historical holiday as a celebration of black community and independence from the white world. Celie's memory speaks collectively to an alternative history of southern African Americans that exists outside of the white mainstream. As Sturken writes, collective memory and history are *"entangled* rather than oppositional" (5). Collective and cultural memory contribute to how history is created, especially the cultural memory of oppressed peoples which is suppressed by white-dominated portraits of southern history designed to reinforce stereotypes and maintain the status-quo of an imagined white hierarchy. Walker's re-designation of a white historical holiday as interpreted by the black community is akin to her revision of blues violence in the novel; traces or sites of memory are reworked to constitute a harmonizing utopia for southern African Americans that breaks the "very bad" cycle of abuse.

At the novel's conclusion, Walker names herself as, not only "author," but also "medium" for the characters. As a medium, Walker presents Celie's individual memory as a voice of the "old ones," similar to singers Mamie, Bessie, and Ma. Like the classic blues divas, Celie's memory makes the public aware of the abuse black women faced, but, in womanist fashion, Celie extends that blues message to include male intimate violence as well—transforming an individual black woman's memory to a cultural memory of Jim Crow brutality. Celie's blues-inspired letters move beyond Ellison's blues "scapegoat" of the "self" to question how the collective blues community internalizes and challenges violence inherited from the white-dominated South. Through Celie's blues memories, Walker asks readers not simply to recognize the power of blues divas, but to uncover the driving force behind domestic and intimate blues violence: the white power structure that can only be transcended by the blues audience's revising of abusive tactics to loving acceptance of one another.

Courtney George, Louisiana State University

Notes

[1] For other readings of blues in the text, see Gunilla T. Kester's "The Blues, Healing, and Cultural Representation in Contemporary African

American Women's Literature" and Keith Byerman's "Walker's Blues."

[2] For specific readings of lesbianism in *The Color Purple*, see Linda Abbandonato's "A View from 'Elsewhere': Subversive Sexuality and the Rewriting of the Heroine's Story in The Color Purple" and Ana Maria Fraile-Marcos' "'As Purple to Lavender': Alice Walker's Womanist Representation of Lesbianism."

[3] For discussions on the critical debate about Walker's men, see Erna Kelly's "A Matter of Focus: Men in the Margins of Alice Walker's Fiction" and Pia Thielmann's "Alice Walker and the 'Man Question.'"

[4] For further readings on the connection between religion and patriarchy in *The Color Purple*, see these compelling essays: James C. Hall's "Towards a Map of Mis(sed) Reading: The Presence of Absence in *The Color Purple*;" Kimberly R. Chambers' "Right on Time: History and Religion in Alice Walker's *The Color Purple*;" Peter Kerry Powers' " 'Pa is Not Our Pa': Sacred History and Political Imagination in *The Color Purple*" and Stacie Lynn Hankinson's "From Monotheism to Pantheism: Liberation from Patriarchy in Alice Walker's *The Color Purple*."

[5] In Steven Spielberg's movie production of the book, the song is actually revised. Shug addresses Celie as "sister", and the song is clearly not about some no-count man, but about her appreciation and love for Celie. While I admire Spielberg's change—the song perhaps more clearly develops the love between the women—I also believe that the scene in the novel better underscores Celie's independent transformation and revision of heterosexual love as a blues audience member.

Works Cited

Allen, Tuzyline Jita. "Women and the (Ab)use of Power in *The Color Purple*" in *Feminist Nightmares, Women at Odds: Feminism and the Problem of Sisterhood*. ed. Susan Ostrov Weisser and Jennifer Fleischner. New York and London: NYU Press, 1994. (88-103).

Brundage, W. Fizthugh. "Introduction: No Deed but Memory" in *Where These Memories Grow: History, Memory, and Southern Identity.* Chapel Hill and London: UNC Press, 2000. (1-28).

Byerman, Keith. "Walker's Blues" in *Alice Walker: Modern Critical Views.* ed. Harold Bloom. New York and Philadelphia: Chelsea House, 1989. (59-66).

Carby, Hazel V. "'It Just Be's Dat Way Sometime': The Sexual Politics of Women's Blues." *Gender and Discourse: The Power of Talk, Vol. XXX.* Ed. Dundas Todd and Sue Fisher. Norwood, NJ: Ablex, 1988. (227-242).

Chambers, Kimberly R. "Right on Time: History and Religion in Alice Walker's *The Color Purple.*" *College Language Association Journal* 31.1 (1987): 44-63.

Christian, Barbara. "The Black Woman as Wayward Artist" in *Alice Walker: Modern Critical Views.* ed. Harold Bloom. New York and Philadelphia: Chelsea House, 1989. (39-58).

Collins, Gina Michelle. "*The Color Purple*: What Feminism Can Learn from a Southern Tradition" in *Southern Literature and Literary Theory.* ed. Jefferson Humphries. Athens and London: U of Georgia Press, 1990. (75-87).

Davis, Angela Y. *Blues Legacies and Black Feminism.* NY: Vintage, 1998.

Davis, Thadious M. "Walker's Celebration of Self in Southern Generations" in *Alice Walker: Modern Critical Views.* ed. Harold Bloom. New York and Philadelphia: Chelsea House, 1989. (25-37).

Fabre, Genevieve and Robert O'Meally. *History and Memory in African-American Culture* (Introduction). New York and Oxford: Oxford University Press, 1994. (3-17).

Ferris, William R. "Alice Walker: 'I Know What the Earth Says.'" *Southern Cultures* (Spring 2004): 5-24.

Fraile-Marcos, Ana Maria. "'As Purple to Lavender': Alice Walker's Womanist Representation of Lesbianism" in *Literature and Homosexuality.* ed. Michael J. Meyer. Amsterdam and Atlanta: Rodopi Press, 2000. (111-134).

Halbwachs, Maurice. *The Collective Memory.* trans. Francis J. Ditter, Jr. and Vida Yazdi Ditter. NY: Harper & Row, 1980.

hooks, bell. "Writing the Subject: *Reading The Color Purple*" in *Alice Walker: Modern Critical Views*. ed. Harold Bloom. New York and Philadelphia: Chelsea House, 1989. (215-228).

Hurston, Zora Neale. "Characteristics of Negro Expression" in *Within the Circle*. ed. Angelyn Mitchell. Durham: Duke U P, 1994. (79-94).

Gussow, Adam. *Seems like Murder Here: Southern Violence and the Blues Tradition*. Chicago: U of Chicago P, 2002.

Hackinson, Stacie Lynn. "From Monotheism to Pantheism: Liberation from Patriarchy in Alice Walker's *The Color Purple*." *Midwest Quarterly: A Journal of Contemporary Thought* 38.3 (1997): 320-8.

Hall, James C. "Towards a Map of Mis(sed) Reading: The Presence of Absence in *The Color Purple*." *African American Review* 26.1 (1992): 89-99.

Harris, Trudier. "On *The Color Purple*, Stereotypes, and Silence." *Black American Literary Forum* 18(1984): 155-61.

Harrison, Daphne Duval. *Black Pearls: Blues Queens of the 1920s*. New Brunswick, Rutgers U P, 1988.

Johnson, Maria V. "'Jelly Jelly Jellyroll': Lesbian Sexuality and Identity in Women's Blues." *Women and Music: a Journal of Gender and Culture 7* (2003): 31-52.

Kelly, Erna. "A Matter of Focus: Men in the Margins of Alice Walker's Fiction" in *Critical Essays on Alice Walker*. ed. Ikenna Dieke. Westport and London: Greenwood Press, 1999. (67-82).

Kester, Gunilla T. "The Blues, Healing, and Cultural Representation in Contemporary African American Women's Literature." *Women Healers and Physicians: Climbing a Long Hill*.
ed. Furst, Lillian R. Lexington: UP of Kentucky, 1997. (114-127).

Lauret, Maria. *Modern Novelists: Alice Walker*. New York: St. Martin's, 2000.

Marvin, Thomas F. " 'Preachin' the Blues': Bessie Smith's Secular Religion and Alice Walker's *The Color Purple*." *African American Review* 28.3 (Autumn 1994): 411-21.

Nora, Pierre. *Realms of Memory*. trans. Arthur Goldhammer. NY: Columbia U P, 1996.

Pinckney, Darryl. "Black Victims, Black Villains." *New York Review of Books* 29 Jan 1987: 17-20.

Powers, Peter Kerry. " 'Pa is Not Our Pa': Sacred History and Political Imagination in *The Color Purple.*" *South Atlantic Review* 60.2 (May 1995): 69-92.

Sturken, Marita. *Tangled Memories: The Vietnam War, the AIDS Epidemic, and the Politics of Remembering.* (Introduction). Berkeley, Los Angeles, and London: U of California P, 1997. (1-18).

Thielmann, Pia. "Alice Walker and the 'Man' Question" in *Critical Essays on Alice Walker.* ed. Ikenna Dieke. Westport and London: Greenwood Press, 1999. (67-82).

Towers, Robert. "Good Men Are Hard to Find." *New York Review of Books* 12 August 1982: 35-36.

Wall, Cheryl. "Writing Beyond the Blues: *The Color Purple*" (Chapter 6) in *Worrying the Line: Black Women   Writers, Lineage, and Literary Tradition.* Chapel Hill and London: UNC Press, 2005. 140-161.

Walker, Alice. "Coming in from the Cold: Welcoming the Old, Funny-Talking Ancient Ones into the Warm Room of Present Consciousness, or, Natty Dread Rides Again!" in *Living by the Word: Selected Writings 1973-1987.* New York: Harcourt Brace,1988. (54-68).

——. "I Know What the Earth Says" in Ferris (2004): 23-24

——. "Womanism" in *In Search of Our Mother's Gardens.* New York: Harcourt Brace,1983. (xi-xii).

——. The *Color Purple.* Orlando: Harcourt Brace, 2003.

Wasserman, Jerry. "Queen Bee, King Bee: *The Color Purple* and the Blues." *Canadian Review of American Studies* 30:3 (2000). 301-317.

White, Matthew B. "'The Blues Ain't Nothin' but a Woman Want to be a Man': Male Control in Early Twentieth Century Blues Music." *Canadian Review of American Studies* 24.1 (Winter 1994): 19-40.

Alice Walker's Revisionary Politics of Rape

Robin E. Field

"Who knows what the black woman thinks of rape? Who has asked her? Who *cares*?" writes Alice Walker in her short story, "Advancing Luna—and Ida B. Wells." "Who has even properly acknowledged that *she* [the black woman] and not the white woman in this story is the most likely victim of rape?"[1] These pointed questions illustrate the limitations of the portrayals of rape and sexual violence in American literature until the late 1970s, when a handful of women writers began to challenge these problematic depictions. Until that point, rape and sexual violence were presented most often through the perspective of the rapist himself, which necessarily obfuscated or entirely ignored the woman's point of view. Walker herself notes: "We have been brainwashed to identify with the person who receives pleasure, no matter how perverted; we are used to seeing rape from the rapist's point of view."[2] With such scenes presented through the perpetrator's perspective, readers viewed rape as a salacious, titillating spectacle of sexualized violence, wherein the woman eventually succumbs to the pleasures of "being mastered." Indeed, adhering to those rape myths, most portrayals of sexual violence were not even considered rape, as the woman did not fight to the death. Rare were the depictions that demonstrated rape as bodily and psychological violence against a woman, and rarer still were those that viewed a rape victim with any kindness or sympathy.

Yet Alice Walker was one of an ever-expanding group of women writers who challenged this inaccurate and demeaning portrayal of rape and rape victims. Referring to the protagonist of *The Color Purple*, Walker writes, "I could have written that Celie enjoyed her abuse and done it in such pretty, distancing language that many readers would have accepted it as normal. But to do this would have been to betray Celie; not only her experience of rape, but the integrity of her life, her life itself" ("Coming In" 58). Walker and these other visionary writers instead demanded that rape be recognized as the violation of a woman's body and psyche, and their fictional depictions registered sympathy and compassion for the rape victim, which ultimately emphasized to the reader that rape was indeed a traumatic experience. Walker explored this topic in several early, but important works of fiction. She used as narrator a (somewhat) sympathetic female friend in "Advancing Luna" (1981) and an omniscient narrator in her novel *Meridian* (1976).[3] Such removed narrational perspectives were typical for these first compassionate renderings of rape victims. Readers were able to view the victim at a safe distance, which proved important when faced with such unfamiliar and disturbing subject matter. Additionally, the omniscient narrator or female friend modeled a more appropriate reaction to the rape victim, another helpful gesture considering the prevalence of rape myths that often blamed the victim as responsible for her violation. Walker's short story and novel also critiqued and revised the identity politics that demanded black women pledge their allegiance to the black community, even if such allegiance meant sacrificing their bodily integrity.

Yet Walker's greatest contribution to the revision of rape in American literature was her much-lauded novel *The Color Purple* (1982). Never before had readers experienced sexual violence through the perspective of the victim herself; someone else had always told the story. In *The Color Purple*, readers are placed *within the victim's consciousness* via the use of a first-person narrative voice. The rape victim gains control of her story, and through her own voice readers learn about the traumatic reality of sexual assault. Hearing such intimate details told with such immediacy proves enlightening to readers; for commonly-accepted rape myths crumble in light of the contradictory experiences of the victim herself. And while hearing the traumatic details of rape was crucial to fostering understanding of the crime, so was learning about a woman's life after rape. Walker's heroine in *The Color Purple* proves that a rape victim could survive sexual violations, heal from this violence, and go on to live a happy and fulfilling life. Through careful analysis of Alice Walker's narrative strategies and revolutionary politics, it is apparent that the author played a crucial role in the revision of the rape story in American literature.

The evolution of Walker's depictions of sexual violence in her early fiction offers important insights into the very fraught arena of African American identity politics in the 1970s. For many African American women, the personal ramifications of rape paled against the political aspects of the assault. The simple act of speaking out against rape—the foremost tactic of the anti-rape movement that began in the early 1970s—was complicated by the history of racial violence in the United States. The primary concern of the black community was protecting young black men from the specious claims of rape, historically made by the white community, which resulted in lynchings and other violence. With such energy focused on combating the stereotype of the black male rapist, charges of rape made by black women against black men were frowned upon. Feminist literary critic Kalí Tal elaborates:

> Race and gender oppression combine to place black women in a double bind. If they speak out against rape and focus on gender issues, they may begin to alleviate the problem of sexual abuse. At the same time, they contribute to the oppressive stereotype of the black male rapist. If they do not speak out, they will continue to be raped and assaulted by the men of their own community. (159)

Many black women, as well as other women of color, chose racial solidarity over gender identification; they remained silent about their personal violations because of a racially prejudiced society and judicial system.[4] In addition, fewer black women than white participated in the anti-rape movement. Historian Maria Bevacqua discusses the disproportionate number of white activists in the movement in her comprehensive study, *Rape on the Public Agenda*. She cites Angela Y. Davis's analysis of why women of color eschewed the organized anti-rape movement:

> According to Davis, women of color distrusted anti-rape organizers on at least two grounds: the belief that majority-white women's groups did not address black women's issues, and the fear that the regulation of rape, particularly by a criminal justice system that they perceived to be racist, would disproportionately target black men, despite the fact that the vast majority of rapes are intraracial. (Bevaqua 40)

Yet as early as 1970, the political imperative of protecting the black community at the expense of personal sanctity began to be examined and, ultimately, critiqued, by black women writers such as Maya Angelou, Toni Morrison, and Alice Walker.

Walker's questions in "Advancing Luna"—"Who knows what

the black woman thinks of rape? Who has asked her? Who *cares*?"—
are quite salient in the mid-1970s, when this story was composed.
Many black women conformed to the politics of the Black Power
movement, which demanded equality for black men in the United
States. Assured that they were included in the category of "black
men," it is no wonder then that black women in those years
maintained the primacy of racial solidarity, rather than gender
identification, in their political activism (Liddell and Kemp 2). Yet
Walker's questions fly in the face of the accepted approach: *do* all
black women believe they should maintain silence if they are raped by
black men, in order to combat negative stereotypes about the black
community? And if so, *should* they? Walker's early fiction delves into
these complex issues. Her texts portray black women's uniquely
complicated relationship to sexual assault, which demands an
acknowledgment of the link between rape and racial violence in the
United States. In particular, "Advancing Luna—and Ida B. Wells"
captures the complex interplay between racial and gender prerogatives
for black women confronted with the problem of rape. The story
relates how a young black woman, the text's narrator, reacts to the
rape of her white friend, Luna, by a black man. Walker underscores
the complexity of the unnamed narrator's response in the story's
content and structure. Just as the women's friendship suffers a rupture
after the rape is revealed, the narrative arc of the story becomes
fragmented and disjointed, echoing the narrator's complicated
reaction to her friend's violation. Ultimately, Walker's story critiques
the rationale for a solely race-based understanding of sexual assault.

  The first section of "Advancing Luna" demonstrates the
primacy of racial identification for the narrator as she relates the rise
and fall of this interracial friendship. The black female narrator and
the white Luna become friends during the summer of 1965 when
working for a black voter registration drive in rural Georgia. The
narrator relates her initial belief that the two would be lifelong friends
whose relationship would "survive everything, be truer than
everything" ("Luna" 95). Yet the personal connection between the
women is shattered when Luna reveals a few years later that she had
been raped by a black activist, Freddie Pye, during the summer in
Georgia. Initially, the narrator experiences horror, incredulity, and
embarrassment after learning about the assault, which literary critic
Nellie McKay contends "signifies empathy and sympathy for her
friend—for the sexual vulnerability and social impotence of all
women to alter their situation."[5] The narrator imagines herself in

Luna's position, hypothesizing that she "would have screamed [her] head off" had she been subjected to such brutality ("Luna" 92). This identification with Luna demonstrates the potential for gender solidarity in countering sexual assault. Rape is acknowledged as a horrifying event that could happen to anyone; and thus women should be able to forge a common alliance, at least in thought if not in deed, against this type of violence.

Yet racial solidarity trumps gender concerns in the narrator's subsequent response to Luna; for her tentative identification with her friend collapses when Luna emphasizes the reasons for her silence during the assault, saying to the narrator, "You know why" ("Luna" 92). From the first Luna realizes, though the narrator temporarily forgets, that the political implications of her assault supersede the possibility of her experiencing any solely personal reaction. Because of her race, Luna's response to the rape implicates her in any subsequent violence that might have occurred had she screamed. Recognizing the power of her voice as a white woman, Luna decides to endure the sexual assault silently rather than place others—other black men—at risk. But despite Luna's strict adherence to racial solidarity with the black community, the narrator feels tremendous anger towards her friend. Rather than bringing the two women together, Luna's revelation emphasizes the power differential between them. The narrator muses: "her power over my life was exactly the power *her word on rape* had over the lives of black men, over *all* black men, whether they were guilty or not, and therefore over my whole people" ("Luna" 95).

The initial sympathy she felt for Luna disappears in the face of the concerns of the black community. McKay notes: "For what the narrator takes seriously is that the survival of the black community depends heavily on its women. How can the black woman be an ally of the white woman as long as the white woman's 'word' remains a sword of Damocles over all black people?" (253). Any gender identification that supersedes race is impossible for the narrator to accept following Luna's revelation. Their friendship immediately becomes strained; and the two never discuss the rape again. The first section of the story ends with an account of the women going their separate ways, their "lifelong" friendship dissolving under the pressure of the narrator's obligations to the black community.

Yet Walker complicates these conclusions about racial solidarity and sexual assault by presenting several more sections in which the narrator continues her meditations about interracial rape.

The narrator is firm about her abhorrence of rape, describing it as "[m]orally wrong," "not to be excused," "[s]hameful," and "politically corrupt" ("Luna" 98). Thus she realizes the problematics of siding with the rapist, especially when rape is used *as a part of rebellion, of 'paying whitey back'* ("Luna" 94). Living in a racist society, however, compels the narrator to stand with the black community unequivocally; for to side with her friend (i.e., "advance Luna") means standing against black men. Her imaginary conversation with Ida B. Wells in the first section of the story validates her conclusion:

> 'Write nothing. Nothing at all. It will be used against black men and therefore against all of us. . . . No matter what you think you know, no matter what you feel about it, say nothing. And to your dying breath!' ("Luna" 94).

Walker again destabilizes this viewpoint, however, pointing out another limitation: that black women significantly compromise their own personal safety when remaining silent about rape. Her narrator notes, "Who has even properly acknowledged that *she* [the black woman] and not the white woman in this story is the most likely victim of rape?" ("Luna" 93). Although Walker delineates the many political implications of a black man raping a white woman, she implies that even more fraught, and thus unmentionable, is the idea of a black man raping a black woman.

The structure of the second half of the story also works to question the whole-hearted embrace of racial solidarity by black women. Walker includes additional discussions about the rape after the initial relation of the events; and in creating this dialogue, she allows the hope of a more unifying resolution. She entitles the first of the subsequent four sections of the story "Afterwords, Afterwards / Second Thoughts." Although the narrator grapples with the same issues in this section as she did in the initial relation, the title implies that she (and perhaps Walker) was left unsatisfied with her preliminary conclusions.

The subsequent sections examine the range of possible understandings about the rape, and the story ends with "Postscript: Havana, Cuba, November 1976." In this title, we see that Luna's rape has troubled the narrator for a decade; however, she continues to share her thoughts with others, opening the discussion up for new opinions and ideas. Walker underscores the viability of reaching such a conclusion through shared dialogue; and in this she implicates the readers of the text, insisting that these questions of race and rape must be taken on by others in order to reach a fruitful conclusion. By deliberately structuring the story with afterwords and addendums, which by their very nature insist upon continued dialogue, Walker emphasizes the importance of breaking silence about rape. McKay concurs: "the successful resolution to this story, which we must write, depends on achieving honest relationships between black and white women and between white women and black men. We can then empower our own words and language, rejecting absolutely the silence of oppression (even of history) that 'empower[s] violence against racial groups and women' by exploiting *all* female sexuality" (257). Thus in "Advancing Luna," Walker demonstrates the power of collective dialogue: not only about the existence of sexual assault (though it was a topic long overdue for discussion), but also of the myriad power struggles of which rape is one violent manifestation, for the black community and, indeed, all of American society.

Given that "Advancing Luna" and *Meridian* were written during the same period of time, it is not surprising that Walker examines similar interests in her novel. Thus in *Meridian*, we read a comparable interracial rape: a black activist rapes a white woman whose politics prevent her from publicly protesting the assault. Yet in this text, Walker even further complicates the political analysis of interracial rape by including the point of view of the rape victim. This perspective is a significant addition; for in 1976 when this novel was published, most fictional accounts of rape had not explored the psyches of their victims, focusing instead on the reactions of the people around her. Walker uses this new perspective to delve more deeply into the individual ramifications of interracial rape, to deconstruct racial and sexual stereotypes, and emphasize the trauma of rape upon the victim, her race and politics notwithstanding.

In *Meridian*, Walker portrays the circumstances of the rape and its individual consequences in much greater detail, which, in turn, places greater emphasis on the personal experience of the assault. The initial disclosure closely resembles Luna's revelation: the white victim, Lynne, attempts to confide to a black woman, Meridian, that she had been raped by a black man, Tommy Odds, while she had been living amongst the black community; indeed, at the time of the assault Lynne was married to one of the black activists, Truman. Meridian is unable to provide compassion and empathy to this white woman, saying, "Can't you understand I can't listen to you? Can't you understand there are some things I don't want to know?"[6] A fervent civil rights activist, Meridian pledges her entire support to the black community, and thus refuses to admit, for entirely political reasons, that this interracial rape could have occurred. Lynne is left to understand and recover from the assault on her own; indeed, she even begins to wonder if she was raped, based on the complete denial she receives from those closest to her, including her husband. She tells Meridian: "I know you're thinking about lynchings and the way white women have always lied about black men raping them. Maybe this wasn't rape. I don't know. I think it was. It *felt* like it was" (*Meridian* 152). The chronology of the novel allows for this doubt to exist initially, for we see the scene between Lynne and Meridian, in which Meridian denies the rape and Lynne herself questions it, before hearing Lynne's experience of the assault. Yet Walker subsequently preempts any doubt that rape occurred by narrating the assault in great detail, using Lynne as the focalizer of the scene. In relating these events so explicitly, Walker deconstructs the rape myths that inform the characters' reactions to the concept of rape, which works to educate the reader as well.

Foremost, Walker demonstrates *what rape is*, knowledge that was largely absent from the collective American psyche until the formation of the anti-rape movement in the early 1970s. Lynne's doubt about her experience stems from the reactions of those around her, who believe the sex must have been consensual. To the rapist, Tommy Odds, "it wasn't really rape. She had not screamed once, or even struggled very much" (*Meridian* 159). Tommy Odds believes that his use of physical and psychological coercion is not rape, simply because Lynne did not fight to the death. Indeed, we soon learn that another black activist, Altuna Jones, holds similar beliefs: "All his life he had heard it was not possible to rape a woman without killing her. To him, in fact, rape meant that you fucked a corpse. That Lynne would actually stoop to sleeping with Tommy Odds meant something terrible was wrong with her, and he was sorry" (*Meridian* 163).

Yet Walker clearly demonstrates how the coercion is indeed rape, and how individual guilt and racial politics allow Tommy Odds to force Lynne to comply. Lynne's presence amongst the black community in this small Southern town had provoked a sniper's gunfire at the black activists, which resulted in the partial amputation of Tommy Odds's arm; and he manipulates her guilt about his disfigurement also by informing her that other women subsequently have refused to have sex with him. Additionally, Tommy Odds knows that Lynne's political solidarity with the black community will lead her to identify with him rather than herself. While he is assaulting her,

Lynne concentrates her thoughts upon her rapist's plight instead of her own: "She lay instead thinking of his feelings, his hardships, of the way he was black and belonged to people who lived without hope" (*Meridian* 160). Yet Walker also does portray Lynne resisting Tommy Odds, physically and verbally: "Please don't do this," she begs, and struggles against him (*Meridian* 159). Tommy Odds responds by pulling her hair until she is lifted off of her feet and pushing her down onto the bed. Lynne is overwhelmed, both mentally and physically, by Tommy Odds and his powerful manipulation.

Given the universal disbelief of her peers, it is not surprising that Lynne herself questions whether she was raped. Yet Lynne is provided affirmation from one crucial source: Alice Walker. For Walker writes definitively that Lynne was raped by Tommy Odds, using the word "rape" without hesitation to describe the experience. The chapter describing the assault begins, "For of course it was Tommy Odds who raped her" (*Meridian* 159). Such authorial verification is important in educating the reader about how to react to rape and rape victims. Foremost, Walker underscores that the victim does not have to die or be beaten violently in order to have suffered rape. The disbelief of Lynne's friends in fact serves as a negative model for how to react to a rape victim. Lynne needs and deserves to experience compassion, reassurance, and kindness, but she does not experience this support. In framing the rape this way, Walker emphasizes the problematics of treating rape as a purely political act, for the victim and her attendant trauma are entirely neglected.

Walker also works to debunk the predominant rape myth plaguing the black community: that of the predatory black rapist. For decades following Emancipation, the lynchings of black men were publicly justified as protection for white women against the insatiable sexual desire of black men. The myth held that black men could not restrain themselves at the sight of a white female body and that rape occurred because of uncontrollable lust. Walker undercuts these ideas, even as she portrays a black man who does rape a white woman[7]. Foremost, she demonstrates that Tommy Odds is entirely in control of his actions and in fact plans his assault—it is no spontaneous outpouring of uncontrollable desire. Tommy Odds comes to the house with the goal of raping Lynne in order to exact revenge: against her specifically because of his arm, and against "whitey" as a group, because of long-standing racial oppression.

He knows the stereotype; indeed, he makes use of it as his "excuse" for rape. Walker writes of him speaking to Lynne: "'You

knows I cain't hep myself,' he said in loose-lipped mockery"
(*Meridian* 159). Using black vernacular to emphasize his race,
Tommy Odds *puts on* the role of the predatory black rapist, rather
than actually embodying it. We also hear that the rape occurs as an
expression of power, rather than sexual desire. Tommy Odds voices
his reasons for raping Lynne aloud the next day, when he brings three
friends to see Lynne, urging them to "[h]ave some of it" and
reminding them that "[c]rackers been raping your mamas and sisters
for generations and here's your chance to get off on a piece of their
goods" (*Meridian* 162, 163). Walker demonstrates the power of this
myth—rape as uncontrollable sexual desire—even to an enlightened
woman like Lynne. Brutalized as she was by her purported friend, she
begins to fear these other three friends as well:

> Lynne looked into the horrified faces of Altuna, Hedge, and
> Raymond. But perhaps, she thought, they are not horrified.
> Perhaps that is not a true reading of what I see on their faces (for
> the first time it seemed to her that black features were grossly
> different—more sullen and cruel—than white). Though none of
> them smiled, she could have sworn they were grinning. She
> imagined their gleaming teeth, with sharp, pointed edges. Oh,
> God, she thought, what a racist cliché. . . . She could not imagine
> they would say no. The whole scene flashed before her. She was
> in the center of the racist *Esquire* painting, her white body offered
> up as a sacrifice to black despair.[8] She thought of the force, the
> humiliation, the black power. These boys were no longer her
> friends; the sight of her naked would turn them into savages.
> (*Meridian* 162)

Walker reiterates the terms of the stereotype in order to emphasize
more strongly the significance of the other three men's response to
Tommy Odds's words: they decline to "have some of it." Indeed, the
response of Altuna Jones underscores his humanity: "It? *It?* . . . What
it you talking about? That ain't no *it*, that's Lynne" (*Meridian* 162).
The other men quickly reassure Lynne that they are not there to hurt
her, and they leave. This response demonstrates to Lynne, and to the
reader, that black men are not predatory and insatiable. It also
emphasizes that the choice that Tommy Odds made in deciding to
rape Lynne: he wanted to exercise power and control over her, rather
than just experience sexual release.

   Walker's emphasis on rape as an expression of power, rather
than sexual desire, ultimately also highlights the political struggle at
hand for the black community: the connection of rape and race. Like
Luna, Lynne does not report the assault in the fear of repercussions

for the entire black community: "She wished she could go to the police, but she was more afraid of them than she was of Tommy Odds, because they would attack young black men in the community indiscriminately, and the people she wanted most to see protected would suffer" (*Meridian* 163). For the safety and protection of the community, Truman and Meridian categorically deny the occurrence of the rape. Lynne never knows if her husband confronted Tommy Odds; and indeed, Walker leaves the possibility nebulous by including an italicized, and thus perhaps imaginary, description of Truman speaking to Odds.

In *Meridian*, then, Walker highlights the same political issues about race and rape, in particular, the need for the black community to stand together to protect black men against lynchings. Yet she also continues to complicate this adherence to racial solidarity in this text by demonstrating the pain and humiliation endured by the victim of the rape. Focusing directly upon Lynne allows us to see the difficulties of an impersonal, solely politicized understanding of sexual assault, because a woman is always hurt during this crime, no matter her politics or racial affiliation. By including the victim's experience of rape, Walker emphasizes how this trauma should be considered alongside the other aspects of the assault. Although she depicts the negative consequences for white women in this novel, she also hints at the problematics of black women protecting black men at the expense of their own safety and self-respect. The importance of this viewpoint is fully developed in her subsequent novel, *The Color Purple*.

Both "Advancing Luna" and *Meridian*, composed as they were in the mid-1970s, underscore the prevalent concerns of 1970s anti-rape movement: demonstrating what rape is, and illustrating the political roots and ramifications of this crime. Yet with such attention focused upon the politics of interracial rape, the sexual assaults themselves, and their attendant bodily and psychological pain, are necessarily downplayed. Walker does acknowledge Lynne's trauma in portraying her rape directly, rather than simply talking about it; but the focus is still primarily upon the racial significance of the attack. However, it is clear that Walker questions political affiliations in which black women subsume their own interests, and that she believes remaining silent about rape in order to protect the community leaves black women open to experiencing further violence. Not surprisingly, Walker's third novel, *The Color Purple*, specifically focuses upon the black woman and *her* experience of sexual assault. Having thoroughly explored the political ramifications of black men committing rape against white women in her earlier texts, she breaks the taboo of speaking about sexual abuse within the black community. Using a first person point of view and other narrative techniques of traumatic realism, she writes the story of Celie's recovery and life after being sexually abused. Ultimately, Walker posits that telling about rape and incest could help to heal the black community as a whole. Literary critic E. Ellen Barker summarizes: "It was Walker's contention that by presenting unrelenting portraits of human weakness, despair, and abuse, she could repair the damage done to the black community in the past, and through *The Color Purple*, 'right [or rewrite] the wrongs' . . . of social and literary history."[9]

Considering the praise lavished upon *The Color Purple* for its groundbreaking depiction of African American women, it seems almost redundant to offer yet another commendation. Yet it is crucial to note the significance of this work to the evolution of portraying rape in American literature. For the first time, we are placed *within the victim's consciousness*, via the use of a first-person narrative voice. It is not the rapist narrating his actions, or a (seemingly) impartial omniscient narrator, or even a sympathetic female friend of the victim. Instead, the rape victim herself gains control of her story, and through her own voice readers learn about her reality of traumatic sexual assault. The use of this first-person narration necessarily shifts the focus of the story to the very personal aspects of rape. Whereas Walker explores the political ramifications of rape upon race relations in "Advancing Luna" and *Meridian*, she largely puts aside these concerns in *The Color Purple* to explore most urgently the physical and psychological consequences of sexual violation upon an individual woman, Celie. Her story focuses primarily upon the healing process Celie undergoes, and secondarily upon the larger political and societal implications of her rape. This focus upon the individual emphasizes not only the self-worth of the rape victim, but also the importance of understanding and affirming her point of view.

Walker's choice to limit her story to the confines of one woman's psychological and physical world is emphasized by the structure of the text as an epistolary novel. As Deborah E. McDowell writes:

> *The Color Purple* fits primarily into the private paradigm, suggested by its choice of the epistolary mode —by definition personal and private—and the finite focus of the Celie letters. One of their most striking features is the conspicuous absence of

any reference to the 'outside' world. . . . Instead, like epistolary
novels generically, *The Color Purple* emphasizes the
psychological development of character. (143)

In accordance with this focus on psychological development,
Walker's novel has also been categorized a bildungsroman. Indeed,
this term is quite apt, in that *The Color Purple* is a "novel of
education" about the personal evolution of a rape victim—but,
significantly, it is the reader who is being educated. In using first
person narration within an epistolary format, Walker is able to
produce Celie's consciousness in great detail, which in turn offers us a
nuanced portrait of the rape victim and her psychological trauma. The
epistolary format also reinforces Walker's use of traumatic realism.
According to Michael Rothberg's formulation, traumatic realism
recognizes the "hole in the real" that is the incident of trauma, as well
as the "complex temporal and spatial patterns" that make this trauma
felt within everyday life (67).

Celie's letters reflect both of these aspects, first in her
inability to express certain aspects of her emotional state, and
secondly in her seemingly mundane descriptions of daily life which in
fact demonstrate her post-traumatic stress. Yet even while Celie's
letters reflect the effects of trauma upon her life, she heals herself
through expressing her emotions to a supportive female community,
and through writing, a technique that certain psychologists, such as
James W. Pennebaker, contend constitutes a crucial step in recovering
from trauma. Thus Walker's novel not only portrays the life of the
rape victim after her violation, a new subject matter in American
fiction, but it also demonstrates the processes through which rape
victims recover.

Walker's traumatic realism incorporates a few of the
traditional aspects of realism, in that she allows Celie to delineate the
events that she endures at the hands of her stepfather. Celie's
straightforward language at first seems to belie Rothberg's notion of
trauma as a "hole in the real." She says: "First he put his thing up
gainst my hip and sort of wiggle it around. Then he grab hold my
titties. Then he push his thing inside my pussy. When that hurt, I cry.
He start to choke me, saying You better shut up and git used to it."[10]
This description allows the reader to comprehend exactly what Celie
experiences—rape. Yet, importantly, a gap exists between the
physical act of rape and Celie's psychological processing of the event;
for Celie herself seems not to understand the rape, or her first
pregnancy, at all.

Before describing the assault, Celie writes in her first letter to God: "Maybe you can give me a sign letting me know what is happening to me" (*Purple* 1). As the ensuing description of her stepfather's actions is so vivid, it seems odd that she does not know "what is happening to [her]." Yet this gap in comprehension persists even until the birth of her child: "When I start to hurt and then my stomach start moving and then that little baby come out my pussy chewing on it fist you could have knock me over with a feather" (*Purple* 2). Celie's seeming incomprehension of sexual intercourse is at odds with the realities of her daily life; for she could not live in a small house and watch her mother bear multiple children without some understanding of sex and pregnancy. Instead, Celie's incomprehension demonstrates the psychological trauma she endures from being raped by her stepfather. Walker does not attempt to express Celie's emotions about rape using mimesis or reference. Instead, she uses the *absence* of representation—that is, Celie's incomprehension—as the device to portray the girl's reaction to trauma. A brief moment at the beginning of the novel does divulge Celie's shifting sense of self due to her exposure to trauma. Her initial words in the first letter state a revision in her belief in her goodness. She initially writes "I am," but then crosses out these two words to write instead, "I have always been a good girl" (*Purple* 1). Because of the sexual abuse, Celie can no longer believe herself to be good; her goodness is relegated to the past, to the time before the rapes began.

Even as absence marks the actual experiences of trauma, Walker allows the symptoms of post-traumatic stress in Celie's daily life to emphasize the depth of her pain. Celie's constant numbness is one very telling sign of her psychological distress. After being married off to Mister, Celie continues to experience forced sex. She explains her reaction:

> I don't like it at all. What is it to like? He git up on you, heist your nightgown round your waist, plunge in. Most times I pretend I ain't there. He never know the difference. Never ast me how I feel, nothing. Just do his business, get off, go to sleep. (*Purple* 78)

The lack of feeling Celie expresses demonstrates her belief in her powerlessness. Psychologist Judith Herman explains that the victim of trauma "escapes from her situation not by action in the real world but rather by altering her state of consciousness."[11] Thus Celie pretends she is elsewhere when Mister has sex with her. Similarly, she passively accepts her husband's physical abuse:

> He beat me like he beat the children. Cept he don't never hardly
> beat them. He say, Celie, git the belt. The children be outside the
> room peeking through the cracks. It all I can do not to cry. I make
> myself wood. I say to myself, Celie, you a tree. That's how come
> I know trees fear man. (*Purple* 23)

In the quotations above, Celie demonstrates that her method of coping
with abuse is to dissociate from her emotions. As the victim of sexual
abuse, she is unable to see herself as someone worthy of love and
respect, even from herself. Both her sister Nettie and her sister-in-law
Kate believe that she deserves a better relationship with her husband,
and tell her she needs to fight for respect from Mister and his children.
But Celie cannot do this: "I don't know how to fight. All I know how
to do is stay alive" (*Purple* 18). Celie eventually confides to her
stepdaughter-in-law Sofia that she no longer feels anger:

> 'I used to git mad at my mammy cause she put a lot of work on
> me. Then I see how sick she is. Couldn't stay mad at her.
> Couldn't be mad at my daddy cause he my daddy. Bible say,
> Honor father and mother no matter what. Then after while every
> time I got mad, or start to feel mad, I got sick. Felt like throwing
> up. Terrible feeling. Then I start to feel nothing at all.' (*Purple*
> 41-42)

At this point, Celie cannot change her situation; all she can do, as
noted above, is "stay alive." Her numbness is a vivid demonstration of
the long-term effects of sexual abuse upon the raped woman who does
survive with her life and her sanity.

Walker's depiction of a black rape victim reflects the
historical significance of rape in the lives of black women in the
United States. As Missy Dehn Kubitschek notes, "Slavery forced
Afro-American culture to see that the woman raped by the master or
used as a breeder did survive, *did* carry on with daily life;
analogously, Afro-American males dealt with the issue on a daily
basis because of the ever-present threat of lynching."[12] Indeed,
Kubitschek posits that the inveterate bodily threat to both sexes posed
by sexual assault allowed African American authors to offer "a more
realistic, complex vision of the meaning of the experience for the
victim and her community" (45). Walker's portrayal underscores how
Celie survives her trauma, for she not only performs, but excels at her
daily routine of keeping house and raising children. Yet Walker
initially places the majority of the emphasis upon the fact that Celie's
emotional and even physical response to personal interactions has

been severely damaged because of the sexual abuse she has endured. She survives, but she is not whole. She feels no emotion towards Mister's children:

> 'Everybody say how good I is to Mr. _____ children. I be good to them. But I don't feel nothing for them. Patting Harpo back not even like patting a dog. It more like patting another piece of wood. Not a living tree, but a table, a chifferobe.' (*Purple* 30)

Celie's use of "another" in regard to wood demonstrates how she still regards herself as wood, even when she is not being beaten. At this point in the novel, Celie truly is more of a victim than a survivor: she may exist on a daily basis, but she admits that she has little to live for.

Yet even as Walker carefully delineates the pain of sexual abuse, she subsequently maps the healing processes that lead to Celie's psychological recovery. Indeed, writer Opal Palmer Adisa locates *The Color Purple* within a group of texts written by black women that "have helped to move and heal many black people from the amnesia and the brutal, historical pain in which so many of us were and are still drowning" (181). The two primary methods of this healing, as dramatized in the text, are the formation of a supportive female community and the use of writing as a means of expressing painful emotions. Herman emphasizes the importance of community to one who has endured a trauma:

> Traumatic events destroy the sustaining bonds between individual and community. Those who have survived learn that their sense of self, of worth, of humanity, depends upon a feeling of connection to others. The solidarity of a group provides the strongest protection against terror and despair, and the strongest antidote to traumatic experience. Trauma isolates; the group re-creates a sense of belonging. Trauma shames and stigmatizes; the group bears witness and affirms. Trauma degrades the victim; the group exalts her. Trauma dehumanizes the victim; the group restores her humanity. (214)

Celie initially feels no emotional connection to those around her, male or female. Yet eventually she forms a bond with her stepdaughter-in-law, Sofia, as the two women share their reactions to the spousal violence they both have endured. When Celie confides her hope of the promise of happiness in heaven, rather than on earth, Sofia offers a radical reconsideration: "You ought to bash Mr. _____ head open, she say. Think bout heaven later" (*Purple* 42). Sofia's suggestion emphasizes the importance of Celie's personal and physical integrity by affirming her right to fight back against Mister. Such an affirmation of her person fills Celie with joy and hope for the first time.

This supportive female community expands to include all of the women associated with Celie's household, such as Squeak, Harpo's mistress, and Sofia's sisters, but especially Shug Avery, a famous blues singer and the mother of three illegitimate children by Mister. Ultimately, it is because of Shug that Celie is able to heal emotionally and sexually. She begins by giving Celie an important gift: public recognition of her personal worth. Shug performs at Harpo's juke joint to a packed audience of community members. She announces the title of a new song—"Miss Celie's Song"—and explains it came to her when Celie was nursing her to health. Celie is awed by this gift: "First time somebody made something and name it after me," she thinks (*Purple* 74). Such public acknowledgment of her importance is crucial in proving to Celie and to the community that she is worthy of love and respect.

Shug continues to validate Celie over the ensuing years, which is of the utmost importance for her process of healing from the traumatic sexual abuse. Barker posits that Shug "enables Celie to evolve into an independent, self-actualized woman, no longer benignly accepting the emotionally crippling conditions that have enslaved her" (55). With Shug's affection and moral support, Celie begins to explore her feelings about her past. For the first time, she tells someone about the sexual abuse she suffered as an adolescent and mourns her experience with tears. Herman notes that an important stage of recovery involves the telling of the story of trauma to an ally (175). Shug provides a sympathetic reaction, encouraging Celie to talk about the abuse. At the same time, she demonstrates the silence that existed within the community about incest: "I thought it was only whitefolks do freakish things like that" (*Purple* 114). Most importantly, Shug then vocally affirms her own love for the grieving woman. With these words, she demonstrates that Celie will be able to experience a deep, meaningful relationship with her. The trust that Celie places in Shug is emphasized by the sexual encounter that follows Shug's words of love. Their homosexual union, Barker argues, represents the culmination of their love for each other: "For Shug, it is an ultimate gift of love, and for Celie, love making and being loved complete her spiritual journey to selfhood" (61). After years of repressing bodily sensations because of the physical and sexual abuse, Celie becomes one with her body, finding it to be a source of pleasure instead of pain. Her newfound capacity for sexual and emotional intimacy demonstrates the progress that Celie has made in her recovery from sexual trauma.

In addition, Shug fosters Celie's independence and creativity by stressing her personal agency. No longer the woman who tolerated Mister's abuses simply because he was her husband, Celie leaves him in order to live with Shug in Memphis. Celie now is able to recognize Mister's manipulations as such and refuses to accept his mistreatment. Though these sentiments were building over the course of the years, they come to a head when Celie and Shug realize that Mister has been withholding Nettie's letters. Celie's love for Nettie and need for communication with her supersedes any feelings of responsibility to her husband. Indeed, she so taps into her anger that Shug must persuade her not to kill Mister. Instead, Celie releases years of suppressed feelings when she announces her departure: "You was all rotten children. . . . You made my life a hell on earth. And your daddy here ain't dead horse's shit" (*Purple* 202). Another key factor that allows Celie to recover her personal agency is the discovery in Nettie's letters that Fonso was not her biological father, but her stepfather; thus her children are not the product of incest. Such knowledge is freeing to Celie; it allows her to make her own choices about her destiny, rather than following the commands of "Pa" to live with Mister as his wife.

While Walker very effectively uses the story and characters of *The Color Purple* to illustrate the importance of female community in healing from trauma, she also emphasizes the significance of writing to this process. James W. Pennebaker delineates the healing power of expressing emotions for an individual: "The health benefits of writing or talking about the traumas . . . are twofold. People reach an understanding of the events, and once this is accomplished, they no longer need to inhibit their talking any further" (103). Writing about her life, and thus about her traumatic experiences, allows Celie to make sense of her past and formulate her future. Most importantly, writing allows Celie to become the agent of her own fortune, in that she constructs her own way of understanding. According to Martha J. Cutter, "Celie's letters allow her to reconfigure the rhetorical situation and create a resistant heroine's text in which she has narratological existence as the author/subject of her own story."[13] Once Celie is in control of her own story, she refuses to stay silent about the abuse she has endured: she forces the community to acknowledge her trauma. In doing so, she bears witness on the behalf of other women who have endured rape and incest. As Herman notes, "moral neutrality in the conflict between victim and perpetrator is not an option" (247). Celie supports and affirms the victims of sexual abuse within the novel; and Walker does so in writing the novel. As she ruminates in the essay "Coming in from the Cold":

> How can you justify enslaving a person like Celie? Segregating or sexually abusing such a person? Her language—all that we have left of her—reveals her as irreducibly human. The answer is you cannot. (64)

By the end of the novel, Walker has emphasized that Celie is a survivor, rather than a victim. She has radically transformed her life from that of an abused woman to the empowered matriarch of a large extended family. She makes her own choices about her friends and sexual partners; even Mister loses his dominance over her and is known as Albert, a friend to chat with on the porch in the evenings. Just before she is reunited with her sister, she writes:

> I am so happy. I got love, I got work, I got money, friends, and time. And you alive and be home soon. With our children. (*Purple* 218)

Overcoming traumatic sexual experiences at the hands of her stepfather and husband, as well as copious physical and verbal abuse, Celie creates a satisfying life for herself. Walker's novel demonstrates the depth of trauma that a rape victim experiences, but also the process of healing and potential for a fulfilling existence in the end. Cutter agrees: "Walker suggests that given the ubiquity of rape in society, women need to learn how to move beyond its victimization into agency and voice" (178).

Alice Walker was instrumental in revising the representation of rape in American fiction. Her fiction offers details about the physical and psychological ramifications of rape, while her centering of the rape victim challenges the political and social attitudes that believe rape is foremost an unpleasant consequence of the power struggles over race relations. Placing the rape victim not only as the central character, but as the narrator of the text as well allows Walker to emphasize that there is more to the story than the actual sexual assault: the victim most often survives the rape, works to heal from the physical and psychological wounds, and recovers to experience a full and satisfying life. But most importantly, Walker's fiction presents significant innovations in form, which work to "share" the victim's pain with the reader. Walker's use of first person narration in *The Color Purple* demands that the reader identify with the pain suffered by the woman being raped, rather than allowing the reader to view the scene of violation voyeuristically. Alice Walker's writing emphasizes how the survivor of rape has a complex and important story to tell.

Robin E. Field, King's College

Notes

[1] Alice Walker, "Advancing Luna—and Ida B. Wells" in *You Can't Keep a Good Woman Down*, 93. All subsequent references to this story are cited as "Luna" and refer to this edition.

[2] Alice Walker, "Coming in from the Cold," in *Living by the Word*, 58. All subsequent references to this essay are cited as "Coming In" and refer to this edition.

[3] Walker wrote "Advancing Luna—and Ida B. Wells" while simultaneously working on her novel *Meridian* (1976), though the shorter piece was not published until 1981, when it appeared in her short story collection *You Can't Keep a Good Woman Down* (Barnett, *Dangerous Desire* 65).

[4] Tal writes: "Though law does not mete justice out to most men who sexually abuse women, communities of American minorities suffer an additional burden of discrimination within the justice system. Women of color are rarely aided by white-controlled courts and police when they are sexually abused. Men of color are most likely to be prosecuted for the crime of sexual abuse when they are accused by abusing white women. Many people of color have learned that it is safest to avoid the U.S. court system entirely, and they often rely on community-based moral and ethical codes, as well as community enforced systems of punishment for infractions to solve their legal dilemmas. Such codes are frequently sexist, yet they often offer more useful guidelines than the dominant white practice of law and order" (*Worlds of Hurt,* 194).

[5] Nellie Y. McKay, "Alice Walker's 'Advancing Luna—and Ida B. Wells': A Struggle Toward Sisterhood" in Lynn A. Higgins and Brenda R. Silver, eds., *Rape and Representation*, 253. All subsequent references refer to this edition.

[6] Alice Walker, *Meridian*, 153. All subsequent references are cited as *Meridian* and refer to this edition.

[7] The stereotype of the insatiable black rapist was portrayed in D. W. Griffith's film *The Birth of a Nation* (1915), where Gus chases Flora until she jumps to her death. While Gender Studies critic Sarah Projansky points out that Gus never actually attempts to rape this white woman, she concedes that "characters in the film, contemporary spectators . . . and many scholars interpret his actions as attempted rape" (*Watching Rape*, 248).

[8] Moments before, Lynne had remembered a painting in *Esquire* that depicted "a nude white woman spread-eagle on a rooftop surrounded by black men," about to be gang-raped (*Meridian* 161).

⁹ E. Ellen Barker, "Creating Generations: The Relationship Between Celie and Shug in Alice Walker's *The Color Purple*" in Ikenna Dieke, ed., *Critical Essays on Alice Walker*, 55. All subsequent references refer to this edition.

¹⁰ Alice Walker, *The Color Purple*, 1. All subsequent references are cited as *Purple* and refer to this edition.

¹¹ Judith Herman, *Trauma and Recovery: The Aftermath of Violence—from Domestic Abuse to Political Terror*, 42. All subsequent references refer to this edition.

¹² Missy Dehn Kubitschek, "Subjugated Knowledge: Toward a Feminist Exploration of Rape in Afro-American Fiction" in Houston A. Baker, Jr. and Joe Weixlmann, eds., *Black Feminist Criticism and Critical Theory (Studies in Black American Literature 3)*, 48. All subsequent references refer to this edition.

¹³ Martha J. Cutter, "Philomela Speaks: Alice Walker's Revisioning of Rape Archetypes in *The Color Purple*," 175-176. All subsequent references refer to this edition.

Works Cited

Adisa, Opal Palmer. "A Writer/Healer: Literature, A Blue Print for Healing" in *Healing Cultures: Art and Religion as Curative Practices in the Caribbean and Its Diaspora*. eds. Margarite Fernandez Olmos and Lizabeth Paravisini-Gebert. New York: Palgrave, 2001. (179-193)

Barker, E. Ellen. "Creating Generations: The Relationship Between Celie and Shug in Alice Walker's *The Color Purple*" in *Critical Essays on Alice Walker*. ed. Ikenna Dieke. Westport, CT: Greenwood, 1999. (55-65)

Barnett, Pamela. *Dangerous Desire: Sexual Freedom and Sexual Violence Since the Sixties.*
New York: Routledge, 2004.

—. "'Miscegenation,' Rape, and 'Race' in Alice Walker's *Meridian*." *The Southern Quarterly* 39.3 (Spring 2001): 65-81.

Bevacqua, Maria. *Rape on the Public Agenda: Feminism and the Politics of Sexual Violence.*
Boston: Northeastern U P, 2000.

Cutter, Martha J. "Philomela Speaks: Alice Walker's Revisioning of Rape Archetypes in *The Color Purple*." *MELUS* 25.3-4 (Fall/Winter 2000): 161-180.

Doane, Janice and Devon Hodges. *Telling Incest: Narratives of Dangerous Remembering from Stein to Sapphire*. Ann Arbor: U Michigan P, 2001.

Herman, Judith. *Trauma and Recovery: The Aftermath of Violence—from Domestic Abuse to Political Terror.* New York: HarperCollins, 1992.

Kubitschek, Missy Dehn. "Subjugated Knowledge: Toward a Feminist Exploration of Rape in Afro-American Fiction" in *Black Feminist Criticism and Critical Theory (Studies in Black American Literature 3).* eds. Houston A. Baker, Jr. and Joe Weixlmann. Greenwood, FL: Penkevill Publishing Co., 1988. (43-56)

Liddell, Janice Lee and Yakini Belinda Kemp, eds. *Arms Akimbo: Africana Women in Contemporary Literature.* Gainesville: U P Florida, 1999.

McDowell, Deborah E. "'*The Changing Same*': Generational Connections and Black Women Novelists" in *Alice Walker.* ed. Harold Bloom. New York: Chelsea House, 1989. (135-151)

McKay, Nellie Y. "Alice Walker's 'Advancing Luna—and Ida B. Wells': A Struggle Toward Sisterhood" in *Rape and Representation.* eds. Lynn A. Higgins and Brenda R. Silver. New York: Columbia U P, 1991. (248-260)

Pennebaker, James W. *Opening Up: The Healing Power of Expressing Emotions.* New York:The Guilford Press, 1997.

Projansky, Sarah. *Watching Rape: Film and Television in Postfeminist Culture.* New York: New York U P, 2001.

Rothberg, Michael. "Between the Extreme and the Everyday: Ruth Kluger's Traumatic Realism" in *Extremities: Trauma, Testimony, and Community.* eds. Nancy K. Miller and Jason Tougaw. Chicago: U Illinois P, 2002. (55-70)

Schwenk, Katrin. "Lynching and Rape: Border Cases in African American History and Fiction" in *The Black Columbiad: Defining Moments in African American Literature and Culture.* eds. Werner Sollors and Maria Diedrich. Cambridge: Harvard U P, 1994. (312-324)

Tal, Kalí. *Worlds of Hurt: Reading the Literatures of Trauma.* Cambridge: Cambridge U P, 1996.

Walker, Alice. "Advancing Luna – and Ida B. Wells." *You Can't Keep a Good Woman Down.* New York: Harcourt Brace Jovanovich, 1981. (85-104)

—. *The Color Purple.* 1982. Orlando: Harcourt, 2003.

—. "Coming in from the Cold: Welcoming the Old, Funny-Talking Ancient Ones into the Warm Room of Present Consciousness or, Natty Dread Rides Again!" *Living by the Word.* New York: Harcourt Brace Jovanovich, 1988. (54-74)
—. *Meridian.* New York: Harcourt Brace Jovanovich, 1976.

Significance of Sisterhood and Lesbianism in Fiction of Women of Color

Uplabdhi Sangwan

Alice Walker's *The Color Purple* (1983) and Beatrice Culleton's *April Raintree* (1984) were published in consecutive years and contend with issues of race, class and gender as their heroines embark on quests for selfhood on the North American continent. Each of these quests is hampered by marginalization that severely limits the female protagonist's access to economic emancipation and class elevation.

Despite the thematic commonality of the protagonists' quests, the authors' treatment of race, gender and class differs. The heroine of *The Color Purple* is black or African American while the heroines of *April Raintree* are of mixed Aboriginal-European descent and reside in Canada (Métis). The authors, Alice Walker and Beatrice Cullerton, have the same ethnicities as their characters. Managing and transcending the differences between the women in the novels require understanding; by examining the similarities and dissimilarities of these novels, a dialogue of discussion in transformative politics emerges. As Indian feminist Rajeshwari Sunder Rajan writes in her book titled *Signposts–Gender Issues in Post Independence India*, "in the interest of a transformative politics, differences must be managed, if not transcended" (3).

Critic Linda Abbandonato, in her essay "A View From 'Elsewhere': Subversive Sexuality and the Rewriting of Heroine's Story in *The Color Purple*," writes that *The Color Purple* is significant because the novel is an act of "conscious rewriting of canonical male texts" (1106). In the novel, Alice Walker foregrounds hitherto marginalized versions of black womanhood aspiring towards a sense of self in the American continent.

Similarly, the novel *April Raintree* is significant because it asserts the developing selfhood of Métis women. The novel was discussed by Sylvia Bowerbank and Dolores Nawagesic Wawia in their review essay "Literature and Criticism by Native and Métis Women in Canada." They write about "a remarkable resurgence of the power and the culture of the First Nations in Canada" (565). Furthermore they impart canonical status to the novel by asserting that "since the publication of Maria Campbell's *Halfbreed* (1979) and Beatrice Culleton's *In Search of April Raintree*, Native and Métis women have been leaders in this cultural resurgence" (566).

April Raintree-A Brief Summary

April Raintree is about two Métis sisters, April who has pale skin and Cheryl Raintree who is brown-skinned. Since the parents of these sisters are alcoholics, the child welfare system separates and places the girls in non-Métis foster homes. At the DeRosiers's home, April is made to clean the family dishes and perform sundry tasks. Her only source of companionship is the family dog. Cheryl, on the other hand, grows up with the Steindalls who April describes as "nice enough" (66). Cheryl demonstrates potential in school and, unlike April, actively seeks authentic information about the Métis history.

As the girls grow older, April attempts to hide her Métis origins. She is embarrassed to be seen with natives (even her sister Cheryl). On the other hand, Cheryl seeks to assert her Métis identity. However, as Cheryl grows to be an adult, she finds herself unable to deal with April's rejection of their heritage and the knowledge of her parent's alcoholism. Cheryl is soon drawn into the cycle of prostitution and alcohol by her lover Mark who seeks to exploit her in his attempt to earn money. Near the end of the novel, Cheryl is so despondent about her life that she commits suicide. Cheryl's story becomes a rendering of the relentless oppression that overwhelms the typical Métis women who as a result of the inferior treatment by society often succumb to the cycle of rape-prostitution-pregnancies-alcohol, etc. Meanwhile, April deals with a divorce from her white husband and is later raped when she is mistaken for Cheryl.

As the novel concludes, April enters into new relationships with a greater acceptance of her Métis heritage. April also discovers the existence of Cheryl's son whom she decides to raise.

While showing April's need for a greater acceptance of her Métis heritage, the novel explores the experience of Métis women. However, the novel concludes without positing a radical socio-political alternative that can provide a respite for Métis women "in search" of their identities (as the very title *In Search of April Raintree* in the first publication suggests).[1]

Like in the women of *The Color Purple*, the women of *April Raintree* undertake a journey in search for more authentic selves on the American continent. The heroines make choices that challenge the limitations thrust upon them on account of their gender, race and class. Nonetheless, the aspiration for a more authentic selfhood is not equally actualized due to these choices. Significantly these choices that reflect the political alternatives suggested by the author become a point of comparison to *The Color Purple*. One of the differences is the role of bonds between women.

The Role of Bonds Between Women in the Colored Woman's Search for Self

Many critics have identified the singular importance of the "bonds between women" in Celie's bildungsroman. However, some scholars have either rendered invisible or been reductive of these bonds— whether erotic or emotional. For example the central tension in *The Color Purple* has been described by scholar Philip Royster in his essay "In Search of our Fathers' Arms: Alice Walker's Persona of the Alienated Darling," as comprising of two poles where "violent black men who physically abuse their wives and children is one of the poles of controversy and [...] depiction of lesbianism is another" (347).

Royster's polarity leads to a simplistic summary of the novel that erases the social, political and emotional role and function of "lesbianism" in the Black woman's history of ideas. Royster's argument appears to focus merely on the sexual aspect of the term "lesbian" while presenting a lesbian as a person suffering from some form of dysfunction. He accuses Walker of being an "alienated writer" and of having the "frustrated psychosexual attitudes" of her characters (349). This accusation suggests dysfunction because the position of "alienated writer" is for Royster an "attitude" that will only "frustrate her goals" and undermine Walker's "commitment to change" (348). He writes:

> The speaker of one of her poems that appears in *The American Poetry Review* (6.1[1977]: 28-29) expresses something of the intensity of Walker's alienation when she asserts: "I find my own/

small person / a standing self/ against the world" (qtd. in Erickson 86 – 87). One of the comforts for the outcast persona is her as-yet-unending search for father figures with whom to be a darling. This search influences Walker's fictions, which portray women with frustrated psychosexual attitudes towards men (Ruth towards Grange, Meridian towards both Eddie and Truman, and Celie towards both Alfonso and Albert), and colors her expressed non-fictional attitudes concerning men. (349)

Royster seems to view lesbianism through what Adrienne Rich describes as the lens of "compulsory heterosexuality" through which the "lesbian experience is perceived on a scale ranging from deviant to abhorrent or simply rendered invisible" (13).

Rich also argues that "lesbianism" can be viewed as a counter-discourse against the "institution" of "compulsory heterosexuality" that traditionally has been used by men to exercise control over women (Rich 13). The control is made possible by assuring "male right of physical, economic and emotional access to the woman" (Rich 26). Thus bonds amongst women of color counter the various forms of power men exercise over women and the means that men deploy to perpetuate such control. Walker offers the idea of "bonds between women" as an alternative when addressing the oppressed status of the black woman. "Womanism," a term coined by Walker, through its inclusive notions of sisterhood and lesbian relations, leads to reformulation of power relations between men and women and engenders social and individual transformation.

In *The Color Purple,* the "bonds between women" also provide strength to the women to recognize and counter the controlling stereotypes such as that of a "mule" and the "jezebel." Critics have interrogated the power relations that racial stereotypes have historically served. Scholar Rupe Simms, in her essay "Controlling Images and the Gender Construction of Enslaved African Women," historically locates the construction of the controlling stereotypes of the Black women as "mules" and "jezebel" as products of "pro-slavery intellectuals."[2] The controlling stereotype of a "mule" enabled the white master and his sons to justify "the exploitation of the female slaves." Simms explains:

[T]hey perceived the enslaved woman as insensible brutes and sub-human beasts who were only to be valued for their labour [...] Because these slaves were viewed as less than human, they could justifiably be beaten to death, worked to death, and otherwise treated as domestic stock (883).

The stereotype that Simms describes shaped Celie's lived experience. As Celie's story shows and as Simms suggests, the stereotype of a "mule" is not merely a product of "white androcentric presentation" of black women (Simms 880). The stereotype has also been exploited by some black men. In *The Color Purple*, the sole purpose of a woman's body, even for some black men, is to serve— sexual or physical. The Celie that readers are introduced to at the beginning of the novel is trapped in the stereotypical role of a "mule." She is further dehumanized through sexual exploitation. Thus, she is valued by her father and Mr. _____, her husband, merely for being able to "work like a man" and perform "hard work" (TCP 8).[3] As these men discuss her as an object of exchange in marriage, she is inspected as if she were domestic stock. Celie's very survival is at risk. Because Celie was financially dependent on her "father," she was vulnerable to constant sexual abuse and pregnancies in her early teens. Her existence is justified by the rigorous service her body could perform for the black male. The fact that the "father" and husband are the ones who exploit the young Celie serves to highlight the fact that a woman, especially a woman of color, cannot rely on men, even if they share her skin color, to protect and nurture her. She will have to look elsewhere for such sustenance.

In the ensuing discussion about Celie, both men refuse to acknowledge the reality of Celie's sexual exploitation even as they acknowledge the fact that she is not "fresh" since she has given birth twice by the age of fourteen (TCP 7). Instead of performing a "fatherly" role, her father constantly evaluates her in a gesture that suggests moral superiority. He describes her as being a "bad influence"—implying uncontrolled sexuality that can corrupt his other girls (TCP 8). Even as Celie delivers his child, he says that he could "stand her no more" and he describes her as "evil and always up to no good" (TCP 3). Even though the choice of engaging in the sexual encounter is denied to Celie, she is blamed for bringing the encounter upon herself. In addition, she bears the blame for the consequences of her rape—her unwanted children. The onus of the pregnancy and the resultant birth is ascribed to her intrinsic moral defects. By accusing her of being lascivious, her father casts her as a "jezebel," a stereotype that according to Simms describes a woman whose "sexual aggression, fertility and libidinous self expression were considered limitless" (Simms 882).

Simms explains this image in historical terms and says that it was this representation that enabled the white slave owners to use the black women slaves as breeders in their plantations. The master and his sons perpetuated the abuse of the black slave woman by explaining that their copulation with her was not defilement; instead they were only "satisfying her natural desires." In other words, they believed that their unwanted attentions were not an act of rape since the African woman truly enjoyed the experience (Simms 883). Celie's "father," upon raping her, appears to employ a similar logic.

This cycle of exploitation is re-created when Mr. _____ decides to "marry" Celie as "the woman he had helping him done quit" (TCP 10). Celie thereafter constantly refers to herself as being employed in activities at not only home but also on the fields. Comparisons between Celie's and Mr. _____'s labor are suggested when she at one time describes that "He wake up while I'm in the field. I been chopping cotton three hours by time he comes" (TCP 26). This attitude where women are condemned to being akin to animals and used as beasts of labor is verbalized when Harpo says "Women work. I am a man" (TCP 21).

As the *The Color Purple* unfolds, Celie breaks through this negative script about the inferiority of the black woman. She is able to gradually move away from being a "mule" and an asexual nurturer to Mr. _____'s children when she meets Mr. _____'s lover, Shug Avery. Shug is a singer and a version of womanhood that rejects controlling stereotypes. Celie is mesmerized by and attracted to this alternative. Unlike Celie who is self-effacing, Shug invests herself with flamboyant clothes. She wears "a red wool dress," "black hat with feathers," "snake skin bag," etc. (TCP 45). Celie describes Shug as being dressed "to kill" and being "stylish."

Through her attire, Shug chooses not to imitate codes that attempt to contain her as a "mule" and she struggles to reclaim her body and acknowledges its desires. The inability of the men in the community to contain her threatens to destabilize the male order, and attempts are made to restrict Shug's influence by dehumanizing her. For example, the parish priest, an upholder of moral order attempts to control her by labeling her as a jezebel through slurs such as a "slut," "hussy" and "heifer" which suggest uncontained animal sexual promiscuity (TCP 44). Celie rejects the priest's sermon and feels that "someone got to stand up for Shug" (TCP 44). Shortly thereafter, Celie begins to love Shug primarily because she opens up the possibility of an alternate definition of selfhood for Celie. Significantly, Celie's first act of resistance occurs when she spits into the glass of water belonging to Old Mr. _____ because he refers to Shug in a derogatory manner.

Nettie, Celie's sister and other women in the novel such as Sophia, the wife of Mr._____'s son Harpo, enable Celie to counter similar controlling stereotypes by enlarging her discursive space beyond her home. They teach her what "go on in the world" through discussions of Africa, politics of the idea of a white God, colonial exploitation of Africa, etc. (TCP 16).

Sophia, Harpo's strong and physically imposing wife, also contributes to Celie's bildungsroman by teaching her the unacceptability of wife battering. Initially, Celie had assimilated and viewed as definitive her sub-human status as a "mule." She does not find her husband's assaults problematic because she has been socialized into believing that as a "wife," she is "stubborn" and that was what "all women were good for" (TCP 22). Not only does Celie accept her inferior status and the right of a man over a woman's body; she also perpetuates this belief when she suggests to Harpo that he should beat his wife in order to control her. The resultant fight between Sophia and Harpo "like two mens" becomes a defining moment in Celie's transformation (TCP 37). Celie finds that she cannot even sleep as she feels intense guilt and shame for having advised Harpo to beat his wife. She overcomes the socialization that naturalizes the practice of wife battering and begins to view it as unjust.

With the aid of Shug, Nettie and Sophia, Celie evolves into a woman capable of envisioning possibilities and therefore seeks to act upon rather than be acted upon. While the Celie that the reader meets at the beginning of the novel is a being who lacks ownership of her own body, the "bonds between women" help Celie challenge the stereotypes; in fact, they are crucial for enabling her to develop a more authentic sense of self. As the novel proceeds, she transforms: From being the "mule" of the masculine figures in the novel, Celie becomes economically independent and capable of making decisions. For example, by the end of the novel, Celie decides to not only keep the "white man" Alphonso got for her store but also to hire Sophia to "wait on colored cause they never had nobody in a store to wait on 'em before and nobody to treat 'em nice" (TCP 280). The former decision is significant because the act of seeking services from a white man suggests a reversal of power equation between the two races. The latter decision suggests a gesture that emanates from the desire to accord dignity to Celie's own race. These decisions show Celie's successful transformation into an entrepreneur.

Celie's bildungsroman suggests that the controlling stereotype of a "mule" and "jezebel" influences the heroine's quest, as it constitutes a pole from which she moves away. Another method of interpreting Celie's transformation is proposed by the psychologist Charles Proudfit. Proudfit theorizes using "psychoanalytic developmental psychology" to argue that Celie's transformation is "clinically accurate" (19). In the novel, Celie forms both sexual and emotional bonds with the various women she interacts. These bondings, Proudfit explains, "range from ministrations of Celie's younger sister Nettie, to Kate and Sophia and to Shug's facilitating Celie's sensual awakening to adult female sexuality and a healthy emotional life" (13). He further elaborates that these female bondings, which occur over an extended period of time, enable Celie, "a depressed survivor-victim of parent loss, emotional and physical neglect, rape, incest trauma and spousal abuse–to resume her arrested development and continue developmental processes that were thwarted in infancy and early adolescence" (19). Such psychoanalytical tools reveal the central role that "bonds amongst women" play in Celie's transformation.

Unlike the women in *The Color Purple*, the women in *April Raintree*, including protagonist April, refuse to challenge the oppressive gender constructions and instead continue to view the constructions of patriarchy uncritically. April's sexuality is envisioned solely in relationship to men. This is despite the history of sexual and emotional violence that she is subjected to. April opts to operate within the paradigm of patriarchy and searches for her "Prince Charming" (83). This fairy tale trope shows April's lack of self-assertion and her willingness to assume the role of a passive and dependent partner. In pursuit of this unrealistic fantasy, she uncritically moves through a series of relationships that turn out to be unfulfilling since the men seek to exploit her sexually and/or emotionally. Thus she enters into a relationship with Jerry Mac Callister, a married man, who desires her only for sexual pleasure.

Similarly the character Bob Radcliff marries April to get even with his mother for breaking up his relationship with Heather. The emotional and sexual violence intensifies when April is raped upon being mistaken for Cheryl. However April continues this pattern of heterosexual relations by leaning upon another lover, Roger, for reassurance (Culleton 167).

Co-sanguine with April's complicity with patriarchy is her acceptance of the associated categorization of women as either a whore or Madonna. Celie, on the other hand, comes to discard these categories as invalidating a black woman's sexuality; her relationship with Shug helps her to revise her relationship with her own body. Instead Celie begins to see her sexuality as a source of pleasure for her own self and not merely as a source of pleasure and power for the men like Mr. _____ or her father. Moreover Celie ceases to believe that the purpose of her body lies only in the service that it could perform for the Black man. In contrast, April does not find constructions of whore or Madonna problematic and she subscribes to these stereotypical labels. Her vocabulary is saturated with notions such as "good girls" or "perfect gentleman" (Culleton 79). The femininity April cultivates is not that of the Métis women whom she considers to be merely "strays" (Culleton 82). Rather, she attempts to be viewed as a refined white woman and towards this end she reads books on "proper etiquette" rather than mix with natives at the Friendship Centre. April's yearning for refinement can be understood in the light of historian Julia V. Emberly's theory on the rhetoric of colonialism. According to Emberley, *aboriginality* is viewed through the notion that all cultures go through stages of "cultural development from the simple to complex" (60). When this Darwinian tale of evolution is "applied to human culture, aboriginal cultures are made to represent an earlier stage of cultural evolution" (60).

In Culleton's novel, Métis are degraded by the white race as "half-breeds" who love to "wallow in filth." Métis girls are stereotyped as morally decadent who engage in "fighting," "running away," pregnancies, "prostitution," etc. (Culleton 26, 48). These stereotypes are treated as authentic and justify racial discrimination, political control, gender and economic oppression. The resultant lack of opportunities and economic independence brought about by these stereotypes compound Cheryl's problems and make her an easy victim for exploitation by men. Likewise the economic independence

April possesses is not derived or sustained by any meaningful economic activity but from divorce settlements and therefore is not a solution available to other Métis women.

Significantly, April and Cheryl provide a means by which the author renders the opposing poles of addressing gender-race-class oppression.[4] The socio-political alternatives implied in both these positions can be compared to the alternative demonstrated by Celie. This comparison reveals that April's and Cheryl's opposing positions, are rendered effete in their inability to effect emancipation. Both positions operate within the paradigm of patriarchy and the associated "institution" of "compulsory" heterosexual relations; therefore, both women are vulnerable to the sexual and emotional violence directed towards them by men. April experiences sexual violence in the form of rape, emotional deception by Jerry and desertion by Bob, while Cheryl is drawn into the cycle of alcohol, prostitution and suicide. Unlike Celie, both siblings fail to draw sustained strength from mutual support or a support group. As individuals, they are not able to access or create economic opportunities for individual growth and therefore are relegated to a life of drudgery. In *April Raintree*, there is no "bond between women."

April Raintree ends where April begins to "accept her identity" (184). However, the resolution *April Raintree* proposes is limited in its potential to effect changes at social, sexual, emotional and economic levels. In an act of writing a counter-discourse to the dominant racial discourse, Culleton asserts the unique Métis identity. However Culleton challenges only the racial and not the patriarchal notions that seek to construct and constrict the identity of Métis woman. The Métis women in the novel continue to be defined by Culleton strictly within the paradigm of patriarchy and its associated institution of "compulsory heterosexuality." Culleton views as normative only those ideas of sexuality and emotional bonds that patriarchy permits. In the novel, emotional and erotic sustenance is available to Métis women only through relationships with men that are based on unequal power relations between the two genders in patriarchy. Therefore, the women in *April Raintree* can never access emotional and erotic fulfillment in an alternate support group based on bonds between women. In contrast, Walker proposes sisterhood and lesbian relationships as emotional and sexual alternatives that can also herald social and economic changes in the lives of black women.

The Colored Woman's Search for Self and Her
Transformed Place

An authentic self requires a supportive place. This essay defines a community as a social/cultural place. Celie's bildungsroman is marked by milestones where she liberates herself from the control of cultural and historical stereotypes. For these milestones to be reached, dismantling of internalized racial attitudes–and not merely gender relations—need to occur within her community. By the end of the novel, Celie's community becomes supportive of the liberated Celie.

As Celie, along with the other black women in her community, emerge from these controlling stereotypes, *The Color Purple* moves towards what critic Molly Hite describes as a "celebration" of family reunion and of the black race (262). Unlike Royster who describes the novel as consisting of two static poles constructed along gendered lines and placed in opposition with each, Hite describes the novel as depicting a state of flux where a "new social order... will supplant the old" (Hite 262). Hite lists several favorable events that proclaim this change including Celie's inheritance of a house and store and learning that her children are not the product of incest. When Shug returns from her last heterosexual fling to find Albert and Celie living in platonic harmony after Albert realizes that "meanness kill." Nettie, her husband Samuel and the children also miraculously return from the sea after their ship had been reported lost at sea.

Royster's polarization of *The Color Purple* presents a static and an irreconcilable picture of the novel's black community. Moreover Royster's misreading also overlooks the depiction of the transformation of tyrannical male figures in the novel. Through this transformation, Walker suggests that the entire black community may transform to become a community where dignity is accorded to all its members—both men and women. According to Walker, the society that enables more fulfilling lives for black women is inclusive of transformed men. Critic Candice Jenkins notes in her essay "Queering Black Patriarchy: The Salvific Wish and Masculine Possibility in Alice Walker's *The Color Purple,*" that Walker reshapes the black family, "in unconventional ways that divest its black male members of a good deal of power..." (970). Thus Albert, Harpo and Samuel experience fundamental modification in their approach to women, thereby suggesting that Walker does not reject men but instead visualizes a more constructive mutual relationship. The conclusion in

The Color Purple is "favorable" not merely because "lesbianism," propelled by distorted sexual instincts, is established.

In addition, the women of *The Color Purple* reevaluate the idea of merging with the white society on egalitarian terms, as not being central to the search for identity; the black women have their own community or space. Moly Hite notes that in *The Color Purple* "the white society figures as profoundly unnecessary" (Hite 261).

April Raintree posits a far more grim view of the Métis community's chances of evolving a counter-discourse than the black community's chances of *The Color Purple*. Celie's transformation is facilitated by support made available to her by other women of the black community who also resist forces that oppress them and more importantly by a simultaneous change within the black community. Transformation in April and Cheryl is far more difficult as both the sisters ultimately struggle as individuals. Even though Culleton depicts the angst of the Métis community, the novel does not depict active acts of resistance. This is due to the extent of destruction the white race has been able inflict upon the Métis people. The white race in the novel, *April Raintree*, has practices such as institutional interventions in the form of the child placement policy that prevent emotional bonds from developing between the two sisters. Such practices help maintain white hegemony and perpetuate the fragmentation of the identities of Métis people as a community and as individuals. The child placement policy, through the practice of placement of Métis children in non-Métis and Native families, serves to severely undermine Métis culture.

Over the years, such a child placement policy also causes a breakdown in the relationship between siblings April and Cheryl. In the early childhood when the sisters are placed in the household of the DeRosiers', a white family, they are able to, with mutual support, offer some semblance of resistance to the humiliation that their foster family lashed out at them. At one time, Cheryl protests that the punishment of cutting April's hair by Mrs. De Rosier's hands is unjust. Subsequently, Mrs. DeRosier in turn punishes Cheryl's defiance by cutting her hair.

However, since the child placement policy imposes years of separation from their own culture, the sisters lack access to their roots and grow to possess divergent attitudes towards their Métis roots. April experiences a sense of shame of her Métis roots and seeks to reject them. Hiding behind her pale skin and assuming the façade of being white, she confesses at one point to not even wanting to have children as "they might turn out looking native" (Culleton 152). Cheryl, on the other hand, is actively engaged in discovering the authentic history of her Métis identity and asserting it.

These differing attitudes alienate them from each other, and the extent of this alienation can be gauged by the fact that April does not even know about the nature of economic activity Cheryl is involved in to sustain herself. It is only when April realizes that Cheryl has been involved in prostitution that she realizes her own disinterest in knowing her sister. Eventually it takes violence— Cheryl's suicide—for April to "accept" her true ethnic identity (Culleton 184).

The colonizers appear to be successful in many ways. They isolate the sisters so that they are deprived of life-saving support system. Cheryl succumbs to the burden of singly dealing with institutionalized oppression and commits suicide. April on the other hand, by the end of the novel, reaches a point where she finally begins to accept her roots. The success of a subsequent journey is, however, difficult to attain since she, unlike Celie in *The Color Purple,* does not have anyone with whom she can share the trauma and burden of this journey. April's approach to dealing with race, gender and class discrimination do not resolve her loneliness. She especially admits to "feelings of loneliness" when Cheryl leaves her (Culleton 96).

Cheryl represents another approach to dealing with the dominant discourse of race, class and gender. Unlike April, she asserts her Métis identity. In fact, her life is marked by a constant assertion of her racial roots. At school, she challenges the version of "history" disseminated by the colonizers that portrays Indians as torturers who massacred brave white explorers. Later, as an adult, she is involved with "events concerning native people" associating with other Métis and Indian people in the Friendship Centre (Culleton 138). When April accompanies Cheryl to the Friendship Centre, Cheryl is introducing April to a racially supportive community. April says:

> 'When we got to the Friendship Centre, we entered a large recreation room, filled with elderly native people. Cheryl mixed among them immediately, with me tagging along behind her. While she conversed with them, I could only smile patronizing smiles and nod when it was expected. I knew that Cheryl saw their quiet beauty, their simple wisdom. All I could see were watery eyes, leathery, brown skin, aged, uneducated natives who had probably not done much in their lives.

> Cheryl explained that some of the people were in the
> city for either medical reasons or they were visiting relatives'
> (139).

Later April meets an old Métis woman. The woman puts her
hands in April's. April says, "Her gaze held mine for I saw in her eyes
that deep simple wisdom of which Cheryl had spoken [. . .]I had this
overwhelming feeling that a mystical spiritual occurrence had just
taken place" (140). Later April says that she "continued to waver back
and forth as to just how I felt abut being a Métis" (141).

Gender, Race and Class

By the end of *The Color Purple,* Celie has moved from the
dependent, victim class to the class of the self-sustaining entrepreneur.
She makes the transformation with the support of black women. Her
business is supported by and serves her community. Her business
employs members of her racial group. Celie makes decisions and
gives directions. Most importantly, she does not depend on the white
community or black men for financial support.

April Raintree asserts that institutionalized oppression
prevents avenues for class advancement for the Métis. Thus when
Cheryl abandons her education at the university, she precludes any
opportunity to gain economic independence especially when non-
status Indians and Métis were having "hard times finding
employment" (Culleton 140). Cheryl is weighed down by her
economic vulnerability and by her knowledge of her family's
abandonment. She is soon drawn into the cycle of alcoholism and later
sexual exploitation when Mark DeSoto, who has himself been unable
to find a stable source of earning, pushes her into prostitution so that
he can use her body as a possible source of income.

Bereft of any agency, her relationship with Mark reflects a
special vulnerability of Métis women—they may be at the receiving
end of violence by the hands of men whose own aspirations have been
frustrated due to lack of sustained employment opportunities and lack
of government intervention to provide for them. Thus, Cheryl
describes Mark, who is only "working the streets," as an "abuser"
(180, 181). Cheryl at one time also explains to April that it was only
the Treaty Indians who got "supposed" benefit and that Non-Status
Indians and Métis only got "welfare" (Culleton 139).[5] Cheryl later has
to deal with the pressure of becoming a single mother. It needs to be

noted that she does not share this fact with April, who in turn becomes aware of the existence of Cheryl's child only at the end of the story.

In concluding *April Raintree* with Cheryl's child being a male, the author appears to refrain from interrogating further the implication of the oppressive forces of race, gender and class on the subsequent generations of Métis women. The text falls silent about suggesting alternatives that will address the continuation of a cycle of suicides that consumes women such as Cheryl and her mother. The child, called Henry Liberty Lee, represents, according to writer Margery Fee, "a new generation" (177). However Fee's reading homogenizes the different experiences of Métis men and women. According to Fee, the baby (a gender-neutral term used by Fee) represents "a new generation that will grow up with a new perspective because of his mother's comprehension of how the dominant ideology can harm him" (177). Unfortunately, such a reading does not acknowledge that Métis men and women might have different realities and experiences.

Also by concluding with Cheryl's suicide, Culleton's novel, reflects the lack of solution to "cultural stress," a term that the critic Lesley Erickson uses to describe aboriginal suicide in her essay "Constructed and Contested Truths." According to Erickson:

> the Royal Commission on Aboriginal Peoples reported in 1995 that status Indians in contemporary Canada suffer a suicide rate three times the total national average, while adolescents are five to six times more likely to commit suicide than their non-Aboriginal age-group peers. The commission concluded that Aboriginal suicide was an outward expression of the 'cultural stress' that accompanied Canada's colonial relations with First Nations. (595-596)

In Culleton's novel, Cheryl's death reflects the continued cycle of "cultural stress" that had consumed her mother. This "cultural stress" is bound to exert itself as long as the Métis woman continues "the experience of having been interpellated by a dominant discourse as a 'second-class citizen'" (Fee 173). It can be argued that Walker's formulation of bonds between women enable the women of *The Color Purple,* to an extent, to deal with such stresses and to use these bonds to play a life-saving role. Unlike April and Cheryl who deal with their personal and racial histories as isolated individuals, Celie and other black women in *The Color Purple,* with mutual support, are able to actively construct their identities along race, gender and class lines.

Culleton's novel concludes however without suggestions of any affirmative action to counter the second-class treatment of Métis women. However, the novel does suggest a rise in awareness of one's Métis identity and recognition of workings of a "dominant ideology" that attempted to distort April as the "Other." The conclusion of the novel at this juncture is a problematic and insufficient because Cheryl, as has been described above, had already possessed an awareness of this identity. The Métis identity is repeatedly shown as being constructed as the "Other" through practices of knowledge formation. This process of knowledge formation includes formally teaching in schools a version of history that constructs the Indians as savage torturers. Although the novel concludes at a juncture where April accepts her origins and heritage, she is not depicted even at the end as engaging and seeking support from members of her community. Contrary to Walker, Culleton does not elaborate upon the role of Métis community in sustaining and preventing possibilities of frustration of April's transformation. Members of Métis community in the novel, such as Cheryl's friend named Nancy, are not depicted as embodying traits that suggest acts of resistance.

Conversely, Walker in *The Color Purple* appears to locate Celie's within the context of the black community. The transformation and self-assertion by black community is equally essential to sustain Celie's transformation. Hence the readers are presented with the celebration by the black community, commemorating itself on the Fourth of July in an act of self-assertion. The assertion of ethnic identities and histories play a central role in formulation of Celie's, Cheryl's and April's identities. However, unlike Celie, Cheryl and April find no space or community–political, institution or physical—for their asserted identity.

The Successful Attainment of Self

Walker's formulation of bonds between women—both sexual and emotional—provides an alternate script of selfhood that erases and demolishes constrictive ideas of womanhood. In the treatment of the theme of racial oppression, Walker visualizes the role of economic independence gained by the black women that overturn the white hegemony. In contrast, the women of color in *April Raintree* continue to operate within the paradigm of patriarchy and lack a support group. Thus no radical counter-discourse emerges that leads to the successful attainment of self.

April Raintree, like *The Color Purple,* concludes with an assertion of racial identity—but the role and function of this assertion in the life of Métis women becomes problematic as the text depicts them as being an easy target of physical, emotional and sexual violence not only from the white men but more significantly from men of their own color. The author does not provide an alternative or interrogate this aspect further. They have no supportive space or community. From the perspective of class, the economic independence gained by Celie enables her to transform from being the muted slave of her "father" and "husband" to becoming a self-sustaining entrepreneur. Unlike *The Color Purple, April Raintree* concludes without proposing any substantial economic resolution that might empower women in material terms. April depends on the alimony that is granted from having been in a heterosexual relationship.

Conclusion

The Color Purple and *April Raintree* depict heroines from different racial backgrounds in the North American continent who are engaged in search for self. Each novel uniquely negotiates issues of gender, race and class. Unlike April and Cheryl, Celie's emotional and erotic bonds with the other Black women facilitate social and individual transformations that also entail financial independence and the dignity from being financially independent. In Walker's novel, the transformation of the black community is required to evolve a counter-discourse to racial and gender oppression.

Walker and Culleton consider assertion of ethnic and racial histories as critical to the heroine's search for self. However April undertakes an individual search for self, and unlike Celie, lacks the support group/space/community that could impart agency to effect and sustain socio-political transformation. April's search for an identity appears ultimately to be self-limiting, problematic and difficult as it continues to maneuver in various degrees within the dominant discourses of gender, race and class. Her search for identity can be described by borrowing the words from Audre Lorde's essay, "The master's tools will never dismantle the master's house."

The Color Purple is far more comprehensive and incisive in confronting the issues and seeking solutions. Thus a cross-cultural reading enables the viewing of the sisterhood and lesbianism in *The Color Purple* as being more than merely emotional or sexual positioning but as an effective counter-discourse to the dominant ideas of race and gender relations.

Uplabdhi Sangwan, Delhi University in India

Notes

[1] Culleton, *April Raintree*.

[2] Simms' research deals with the production of the first three hegemonic stereotypes by pro-slavery ideologues in six realms, namely religion, natural science, popular literature, social science, politics and law and philosophy.

[3] Walker. *The Color Purple*. All quotes that follow from this text are from this edition.

[4] Margery Fee reads the two sisters April and Cheryl as representing the "choice of assimilation and oblivion." Where Fee reads the siblings in terms of a literary trope that uses two sisters as representing two attitudes to racial oppression, this paper suggests that the trope can be read to have been deployed to read two attitudes to race, class and gender.

[5] < http://www.cbc.ca/news/background/aboriginals/faqs.html > This site briefly discusses that the "federal government's Indian Act divides Indians into two categories: Status and Non-Status Indians. Status Indians are people who qualify for registration on an official list maintained by Ottawa. The reason this matters is that Status Indians are entitled to certain rights and payments not available to other Canadians–depending on the terms of their treaty. There are rules that determine who qualifies as a Status Indian–usually based on evidence of descent from people Ottawa recognizes as members of an Indian band." "Non-Status Indians are people who consider themselves Indians though Ottawa does not recognize them as such. This is usually because they can't prove their status or have lost their status. Non-Status Indians are not entitled to the same rights and benefits available to Status Indians."

Works Cited

Abbandonato, Linda. "A View from 'Elsewhere': Subversive Sexuality and the Rewriting of Heroine's Story in *The Color Purple*," *PMLA* 106 (1999): 1106-1115. On line at http://www.jstor.org/search (consulted 18 June 2007).

Bowerbank, Sylvia and Dolores Nawagesic Wawia. "Review: Literature and Criticism by Native and Métis Women in Canada" Review of *Kôhkominawak Otâcimowiniwâwa/Our*

Grandmothers' Lives as Told in Their Own Words by Glecia Bear, Irene Calliou, Janet Feitz, Minnie Fraser, Alpha Lafond, Rosa Longneck and Mary Wells; edited and translated by Freda Ahenakew and H. C. Wolfart. Saskatoon, Saskatchewan (CA): Fifth House Publishers, 1992. (566)

Brah, Avtar."Diaspora, Border and Transnational Identities" in *Feminist Postcolonial Theory – A Reader.* ed. Reina Lewis and Sara Mills. Edinburgh: Edinburgh U P, 2003. (613 – 634)

Calhoun, Cheshire. "The Gender Closet: Lesbian Disappearance under the Sign 'Women'" *Feminist Studies* 21 (1995): 7 - 34.

Christian, Barbara. "The Race for Theory" in *The Black Feminist Reader* ed. Joy James. Massachusetts: Blackwell, 2000. (11-23)

Culleton, Beatrice. *April Raintree*. Canada: Pemmican, 1991.

Emberley, Julia V. "The Bourgeois Family, Aboriginal Women, and Colonial Governance in Canada: A Study in Feminist Historical and Cultural Materialism" *Signs* 27.1 (2001): 59-85. On line at http://www.jstor.org/search (consulted 20 August 2007).

Erickson, Lesley. "Aboriginal Suicide, Law, and Colonialism in the Canadian West(s), 1823–1927" *The Canadian Historical Review* 86 (2005): 595-618. On line at http://muse.jhu.edu (consulted 21 August 2007).

Fee, Margery. "Upsetting Fake Ideas" in *Native Writers and Canadian Writing.* ed. William H. New. Vancouver, BC: UBC Press, 1991. (168 -180)

Hite, Molly. "Romance, Marginality, Matrilineage: Alice Walker's *The Color Purple* and Zora Neale Hurston's *Their Eyes Were Watching God*" *Novel: A Forum on Fiction* 22 (1989): 257-273. On line at http://www.jstor.org/search (consulted 15 July 2007).

Jenkins, Candice M. "Queering Black Patriarchy: The Salvific Wish and Masculine Possibility in Alice Walker's *The Color Purple*" *Modern Fiction Studies* 48 (2002) : 970. Online at http://muse.jhu.edu (consulted 15 July 2007).

Lorde, Audre. "The Master's Tool Will Never Dismantle the Master's House." *Feminist Postcolonial Theory—A Reader.* Eds. Reina Lewis and Sara Mills. Edinburgh: Edinburgh U P, 2003. (25-28)

Proudfit, Charles L. "Celie's Search for Identity: A Psychoanalytic Developmental Reading of Alice Walker's *The Color Purple*" *Contemporary Literature* 32 (1991): 12-37. On line at http://www.jstor.org/search (consulted 18 June 2007).

Rajan, Rajeshwari Sunder, ed. *Signposts – Gender Issues in Post Independence India.* New Brunswich, NJ: Rutgers U P, 2001.

Rich, Adrienne Cecile. "Compulsory Heterosexuality and Lesbian Existence" *Journal of Women's History* 15 (2003): 11 – 48. Online at http://muse.jhu.edu (consulted 21 August 2007).

Rosa, Deborah De. "Womanism" in *The Oxford Companion to Women's Writing in the United States.* ed. Cathy N. Davidson. New York: Oxford U P, 1995. (928-929)

Royster, Philip M. "In Search of our Fathers' Arms: Alice Walker's Persona of the Alienated Darling" *Black American Literature Forum* 20 (1986): 347 -370. On line at http://www.jstor.org/search (consulted 20 August 2007).

S. H. Brown, Jennifer. "Métis, Halfbreeds, and Other Real People: Challenging Cultures and Categories" *The History Teacher* 27.1 (1993): 19-26. On line at http://www.jstor.org/search (consulted 25 August 2007).

Sawchuk, Joe. "Negotiating an Identity: Métis Political Organizations, the Canadian Government, and Competing Concepts of Aboriginality" *American Indian Quarterly* 25.1 (2001):73-92. On line at http://www.jstor.org/search (consulted 25 August 2007).

Simms, Rupe. "Controlling Images and the Gender Construction of Enslaved African Women" *Gender and Society* 15 (2001): On line at http://www.jstor.org/search (consulted 18 June 2007). : 879 – 897. On line at http://www.jstor.org/search (consulted 25 August 2007)

Stoneham, Geraldine. "It's A Free Country: Visions of Hybridity in the Metropolis" in *Comparing Postcolonial Literature.* ed. Ashok Bery and Patricia Murray. New York: St. Martin's Press, 2000. (81-92)

Walker, Alice. *The Color Purple.* Orlando: Harcourt, 2003.

The Spirit of Space

Homeward Bound: Transformative Spaces in *The Color Purple*

Danielle Russell

> The body is subject to the whim of locations, imponderable twists
> of fate that lead to doom or survival. (Eagleton 305)

The opening quote serves as a succinct statement about the
interchange between the central character of *The Color Purple* and the
spaces she inhabits. The line was actually taken from a study by
feminist critic Mary Eagleton of the life and work of American poet
Adrienne Rich. Eagleton hones in on the relationship between identity
and location: identity is intimately and irrevocably entwined with
place. Neither Rich nor Eagleton directly addresses the fiction of
Alice Walker in their work, but the three writers share a perceptive
awareness of the power of settings to shape characters—real or
fictional. Locations and relocations have a strong impact on identity.
Survival rates can hinge on geography. To live in a refugee camp in
Darfur or a home in the Gaza Strip is to occupy more than a space
located by latitude and longitude on a map. Such areas, like countless
politically and economically unstable sites around the globe, are
fraught with risks to life, limb, and liberty. Visual images beamed
around the world graphically illustrate the vulnerability associated
with geographic location.

Place is not just experienced objectively; there is a subjective
quality to the interaction. Writer Eudora Welty addresses this issue in
"Place in Fiction":

> Place has the most delicate control over character [...] by
> confining character it defines it [....] Place in fiction is the named,
> identified, [...] gathering spot of all that has been felt, is about to
> be experienced, in the novel's progress. (122)

Welty emphasizes the shaping power of fictional settings. The control is "delicate," but inescapable. Welty's compelling point that place is the "named, identified," however, signals the fact that the interaction is not one-sided: both the individual and the space are defined. Place is humanized space.

Shifting locations can lead to changes in character. This potential is illustrated through Celie, Walker's central figure; Celie is not presented as possessing a fixed or static identity. Celie's body is subject to the whim of locations that Eagleton identifies in Rich's work. Through imponderable twists of fate—specifically rejuvenation in the arms of her husband's mistress, the recovery of lost loved ones, and a reconciliation with her estranged husband Albert—Celie not only survives, she thrives. Significantly, Celie does so in a space that is initially a hostile one: the home. Her early experience of home—both in her family and marital homes—is one of vulnerability and violence, but the introduction of Shug Avery proves to be a catalyst in Celie's life. Shug recognizes the importance of a genuine home—a place of comfort and creativity—being at "home" in one's body, and the need to adopt a malleable concept of family.

The lessons are invaluable to Celie; internalizing and acting on them aid in her growth from a voiceless victim to a self-asserting individual. That process, by necessity, also entails a series of spatial movements; Celie shifts from her imprisoning childhood home to the slightly less smothering abode of Albert. The dwelling is not, initially, all that different, but the potential for positive change is raised by the presence of Shug Avery. Moving out of these oppressive sites, and into the more open home of Shug and, finally her own home, Celie discovers the transformative power of space.

The negative spaces Celie has been forced into, first by her stepfather and then her husband clearly have shaped her identity. Celie's gesture of negating "I am" in favor of "I have always been a good girl" in her opening letter to God, signals the shift in her sense of self (1). The act of incomprehensible brutality seemingly has changed the young girl; she hesitates in describing her moral state. Positive transformation will, however, be achieved through an amelioration of the (concept and reality of) home. Celie's journey takes her through a series of domestic dwellings: from a site of perverted relationships (stepfather's control); to a socially sanctioned, but no less exploitative connection (marriage); to a tender, but tenuous partnership (Shug is not committed to monogamy); to a personal home that is self-defined (Celie establishes the boundaries). She comes full circle, returning to a transformed family home purged of the perversion and the violence, and a transformed family that is expanded and connected by love, not hostility. The main focus in *The Color Purple* is Celie's transformation, but it is mirrored, in varying degrees, by several peripheral characters connected to her: Nettie and Albert are also transformed by their experiences of domestic spaces.

Houses of Horror: Home as a Hostile Space

Home is a complex place: it can comfort or confine. A home has both a physical presence and an emotional resonance. Ideally, it functions as a sheltering space, particularly for children. At its best, the home is a personal sanctuary that fosters and encourages personal development. At its worst, it is an oppressive and suffocating entity. Philosopher Gaston Bachelard's work on "felicitous space" has played a key role in shaping discussions of the home (xxxii). It is difficult to find a work on the theory of space that does not acknowledge (to varying degrees) Bachelard's *The Poetics of Space*. In particular, Bachelard's definition of the home as "a space for cheer and intimacy, space that is supposed to condense and defend intimacy," has established an idealized concept that emphasizes human interactions within the dwelling (48). While acknowledging that negative examples of the home exist, Bachelard does not address the existence of "hostile space" or the "space of hatred and combat" in any detail (xxxii). He insists these destructive houses can only be "studied in the context of [...] apocalyptic images" (xxxii). Walker's novel insists on recognition of the detrimental experience of the home. *The Color Purple* also affirms that the combat can take a more subtle form and lead to the creation of felicitous space.

Initially Celie's natal home is a place of disconnection, vulnerability, and violence in her (and by implication Nettie's) experience. The precarious situation of the sisters is exacerbated by, and reflected in, their position within the house. Celie describes the arrangement to Shug, "the girls had a little room...off to itself, connected to the house by a little plank walk" (113). Physically detached from the family dwelling, what should be a sheltering space becomes a site of exploitation; bedroom as private sanctuary is obliterated by the stepfather's intrusion. The secluded location— "nobody ever come in there but Mama"—permits an act of perversion (113). Memories of this initial home are painful; they haunt Celie rather than sustain her in subsequent experiences. In fact, the acts of betrayal she endures in her family home set Celie on a potentially destructive path. The most significant act is clearly the sexual assaults, but her mother's hostility during Celie's pregnancy—"She scream at me. She cuss at me" (2)—is also a betrayal (albeit one fueled by her own illness). The key adult figures in her life have misused their power over Celie.

The movement to her husband's house affords even less chance for Celie to escape the pattern of abuse. The result of an arrangement between her stepfather and Mr.__, the move signals a continuation of Celie's disempowerment. It is a relocation which simply adds to Celie's workload. The new home is a site of continued exploitation and violence. The dwellings cannot be construed as Bachelard's "space of cheer and intimacy"; the actions of the men are dehumanizing, thereby creating spaces of threats and alienation.

Shug Avery's later presence in the home will raise the possibility of a connection that Celie has not experienced since the loss of Nettie. Celie's instinctive response to the sight of the sick singer is one of welcome:

> Come on in, I want to cry. To shout. Come on in. With God help, Celie going to make you well.' (45)

Celie remains silent, however, because "It not my house" (45). Despite the fact that it is her marital home, Celie does not have the authority to speak. Like the silence imposed by the stepfather, the home (and her husband) imposes a silence Celie cannot even struggle against at this point in her life. Shug feels no such compunction, saying to Celie, "You sure *is* ugly" (46). The mistress is more at home—and vocal—than the wife.

The Practical Effects of Place: Marginalization and the Vulnerability to Violation

Frequently identified as an epistolary novel, *The Color Purple* actually begins in a space beyond the boundaries of the genre. A threatening voice issues the opening sentences—"*You better not never tell nobody but God. It'd kill your mammy*"—not the voice of the central character Celie, but the catalyst for her letter writing, her rapist stepfather (1). Walker's technique of delaying the protagonist's statement of identity mirrors Celie's marginalized position. Her authority as the author of her own story (and indeed of her life) is challenged by the stepfather's intrusion; his looming presence reflects the physical and psychological legacy of his penetration of Celie's private space—her bedroom and her body. The reader is thrust into an intimate emotional and psychological space: a young girl's painful memory of abuse. The impact of the man's brutality is revealed in the first letter (and reinforced through subsequent ones). Celie does indeed turn to God, and there is poignancy to the details she offers her omniscient audience:

> I am fourteen years old. I am I have always been a good girl. Maybe you can give me a sign letting me know what is happening to me. (1)

Celie's subsequent accusation to God that "you must be sleep," can be read as a step towards claiming her own authority (178). The choice to stop writing to God, in favor of Nettie, is an act of defiance: the ultimate authority has lost his authority.

The facts Celie knows in the opening passage, however, are basic in contrast with her bewilderment over her predicament. Isolated and intimidated, Celie's very identity is under assault. The gesture of crossing out "I am" in favor of "I have always been" indicates her uncertainty about her moral status. It is also a seeming negation of identity, of being. The violation of her body ruptures Celie's sense of reality. Unable to comprehend, let alone articulate what she is enduring, Celie is forced to retreat into the interior space of the letter. It, like Celie herself, occupies a state of limbo: recorded (and therefore potentially for public consumption) yet hidden (a private document addressed to God which is simultaneously a confession and a testament to Celie's existence—as she will defiantly tell her husband, "I'm here") (210). The letters become a tangible representation of Celie's inner thoughts and emotions. She cannot articulate, or act on, these sentiments, but finds a release through the process of writing.

Moving out of the Margin: Envisioning Alternative Spaces

Asserting her identity will require a series of spatial movements on Celie's part; the movements will entail both physical and imaginative relocations. The first is stepping into the imaginative space created by a photograph of Shug Avery. Initially, Celie is merely curious about the woman associated with her potential husband. Her focus will, however, shift:

'An all night long I stare at it. An now when I dream, I dream of
Shug Avery. She be dress to kill, whirling and laughing.' (6)

The picture opens a space of fantasy for Celie. Physically confined in
Albert's home, and constrained by her marriage, Celie can only find
freedom in the fantasies the image triggers. Dreams of Shug bring a
much needed escape outlet, anticipating their subsequent relationship.
The thought of Shug also helps Celie cope with her wedding night: "I
know what he doing to me he done to Shug Avery and maybe she like
it. I put my arm around him" (12). Oddly, the mistress bridges the
distance between husband and wife—temporarily and tenuously at
this point, but later in their lives Shug will provide the common
ground that permits a friendship between Celie and Albert. The image
of Shug Avery introduces an alternative space from the space of
oppression and disconnection Celie inhabits. In her dreams, Celie
discovers a different vision of life—one she cannot personally access
at this point in her waking life. Shug's actual entry into the Albert's
home will trigger an end to the domestic violence and powerlessness
Celie endures, but Celie cannot anticipate this altered reality.

The triangular relationship between Albert, Shug and Celie
would suggest a severance of a marital bond. It cannot, however, be
construed as a romantic triangle in the traditional sense since Celie
has no desire for Albert. Celie's desire is directed towards Shug. In
Walker's text, the inclusion of a third party is actually a means of
creating solidarity between Celie and Albert. The couple share an odd
moment of connection when they unite in defense of Shug from an
attack by Albert's father: "Mr.___look up at me, our eyes meet. This
is the closest us ever felt" (55). All they have in common is a desire to
protect Shug; she functions, at this point at least, as a unifying force.
For Celie, the expanded relationship leads to a new awareness of the
world:

'First time I think about the world. [...] I see myself sitting there
quilting tween Shug Avery and Mr. ___. Us three set together
[....] For the first time in my life, I feel just right.' (57)

Harmony springs from a position of entrenchment. The trio forms a
family of their own in defiance of the expectations of Albert's father.
It remains, however, an uneasy alliance. Although Celie articulates a
feeling of contentment, the household is still fraught with danger.

The concept of home as a protection against a hostile world is
problematic in Walker's novel. Celie's vulnerability in the home
stems from the personal-in Celie's case a loveless marriage to a self-

centered and violent man-and the public-systemic racism. The history of the home in America is not uniform. The possibility of ownership, of creating autonomous space, is complicated by the legacy of slavery, the realities of poverty, and the obstacles that stem from racial discrimination. Feminist bell hooks' work on the "subversive value of homeplace, of having access to private space" free from direct encounters with "white racist aggression" illustrates the potential of the home to nurture alternative versions of a family (47). The nuclear family is not the dominant structure in hooks' assessment of the home. By necessity the family is more flexible; its malleability creates the potential for greater accommodation.

White racist aggression is part of *The Color Purple*— lynching, miscarriages of justice, rape, imperialist practices—but it is not Walker's direct concern. The spotlight is focused on the black community and its acts of cruelty and compassion. Domestic space in the novel is not an overt site for the political solidarity hooks envisions; personal connections are the focus in the homes Shug and Celie establish. The people they welcome into their homes are bound to the women by love, compassion, and companionship. So marginalized groups can find collective power in domestic spaces; in this context, domesticity can be a subversive act. Survival is found in a space of resistance. Celie is in desperate need of a personal sanctuary, but for much of the novel she cannot even envision one.

The home as a personal place, a defense against the world, and a place of nurturing, is painfully absent in Celie's life and imagination. The tactic of silent submission she has adopted negates the belief of a home as a healing space. She will eventually unlearn this tactic of silent submission from her daughter-in-law Sofia:

> 'All my life I had to fight [...] my daddy [...] my brothers [...] my cousins and my uncles. A girl child ain't safe in a family of men. But I never thought I'd have to fight in my own house.' (40)

Although home should offer a respite from life's battles, Sofia shows that this is not the case. Significantly, the hostility she describes stems from the private (her family) rather than the public (strangers) world. That is not to suggest that threats do not emanate from outside the home—Sofia will also be forced to deal with such repercussions later in the novel—but that they also originate within the home.

The Healing Power of Home: Discovering a Place of Her Own

As a mere possession, or symbol of power, a home can function as an oppressive site. If the individuals within the household are connected only tenuously—as Celie is with Albert during their marriage—then the place can be akin to a prison. It is clearly Albert's home; Celie is little more than a poor substitute for the woman Albert really desired. Once it incorporates responsibility and affection, however, the home can become a communal place and source of inspiration. The emotional power of the home requires intimacy and nurturing to be sustained; it is a collective process. A home is the "immediate setting that is personalized, lived in, and 'made,'" writes literary critic Arnold Weinstein in his comprehensive study of the home in American writing, *Nobody's Home: Speech, Self, and Place in American Fiction from Hawthorne to DeLillo,* "but also and no less crucially the larger human nexus, the family that one lives in, that one both inherits and 'makes'" (5). In *The Color Purple,* the human connection associated with a protective family dwelling has been denied Celie; indeed it is beyond her comprehension for much of her early life.

Celie learns that the home is a place for nurturance and intimacy. The source of this crucial lesson for Celie is her husband's mistress. Initially, Celie is the nurturing figure in the unlikely pairing: she bathes and feeds the weakened Shug. Shug stirs a new passion within Celie:

> 'I got full sight of Shug Avery long black body with it black plum nipples, [...] I thought I had turned into a man. [...] I wash her body [...] My hands tremble and my breath short.' (49).

It is an intimate act, but not one that immediately triggers intimacy because Shug remains hostile. Initially tenderness is one-sided in these interactions, but eventually Shug does make a public offering of "Miss Celie's Song"—"First time somebody made something and name it after me" Celie acknowledges (74).

As their friendship develops, Shug will help Celie negotiate a place for herself in Albert's house. Shug is the first person to successfully intervene on Celie's behalf; she confronts Albert about his abuse thereby negotiating a kind of truce. Her protective impulse increases the more Shug learns about Celie's past; Shug's arms will become a healing space for the wounded Celie. Painful memories, repressed for so long, are finally released in the sheltering (and non-judgmental) embrace Shug and Celie share. Shug's removal of Celie to her own home in Memphis later in the novel continues this process of opening up an intimate space. Shug reassures Celie, "I brought you here to love you and help you get on your feet" (214). The "big and pink" home is the first dwelling that provides Celie with a personal space: "Shug give me a big back bedroom overlook the backyard and the bushes down by the creek" (211). The rationale behind the placement is that she knows Celie is "use to morning sun" (211). It is the only time that anyone has given some thought to where Celie will be comfortable.

Financial independence will come for Celie in the form of "Folkspants, Unlimited. Shug Avery Drive," the business she forms in Shug's dining room (217). Sewing begins as a substitute for violence, "a needle and not a razor in my hand," thinks Celie (147). The rage must be redirected if Celie is to survive. Celie discovers a passion and a purpose in the process of designing pants. Shug's home encourages an independence that Celie's previous homes have stifled.

While the large square dwelling is not Shug's ideal, it serves a therapeutic function for Celie. Shug's desire for a round house has been thwarted—"everybody act like that's backward"—but she has drawn up the plans for the future (211). A mud dwelling, it too will be pink and, in Celie's eyes "look sort of like some kind of fruit" (211-212). It visually echoes Nettie's African hut. Nettie describes her home as "all colorful and warm and homey"; all it lacks are windows and a picture of Celie (160). In each instance, the structure is an overtly feminine space that mirrors the female form; as Shug points out, "I just feel funny living in a square. If I was square, then I could take it better" (212). The round homes are vulnerable spaces: Nettie's round home is destroyed by developers and Shug's concept meets with derision. Natural in design and construction, by the time Celie and Shug finish improving the design, "our house [observes Celie] look like it can swim or fly" (212). The blueprint for Shug's dream house remains a mere vision, but its spirit of accommodation, cooperation, and creativity will be sheltered in the home Celie prepares for her long-lost family.

Celie's final home is the legacy of her long-lost family: the mother lost to illness and then death, and the father lynched before a memory of him could form. Alphonso's usurpation of her property rights is temporary, and Celie is granted her rightful inheritance upon his death. In an instant, Celie is the owner of a home, land, and a store. It is an overwhelming prospect, "Just to think about having my own house enough to scare me" (249). Significantly, it is not the house Celie grew up in; the stepfather "got an Atlanta architect to design it" (250). Shug and Celie purify it with cedar sticks "chasing out all the evil and making a place for good" (250). Now possessing room enough for the extended family—Nettie, the children, Nettie's husband and Shug—Celie envisions a shelter for all her loved ones. In doing so, Celie moves beyond the confines of a mere structure and assumes responsibility for the ongoing "creation" of the home. As geographer Holly Youngbear-Tibbetts theorizes in her work on the emotional and imaginative role of the home, home "in the most replete sense of the word, is not about the confines of place and community [...] it is a created place, secured not by nativity, entitlement, or endowment but by continual and careful creation and recreation [...]" (36). Celie's "ownership" of the home (literally and emotionally) opens it up to those with whom she shares a genuine connection.

The Personal Made Political: Redefining the Domestic Household

Race and gender complicate ownership, autonomous space, and definitions of domestic households in *The Color Purple*. Despite these obstacles, the novel offers a compelling alternative to the home as a site of oppression. Celie's establishment of her own home marks a personal victory. It can also be read as fulfilling hooks' radical political dimension. "Black women," hooks contends, "resisted by making homes where all black people could strive to be subjects, not objects, where we could be affirmed in our minds and hearts despite poverty, hardship, and deprivation" (42). Celie's home provides a respite, for both family and friends, from the pain of poverty and hardship. It opens the space of resistance bell hooks identifies. Celie's defiant statement to her husband as she left him—"I'm pore, I'm black, I may be ugly and can't cook [....] But I'm here"—is concretized, and softened in her home (210). The element of the curse has been eliminated; neither Celie nor Albert is a threat to the other in the later years of their lives.

Celie discovers a sense of peace and contentment in her new home and, in the process, opens the space for a new family dynamic. Moreover, she and Albert achieve a mutually nurturing relationship. Once again this is prompted by Shug Avery; the shared loss of the lover leads to a friendship: "the old devil put his arms around me and just stood there on the porch with me [....] I bent my stiff neck onto his shoulders" (276). Although compassion and understanding have been noticeably absent from their past interactions, by sewing together Celie and Albert achieve a degree of intimacy. The extent of their reconciliation is evident when the long awaited reunion with Nettie and the children occurs. Celie points "up at my peoples. This Shug and Albert" (293). By establishing her own home and business, Celie has successfully redefined her family. The new family dynamic is a community of choice not determined by genetics.

Significantly, Celie is not the only one altered by her movement out of the marital home. Albert is also humanized; he too discovers a sense of contentment impossible in his previous pattern of behavior. His vulnerability after Celie's curse and Shug's departure creates an opening for Albert to connect with the son he has bullied. Harpo "clean the house, got food. Give his daddy a bath" (227). The tender treatment is also essential in rekindling Sofia's love for Harpo. She observes the father and son "laying there on the bed fast asleep. Harpo holding his daddy in his arms. After that, I start to feel again for Harpo, Sofia say" (227). Fulfilling his father's needs, Harpo once again becomes the man Sofia can love.

Celie and Albert reach a different, but no-less compelling connection. Celie cannot hate Mr.__ because of Shug, but she also recognizes that "he trying to make something out of himself [....] when you talk to him now he really listen" (264). The epiphany permits the previously-alienated husband and wife to establish a companionate relationship. As bell hooks perceptively theorizes, a home is a healing space that permits collective regeneration. Under Celie's guidance, the home is expansive enough to accommodate a variety of nurturing relationships devoid of power conflicts. The conclusion of *The Color Purple* ameliorates both the family home and the family.

The final moments of the novel reveal a home free of violence and exploitation. Celie also discovers a familial structure contingent on affection rather than power struggles. For the most part, marriages in the novel have been arrangements by men for their benefit (most significantly the stepfather/Albert negotiation of Celie's fate), but the final pages offer a spiritual/emotional bond at the heart of the extended family. It is a peace achieved through rebellion and reconciliation. Nature plays a significant role in Celie's journey away from oppressive social institutions. The long fermenting confrontation with Albert strikes Celie as coming from a connection to a natural entity:

'it […] seem to come to me from the trees [….] I say, You better
stop talking because all I'm telling you ain't coming just from me.
[…] when I open my mouth the air rush in and shape words.'
(209)

It is cast as an out-of-body experience; Celie only comes to herself
when Shug shakes her. The defiant moment is powerful and yet oddly
enough it undercuts Celie's agency. She is almost a conduit for nature
as she taps into a source of strength and inspiration. The "self" she
comes to is still a work-in-progress. Celie must move out of the home
in order to forge a functioning identity of her own.

   A key step in Celie's rejecting the role of victim is a
reconnection with her abused body; first she looks at herself and then
she embraces Shug's healing touches. Celie has never been at "home"
in her own skin. The disconnection from her body is a direct legacy of
abuse. In her role as wife, Celie's survival tactic has been continued
detachment, to "pretend I ain't there" (78). More than pleasure, the act
of intimacy affords a lesson in self-love which leads to a reconnection
with the self—the most intimate of "homes."

   The relationship between the individual and the spaces Celie
occupies is especially evident in the setting in *The Color Purple*.
Domestic, spiritual, and sensual spaces trigger painful, but
empowering experiences for Celie. Intimacy is ultimately achieved
through spatial experiences. Celie discovers the therapeutic powers of
transformative spaces. Healing is found in the arms of a lover and
friend. The body Celie has been taught to distrust ultimately proves to
be a transformative space that leads her "home."

Danielle Russell, York University and Glendon College

Works Cited

Bachelard, Gaston. *The Poetics of Space* translated by Maria Jolas.
      Boston: Beacon Press, 1969.
Eagleton, Mary. "Adrienne Rich, Location and the Body" *Journal
      of Gender Studies* 9 (2000): 299-312.
Friedman, Marilyn. "Feminism and Modern Friendship: Dislocating
      the Community" in *Explorations in Feminist Ethics: Theory
      and Practice*. eds. Eva Browning Cole and Susan Coutrap-
      McQuin. Bloomington: Indiana University Press, 1992. (89-
      97)

Hall, James. C. "Towards a Map of Mis(sed) Reading: The Presence of Absence in *The Color Purple.*" *African American Review* 26.1 (1992): 89-97.

hooks, bell. *Yearning: Race, Gender, and Cultural Politics.* Boston: South End, 1990.

Powers, Peter Kerry. "'Pa is Not Our Pa': Sacred History and Political Imagination in *The Color Purple*" *South Atlantic Review* 60.2 (1995): 69-92.

Selzer, Linda. "Race and Domesticity in *The Color Purple*" *African American Review* 29.1 (1995): 67-83.

Walker, Alice. *The Color Purple.* Orlando: Harcourt, 2003.

Weinstein, Arnold. *Nobody's Home: Speech, Self, and Place in American Fiction from Hawthorne to DeLillo.* Oxford: Oxford University Press, 1993.

Welty, Eudora. *The Eye of the Story: Selected Essays and Reviews.* New York: Random House, 1979.

Youngbear-Tibbetts, Holly. "Making Sense of the World" in *Making Worlds: Gender, Metaphor, Materiality.* eds. Susan Hardy Aiken, Ann Brigham, Sallie A. Marston, Penny Waterstone. Tuscon: The University of Arizona Press, 1998. (31-44)

A House of Her Own: Alice Walker's Readjustment of Virginia Woolf's *A Room of One's Own* in *The Color Purple*

Turgay Bayindir

Virginia Woolf has been widely recognized as one of the most influential feminist writers of the twentieth century. In fact, Woolf's book length essay, *A Room of One's Own* (1929)[1], is still studied as one of the constituting texts of the early twentieth century feminism; it has been productively used within the various twentieth century feminist movements in eliminating the common prejudice that women are by nature inferior to men and also in exploring the real reasons why prior to the beginning of the twentieth century, women have not contributed to the arts and sciences as much as men have. In this lengthy essay, addressing the specific issue of the scarcity of women writers in canonical literature up to her own time, Virginia Woolf argues that "a woman must have money and a room of her own if she is to write fiction" (4).

Several contemporary American women writers have adopted Woolf's feminist rhetoric in their fiction, and it has been especially popular among minority women writers. For example, famous Mexican American writer Sandra Cisneros titles the second to last section of her novella, *The House of Mango Street* (1984)[2], as "A House of My Own," a vignette in which the main character Esperanza ruminates over the possibility of one day living in a house of her own: "Not a flat. Not an apartment in back. Not a man's house. Not a daddy's. A house all my own" (108). Another American woman writer to adopt Woolf's polemical strategies in her own fiction is the African American writer Alice Walker. An especially salient connection can be traced between the feminist ideas presented in Woolf's essay and Alice Walker's Pulitzer Prize-winning novel *The Color Purple* (1982). Writing in early 1980s, Walker reformulates Woolf's idea of "a room of one's own" in this historical novel.

Through the example of her female protagonists, Alice Walker demonstrates that a room of one's own is not sufficient for African American women to truly free themselves from the stifling influence of patriarchy. Almost identical to Esperanza's thoughts in Cisneros' novella, the only solution Walker offers in *The Color Purple* to black women's independence from patriarchy is a house of their own where they can live free from the confines of men regardless of whether that man is a father or a husband.

In *A Room of One's Own*, Virginia Woolf sets out to answer the questions 'Why was one sex so prosperous and the other so poor? What effect has poverty on fiction? What conditions are necessary for the creation of works of art" (25). Through an ingenious historical analysis and her trademark rhetorical strategies, Woolf proves that the lack of equal female involvement in arts and sciences is not due to their inherent inferiority to men as had been claimed by many male scholars, but instead can be attributed to the fact that, throughout the centuries, they have been kept at a socially disadvantaged position by men. From these premises, Woolf arrives at the conclusion that in order for women to create genuine works of art, they need not only a stable income enough to live on, but also a room of their own where they can free their minds of the mundane works of domestic life such as cooking, cleaning, taking care of children, and most of all, serving the male members of their family, so that they can concentrate all their creative energies on writing.

Later on in the essay, Woolf also argues that the myriad of powerful female figures in canonical western literature might give readers the wrong idea about the position and role of women in western society. Giving a long list of heroines from classics of western literature ranging from Antigone and Medea to Lady Machbeth and Madame Bovary (all created by male writers), Woolf remarks that, "[i]ndeed, if woman had no existence save in the fiction written by men, one would imagine her a person of the utmost importance; very various; heroic and mean; splendid and sordid; infinitely beautiful and hideous in the extreme; as great as a man, some think even greater" (45). "But" Woolf adds, "this is woman in fiction" and in reality, she asserts, "she was locked up, beaten and flung about the room" (45). Therefore, she concludes that it seems "pure waste of time to consult all those gentlemen who specialize in woman and her effect on whatever it may be—politics, children, wages, morality—numerous and learned as they are. One might as well leave their books unopened" (31).

As a solution to the misrepresentation of women in literature created by male writers, Woolf suggests, "What one must do to bring her to life was to think poetically and prosaically at one and the same moment, thus keeping in touch with fact" (46). Woolf's statement is a clear call for women to write about their own experiences in their own words. As stated earlier, one contemporary American woman writer to answer Woolf's call in her writing is Alice Walker. In several of her non-fictional writings, Walker discusses Woolf's relevance for African American women.[3] For instance, her famous essay "In Search of Our Mother's Gardens" demonstrates how Walker follows Woolf's seps in unearthing earlier black women writers. Directly addressing Woolf's ideas regarding the issue of the woman writer's position in society, Walker asks:

> What then are we to make of Phyllis Wheatley, a slave, who owned not even herself? This sickly, frail black girl who required a servant of her own at times—her health was precarious —and who, had she been white, would have been easily considered the intellectual superior of all the women and most of the men in the society of her day. (235)

As the title of her essay clearly shows, Walker's career as a writer is a search for a female tradition within the African American literary history. She has not only produced fictional works with black women as the central characters but also done extensive scholarly research on the works of earlier black American women writers such as Phyllis Wheatley, Nella Larsen and Zora Neale Hurston.[4] The use of the word "womanist" in the subtitle to her collection of essays *In Search of Our Mothers' Gardens: Womanist Prose by Alice Walker* is also reflective of Walker's active involvement in this Woolfian project. As Phil Williams reminds us, "the term 'womanist' was popularized by Pulitzer Prize-winning author Alice Walker in her book *In Search of Our Mothers' Gardens*, and it refers specifically to feminism as seen and studied by women of color." Although the term "womanist" can be applied to many "women of color" such as Audre Lorde, Sandra Cisneros and Gloria Anzaldua, Alice Walker occupies an especially significant place among them since, collectively, the central concern of her body of works is the position and roles of black women in the contemporary world, both in the United States and in Africa.

The Color Purple can be considered as the culmination of Walker's dedication to the specifically womanist project of representing black women's lives. The novel, which made Alice

Walker famous almost overnight, is the life story of its African-
American female protagonist Celie. The story is set in early twentieth
century, in the rural American south, mainly in Georgia, thus
deserving the label "historical novel", a description given by Walker
herself in the article "Writing *The Color Purple*" (355)."[5] The novel is
written in epistolary form; that is. In the first half of the novel, the
letters are written by Celie addressed to God. In the second half, on
the other hand, the majority of the letters represent written
correspondence between Celie and her sister Nettie who is on a
religious mission in Africa although there are still some letters
interspersed in between, written by Celie addressed as "Dear God"
(144,146,148, 177).[6] The first letter is from the time when Celie is
fourteen years old and the rest of the letters follow the development of
her self-realization up to her mid-fifties when she finally inherits her
step-father's house and reunites with her sister Nettie who comes back
from her missionary post in Africa. Throughout the novel, Celie
develops from a young girl occupying total object position to a mature
woman who has the agency over the direction of her own life.

      During her early teenage years, Celie is repeatedly raped by
her father, and furthermore, she is not given any say over the choice of
the man she is going to marry. Similar to the way Woolf demonstrates
from English history in *A Room of One's Own*, Celie is treated like an
animal that could be bartered and traded between men.[7] Her father's
total objectification of her body is most acutely present in the repeated
episodes of rape, starting before the beginning of the narrative when
she is fourteen. He does not treat her as a human being, let alone as his
own daughter; for him, she is only a young and available female body
that could be used for the satisfaction of his carnal desires. The first
time he rapes her, he says, "You gonna do what your mammy
wouldn't" (1). During these episodes of rape, when she starts crying,
he tells her, "You better shut up and git used to it" (1). He also takes
away Celie's two children as soon as they are born, leading her to
believe that he killed them although he sells them to a couple for
adoption. At this point in the narrative, neither Celie nor the reader
knows that he is not her biological father but only the second husband
of her mother. Since Celie is not aware of this fact, the letters reflect
her complex emotions resulting from her experience of rape coupled
with what she considers incest. Moreover, she cannot experience any
joy of motherhood not only because her children are born out of rape
but because they are immediately removed by her father so that he
will not have to support them. Although we do learn later, together

with Celie, that he is not her biological father, it does not make the experience any less painful either for Celie or, indeed, for the reader.

Soon after her mother dies and her second child is taken away by her father, she is sent off to live with Mr. ____, a much older man with several children. Although Mr.____ takes Celie as his wife, the way the marriage contract takes place between Mr.____ and Celie's father reads more as if they are dealing with the transaction of a slave or a horse:

> 'Pa call me. *Celie*, he say. Like it wasn't nothing. Mr. ____ want another look at you.
> I go stand in the door. The sun shine in my eyes. He's still up on his horse.
> Pa rattle his newspaper. Move up, he won't bite, he say.
> I go closer to the steps, but not too close cause I'm a little scared of his horse.
> Turn round, Pa say.
> I turn round.' (10-11)

The fact that he never gets off his horse reveals the power positions between Celia and her husband Mr.____ from the very beginning of their relationship. Significantly, her husband is not named until the end of the novel; he remains as Mr. ____ for most of the novel. It is important that Celie calls him Mr. ____ in her letters even after they have been married for a long time because she does not feel any more intimate with him than she was before the marriage although he satisfies his sexual needs on her every night. She writes in one letter: "But I don't cry. I lay there thinking bout Nettie while he on top of me, wonder if she safe" (12). The fact that he is not named is also important because it was not Celie who picked him as her husband; she simply had to marry him in order to save her little sister Nettie from a similar fate. From the very beginning, Celie knows that Nettie is the one he intends to marry because she is more attractive. As African American critic Thadious Davis states in her article "Walker's Celebration of Self in Southern Generations," the husband becomes "Albert" only after "he discovers reflection which makes him a defined person who can accept the responsibility for his mistakes and the suffering he has caused" (31). These two factors together explain why he remains as Mr.____ as long as Celie is kept in bondage to him within the contract of marriage officiated by her father.

In the many letters Celie writes after she is married, Mr.____ is described not simply as an insensitive and indifferent husband and father, but also as a violent man who resorts to beating his wife and children frequently. In other words, he fully replaces Celie's stepfather. In one of the letters, which describes the earlier stages of their marriage, Celie says,

> 'He beat me like he beat the children. Cept he don't never hardly beat them. He say, Celie, git the belt. The children be outside the room peeking through the cracks. It all I can do not to cry. I make myself wood. I say to myself, Celie, you a tree. That's how come I know trees fear man.' (22)

This touchingly naïve description of the husband's brutal beatings from the perspective of Celie serves for Alice Walker exactly the purpose of "keeping in touch with fact" (46) that Woolf suggests should be the aim of the woman novelist. As discussed earlier, in *A Room of One's Own*, Woolf argues that women are not presented realistically in fiction written by men, so it is useless to look for true representations of women's lives in their books. Like the Harlem Renaissance writer Zora Neale Hurston's novel *Their Eyes Were Watching God* (1937)[8], Walker's novel presents a black woman suffering in the hands of a black man, rather than the more accepted African American tradition of presenting black people suffering the wrongs of the white race. As Mary Ellen Washington writes in the "Forward" to Hurston's novel, Hurston was roundly criticized by the dominant black writers of the period for focusing on a black woman "searching for self-realization" (x). Richard Wright, for example, saw Hurston's novel as arch treachery. He writes in a review, published in *New Masses*, "In the main, her novel is not addressed to the Negro, but to a white audience whose chauvinistic tastes she knows how to satisfy. She exploits that phase of Negro life which is 'quaint,' the phase which evokes a piteous smile on the lips of the 'superior' race" (23).[9] Walker, however, champions Hurston in her own works. Maria Lauret states in her book *Alice Walker*, (an overall evaluation of Walker's achievement as a writer), that "Hurston's example enables Walker to articulate her critique of race and gender relations in the feminist post-Civil Rights era and to theorize it in the concept of womanism" (18). In other words, basing her main character's journey into selfhood on Hurston's model, Walker effectively declares that she has embraced Hurston as her predecessor and rejected the male models of activist black writers such as Richard Wright or Ralph Ellison.

The Color Purple's representation of black women's sufferings in the hands of their own men does not end with physical violence and rape. Celie's husband Mr.____ also keeps an open door policy with his long-term mistress Shug Avery, an unconventional female blues singer. Celie, however, is not upset by this fact, partly because she does not feel any emotional attachment to her husband and partly because she, herself, takes an ineffable liking to Shug. In the end, it is through the agency of Shug Avery, a woman of her own, that Celie comes to realize herself not simply as a woman but, as Walker's definition of the word "womanist" in *In Search of Our Mothers' Gardens* puts, as "a woman who loves other women, sexually and/or nonsexually" (xi). The theme of love and eroticism between women is often considered to be the uniting element of 'womanist' fiction although it is not necessarily an essential component of it.[10] In *The Color Purple*, however, it is very significant that Celie discovers what sexuality means only after she experiences it with Shug. Talking about sex, she says, "I don't know nothing bout it. Mr.____ clam on top of me, do his business, in ten minutes us both asleep. Only time I feel something stirring down there is when I think bout Shug" (65). That is, up to that point, Celie's only experience with sex has involved her being used as a sexual object first by her stepfather, and later by her husband.

Through the example of Celie's awakening into womanhood in *The Color Purple*, Walker seems to suggest that the solution to patriarchal oppression is the formation of bonds between women— sexual or nonsexual. Walker seems to argue that only another woman can truly understand and appreciate the experience of being a woman. Thus, one purpose of 'womanist' fiction could be summarized as locating the source of empathy for women in other women since men lack authenticity of female experience. For this reason, just as Zora Neale Hurston was criticized by Richard Wright and Ralph Ellison for writing realist and celebratory accounts of African-American women's lives, Alice Walker has been accused of being a man-hater, an argument that could be read into Celie's statement that even "trees fear man" (22). For example, when reviewing the Spielberg film adaptation of *The Color Purple* (1985), Pauline Kael accused Walker of "rampant female chauvinism" (69). The assumption behind such negative criticism towards Hurston's and Walker's novels has been that portraying black men negatively would only perpetuate the white prejudice against African-Americans. In other words, prejudiced readers—particularly white Americans—could easily reach the faulty conclusion that the male characters portrayed negatively in these works represent all black men. However, both Hurston's and Walker's agenda is the realistic portrayal of women's lives; and therefore, they should be given credit for "keeping in touch with fact" as Woolf has demanded of women writers writing about women's lives.

As soon as Celie discovers her womanhood—thanks to the friendship and love of Shug—she starts becoming more independent and less servile to Mr. ____:

> 'Now that my eyes opening, I feels like a fool. Next to any little scrub of a bush in my yard, Mr.____'s evil sort of shrink. But not altogether. Still, it is like Shug say, You have to git man off your eyeball, before you can see anything a'tall.' (204)

As reported by Celie, Shug's attitude towards men exemplified here demonstrates the general mood of 'womanist' fiction:

> 'Man corrupt everything, say Shug. He on your box o grits, in your head, and all over the radio.
> He try to make you think he everywhere. Soon as you think he everywhere, you think he God. But he ain't. Whenever you trying to pray, and man plop himself on the other end of it, tell him to git lost, say Shug.' (197)

Although this might sound not only harsh but, more importantly, overly generalized, the affective value and validity of these statements for the women in the novel cannot be denied. Similarly, Virginia Woolf states in *A Room of One's Own* that "[w]omen have served all these centuries as looking-glasses possessing the magic and delicious power of reflecting the figure of man at twice its natural size" (35). Therefore, the essential goal of the patriarchal institution, in order to maintain men's already-existing superiority over women, would be to protect the established assumption that women are innately inferior to men. The discourse of men with god-like powers that Shug criticizes in the above excerpt as well as the common perception of God in the male persona as "He" is so pervasive in Celie's psyche that, initially, she simply crumbles under the pressure of going against it. She says, "this is hard work, let me tell you. He been there so long, he don't budge. He threaten lightening, floods and earthquakes" (197).

Together with her newly-born subjectivity, Celie also discovers her creative side. As women's studies scholar Keith Byerman points out, upon Shug's encouragement, "Celie begins making pants, especially purple ones (a color associated with Shug's regal bearing), for herself and others" (65). The for-women-only quality of the pants is significant in the novel as wearing pants would symbolically impart agency to the women who wear them. That is why, for example, the first time Shug suggests that Celie should wear pants, Celie responds, "Mr.____ not going to let his wife wear pants" (146). Moreover, just as the quilt in other fictional works of Walker represents female bonding[11], the pants in *The Color Purple* act as a symbol for female bonding. Although the pants are made by one woman only, they are shared among many women. Celie takes an exception to the for-women-only rule when she makes pants for Shug's son Jack too, because she explains, "Jack is tall and kind and don't hardly say anything. Love children. Respect his wife, Odessa, and all Odessa amazon sisters. Anything she want to take on, he right there" (213). Another example of a positive male character in the novel is Mr.____'s son Harpo. Harpo's relationship with his wife Sophia and the way he treats women in general is the polar opposite of his father's relationships with women.[12] This and other positive examples of male characters treating women decently in the novel show that Walker is not in fact a man-hater, but she is depicting the doubly oppressed position of African-American women in the hands of both whites and the oppressive and violent black men. Editor Harold Bloom quotes Alice Walker saying,

> We live in a society, as blacks, women, and artists, whose contests we do not design and with whose insistence on ranking us we are permanently at war. To know that second place, in such a society, has often required more work and innate genius than first, a longer, grimmer struggle over greater odds than first. (1)

As her own words clearly demonstrate, Alice Walker's feminist discourse is in line with Woolf's propaganda in *A Room of One's Own* for creating the necessary social conditions so that women can participate in all areas of life as much as men do. In a similar vein, Walker's essay "In Search of Our Mothers' Gardens" asks, "What did it mean for a black woman to be an artist in our grandmothers' time? In our great-grandmothers' day? It is a question with an answer cruel enough to stop the blood" (233). Therefore, Walker's depiction of Celie's struggles in *The Color Purple* could be considered as symbolizing the struggles of black women artists to survive and produce creative works of art in a society that is not only racist but sexist as well.

The first action Celie takes after discovering her selfhood as a woman is to move out of her husband's house to Shug's house in Memphis, leaving her husband behind. The implication of this, of course, is that as long as she stays under the roof of a dominant male figure as her husband, she cannot realize her creative potentials. Thus, Shug and Mr.____ are juxtaposed as polar opposites in terms of their influence on Celie's life; while her husband's presence is a stifling influence on Celie's creativity, Shug's presence only nurtures it and allows it to reach its full potential. From the very beginning of their cohabitation, Celie's relationship with Shug is put in contrast to her former relationship with her husband. In her marriage to Mr.____ , Celie was in the position of a house servant. On the other hand, once Celie moves in with her, Shug is quick to remind her: "You not my maid. I didn't bring you to Memphis to be that. I brought you here to love you and help you get on your feet" (211). As seen in her attitude towards Celie in this passage, Shug not only considers Celie as her equal but also indicates that she is acting as Celie's mentor so that she could become like herself, a woman of her own.

When Celie says that she feels the need to earn her own living, Shug reminds her that she is already earning her living with the sale of the pants that she has been making: "You making your living, Celie, she say. Girl, you on your way" (214). The letter that immediately follows this letter in the novel opens with Celie's projecting a positive mood for the first time: "I am so happy. I got love, I got work, I got money, friends and time" (215). It is significant that Celie puts forth her own income as a source of happiness; it would not be far-fetched to conclude that Celie could not have uttered this when her life was bound to that of Mr.____ because he had to power to tell her who to see and what to do. In *Three Guineas* (1938), Virginia Woolf argues that women should attain "freedom from unreal loyalties" (80) to men and patriarchy[13]; in other words, as long as women are financially dependent on men, they cannot claim to have an independent mind and thus, will not be able to produce creative works of art. In "In Search of Our Mothers' Gardens," speaking of previous generations of black women writers, Walker arrives at the same conclusion: "when we read the novels of Nella Larsen or the oddly false-sounding autobiography of that freest of all black women writers, Zora Hurston—evidence of 'contrary instincts' is everywhere. Her loyalties were completely divided, as was, without question, her mind" (236). Similarly, Celie's creative outburst occurs only after she strips herself of the servile position that she occupied in relation to Mr.____ and is able to stand on her own feet with the help of the money she earns herself.

Having freed herself from the "unreal loyalties" to the patriarchal society at large and the obligations to her husband in particular, Celie can now stand on her own feet and assert her agency over her own life as represented in her newly-gained power over the selection of who to associate with and who to choose as her lover. At this point in the novel, Walker gives Celie the ultimate symbol of her complete freedom from male dominance: a house of her own. After Celie's stepfather dies, it is revealed that the house he lived in legally belonged to her mother; therefore, as her only surviving children, Celie and Nettie inherit the dwelling. At first, Celie does not know what to do with it: "But I never had no house, I say. Just to think about having *my own house* enough to scare me" (245, my emphasis). Although this ending might sound a bit unrealistic and contrived from a craft perspective, it has very important implications for Walker's agenda in this novel. As writer Mae G. Henderson quotes from an interview, Walker says of Celie, "I liberated her from her own history [...]I wanted her to be happy" (67). In this sense, the novel not only serves as a realistic representation of black women's lives in the past as a proper historical novel should, but it also presents contemporary black women an ideal to strive for.

The fact that, in the conclusion of the novel, Alice Walker gives Celie a house of her own is not only a remarkable reference to Woolf's essay but it also reveals that Walker consciously uses the house as a symbol for Celie's ultimate achievement of freedom from patriarchy. Although she shares the ownership of the house with Nettie, this does not pose any threats for either Celie or Alice Walker because the 'womanist' nature of the novel propagates the idea that female bonding only enriches and supports female freedom from patriarchy. Feminist critic Barbara Christian argues that "Celie's attainment of freedom affects not only others of her sisters, but her brothers as well" (53). At the end of the novel, Celie opens the doors of her house to not only Shug, Nettie and her other female friends, but also the male members of their family, who treat women with respect and, therefore, do not constitute a threat to female freedom. Moreover, even her husband goes through a transformation for the better, which is also indicated, as stated earlier, with the switch from "Mr.____" to "Albert" in the text. As scholar Candice M. Jenkins states, he "learns to relinquish his power to dominate in order to engage in more human and egalitarian relationships with everyone around him" (994). In a way, as feminist scholar Barbara Christian points out, the freedom of women also frees the men from their bondage to patriarchy and the strictly defined roles of manhood that they have come to perform without questioning.

Alice Walker's novel *The Color Purple* is arguably not the greatest novel ever written when looked at from the perspective of writing as craft. At times it seems, as William Willimon argues, that it "could only have been created by a writer more interested in writing a polemic than a novel" (319). On the contrary, Walker's 'womanist' polemic in *The Color Purple* should hardly be considered as a shortcoming. Activist African American women like Alice Walker in the post-Civil Rights Act era did not have the luxury of subtlety since the urgency of their cultural context required them to take action in the more direct routes. Virginia Woolf was similarly accused of employing too much polemic by male critics in the 1930s regarding both her fiction and her anti-patriarchal position in her book-length essays *A Room of One's Own* and *Three Guineas*. In *Virginia Woolf as Feminist*, feminist scholar Naomi Black points out that these hostile reactions can be summarized in the words of Woolf's nephew and first biographer Quentin Bell who wrote that *"Three Guineas* was an irrational cry of feminist anguish" (5). Woolf was writing in the aftermath of the passing of the universal suffrage law in England in 1919, and an important component of Woolf's intention in writing these polemical works is to demonstrate that simply because women are equal to men in law did not mean women's fight to get equal rights should be over since the law did not guarantee equality for women in everyday life. In other words, unlike male critics, Naomi Black, for example, thinks that Woolf's goal in these polemical writings was "to document the details of continuing sexism" (5).[14]

Alice Walker ingeniously contrives to adopt Woolf's feminist concept of "a room of one's own" to fit into her own specific context of African-American women's experiences in *The Color Purple*. The story of Celie's journey from a doubly oppressed position to complete freedom and agency over her own life serves the purpose of both exemplifying black women's lives from the past and pointing out to contemporary and future generations of black women that they can also be liberated "from [their] own history" (Walker quoted in Christian 67). Since Walker was working in the wake of the Civil Rights Act of 1964, *The Color Purple* can be read as part of her overall feminist agenda to help African American women claim the rights that have already been given them by law but had not been achieved in real life. It is the work of such free spirited, activist women writers as Virginia Woolf and Alice Walker that has brought about more gender equality in their respective societies by increasing consciousness among women and men alike. To conclude, as scholar Maria Lauret states, "Woolf's polemical work, in other words, is productive for African American writers like Alice Walker, whilst at the same time our engagement with Walker illuminates Woolf" (24). *The Color Purple* can be read as the product of this dialogue between Virginia Woolf and Alice Walker; yet, as Lauret's statement implies, there is room for further investigation into this dialogue, particularly to see how our engagement with Walker can shed light on our understanding of Woolf.

Turgay Bayindir, Purdue University

Notes

[1] *A Room of One's Own* is a lengthy essay, first published in 1929. The printed version is based on two papers Virginia Woolf read to the Arts Society at Newnham College and the Odtaa at Girton College in 1928. Newnham and Girton are two of the earliest women's colleges at Cambridge University.

[2] *The House on Mango Street* is a coming-of-age novella, written in the form of a series of vignettes. It focuses on the life of a Latina girl, Esperanza, in a predominantly Chicano neighborhood of Chicago. Cisneros dedicated the book "A las Mujeres" (To the Women) (vii).

[3] In terms of Walker's discussion of Virginia Woolf, of particular significance are the two essays, "In Search of Our Mothers' Gardens" and "One Child of One's Own," both of which are printed in *In Search of Our Mothers' Gardens*.

[4] Walker talks about her extensive search in the 1970s for the then-forgotten African American woman writer Zora Neale Hurston in the two essays, "Zora Neale Hurston: A Cautionary Tale and a Partisan View" and "Looking for Zora." Both of these essays also appear in *In Search of Our Mothers' Gardens*.

[5] In "Writing *The Color Purple*," also printed in *In Search of Our Mothers' Gardens*, Walker explains how the story first germinated in her mind as a historical novel.

[6] Interestingly, a stretch of seven letters written by Celie to Nettie in the second half of the novel end with "Amen" (192-225) while the letters addressed as "Dear God" do not have this adage. The only exception to this is the very last letter which is addressed as "Dear God. Dear stars, dear trees, dear sky, dear peoples. Dear Everything. Dear God" (285).

[7] In the oft anthologized "Chapter Three" of *A Room of One's Own*, Woolf narrates the imaginary story of Shakespeare's sister to prove that "it would have been impossible, completely and entirely, for any woman to have written the plays of Shakespeare in the age of Shakespeare" (48) since such genius could not "have been born among women whose work began, according to Professor Travelyan, almost before they were out of the nursery, who were forced to it by their parents and held to it by all the power of law and custom" (50).

[8] In *Their Eyes Were Watching God*, the main character Janie Crawford, an African American woman in her forties, retrospectively narrates her life story which takes places around the first quarter of the twentieth century. The novel is set in central Florida, mainly in Eatonville which is a historically existing town that was one of the first all-black communities in the US. For an in-depth discussion of Hurston and *Their Eyes Were Watching God*, see *Zora Neale Hurston: Critical Perspectives Past and Present* eds. Henry Louis Gates Jr. & Kwame Anthony Appiah.

[9] Another hostile criticism of the novel comes from the famous Harlem Renaissance intellectual Alain Locke, who wrote in *Opportunity*, "when will the Negro novelist of maturity, who knows how to tell a story convincingly—which is Miss Hurston's cradle gift, come to grips with motive fiction and social document fiction?" (22).

[10] In the epigraph to *In Search of Our Mothers' Gardens* (xi-xii), Walker provides four different definitions of the word "womanist," only one of which containing references to eroticism between women.

[11] Of particular interest is the short story "Everyday Use," included in Walker's short story collection *In Love & Trouble: Stories of Black Women* (1973). The story uses the quilt as a symbol of mother-daughter bonding and a ritualistic tool for female initiation.

[12] The complex relationship between Harpo and Sophia and their norm-defying marriage deserve an in-depth analysis that is beyond the scope of this paper. For this and other masculine gender related aspects of the novel, see Candice M. Jenkins, "Queering Black patriarchy: The Salvic wish and masculine possibility in Alice Walker's *The Color Purple*."

[13] *Three Guineas* is a collection of three essays Woolf wrote in response to three different letters from three different societies appealing to Woolf for financial contribution. Unlike Woolf's earlier works, these essays are overtly political, which shows Woolf's increasing desperation in the face of growing fascism in Europe and the looming catastrophe of another world war.

[14] Naomi Black's recent book *Virginia Woolf as Feminist* is an insightful study of the non-fictional feminist writings of Woolf. In this valuable work, Black particularly reclaims *Three Guineas* as one of the founding texts of twentieth century feminism.

Works Cited

Bloom, Harold, ed. *Alice Walker* New York: Chelsea House, 1989.

Black, Naomi. *Virginia Woolf as Feminist* Ithaca, NY: Cornell U, 2004.

Byerman, Keith. "Walker's Blues" in Bloom (1989): 59-66.

Christian, Barbara. "The Black Woman Artist as Wayward" in Bloom(1989): 39-58.

Cisneros, Sandra. *The House on Mango Street* New York: Vintage Books, 1984.

Davis, Thadious M. "Walker's Celebration of Self in Southern Generations" in Bloom (1989): 25-37.

Gates, Henry L. Jr. and K.A. Appiah eds. *Zora Neale Hurston: Critical Perspectives Past and Present* New York: Amistad, 1993.

Henderson, Mae G. "*The Color Purple*: Revisions and Redefinitions" in Bloom (1989): 67-80.

Jenkins, Candice M. "Queering Black Patriarchy: The Salvic Wish and Masculine Possibility in Alice Walker's *The Color Purple*" *Modern Fiction Studies* 48:4 (Winter 2002): 969-1000.

Kael, Pauline. "Current Cinema: Sacred Monsters." *The New Yorker* (30 December 1985): 69.

Lauret, Maria. *Alice Walker* New York: St. Martin's, 2000.

Locke, Alain. "Literature by and about the Negro." *Opportunity* (1 June 1938): 22.

Walker, Alice. *The Color Purple* (1982) Orlando: Harcourt, 2003.

—. "Everyday Use" in *In Love & Trouble: Stories of Black Women* Orlando, FL: Harcourt, 1973. (47-59)

—. "Looking for Zora" in Walker (1983): 93-116.

—. "One Child of One's Own: A Meaningful Digression within the Work(s)" in Walker (1983): 361-83.

—. *In Search of Our Mothers' Gardens* New York: Harcourt, Brace, Jovanovich, 1983.

—. "In Search of Our Mothers' Gardens" in Walker (1983): 231-43.

—. "Writing *The Color Purple*" in Walker (1983): 355-60.

—. "Zora Neale Hurston: A Cautionary Tale and a Partisan View" in Walker (1983): 83-92.

Washington, Mary Helen. "Foreword" in *Their Eyes Were Watching God* (1937) New York: Perennial Classics, 1998. (ix-xvii)
Williams, Phil. "Subscribing to the Theory" On line at: http://www.uga.edu/columns/000522/campnews.html (consulted 3 May 2005).

Willimon, William H. "Seeing Red over *The Color Purple*." *Christian Century* (2 April 1986): 319.

Woolf, Virginia. *A Room of One's Own* (1929) New York: Harvest / HBJ, 1959.

—. *Three Guineas* (1938) New York: Harvest / HBJ, 1966.

Wright, Richard. "Between Laughter and Tears." *New Masses* (5 October 1937): 22-23.

Adapting and Integrating: *The Color Purple* as Broadway Musical

Kathryn Edney

Although it became a Broadway smash in 2006, the musical version of *The Color Purple* was never assured of becoming a sure-fire hit. While the show followed the recent trend of adapting non-musical films for the musical stage, it remained a risky financial and artistic proposition for many reasons. Broadway musicals have always been incredibly expensive to produce, much more so than straight plays. Many shows struggle to break even; in fact, statistics show that four out of five musicals never make a profit (Adler 15-16; Berfield 104; Rosenberg and Harburg 12-15). In addition, the musical version of *The Color Purple* threatened to attract the same types of criticisms regarding the legitimacy of the adaptation that had haunted Steven Spielberg's film version of Alice Walker's novel. Indeed, given the popular notion that musical theater equates to "light and fluffy," fears about how appropriate it was to musicalize Celie's story were perhaps a given.

The Color Purple also posed significant concerns for fans of musical theater at a time when the trend of recycling familiar films into musical theater productions led critics once again to question the very future of musical theater: didn't Broadway have anything new and original to offer as it had in previous decades? Along with this fear regarding a lack of original ideas, the nature of the creative team behind *The Color Purple:* troubled traditional theatergoers. In particular, *The Color Purple* used three composers working collaboratively—Brenda Russell, Allee Willis, and Stephen Bray—none of whom had experience in writing for a Broadway show. Moreover, the man responsible for bringing *The Color Purple* to the stage, Scott Sanders, was white, and he too had no experience with musical theater. This combined lack of experience, which signified to many that the music component of this new musical would be neglected for visual spectacle, coupled with *Purple*'s huge cast, recalled the standardized European megamusicals pioneered by Andrew Lloyd Webber and Tim Rice in shows such as *Cats* (1982) where (to the minds of many) soft rock and exotic scenery trumped both music and a convincing narrative.

   To help offset the many financial risks, the creators of *The Color Purple* therefore followed the practice of developing and refining the musical play in a regional production space—Atlanta's Alliance Theater—out of the direct line of sight of New York drama critics (Adler 15-17; Hughes W9).[1] By opening in Atlanta, composers new to Broadway would have the opportunity to test out their music and discover ways of integrating their songs into the narrative of the show. Developing the musical out-of-town also provided producers with the opportunity to create "buzz" for the show, creating demand for *The Color Purple* long before its official debut in New York City. The history that surrounded the source material—novel and film—although potentially problematic, did guarantee that the original production of the musical would garner a lot of media attention (Hutcheon 5). All this initial attention became even more intense as the show made the transition from the Alliance Theater to Broadway, and once Oprah Winfrey decided to invest in the production, the intense scrutiny turned into a feeding frenzy.

   But there is something intriguing about the rhetoric employed by the multiple co-creators of *The Color Purple* to deal with the perhaps understandable skepticism of the press and public. Everyone, including the show's three songwriters and the actors, and finally even Oprah herself, argued that this musical with its all-black cast and focus on a loving lesbian relationship fell squarely within the classic model of the "integrated musical" pioneered by Richard Rodgers and Oscar Hammerstein. They all defined *The Color Purple* as "universal" and as "old-fashioned" as 1943's *Oklahoma!* This impulse to place *The Color Purple* within a "universal" genre framework ignored the musical's connections and similarities to other all-black musicals such as *Jelly's Last Jam* (1992), *Dreamgirls* (1981), and even *Shuffle Along* (1921), and so removed the show from the problematic relationship African Americans have historically had with the Great White Way. Only very rarely did reviewers or cultural critics, from either white or African American media outlets, make this larger history visible.

   A closer analysis of *The Color Purple* will thus open up a reexamination of the problematic relationship between blacks and Broadway. This essay will first examine the text and music of *The*

Color Purple in relation both to the general history of representations of blackness on the Broadway stage and to specific earlier all-black musicals. Second, it will explore the critical and promotional rhetoric surrounding the musical before and after it opened on in New York City. Specific attention will be paid to how *The Color Purple* was rhetorically "normalized" to align it within the genre conventions of the idealized Broadway musical epitomized by the works of Rodgers and Hammerstein. By so doing, the co-creators of *The Color Purple* not only removed the show from the segregated history of Broadway, they also simultaneously worked to separate the musical from the British megamusical subgenre, thus emphasizing its Americaness.

Some Definitions

Allen Woll correctly points out that the term "black musical":

> has defined a variety of theatrical presentations. At times these words connote an entirely Afro-American creation: blacks onstage and behind the scenes shaping the final work for black audiences. On other occasions [...] black artists created these shows for predominantly white audiences." (xiii)

The African American playwright and director, Douglas Turner Ward defined "black theater" as "by, about, with, for and related to blacks" (qtd. by Blau 17), but also he noted that for a production to be classified as black theater not all of these attributes needed to be present, just some of them. The question of what a black musical "is" becomes further complicated by the historical relationship between blackface performance, (white) American musical theater, the black musical, and the politics of representation these relationships entail.

This concern over what, precisely, is meant by "black theater" much less "black musical theater" is certainly not recent. As a result of the Great Migration from southern rural to northern urban states that began in the 1910s, African American artists and intellectuals of all kinds experienced a collective creative surge that lasted from the 1920s through the 1930s. Known now as the Harlem Renaissance—a misnomer since the movement was not limited to New York—the period saw a dramatic surge of artistic output from African Americans and a corresponding surge of interest in that art from many white (upper middle class) Americans (Douglas; Hutchinson 14-25). Although the literature, paintings, and sculptures of the Harlem

Renaissance tend to dominate scholarly discourse surrounding the movement, it should not be forgotten that 1926 saw the establishment of the Krigwa Little Theater Movement, thus answering the call from black intellectual leaders—including W.E.B. DuBois, Langston Hughes, and Theophilus Lewis—for a "Negro national theater" about, by, and for African Americans. Unfortunately, Krigwa was only moderately successful, and white American representations of black American lives, with its roots in nineteenth century blackface minstrelsy, continued to dominate the theatrical stage during the 1920s and 1930s, and indeed throughout the twentieth century (Douglas 100; Johnson 166-68; Sanders 20-21).

As many scholars have noted, modern American musical theater is a mongrel art with a long and extensive pre-history; its sources of influence can be traced to European comic operas, Gilbert and Sullivan operettas, burlesque shows, and blackface minstrel shows. Over time, each of these different genres of entertainment added different elements—pretty chorus girls in tights, comic plots, a particular use of music, and formal structure—to what we now consider to be modern American musical theater. And during the 1970s and 1980s, these same elements were worked and reworked by men such as Stephen Sondheim and Andrew Lloyd Webber, who attempted to breathe new life into what by then seemed to be outworn traditions that had little place in modern popular culture (Preston 3-28; Sternfeld 1-13).[2]

Minstrel shows in particular had a profound influence on musical theater with their use of popular songs grounded in African American music (or, at least, an Anglo-American perception of African American music). Just as important, this music, quite distinct from the models of Anglo-European entertainment, reacted to and was shaped by American concerns. As Eric Lott has demonstrated, blackface minstrelsy was not just rehearsing wider national anxieties about race, but also about gender and class as well (89-107). Minstrel shows were part of American popular culture that quickly reacted to changing events within society—everything from women's suffrage to international politics—through music, dance, and satire (Lhamon 150-208). And because minstrel shows were effectively variety shows, they had the ability to add and discard certain acts or songs as the circumstances demanded without damaging the overall structure of a production. Sketches and songs were only very loosely connected; there was rarely a coherent narrative in place. This basic function and structure of minstrel shows profoundly influenced the shape and sounds of the modern American musical until 1943's *Oklahoma!* by Richard Rodgers and Oscar Hammerstein, although that influence often remains unacknowledged.

Prior to *Oklahoma!*, musicals tended not to worry overmuch about whether or not its songs functioned logically within the context of the story, although the plots of pre-1940s musicals tended to be rather simple. A specialty number or a romantic song would be sung directly to the audience ("presented") as if the singer was in a concert setting rather than a character in a show. In other words, songs in these earlier musicals literally stopped the show, rather than forwarding the plot or deepening character development. In addition, to a certain extent, prior to *Oklahoma!*, much of mainstream musical theater might have been characterized as "black musical theater," given the influence of African American musical ideas on the form. Whereas musicals of the 1910s-1930s tended to focus on comedy, and urban contemporary life and musical sounds—the shows of George and Ira Gershwin are a prime example—*Oklahoma!* set the American musical in America's heartland of the nineteenth century, deploying Western musical motifs that borrowed very little, if at all, from the African American musical tradition (Sears 120-28).

But what *Oklahoma!* is best known for is its "integration," not in terms of the racial make-up of its cast, but rather in terms of the structure of the musical. The songs did not come from "out of nowhere" and stop the action; instead, the songs worked with the narrative to help further its message. Rodgers and Hammerstein consciously worked toward this goal of turning the musical comedy, where no explanation for a song was ever needed, into the musical play, where the use of a song needed to be motivated, needed a reason to exist. This is not to say that musicals prior to 1943 had never attempted such integration; *Showboat* (1927), *Porgy and Bess* (1935), *Pal Joey* (1940), *Lady in the Dark* (1941), could all lay claim to the title of "the first" integrated musical in terms of the attempt to find a reason for a song, but it was *Oklahoma!* that captured the imaginations and changed the expectations of audiences where, for whatever reasons, these earlier shows had not. Nor is it possible to say that all musicals following in the wake of *Oklahoma!* aspired to or achieved the idealized "integration" attributed to this musical. Indeed, recently some scholars, such as Scott McMillin, have begun to dismantle the idea that *Oklahoma!*, or any musical, is "integrated," given the particular ways in which songs and music function within the context of any theatrical piece. But, it is the case that *Oklahoma!*

is still generally held up as the standard, as the first and best example, of the ideal of the "integrated musical," especially within the popular imagination.

Brief History and Patterns of the Black Musical

As the (white) American musical developed in New York City over the course of the nineteenth and into the twentieth century, the black American musical slowly evolved along a parallel, but very similar line as its mainstream rivals. Because African Americans were living in a segregated society, few had the opportunity to perform on mainstream stages in an integrated cast. The few who were afforded the opportunity—Bert Williams is one central example—were required to darken their faces when performing, essentially acting and singing a version of the blackface minstrelsy begun by white entertainers in the nineteenth century. The power structure on Broadway also meant that all-black cast musicals had to find their own stages off-Broadway on which to perform; if the musical "crossed over" to white, mainstream success, then a show might be transferred to Broadway proper (Woll 58).

The relative success of the black musical during the 1920s and 1930s had quite a lot to do with the Harlem Renaissance and the fact that African American culture was "in vogue" with upper and middle-class white Americans during this period. The desire of whites to see what blacks were "really like" had earlier manifested itself in the attendance of blackface shows where white men darkened their faces with burnt cork, but suddenly expanded to include the consumption of African American literature, art, music, and drama (Fisher 115-117). As Langston Hughes famously said, it was a time when "the Negro was in vogue" and white Americans would make trips down into Harlem clubs to experience a different way of life (77-80).

And, if someone was not brave enough to venture onto the unfamiliar streets of Harlem, then the theater could provide some measure of what blacks were "really" like. *Shuffle Along* (1921), although not the first all-black musical, is certainly one the most famous from this period, and was credited by Langston Hughes with kicking off the Harlem Renaissance (Hughes 77-80). Eubie Blake, Noble Sissle, Flournay Miller and Aubrey Lyles created the show, loosely based on an older vaudeville skit entitled "The Mayor of Dixie," created by Miller and Lyles. The skit eventually expanded to involve a contested mayoral race, political corruption, and love across class lines. The musical score was built around jazz—it featured the song "I'm Just Wild About Harry"—but because the setting of the show was the Deep South, the cast spoke in a thick regional dialect. Thus, although groundbreakingly modern in many regards, *Shuffle Along* also perpetuated many of the performance stereotypes rooted in blackface minstrel shows (Woll 57-60). Not surprisingly, the show also spawned a fair number of sequels and imitations, but black theater also suffered the same fate of much of black art and literature after the Great Depression took hold of the United States. The Negro fell out of the mainstream's field of interest.

The difficulty of representing an "authentic" African American experience that did not cater to white expectations continued to haunt black musical theater throughout its history. Later revues or celebratory shows such as *Ain't Misbehavin'* (1978) or *Five Guys Named Moe* (1992) were often characterized as being too positive by critics, as both neglecting a history of racism and the history of white representations of blacks on stage and off. The "feel good" music and nostalgia for an earlier, seemingly less complicated era, took the place of historical realities. In addition, these productions, as revues, were generally plotless and relied on ready-made compositions from famous artists placed within a slim narrative framework. Sometimes called "jukebox musicals"—where a show consists of already familiar songs rather than new compositions—their performances were thus not truly musicals in the *Oklahoma!* sense of the term. Jukebox musicals, as Holden notes, had no original musical and often had very little, if any, plot (A15).[3]

More serious shows like *Dreamgirls* (1981)—about the rise and fall of a 1960s era all-girl singing trio—can be categorized as fitting within the ideal of the integrated musical. It used a very particular musical vocabulary, Motown, without simply forcing pre-existing Motown songs into the narrative. However, it was artistically controlled and created by whites, perhaps throwing into question its status as a "black musical." *Jelly's Last Jam* (1991), created by the African American playwright George C. Wolfe about the life of jazz composer Jelly Roll Morton, is one of the very few modern American musicals not only created by a predominantly black creative team and featuring an nearly all-black cast, but also dealing explicitly with the influence of blackface in American entertainment and the importance of African and African American history in popular culture. Although the music of Morton was used, composer Luther Henderson adapted the jazz music to fit the needs of the show.

Although very different structurally and politically, there is one crucial link between these various black musicals of the late twentieth century. Whether they were "jukebox" or integrated shows, these musicals attempted to emphasize the importance of African American music in the wider American culture and to use different musical styles as a means to delineate particular historical periods. Of course, as noted above, the ways in which African American music was showcased in different productions could fall within a wide spectrum from apolitical to obviously political. A show like *Ain't Misbehavin'* was content to simply introduce the music of a composer like Fats Waller to an unknowing audience with little narrative or historical context. In contrast, *Jelly's Last Jam* embedded its music within the larger histories of slavery, segregation, and exploitation through a fictionalized biographical narrative.

The Color Purple – Music and Plot

The plot of the musical version for *The Color Purple* largely follows the novel on which it is based. Indeed, the musical follows the book so closely that reviewers either criticized librettist Marsha Norman for overstuffing the narrative, or praised her for including so many important elements crucial to Walker's novel. Richard Kislan notes that there are five major elements in a musical's book (that is, its script): characters, plot, situation, dialogue/language, and theme (177). What is important to notice here is that the plot is secondary to the characters. This is not to say that the plot is not important to a musical, but rather that a musical generally cares more about the emotional development of its characters—and it is through music and dance that much of this emotional exploration takes place—than it does about a complex story.

Although there have certainly been many musicals that engage with complex issues and/or plots, there is some truth to the cliché that musicals tend to be variations on the "boy-meets-loses-finds-girl" theme. Music and dance takes up much of the space that is normally occupied by plot twists within a non-musical play, resulting in more streamlined stories for musicals. In contrast, *The Color Purple* is a commentary on the struggles of African American women that spans decades, but it also encompasses child abuse and incest, the meaning of family, contemplations about women's relationship to

God, and often a consideration of heterosexual and homosexual love. The first act, in seven scenes, covers Celie's early childhood up until the point when she discovers the letters from her sister Nettie that Mister had hidden from her. In an unusual modification for a second act in a musical, the culminating act is one scene longer than the first, and begins with Çelie's reading the letters and recreating Africa in her mind from Nettie's descriptions of it. The show then moves swiftly through the end of Celie and Mister's marriage, the relationship between Celie and Shug, and Celie's coming into her own as an independent woman. The show concludes when Celie and Nettie are finally reunited, with Celie rediscovering her faith in God indicated by the final reprise of the song "The Color Purple." Within this main story, the love triangle between the secondary characters Sofia, Harpo, and Squeak is included, although, as in the movie, Squeak is little more than an obstacle between Sofia and Harpo.

Whether one feels that the plot of the musical is "overstuffed" or "oversimplified," it is still the case that in adapting from one medium to another the structural and/or genre requirements of the medium needs to be taken into account. For example, in considering the adaptation of *The Color Purple* for the movie screen, it is crucial to realize one of the fundamental differences between a movie and novel: the former relies on images over words to relate its message. While this point may seem incredibly obvious, it does help to keep in mind that during the process of adaptation, there is no such thing as perfect fidelity to the original text because modes of expression vary between different forms of art. Thus, when considering the transformation of *The Color Purple* into a musical theater text, it is important to understand that integrated musicals realize their fullest emotional expressions through song and dance performed in real time, and only secondarily through visual spectacle and dialogue (Hutcheon 1-13).

It is the transformation from written text to performative text that necessitated the largest changes to *The Color Purple*, not in terms of thematics or narrative so much as in terms of meeting the pressures of the genre of musical theater which require that all of the important characters are given their own voice and their own songs. Although *The Color Purple* as a novel is, as scholar Maria Lauret has noted, indebted to African American musical forms and although its musicality is embedded within the language and rhythms of Walker's text, the jazz and blue motifs contained within the novel are all filtered through Celie's, and later her sister Nettie's, uniquely written voices (101-120). In contrast, *The Color Purple* as a musical show must allow for a greater multiplicity of voices, all of whom relate their own points of view using their own particular musical motifs.

The short overture for *The Color Purple* prepares its audience for the music it should expect to hear throughout the course of the show; the first strains of the music are lush and dominated by the bright sounds of trumpets. The music then segues into a bluesy riff, prominently featuring the piano and muting the final notes of the horns. But immediately following this bit of raucous blues, the smooth pop sounds come to the forefront once again, before the show launches into the first song, "Huckleberry Pie."[4] Overtures for musicals generally function to familiarize an audience with the songs they are about to hear as the show progresses. Further, the overture prepares the audience for the type of musical they are about to see by foreshadowing the tone of the show through the use of -particular songs from the production (Kislan 221-222). However, the overture for *The Color Purple* is rather unusual in meeting this requirement as it features only three songs: "What About Love?," "Push Da Button" and "The Color Purple," but it serves its purpose remarkably well, setting up the blueprint for the musical as a whole.

The overture highlights the importance of pop music to the show and the subservient position other forms of music will take in relation to the soft rock palette. This fact is highlighted by the relative importance of the three songs featured within it. Both "What About Love?" and "The Color Purple" are central to the emotional progression of the musical as a whole, and both will be featured in reprises. They are sung by Celie and highlight her as the central character and star. "Push Da Button," while an entertaining number and providing the opportunity for characters to cut loose in song and dance, could be removed from the musical without harming the narrative or the emotional development of its characters. The song occurs within the context of a jook joint performance and is therefore a moment of spectacle; in fact it is a celebration of pure performance for performance's sake. This is not a meant as a criticism of the number itself rather the purpose here is to highlight how "Push da Button" functions within the overall context of the musical version. While not out of place within the show, it is simply not as important as either "What About Love" or "The Color Purple" to either the story or the characters.

Although *The Color Purple* does employ musical motifs from blues, jazz, gospel, and work songs, they are used in very particular ways and generally restricted to secondary characters. For example, blues music is closely associated to Shug Avery to suggest her sexual prowess (and perhaps her independence as well); conversely, in the song "Hell No!" Sofia first uses the blues and then gospel music to demonstrate her strength, independence, and authenticity as a black woman. These various musical styles are also occasionally used to mark a historical progression as the story moves forward in time; a shift from 1910s-sounding blues to the more complex sounds of 1940s jazz indicates a clear change in the historical period from the first act to the second. In contrast, the pop sounds are both ahistorical and anachronistic, occurring consistently throughout the musical and overwhelmingly sung by Celie when she is considering romance or making major decisions in her life.

However, since the pop sounds are so generic, Celie's musical motifs tend to rob her of her particularity as a character. Musically, and to a certain extent lyrically as well, Celie's songs could be sung by superstar Beyoncé Knowles with few alterations. In contrast, it is difficult to imagine "Hell No" being performed by anyone other than the character of Sofia. Thus, while Celie is clearly in the process of finding her own voice and the means to tell her own story in the novel version of *The Color Purple*, she very nearly disappears from the musical version by virtue of the music she sings.

The three individual composers/lyricists of *The Color Purple*—Russell, Willis, and Bray—are all accomplished pop songwriters; each one had previously worked with a variety of performers including Sting, Mary J. Blige, The Pointer Sisters, and Madonna (Funderburg, *Memory Book* 18-20). It is therefore not all that surprising that much of the score for *The Color Purple* sounds as if it belonged on a Top 40 radio station. However, in terms of the larger history of musical theater, the use of more or less generic sounding pop music within *The Color Purple* is not atypical for this current period of musical theater history. Since the rise of the megamusical during the 1980s, generic rather than particularized musical sounds have tended to predominate on the American musical stage. This tendency toward generic sounds is usually attributed to megamusicals, such as *Cats* or *Les Miserables*, which were created by Europeans and meant for a mass, international market. The more familiar—or generic—the music, the easier it is to transport (and translate) a production from country to country. Over the course of the 1990s and through the early part of the twenty-first century, American creators of musicals began to borrow from the European megamusical model because they recognized its enormous popularity. The result are shows like *The Producers* which, while solidly American in tone and subject matter, has what many have characterized as a forgettable musical score (Sternfeld 339-352). Using music that is particularly associated with African Americans within *The Color Purple* thus ensured that the show would not be mistaken for its European counterparts and guaranteed the show's "authentic" black pedigree.

As Portia K. Maultsby (as have many others) has demonstrated, one cannot say that American pop music is separate from African American music (183-184). In fact in the United States, music from black performers and communities has crossed over and influenced the music of white performers and communities since slavery (Riis 3-6). However it is also true that historically, in terms of how music is marketed and sold in the United States, there has been a very clear divide between white and black popular musical performance. One place where this divide is particularly evident is in the changing ways in which the Billboard charts attempted to map out the tastes—and corresponding races—of American audiences. For example, in 1972, Billboard executives debated the differences between "rhythm and blues" and "rock and roll" music; implicitly the debate was over degrees of "whiteness" and "blackness" represented by these two genres (Redd 31). It is therefore possible to say that the perceived differences between white American and black American musics have been artificially hardened by marketing executives and/or are a hold-over from an earlier era in America's legally segregated society. However, musicologists have also shown that African American popular music has rhythms and tonal structures—with its roots in African societies and modes of music-making—that makes it distinct from white American and European popular music more generally (Maultsby 183-184).

The Color Purple is less tightly bound to the history of African American popular music than its recent all-black predecessors, including *Dreamgirls*, *Jelly's Last Jam*, and *Ain't Misbehavin'*. Both *Ain't Misbehavin'* and *Jelly's Last Jam* were predominated by jazz and blues music; the former focused on solely the music of Fats Waller, while the latter used the music of Jelly Roll Morton and other jazz greats to tell a musical biography and a history of the African American experience. Neither show employed a modern "Top 40s" popular music sound, although obviously the music used in each was considered popular at one time. *Dreamgirls* is the most modern sounding of the three, and it is possible to characterize the score as being located solidly within the Top 40 tradition. However, *Dreamgirls* is rooted in the Motown sound of the 1950s and 1960s. While Berry Gordy, the founder of Motown, very deliberately tailored and marketed Motown artists to the expectations of white audiences, the groups and artists he groomed for success had deep roots in the African American musical traditions of gospel, soul, and four-part harmony, as well as solid roots within the segregated community of Detroit (Smith 136). All three of these previously mentioned musicals, and many like them, focused on the ways in which African American musical forms could help tell uniquely African American stories. In contrast, the music of *The Color Purple* does not quite function in this way. Although the composers were certainly aware of the importance of particularized musical idioms so in order to create a show that was "a completely authentic experience, not blasphemous at all to the period," the predominance of pop sounds overall disconnects the music from the historical and cultural context of Walker's narrative (Brock M1).

In a 2004 interview with the *Atlanta Journal-Constitution*, Alice Walker discussed her initial reservations when Scott Sanders, a white man, suggested to her that her novel would translate well onto the musical stage:

> Early on Scott was bringing me music by very famous people because he was starting at the, quote 'top'. But I didn't care for them. [...] I listened to it and I said 'It doesn't have the soul, it doesn't have the heart, and it's not really in the African-American sensibility." (Bentley C7)

However, when she heard a recording of Allee Willis, Brenda Russell and Stephen Bray's impromptu rendition of "Shug Avery's Coming to Town," she "knew right away that that's who could do the music, because they had the heart and they had the soul" (Bentley C7). However, it is important to note that Walker herself, in discussing the musical version of her book, highlighted the all-inclusive nature of its themes over the unique characteristics of her original story: "the novel is [...] about helping people see that we are just human beings here" (Walker 11).

The Rhetoric Surrounding *The Color Purple*

An important aspect in understanding any piece of musical theater is to recognize what an intensely collaborative effort such an undertaking is. In this way, creating a musical theater show has much in common with creating a film, although in the case of a theatrical production, the work is never completely final since the show is performed live night after night. In general, while multiple people may have had a hand in writing the libretto (that is, the story and dialog) and several people may have contributed to writing the lyrics, it is quite uncommon for more than one composer to be responsible for the music. Further, the composer is very rarely also the same person who wrote the book for the show, nor is the person who composed the music always the same person who wrote the lyrics. It is therefore common practice to refer to a "Sondheim musical" or a "Lloyd Webber show," that is, to refer to a production as belonging to the composer of a musical, even when many others contributed to its creation. And this convention, of course, completely leaves out the choreographer, director, producer, and sundry other people involved in the creative process of a musical.

The collaborative nature of musical theater has been highlighted here because of the nature of the discourse surrounding *The Color Purple* and the ways in which the media reported on precisely what kind of musical the show was. This discourse had three distinct phases. The first wave of discussions over the show occurred prior to its move from Atlanta to New York City. Much of the ink spilt during this phase of the musical's life had to do with how the show was created and its connection to Alice Walker. The second wave occurred when it became clear that Oprah Winfrey would contribute a significant amount of money to the New York production, and predictably the discussion highlighted her previous involvement as an actor in Spielberg's version of the book as well as on her power within American culture generally. The final phase of discourse surrounding the show occurred once it had opened in New York and mainly took the form of reviews either praising or panning the production. There have also been subsequent discussions of the show that followed the New York premiere that have to do with the influx of new—typically *American Idol*—stars into various roles and their impact on the show.[5]

The divisions between these phases of media coverage is not quite so cut and dried as presented here. For example, very often stories regarding the creative team that circulated prior to the show's opening in Atlanta were retold once the show reached Broadway, and Oprah's unique involvement was frequently raised during the course of a review. And the "memory book"[6]—a glossy coffee-table book about the show that includes a copy of the script—published as a media tie-in for the show canonizes an official version of how *The Color Purple* (the musical) came to be. However, these divisions are useful in that they do highlight the evolving nature of the discussion surrounding *The Color Purple* as a musical, as its own entity separate from the book or the movie.

Before *The Color Purple* opened on Broadway, indeed before it even had its opening night in Atlanta, there was a substantial amount of press coverage for the show. The *Atlanta-Journal Constitution*, not surprisingly, was at the forefront of this media attention. This local newspaper spent considerable time documenting how the musical came to be and the various people involved with its genesis. In particular, the newspaper highlighted the collaborative nature of musical theater overall within the context of the novelty of the show having three composers, none of whom had ever been involved with a musical before. Thus by focusing on the collaborative nature of musical theater in general, the team of three inexperienced composers was enveloped by a clearly established idea about the process involved in creating a new musical. This formulation obscured Russell, Willis, and Bray's collective status as novices and resituated them as descendents of Rodgers and Hammerstein.

In a long feature piece written while *The Color Purple* was still in rehearsals, for example, the word "collaboration," references to teamwork and the large number of people involved in the production, abound: "'Purple' boasts three composer-lyricists, a book writer, a choreographer, a music director, and a full cadre of designers" (Brock, "The Making of a Broadway Musical" M1). Apart from the number of composer-lyricists, the number of collaborators involved with the production is not at all unusual for a musical, and yet Bock's critique implies that the number of collaborators involved with *The Color Purple* is evidence of its integrated nature. And it is this "integrated" aspect of the production that subsequently connects *The Color Purple* very closely with the idealized model of musical integration: *Oklahoma!* In the case of this July 2004 feature, integration refers not to the narrative and musical structure of the show itself, but instead refers to how everyone involved behind the scenes worked together:

> there was once a process like the one happening now with *The Color Purple*. For their hit musicals, composer Richard Rodgers and lyricist/librettist Oscar Hammerstein collaborated to create never-before-heard material—sometimes with additional book

> writers (*South Pacific*) and sometimes not (*Oklahoma!*). Songs
> and scenes were written and rewritten [...] Rodgers and
> Hammerstein did not carry the Apple computers and iPods that
> *The Color Purple* team does. [...] They used pencil, paper, rubber
> erasers. But that sense of mystery, of something new being
> generated from the raw random energy of its creators, was the
> same. You get something of that vibe from Russell, Willis and
> Bray—Los Angeles-based pop songsmiths who have never
> written for musical theater before. (Brock, "The Making of a
> Broadway Musical" M1)

There are several important issues to point out regarding this
description of the process behind *The Color Purple*. The phrase "there
was once a process like the one happening now" implies that other
current musicals, unlike *The Color Purple*, are not following in the
same collaborative creative method that was so successfully
established by Rodgers and Hammerstein. *The Color Purple* is thus
constructed as being a direct descendent of *Oklahoma!*, if not in terms
of technology (pencil vs. computer), then in terms of energy and
spirit. And the "vibe" connecting these two vastly different
collaborative teams across time also subtly works to characterize *The
Color Purple* as more like *Oklahoma!* than any, never-mentioned,
African American musicals that appeared in the past. The show and its
narrative are implicitly universalized, thus folding it within the history
of a white tradition of American musical theater, leaving the history of
black musical theater as unmentionable and forgotten.[7]
        Of course, all of the upbeat pre-opening press did not
necessarily mean that the show itself would be received positively.
The reviews of *The Color Purple* in both its original Atlanta and its
revised New York versions were both quite mixed. However,
reviewers consistently made comparisons and connections to past
(white) musicals, regardless of whether or not the Atlanta version was
received positively. Comparing new musicals to old is nothing
unusual; however, it is noteworthy that, given its all-black cast, the
mainstream white press perceived *The Color Purple* as falling within
the "white musical" tradition. Indeed, one criticism about the show
was that it was closer in spirit to British, rather than American,
musical theater: "it's not so much different from so many other
uninspired, assembled-by-committee extravaganzas that have come to
dominate the Great White Way in the 23 years since *Cats*" (Brock,
"Review" G1). Even when the reviewer for the *Atlanta Constitution*,
Wendell Brock, spotlights "the stunningly designed and danced Africa
sequence," there is no sense that the number or the show as a whole

might be part of a different tradition of musical theater or subject to different pressures than a musical cast with white, rather than black, Americans.

Once the musical was ready to move from Atlanta to Broadway, dual impulses manifested themselves in the media coverage, often within the same article. On the one hand, the impulse to universalize the show and contain it within a mainstream tradition persisted. On the other hand, Oprah Winfrey's decision to invest in the production and heavily promote it on her talk show program pushed cultural critics and pundits to briefly reflect on the "unusual" story *The Color Purple* told within the frame of musical theater. An article in the *New York Post* demonstrates this schizophrenia quite well. The article begins with outlining the particulars of *The Color Purple*'s narrative: "a tale rife with rape, racism, poverty and abuse. Hardly the stuff of a big Broadway musical," but then a few sentences later describes the story as really "about adversity, faith and redemption" ("How Purple Rose to B'Way" 80). After outlining Winfrey's involvement in Spielberg's movie version, this theme of "great truths" is rearticulated when explaining why producer Sanders wanted to turn *The Color Purple* into a musical: "the story of a poor, Southern black woman's journey to self-awareness and pride seemed 'universal'" ("How Purple Rose to B'Way" 80). The mantra of "the universal" shining through the particular "unlikely" elements of the narrative was repeated in many different sources nationally, including Winfrey's magazine *O*: "Celie's story belongs to all of us, as Marsha Norman [the librettist] said, because we at once fear and embrace it" (Funderburg, "*The Color Purple* [*O* Anticipation List]" 76). But what, precisely, are "we" embracing through Celie's story? The implicit answer provided by the article is that the audience embraces the color-blind idea of triumphing over adversity without specifically articulating what that "adversity" might be.

Winfrey's involvement with *The Color Purple* is a long and complex one. She admits that the novel is one of her favorites, and her role as Sofia in the film version brought her into the public eye long before her talk show gained its popularity. Her production company, "Harpo" is a play on her own name but is also coincidentally the name of one of the secondary characters in *The Color Purple*. All of these facts were rehearsed to a greater or lesser extent in the media and lent an air of inevitability to her investing in the show, something which Winfrey herself encouraged:

the fact that the theater where a new musical version of *The Color
Purple* is slated to open turns out to be across the street from *O*
magazine is no accident, either. [...] There's something deeply
magical, connected to a spiritual force I cannot explain,
surrounding *The Color Purple*. I no longer question it. I surrender
to it and feel blessed to be a part of it in its new voice on
Broadway." (Winfrey 72)

That the New York premiere of *The Color Purple* coincided with the
end of the sixteen-year feud between David Letterman and Winfrey,
with the talk-show host ending their interview by escorting her from
his soundstage to the theater, only seemed to heighten the sense that
musical was not just integrated in the *Oklahoma!* sense, but capable of
integrating very disparate types of people, at least in terms of its
audience if not in terms of who was represented on the stage.

Of course, once *The Color Purple* opened on Broadway and
was available to critics to review, the discourse about the show did
shift somewhat, although only a very few publications, such as the
New Yorker, directly connected the show to a history outside of white,
mainstream musicals. Critic Burt Lahr notes that while music is of
course central to a Broadway musical, "for the African-American
story it's doubly important, linked as it is to the achievement of
individuality through centuries of subjugation" (115). Ironically,
however, the prevalence of pop music throughout *The Color Purple*,
however, did not allow for any individuality to shine through. Indeed,
Lahr implicitly rejects the heavily promoted idea that *The Color
Purple* is an integrated show when he comments that, "this noisy
production is about presentation not penetration" (115). For Lahr, the
music had no real connection to the arc of the narrative within the
show; instead many of its songs were performed as if the characters
were in a rock concert.

Other critics, with varying degrees of warmth, reviewed *The
Color Purple* without explicitly highlighting the relatively unusual
fact that the cast was all black or calling any attention to the longer
theatrical history behind the show. At one level, this lack of
acknowledgement regarding race may be viewed as heartening,
indicating that reviewers were judging the show on its merits, rather
than on racial politics. However, that the relative absence of African
Americans on mainstream Broadway stages in general went entirely
without mention at all, an omission that suggests a reluctance to raise
the issue and thus draw attention to it. Indeed, in the few instances
when the racial make-up of the cast was confronted as an important
issue, the references were typically done in terms of audience

attendance. African Americans, who generally do not attend Broadway musicals, came to see *The Color Purple* in large numbers alongside the more typical white audience members. But even then, the discussion turned back to integration, in this case the happy result of an integrated Broadway audience brought about through *The Color Purple* rather than then leading to a discussion about why black audiences might generally avoid Broadway (Barnes B1; Berfield 104).

Conclusion

Paradoxically, one reason for focusing on the "universal" qualities of *The Color Purple* is its very particular nature. To help guarantee that white, mainstream audiences would attend this all-black musical, its similarities to other, more familiar musicals and those elements of the plot that would resonate with a white audiences familiar with the stories and conventions of Broadway musicals were highlighted. The much less well-known past of African-American musicals, was by necessity of market forces, left behind. The show was thus effectively folded within a larger history of American musical theater discourse by concentrating on how the creation of *The Color Purple* was really not so very different from what had happened in the past. That Oprah Winfrey, a revered national figure, "a knowledgeable businesswoman who seems to have her finger on the pulse of the nation," had decided to invest her money and her approval in the show, served to further bridge the gap for white audiences between a potentially unsettling theatrical experience and a "universally" uplifting one (Butler 1B).

The main concern over the transformation from the page to the stage did not seem to one of fidelity to the style of the original text, since it seemed more acceptable to contemplate the book being transformed into a straight dramatic play (Leitch 161-163). Instead, the skepticism over adapting the novel to the stage had much more to do with the genre of musical theater than with the wider genre of live performance. Of course, this assumption that the racially and sexually charged themes of Walker's novel would be rendered far too "light" by musical adaptation ignores musicals such as *Carousel*—which explicitly deals with spousal abuse—or *Sweeny Todd*—whose plot revolves around a corrupt legal system, rape, and bloody revenge. Even *Oklahoma!*, with its rhetorical status as the one musical against which all others are judged, encompasses dark sexual desires and murder. In other words, although its status in public memory is largely structured around the idea of "boy-meets-girl," the musical is itself much darker and more complicated than is typically acknowledged. A clearly simplified plot structure determined by the genre's demands for song and dance does not necessarily equate to simplistic or non-controversial issues or themes.

Indeed, on the surface, in its transformation from written to performative text, very little of the plot elements of *The Color Purple* were substantially altered. One of the praises earned by the musical adaptation in contrast to its filmic adaptation was the more fully rounded characterization of Mister, Celie's abusive husband. By having him sung about and giving him songs to sing, Mister's transformation from villain to man had an emotional resonance and reality that had not been achieved on the screen (Funderburg 25). Unintentionally, the emotional reality achieved by many of the characters by the adaptation from book to stage was not realized in the character of Celie. By giving her the most "universal" music to sing as a means of transforming her into a more relatable character, the creators of *The Color Purple* drained Walker's heroine of what makes her such a compelling character in the first place: her unique voice.

Kathryn Edney, Michigan State University

Notes

[1] The Disney musical *Aida* also premiered at the Alliance Theater—and was considerably reworked—prior to its opening on the Broadway stage. Kathy Janich, "On Theater: 'Purple' Hued Chance for an Alliance Coup?" *Atlanta Journal-Constitution* (19 October 2003): M4.

[2] There are many book-length histories of musical theater; Preston's piece is one of the most concise.

[3] There are exceptions to the plotless jukebox musical, with *Mamma Mia!* (2001)—a show built around the songs of ABBA— is one key example.

[4] These observations regarding the music are taken from my listening to the CD cast recording of the show and from my observing a performance of the show in Chicago May 19, 2007.

[5] While the habit of American Idol discards crossing over and finding success on Broadway is an interesting phenomenon, it falls beyond the scope of this essay.

[6] Lise Funderberg is the general author, compiler and interviewer of the "memory book." See Works Cited.

[7] It is important to note that Rodgers and Hammerstein, as was the case with many of the creators of Broadway musicals, were ethnically Jewish. As Andrea Most has demonstrated in *Making Americans*, shows such as *Oklahoma!* worked through concerns over ethnic assimilation within the Anglo-dominated American culture of the 1940s. The phrase "white tradition" in this context therefore, refers more to the

popular discourse and perceptions surrounding these shows rather than to the precise ethnic or racial heritage of any particular composer or lyricist.

Works Cited

Adler, Steven. *On Broadway: Art and Commerce on the Great White Way*. Carbondale, IL: Southern Illinois UP, 2004.

Barnes, Brooks. "'Color Purple' Proves Black Themes Can Make Green on Great White Way" *Wall Street Journal* (1 December 2006): B1.

Bentley, Rosalind. "*The Color Purple* Premiere: Q&A/Alice Walker" *Atlanta Journal-Constitution* (18 September 2004): C7.

Berfield, Susan "The Making of *The Color Purple;* Behind the Scenes as a Masterpiece becomes a Musical" *Businessweek* (21 November 2005): 104.

Blau, Eleanor. "The Negro Ensemble Company is on the Move" *New York Times* (31 August 1980): D3, D17.

Butler, Tim. "The Purple Tony Eater," *Tri-State Defender* (Memphis) (3 June –7 June 2006): 1B.

Brock, Wendell. "Review: Color it Splashy" *Atlanta Journal-Constitution* (2 December 2005): G1.

—. "The Making of a Broadway Musical: Behind the Scenes as a Masterpiece becomes a Musical" *Atlanta Journal-Constitution* (25 July 2004): M1.

Douglas, Ann. *Terrible Honesty: Mongrel Manhattan in the 1920s*. New York: Farrar, Straus, and Giroux, 1995.

Fisher, Rudolph. "The Caucasian Storms Harlem" in *The Portable Harlem Renaissance Reader*. ed. David Levering Lewis. New York: Viking P, 1994. (110-117)

Funderburg, Lise. "*The Color Purple* [O Anticipation List]" *O: The Oprah Magazine*. 6.12 (December 2005): 72,74,76.

—. *The Color Purple: A Memory Book of the Broadway Musical*. New York: Carroll and Graf, 2006.

Hoffman, Barbara "How Purple Rose to B'Way" *New York Post*. (27 November 2005): 80.

Holden, Stephen. "A 'Let's Try this' Approach to Musicals," *New York Times* (6 October 2002): A15.

Hughes, Langston. "When the Negro was in Vogue" in *The Portable Harlem Renaissance Reader*. ed. David Levering Lewis. New York: Viking P, 1994. (77-80)

Hutcheon, Linda. *A Theory of Adaptation*. New York: Routledge, 2006.

Hutchinson, George. *The Harlem Renaissance in Black and White*. Cambridge, MA: Harvard UP, 1995.

Janich, Kathy, "On Theater: 'Purple' Hued Chance for an Alliance Coup?" *Atlanta Journal-Constitution* (19 October 2003): M4.

Johnson, Lewis D. "The Jewel in Ethiope's Ear" *Opportunity* 6.6 (June 1928): 166-168.

Kislan, Richard. *The Musical: A Look at the American Musical Theater*. Englewood Cliffs: Prentice Hall, 1980.

Lahr, Burt. "Artificial Respiration; Accentuating the negative in *The Color Purple* and *Miss Witherspoon*" *New Yorker* (12 December 2005): 115.

Lauret, Maria. *Modern Novelists: Alice Walker*. New York: St. Martin's P: 2000.

Leitch, Thomas. "Twelve Fallacies in Contemporary Adaptation Theory" *Criticism* 45.2 (Spring 2004): 149-171.

Lewis, David Levering. *When Harlem was in Vogue*. New York: Alfred A. Knopf, 1981.

Lott, Eric. *Love and Theft: Blackface Minstrelsy and the American Working Class*. New York: Oxford UP, 1995.

Lhamon, W. T. *Raising Cain: Blackface Performance from Jim Crow to Hip Hop*. Cambridge, MA: Harvard UP, 1998.

McMillin, Scott. *The Musical as Drama*. Princeton: Princeton UP, 2006.

Preston, Katherine K. "American Musical Theater before the Twentieth Century" in *The Cambridge Companion to the Musical*. eds William A. Everett and Paul R. Laird. Cambridge: Cambridge UP, 2002. (3-28)

Maultsby, Portia K "A Map of the Music" *African American Review*. 29.2 (Summer 1995): 183-184.

Most, Andrea. *Making Americans: Jews and the Broadway Musical*. Cambridge: Harvard UP, 2004.

Redd, Lawrence N. "Rock! It's Still Rhythm and Blues" *The Black Perspective in Music*, 13.1 (Spring, 1985): 31-47.

Riis, Thomas L. *Just before Jazz: Black Musical Theater in New York, 1890-1915*. Washington, D.C.: Smithsonian Institution P, 1989.

Rosenberg, Bernard, and Ernest Harburg. *The Broadway Musical: Collaboration in Commerce and Art*. New York: New York UP, 1993.

Sanders, Leslie Catherine. *The Development of Black Theater in America: From Shadows to Selves*. Baton Rouge: Louisiana State UP, 1988.

Sears, Ann. "The Coming of the Musical Play: Rodgers and Hammerstein" in *The Cambridge Companion to the Musical*. eds William A. Everett and Paul R. Laird. Cambridge: Cambridge UP, 2002. (120-136)

Smith, Suzanne. *Dancing in the Street: Motown and the Cultural Politics of Detroit*. Cambridge: Harvard UP, 1999.

Sternfeld, Jessica. *The Megamusical*. Bloomington and Indianapolis: Indiana UP, 2006.

Walker, Alice. "The Journey Begins" in *The Color Purple: A Memory Book of the Broadway Musical*. New York: Carroll and Graf, 2006.

Winfrey, Oprah. "Live, from Broadway, It's...*The Color Purple!*" *O: The Oprah Magazine*. 6.12 (December 2005): 71-72.

Woll, Allen. *Black Musical Theatre: From* Coontown *to* Dreamgirls. New York: Da Capo P, 1989.

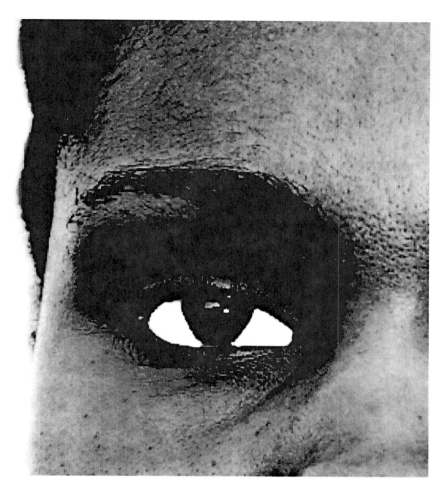

The Classic Beneath the Polemic

Alice Walker's Womanist Reading of Samuel Richardson's *Pamela* in *The Color Purple*

Apryl Denny

When asked what she "considered the major difference between the literatures written by black and white Americans," Alice Walker responded,

> I had not spent a lot of time considering this question, since it is not the difference between them that interests me, but, rather the way black writers and white writers seem to me to be writing one immense story - the same story, for the most part - with different parts of this immense story coming from a multitude of different perspectives. ("Saving the Life" 5)

The Color Purple and Samuel Richardson's *Clarissa*

Taking their cue from Walker's suggestion that all stories can be read as parts of a larger whole, some critics have read *The Color Purple* as offering a "different perspective" on the stereotype of the "heroine" originated in the eighteenth-century English novel. For example, feminist literary critic, Linda Abbandonato, in "A View from 'Elsewhere': Subversive Sexuality and the Rewriting of the Heroine's Story in *The Color Purple*," applies feminist psychological and linguistic theory to read Walker's novel as a challenge to the canonical depiction of the heroine in eighteenth-century novels like Samuel Richardson's *Clarissa*.[1] "Richardson himself (at least as constructed in our literary histories)," Abbandonato explains,

> perfectly symbolizes white patriarchy: the founding father of the novel (by convention, if not in fact), he tells the woman's story, authorizing her on his terms, eroticizing her suffering, representing her masochism as virtue and her dying as the emblem of womanly purity. (1107)

According to Abbandonato, Celie, the "heroine" of *The Color Purple* challenges *Clarissa's* white male perspective by being a linguistic and sexual revolutionary. By having Celie write her letters in "black vernacular" rather than "standard (white) English" and by depicting her as lesbian in a "system [...] of compulsory heterosexuality" that defines lesbianism as a "sickness," Walker's novel subverts Richardson's worldview and "relegate[s] man to the margins of a world he has always dominated" (Abbandonato 1112).

In response to Abbandonato, Dror Abend-David, a scholar of eighteenth-century British literature, defends *Clarissa* from what he calls an "occupational hazard" of feminist theory. Abend-David explains that Abbandonato has failed to see Richardson's novel in its historical context and demonstrates in Clarissa's narrative her "critique of the patriarchal system, her denial of the commodity value of women, and her creation of female self-sufficiency in the terms of sexual and moral independence from male domination" (18). Abend-David asserts that, by polarizing *Clarissa* and *The Color Purple*, respectively, as "the prototype of chauvinist literature" and "the epitome of feminist writing," Abbandonato has not only misread *Clarissa* but has failed to recognize that "the ideological achievement of *The Color Purple* is not [...] in denouncing a male-dominated society, but in describing the possibilities in the absence of such domination" (19).

It is apparent that Abend-David, despite his own determination to polarize his and Abbandonato's interpretations on the basis of their historical legitimacy, has recognized what Walker means when she says that we are all writing "one immense story" from "a multitude of different perspectives." Walker's novel does not oppose Richardson's but, rather, builds on his critique of the eighteenth-century gendered class system. The problem with Abend-David's argument is that in discrediting rather than building on Abbandonato's reading, he too loses an historical piece that is essential to understanding Walker's novel. Joining Abbandonato's analysis of sexual subversion with Abend-David's historicized reading of "domination" reveals that Walker's novel can be read as a response not to *Clarissa* but to Richardson's first novel, *Pamela*. In order to describe the possibilities of a world without "domination," Alice Walker's *The Color Purple* builds on and revises a "sexual subversion" established in Richardson's *Pamela*.

The Color Purple and Gendered Authority in Richardson's *Pamela*

At first glance, *Clarissa*'s influence on *The Color Purple* seems quite believable. Clarissa's rape obviously connects her to the heroine of Walker's novel. Although she is a rural, African-American girl raped and impregnated at the age of fourteen by her step-father, Celie is like Clarissa in that she strives to define herself rather than to be defined by a sexist and classist social system that devalues her because of her rape. On the other hand, in telling the story of the servant-class girl who *didn't* get raped, or the good girl who, through the power of her unfaltering virtue, avoids destruction and converts her would-be rapist into the ideal husband, Richardson's *Pamela* is more like Celie's story than Clarissa's story is.

Pamela, like *Clarissa*, was very widely read and influential in modeling how women were to behave in eighteenth-century England. As Margaret A. Doody explains, *Pamela* was

> a "best seller"[...] Everybody read it; there was a Pamela rage, and Pamela motifs appeared on teacups and fans. Many praised the novel [...] enthusiastically [...] for its [...] morality, but some condemned it for its "leveling" tendency. (7)

Pamela's "morality," like *Clarissa's*, stresses the importance of women's chastity, but the "leveling tendency" that Doody calls attention to is what sets *Pamela* apart from *Clarissa*. *Pamela*, unlike Richardson's subsequent novel, features a servant-class heroine who challenges a social code that demands chastity of "middle- and upper-class young ladies" but which has accepted that "lower-class girls are not supposed to set any such value on themselves—they are there for sexual convenience" (Doody 14). Pamela, in maintaining the moral values expected of a woman far above her class, is ultimately elevated into that higher status precisely because of her morals. This challenge to the rigid class stratifications of eighteenth-century English society made *Pamela* a best seller, and it is precisely what influences Walker's novel.

In *The Color Purple*, Walker builds on the analysis of class and gender issues in *Pamela* to include the "different perspectives" of race and sexual orientation. In reinventing the male-identified, working-class, women depicted in *Pamela*, Walker creates a network of Womanist characters who guide her novel's heroine toward a personal growth that leads to social transformation.

Pamela, like *The Color Purple,* is written from its female hero's point of view. Composing his novel as a collection of letters written by a fifteen-year-old servant-class girl to her parents upon the death of the kind mistress she has served for three years, Richardson employs a generic device popular in his time and presents himself as the editor of letters he claims to be genuine. No reader in Richardson's day would have been fooled by this device, but in using it, he makes clear his goal is to present an individual, working-class woman's point of view. Pamela's personal predicament, as the letters quickly reveal, is that her mistress' son, known only in the text as Mr. B, sees himself as having inherited all of Pamela's potential services. Pamela's personalized commentary on Mr. B's attempt to take her as his mistress has been called the first English novel and is still seen as an early sign of the push toward individualism that defines the Romantic period in English literature yet to come.

But upon its publication in 1740, the story of Pamela's private struggle to maintain her chastity also found its place in a contemporary debate on the meaning of authority. In the context of this dialogue, Pamela can be seen as an eighteenth-century, servant-class "Everywoman." According to literary scholar Jeremy W. Webster, once Pamela becomes a part of Mr. B's "family," he expects her to serve him as is "articulated in Robert Filmer's *Patriarcha*" (57). Filmer, a firm Royalist knighted by Charles I, articulated the seventeenth-century philosophy of natural rights in his *Patriarcha, or The Natural Power of Kings.* According to Filmer, the absolute power of the father over the family and its servants enacted by the Old Testament patriarchs is the true model for all forms of government, familial as well as political. As Webster explains, "the word *family* means at least two different things in the eighteenth century. On the one hand it means roughly what it does today, that is, parents and their children," and on the other it "can also mean the entire household, including servants" (56). Webster writes that "Mr. B. repeatedly asserts his right as head of household [head of the family] to use Pamela [his servant] as he sees fit in keeping with traditional patriarchy" (57). It is Mr. B's presumed right to use her that Pamela, as Everywoman, challenges; her attempt to avoid Mr. B's unchaste advances is her plea for self-governance no matter her social class. During an altercation with Mr. B early in the novel, Pamela exclaims:

> 'When a master of his honour's degree demeans himself to be so free as *that* [kissing Pamela] to such a poor servant as me, what is the next to be expected?—But your honour went farther, so you

did; and threatened me what you would do, and talked of
Lucretia, and her hard fate.— Your honour knows you went too
far for a master to a servant, or even to his equal; and I cannot
bear it.' (Richardson, *Pamela* 29).

Mr. B, as justice of the peace and, therefore, the law in
Pamela's home and community, acts on the assumption that whatever
his "honour" chooses to do is "honourable." As Pamela says of Mr.
B's Lincolnshire housekeeper, Mrs. Jewkes, who holds Pamela
captive and assists Mr. B in his plot to rape her:

> 'she [Mrs. Jewkes] praises [...] the author of my miseries [Mr. B],
> and his *honourable* intentions, as she calls them; for I see, that
> she is capable of thinking, as I fear *he* does, that every thing that
> makes for his wicked will is honourable, though to the ruin of the
> innocent.' (Richardson, *Pamela* 121)

In *The Color Purple,* Walker takes up this same debate on
authority and applies it to the role of the father in the African-
American home in the American South of the early twentieth century.
Like Pamela's Mr. B, Celie's step-father, Alfonso (*The Color
Purple's* first Mr. ____) holds that everyone in the family is his
personal property to use or sell as he sees fit. Celie's first letter
confides to God that Alfonso has begun to ritually rape her on the
premise that "You gonna do what your mammy wouldn't" (Walker,
TCP 1). Shortly thereafter, when she has "breasts full of milk running
down [her]self" because Alfonso has sold the child he fathered, Celie
observes that he has begun to target another more "decent" family
member, her younger sister, Nettie. "I keep hoping he find somebody
to marry. I see him looking at my little sister. She scared" (Walker,
TCP 3). Four years later, Albert (the novel's second Mr. ____, another
patriarch in the tradition of Filmer) comes "courting" Nettie, but
Alfonso, clearly a better horse trader than Albert, makes him settle for
a cow and Celie, "the better wife," rather than hold out for the sexual
allure of the younger and unspoiled Nettie (Walker, *TCP* 8).

Walker's depiction of woman as commodity in these scenes is
reminiscent of Pamela's exploitation and rebellion. Both Celie and
Pamela are subject to Filmer's philosophy of the family, and both take
action against this ideology, but Richardson's interpretation of
Filmer's ideology focuses on gender, whereas Walker's emphasizes
race and sexual orientation. As feminist literary critic Nancy
Armstrong explains in her discussion of Richardson's novel:

Pamela's successful struggle against the sexual advances of Mr.
B transformed the rules of an earlier model of kinship relations
into a sexual contract that suppressed their difference in station.
Rather than that of a master and servant, then, the relationship
between the protagonists [...] [came to] be understood as that of
male and female. (110)

Armstrong closely analyzes the financial contract that Mr. B
offers Pamela in lieu of marriage midway through the novel to show
that Pamela refuses to allow Mr. B the *male* power to define her
chastity as a commodity, to own or to trade her to another man,
Reverend Williams. In other words, Armstrong argues that
Richardson has re-envisioned a class-struggle between servant and
master as a gender struggle between man and woman. In creating a
two-columned debate between Pamela and Mr. B, Richardson:

insert[s] Pamela's voice into the field dominated by Mr. B's
contract. [...] In allowing her the grounds for negotiating such a
contract [...] [Richardson] modifies the presupposition of all
previous contracts, namely, that the male defined and valorized
the female as a form of currency in an exchange among men. [...]
Richardson's version of consensual exchange [depicted in
Pamela] empowers the female to give herself in exchange with
the male. (Armstrong 112)

Whereas Armstrong's assessment of *Pamela* as a study in
gender relations is accurate, her reading of Pamela as empowered
through contractual language is less convincing. A twenty-first-
century reader, despite Armstrong's claim to the contrary, cannot help
but notice that Pamela's gift "to give herself in exchange with the
male" is bestowed upon her not because of her independence from
male authority but precisely because of her unflagging obedience to it.
Granted Pamela challenges Mr. B's right to own her body, but she
does so by declaring her allegiance to a male authority higher than
Mr. B, God. In effect, then, Pamela does not challenge the rule of
external, male authority but, rather, only challenges Mr. B's
legitimacy as an authority figure. Pamela explains to Mr. B, "my *soul*
is of equal importance with that of a *princess*" (Richardson, *Pamela*
164). "May God Almighty [...] touch your heart and save *you* from
this *sin* and *me* from this *ruin*!" (Richardson, *Pamela* 202). From
Pamela's point of view, God endorses a woman's sexual obedience to
a man (regardless of their social ranks) only when a legitimate
contract, created and endorsed by a male institution, is in place.

According to Pamela, neither she nor Mr. B has the right to exchange themselves without the approval of the State and the Church.

Critics like Armstrong and Abend-David who read Pamela's story as a triumphant gender and class victory against Mr. B are invariably disappointed by the last third of the novel in which Pamela takes her place as the dutiful wife to the converted Mr. B and takes pride in never challenging his authority, even when he reveals the existence of his former mistress and their illegitimate daughter. This disappointment results from a failure to see Pamela's struggle in its fuller context in the novel as a commentary on how to determine the legitimacy of male authority. Mr. B's choice not to rape Pamela, but to marry her instead, legitimates him as an authority figure, just as the marriage itself legitimates his sexual advances. In effect, Pamela's story is seen clearly in its final third not as challenging gendered authority as a political organizing principle but as demonstrating how to ascertain and dutifully follow legitimate male authority.

In *The Color Purple,* however, Walker does not fail to understand the significance of the last third of *Pamela.* As a self-reflexive black woman living in a white heterosexist society, Walker recognizes that male authority is bound up with institutional power of all kinds, and *The Color Purple* takes up where *Pamela* leaves off to challenge the male definition of authority by replacing its patriarchal model with a new kind of organizing principle that Walker calls "Womanism."

The Color Purple, Womanism, and *Pamela*

The Color Purple reveals to us what the world might look like if we moved from the paradigm of male power and authority depicted in *Pamela* to one of female connection and mutual support based on the doctrine Walker has termed "Womanism." In rewriting the scenes from *Pamela* in which Mr. B attempts to buy Pamela's sexual compliance or to trade it to his underling, the Reverend Williams, Walker introduces the idea that women might unite to gain control of themselves rather than compete with each other to be the best commodity on the male-owned market. Albert and Alfonso's transaction defines Nettie and Celie as competitors for the "privilege" of marrying Albert, but the two sisters refuse to be pitted against each other and, instead, unite in a plan to transform Celie's commoditization into the means to Nettie's liberation from Alfonso.

Once married, Celie, although not much better off as Albert's possession, is at least free of the incest she has been subjected to under Alfonso's roof. Furthermore, Celie's marriage allows her to preserve Nettie from a similar fate:

> 'Nettie here with us. She run away from home. She say she hate to leave our stepma, but she had to git out, maybe fine some help for the other little ones. The boys be alright, she say. They can stay out his way. When they git big they gon fight him.' (Walker, *TCP* 16).

In this scene, Celie and Nettie see themselves as the beginning of a community of "sisters" united to help one another. As feminist literary critic Ana Maria Fraile-Marcos points out, this scene also "reverberates with echoes of the slavery era" (120). In making "Celie turn around in front of Albert as he ponders whether to take her or not," this scene recalls the "the auction block" (Fraile-Marcos 120) and reminds us that the union of sisters in this novel is a network of *black* women who are defined as slaves both by the black men who unite with them in the family and by the white men and women who segregate them in the community.

Richardson's *Pamela* reads class oppression in the light of gender bias in order to challenge the authenticity of authority, but in *The Color Purple*, Walker builds on Richardson's analysis and offers an alternative to authority that she sees coming out of the experience of black lesbians. As Fraile-Marcos explains, Alice Walker's theory of Womanism evolved in the context of a contemporary debate on the definition of black lesbianism (112). In her 1977 article, "Toward a Black Feminist Criticism," black, lesbian writer and activist Barbara Smith defines as black "lesbian" fiction any fiction written by a black woman that depicts "the relationships between girls and women" as "essential" and that maintains a "consistently critical stance toward the heterosexual institutions of male/female relationships, marriage, and the family" (165). Three years later, in 1980, Deborah McDowell's "New Directions for Black Feminist Criticism" challenged Smith's definition for being "vague and imprecise" (190); and four years after that, in 1984, Barbara Christian redefined the term *lesbian* as "women who find other women sexually attractive or gratifying" (189). In the midst of this discussion Walker wrote:

> Womanist 1. From *womanish*. (Opp. Of "girlish," i.e. frivolous, irresponsible, not serious.) A black feminist or feminist of color. From the black folk expression of mothers to female children,

"You acting womanish," i.e. like a woman. Usually referring
to outrageous, audacious, courageous or *willful* behavior.
Wanting to know more and in greater depth than is considered
"good" for one. Interested in grown-up doings. Acting grown up.
Being grown up. Interchangeable with another black folk
expression: "You trying to be grown." Responsible. In charge.
Serious.

...

2. *Also:* A woman who loves other women, sexually and/or
nonsexually. Appreciates and prefers women's culture, women's
emotional flexibility (values tears as natural counter-balance of
laughter), and women's strength. Sometimes loves individual
men, sexually and/or nonsexually. Committed to survival and
wholeness of entire people, male *and* female. Not a separatist,
except periodically, for health. Traditionally universalist, as:
"Mama, why are we brown, pink, and yellow, and our cousins are
white, beige, and black?" Ans.: "Well, you know the colored race
is just like a flower garden, with every flower represented."
Traditionally capable, as in: "Mama, I'm walking to Canada and
I'm taking you and a bunch of other slaves with me." Reply: "It
wouldn't be the first time."

...

Loves music. Loves dance. Loves the moon. *Loves* the Spirit.
Loves love and food and roundness. Loves struggle. *Loves* the
Folk. Loves herself. *Regardless.*

...

Womanist is to feminist as purple is to lavender (*In Search* xi-
xii).

Fraile-Marcos reads Walker's description of Womanism as
"compris[ing] each of the definitions of lesbianism" that Smith,
McDowell, and Christian originate. Womanism, Fraile-Marcos
explains, "seeks to be the comprehensive 'ideology' that absorb[s] the
basic principles of feminism about women's equality" and "names the
reality of black women, which was either misrepresented or not
represented at all within the parameters of either feminism or
lesbianism" (113). Fraile-Marcos' interpretation is convincing, but
Walker's Womanism can also be read as emerging from her writing of
The Color Purple and its response to Richardson's depiction of
lesbian love in *Pamela*.

The Color Purple, published in 1982, precedes and
concretizes Walker's later definition. As Fraile-Marcos points out, the
novel is densely populated with Womanist characters who help Celie
to evolve into a "full person" (122). With the support of her sister
Nettie, Sophia Butler (the wife of Abert's son, Harpo), Mary Agnes
(Harpo's girlfriend), and Shug Avery (the woman Albert first sought

to marry, even before Nettie and his first wife, Annie Julia), Celie
develops:

> from the meek, subdued, obedient, and accepting person she was
> [...] to a self-conscious human being who is just starting to
> appreciate her own worth. [...] Her inferiority complex, due to
> violence, to male chauvinism, and to poverty, is being erased
> because of the supportive bonds between black women in the
> novel (Fraile-Marcos 122).

The one woman among these supporters who is most
responsible for Celie's growth, of course, is Shug Avery. Fraile-
Marcos has identified Shug as the "active agent in Celie's life" who
"provokes a positive evolution in Celie's progress" by means of a love
that is at once maternal and sexual (124).

> After portraying heterosexual relationships dominated by
> infidelity, violence, sexual abuse, and incest, homosexuality
> between Shug and Celie appears as the only healthy sexual
> relationship, because it is based on sympathy and understanding,
> as well as on Shug's desire to help. (Fraile-Marcos 126-27)

This Womanist relationship between Shug and Celie can be read as
developing at least in part from an embryo in Richardson's *Pamela.*

Pamela and Lesbian Love

To call *Pamela* a lesbian novel is, of course, to stretch a point far
beyond even Barbara Smith's generalized definition. In fact, to use the
term "lesbian" to refer to the sexual identity of a person (much less of
a text) prior to the late 1870s is anachronistic since, as theorist Arnold
I. Davidson explains, sexuality was not yet associated with essence
(23). In Richardson's world, one might practice what we today would
call "lesbian" or "gay" sexual activity, but people would not identify
themselves or be identified as "lesbian" or "homosexual" until "the
psychiatric style of reasoning" that connects sex and essence in the
way that we understand it today first emerged in the nineteenth
century (Davidson 25). Nonetheless, as Jeremy Webster explains, the
depiction of *Pamela's* Mrs. Jewkes, Mr. B's Lincolnshire
housekeeper, "represents" a "system of thought" that includes
"lesbian [...] and premarital sex" (61). Mrs. Jewkes openly expresses
her attraction to Pamela in one of their earliest encounters in the

novel. Before Pamela even arrives at Mr. B's country house where
Mrs. Jewkes will imprison her for nearly two months, Pamela writes,

> 'Every now and then she would be staring in my face, in the
> chariot, and squeezing my hand, and saying, Why, you are very
> pretty, my silent dear! And once she offered to kiss me. But I
> said, I don't like this sort of carriage, Mrs. Jewkes; it is not like
> two persons of one sex.' (Richardson, *Pamela* 109).

Pamela is repulsed by Mrs. Jewkes and her sexual overtures. She calls
the housekeeper a "broad, squat, pursy, *fat thing,* quite ugly"
(Richardson, *Pamela* 116) and refers to her as "filthy'" and as a
"wicked procuress" (Richardson, *Pamela* 109).

   Pamela tries her best to avoid Mrs. Jewkes' advances, but,
despite the girl's best efforts, the housekeeper continues to prey on
her. As psychological literary critic John A. Dussinger points out,
"Sexual love radiates its force mysteriously in the text [of *Pamela*],
charging every material thing with erotic significance [...] even pen
and ink" (525). Mrs. Jewkes' attempt to control Pamela's writing is
clearly sexualized. She guards Pamela's use of paper and ink like a
jealous husband monitoring his wife's virtue. Mrs. Jewkes makes
Pamela account for every drop of ink and piece of paper she uses,
forbids her to write anywhere except in the housekeeper's presence,
and forces her to reveal every word she writes. Pamela feels violated
by Mrs. Jewkes' surveillance and by the sexual innuendoes that
accompany it. From Pamela's point of view, Mrs. Jewkes is an Argus
with "a hundred eyes [all] set to watch" (Richardson, *Pamela* 125)
and, thereby, to participate in, Pamela's sexuality. "I'll send [Mr. B]
word [my italics] to come and satisfy you," Mrs. Jewkes scoffs. "If I
was he, I would not be long away [...] I would come, if I was he, and
put an end to all your fears" (Richardson, *Pamela* 126). Mrs. Jewkes
makes it clear that her "word" is more powerful than Pamela's ink,
because her alliance with Mr. B can bring about the rape that Pamela
hopes to prevent by writing her letters. "Horrid creature," Pamela
replies. "Can'st thou not stab me to the heart? I'd rather thou
would'st, than say such another *word*!" (Richardson, *Pamela* 126).
   Shortly thereafter, Pamela and Mrs. Jewkes go fishing, and in
another oddly sexualized scene, Pamela compares the carp she hooks
to her own role as both Mr. B's and Mrs. Jewkes' sexual prey:

> 'O Mrs. Jewkes! Said I, I was thinking this poor carp was the
> unhappy Pamela. I was likening you and myself [as we reeled the
> fish in together] to my naughty master. As we hooked and
> deceived the poor carp, so was I betrayed by false baits; and
> when you said Play it, play it, it went to my heart, to think I
> should sport with the destruction of the poor fish I had betrayed.'
> (Richardson, *Pamela* 134).

Although Pamela's metaphor decries her sexual vulnerability, it also
makes her, even if only momentarily, complicit in her own seduction.
After all, in the metaphor, it is she (not merely Mr. B and Mrs.
Jewkes) who holds the phallic fishing rod that "betrays" her.

In both the fishing and writing metaphors, Mrs. Jewkes stands
in for Mr. B in his role as potential rapist. Mrs. Jewkes literally holds
the fishing rod that Mr. B metaphorically uses to hook Pamela, and
Mrs. Jewkes' "word" quite literally in the context of the novel brings
Mr. B to Lincolnshire to attempt the worst. Richardson plays out Mrs.
Jewkes' sexual attraction to Pamela, as might be expected in 1740, as
an aggressive and predatory conquest, but the corruption he depicts,
like that of Mr. B, seems to lie not in what we today would call sexual
orientation but in Mrs. Jewkes' refusal to hear the word "no." Mrs.
Jewkes' perversion, like Mr. B's, is her failure to distinguish between
sex and rape. As Pamela explains,

> 'She came to me, and took me in her huge arms, as if I was a
> feather: Said she, I do this to shew you what a poor resistance
> you can make against me, if I please to exert myself; and so,
> lambkin, don't say to your wolf, I *won't* come to bed! [...] But
> undress, undress, I tell you' (Richardson, *Pamela* 204).

Despite Richardson's equation between lesbian sexual activity
and rape in his creation of Mrs. Jewkes, all of the lesbian interactions
depicted in the novel are not predatory. Richardson's depiction of the
homoerotic attachment between Pamela and Mr. B's Bedfordshire
housekeeper, Mrs. Jervis, demonstrates that lesbian sex might involve
nurturing rather than conquest. The antithesis to Mrs. Jewkes,
Pamela's first "bedfellow" is referred to as "good Mrs. Jervis" over
and over again. "You may see," Pamela writes to her parents,

> 'what sort of woman that this Mrs. Jewkes is, compared to good
> Mrs. Jervis;...if I was not safe with good Mrs. Jervis [...] what a
> dreadful prospect have I now before me, in the hands of a woman
> that seems to delight in filthiness [Mrs. Jewkes]' (Richardson,
> *Pamela* 109).

Although Pamela's concern for her safety in this passage directly alludes to her potential rape at the hands of Mr. B, her comments closely tie both Mrs. Jewkes and Mrs. Jervis to her sexual initiation, but with two very different effects.

Richardson deliberately parallels Mrs. Jewkes' predation and Mrs. Jervis' nurturing to make it clear that Mrs. Jervis also possesses lesbian desire, but of a type very different from that of Mrs. Jewkes. The novel's earliest scenes between Pamela and Mrs. Jervis can be read as a gentle, loving lesbian connection between the two. Upon the death of Mr. B's mother, Mrs. Jervis nurtures and protects Pamela and hopes that Mr. B's pursuit of her might result in marriage. Less hardened than Mrs. Jewkes, Mrs. Jervis is watchful of Pamela, but feels convinced that her master would never attempt "the worst." After suffering Mr. B's first attack at the summer house, Pamela longs to tell Mrs. Jervis her fears but worries "it would be a sad thing to bring his displeasure upon her for my sake." Rather than admit the truth that she believes Mr. B will enter her bedroom if she is alone, Pamela "beg[s]" Mrs. Jervis to "be permitted to lie with her on nights," giving as her excuse a fear "of spirits." Skeptical of Pamela's explanation but kind-hearted and generous, Mrs. Jervis responds "you shall be my bed-fellow with all my heart [...] let your reason be what it will." Once they are alone, Pamela tells Mrs. Jervis "all that had passed" between her and Mr. B and "shew[s]" her the letters that she later hides from Mrs. Jewkes (Richardson, *Pamela* 18). Mrs. Jervis' loving connection with Pamela is the antithesis to Mrs. Jewkes' coercion of her. Whereas Mrs. Jewkes must force Pamela into her bed, she lies willingly with Mrs. Jervis. Whereas Mrs. Jewkes must force Pamela to relinquish her letters, she offers them to Mrs. Jervis unasked. And whereas Pamela avoids the surveillance of Mrs. Jewkes, she confides her secrets without encouragement to Mrs. Jervis.

Granted, the affection Mrs. Jervis bestows on Pamela seems more maternal than sexual, and clearly these two characters never overtly consummate their love in the novel. But as Barbara Smith explains in her discussion of Toni Morrison's *Sula,* feminist critics need to "re-evaluate the meaning of intense yet supposedly non-erotic connections between women" in literature (171). Just because an author does "not intend the reader to perceive [...] [a] relationship as inherently lesbian" doesn't mean we cannot "at least consider [...] this level of the novel's meaning" (Smith 170). In fact, Smith argues, "this lack of intention only shows the way in which heterosexist assumptions can veil what may logically be expected to occur in a work" (170).

In keeping with Smith's assessment of "what may logically be expected to occur," Richardson's novel structure suggests that he may actually intend for us to consider the possibility of a genuinely loving lesbian relationship between Mrs. Jervis and Pamela as a healthy antithesis to the lecherous predation of either Mrs. Jewkes or Mr. B. Mrs. Jervis and Pamela's love might appear latently sexual, but the structure of the novel equates the willing bond that Mrs. Jervis and Pamela share with the forced bond between her and Mrs. Jewkes to reveal a homosexual connection that transcends the stereotype of predatory lesbian sex. What has generally been read as a sexual opposition between the two housekeepers (Mrs. Jervis, the good servant who denies her own needs, sexual and otherwise, for those of the one she serves, set against Mrs. Jewkes, the fallen woman who courts sexual activity without regard for those who serve her needs) might be read as two very intentional depictions of lesbian attachment, one heterosexist and the other genuine.

In fact, two parallel closet scenes in the novel further emphasize these opposing expressions of lesbian attachment in the novel by depicting each of the housekeepers in a separate triangle with Pamela and Mr. B. The predatory nature of Mrs. Jewkes is presented through her association with Mr. B in a violent closet scene midway through the novel and is set against an earlier scene in which Mrs. Jervis interacts with Mr. B in an attempt to provide for Pamela.

In the novel's most graphically violent scene, Mrs. Jewkes and Mr. B work together to attempt to rape Pamela. Mr. B, dressed in Mrs. Jewkes' clothes, hides in Pamela's closet and comes to her bed pretending to be the under-servant, Nan. He pins Pamela on the bed and holds her left hand down while "the vile procuress" holds her right. Pamela, realizing the true identity of her rapist, screams out "in such a manner, as never anybody heard the like" (Richardson, *Pamela* 212), prays to God to "deliver [her] from this distress! or strike [her] dead this moment" (Richardson, *Pamela* 213), and then falls into a fit. Once she faints, Mr. B relents, but, as she is regaining consciousness, Pamela overhears Mrs. Jewkes urge him on: "And will you, sir, said the wicked wretch, for a fit or two give up such an opportunity as this?—I thought you had known the sex better. She is now, you see, quite well again!" (Richardson, *Pamela* 213). Mrs. Jewkes seems to be even more erotically engaged in this scene than Mr. B is, and the fact that he is dressed in Mrs. Jewkes' clothes symbolically suggests that she is more the author of this debauch than he is.

Through her identification with Mr. B in this scene, Mrs. Jewkes vicariously seeks to rape Pamela, but in a parallel closet scene earlier in the novel, Mrs. Jervis attempts not to rape but, rather, to provide for Pamela through the vehicle of Mr. B. When Mr. B decides to turn Pamela out of his house for what he terms her "insolence," Mrs. Jervis brings him secretly to her closet so that he can overhear for himself that Pamela does not covet his money or wish to demean his authority. Mrs. Jervis believes that witnessing Pamela's virtue will make Mr. B "ashamed of what he has done" and will teach him never "to offer the like to [her] again" (Richardson, *Pamela* 19). She hopes to make it possible for Pamela to remain with her at Bedfordshire and, perhaps, eventually to marry the master. In the closet, Mr. B overhears Pamela's decision to reject the expensive parting gifts he offers and her declaration that she must return home because remaining in the house after his lewd advances might seem like an invitation to more affront. Although somewhat affected by Pamela's honesty, Mr. B is appalled to be the subject of gossip among servants. Mrs. Jervis hoped that inviting Mr. B into Pamela's closet would engender in him the same loving desire that she feels for Pamela, but his pride forces him, instead, to reveal himself, to enter into a confrontation with the two women, and to attempt to force himself on Pamela. Mrs. Jervis's love for the girl leaves her no alternative but to protect her "dear lamb" (Richardson, *Pamela* 60). She "clasps [Pamela] around the waist and shouts to Mr. B, "Are there not [...] enough wicked ones in the world, for your base purpose, but you must attempt such a lamb as this?" (Richardson, *Pamela* 60). Mr. B blames Mrs. Jervis for making Pamela "more afraid of [him] than she had occasion" (Richardson, *Pamela* 63) and eventually dismisses the housekeeper for her betrayal.

Mrs. Jervis' love for Pamela is ultimately impotent because she is unable to conceive of a viable future for her friend other than marriage to Mr. B. By remaining complicit with Mr. B's attempt to own Pamela (either as mistress or wife), both Mrs. Jewkes and Mrs. Jervis become "procuress[es]." Even Pamela herself complies with Mr. B by keeping herself "honest" and holding out for marriage; her chastity makes her a more valued commodity, and in her role as wife she makes clear that she still sees Mr. B as her "master." Mrs. Jewkes' and Mrs. Jervis' desire for Pamela, and hers for Mr. B, remain tied to his power over them all. It is this problem in the novel that Walker addresses by collapsing the strength of Mrs. Jewkes and the tenderness of Mrs. Jervis into a new kind of love object, the Womanist, Shug Avery. Because Shug is both powerful and nurturing, she represents a lesbianism that defines women's relationships as ends in themselves rather than as the means to acceptance or comfort in a male-defined world. In *The Color Purple*, the impotence of the genuine lesbian relationship between Pamela and Mrs. Jervis is transformed into the revolutionary love match between Celie and Shug that permeates the social fabric of the novel and changes the way that everyone, male and female, lesbian and heterosexual, black and white, interacts with each other.

The Color Purple and Lesbian Love

In *The Color Purple*, Walker rewrites the two versions of lesbian sexuality presented in *Pamela*. Whereas Mrs. Jewkes' sexuality is predatory and Mrs. Jervis' is concealed by her role as the good mother, Shug reverberates with the sexual potency of a Mrs. Jewkes tempered by the maternal tenderness and intimacy of a Mrs. Jervis. From her first glimpse of Shug in the picture that falls from Albert's wallet, Celie responds to Shug on both a sexual and a maternal level.

> 'Shug Avery was a woman. The most beautiful woman I ever saw. She more pretty then my mama. She bout ten thousand times more prettier than me. I see her there in furs. Her face rouge. Her hair like something tail. She grinning with her foot up on somebody motorcar. Her eyes serious tho, Sad some' (Walker, *TCP* 6).

Celie immediately connects Shug with her own mother and with herself and identifies with the pain that lies behind Shug's "grin." The moment Shug arrives at Albert's house, looking "like she ain't long for this world but dressed well for the next" (Walker, *TCP* 45), Celie makes it her business to nurture Shug. Celie offers her the careful mothering she never received herself—feeding Shug, combing her hair, and bathing her. But, clearly, Celie's maternal response is infused with sexual attraction.

> '[Albert and Shug] made three babies together but he squeamish bout giving her a bath. Maybe he figure he start thinking bout things he shouldn't. But what bout me? First time I got the full sight of Shug Avery long black body with it black plum nipples, look like her mouth, I thought I had turned into a man.' (Walker, *TCP* 49)

This scene is often read as the moment of Celie's sexual awakening, and it is no accident that the epiphany reveals both Celie's maternal and sexual impulses. Albert's sexual desire for Shug is disconnected from his need to care for her (made evident in his feeling "squeamish" at the thought of bathing her), but Celie's sexual desire is closely linked with her maternal feelings. In fact, the consummation of Celie and Shug's love is depicted in a metaphor of reciprocal mothering:

> 'Us kiss and kiss till us can't hardly kiss no more. [...] Then I feels something real soft and wet on my breast, feel like one of my little lost babies mouth. Way after while, I act like a little lost baby too' (Walker, *TCP* 113).

Because Shug possesses both the open sensuality of Mrs. Jewkes and the nurturing capacity of Mrs. Jervis, she is able to mother Celie as well as to be mothered by her. Shug protects Celie from Albert by threatening to leave if he continues to beat her; Shug reunites Celie with her sister Nettie by discovering the letters Albert has been hiding; and Shug prevents Celie from murdering Albert by taking a weapon from her hand and placing a needle in it instead. When Celie realizes that Albert has hidden her sister's letters in order to make her believe that Nettie is dead, Celie finds herself "standing hind his chair with his razor open" (Walker, *TCP* 120).

This violation of Celie's letters recalls Mrs. Jewkes' and Mr. B's metaphorical rapes in *Pamela* as they force Pamela to reveal what she has written. In Richardson's novel, reading Pamela's letters without permission is equated with rape. In addition to Mrs. Jewkes' demand to see the letters and her highly sexualized voyeurism as she watches Pamela write is a parallel scene in which Mr. B threatens to strip Pamela to get at her hidden letters:

> 'I have searched every place above, and in your closet, for them, and cannot find them; so I will know where they are. Now, said he, it is my opinion they are about you; and I never undressed a girl in my life; but I will now begin to strip my pretty Pamela; and I hope I shall not go far before I find them' (Richardson, *Pamela* 245).

The corresponding scene in *The Color Purple*, as Celie stands behind Albert with an open razor in her hand ready to take revenge on Albert for stealing her letters, makes it clear that Celie also experiences Albert's violation of her letters as a metaphorical rape. It is no coincidence that Celie chooses a razor as her weapon against Albert. Her stepfather, Alfonso, used a haircut as his pretext for raping Celie (Walker, *TCP* 111-12), so in choosing to wield a razor, Celie's momentary fantasy of murder seeks revenge on both her literal and metaphorical rapists.

Shug, however, does not encourage Celie's desire to get even. Shug removes the razor from her hand and takes Celie immediately to her bed. "Nobody feel better for killing nothing" (Walker, *TCP* 145), she tells Celie. Although their conjugal life is interrupted by Celie's trauma, Shug continues to "snuggle" and "hug" Celie and suggests "Times like this, lulls, us ought to do something different. [...] let's make you some pants" (Walker, *TCP* 146). Celie agrees, and with a "needle and not a razor" (Walker, *TCP* 147), begins to remake her life. Her talent for sewing frees Celie from the slave- and marriage-markets that would make her a commodity. Like Shug's singing, Celie's sewing creates her self-determination and prevents her from being owned. As Shug tells Celie when they arrive in Memphis, "You not my maid. I didn't bring you to Memphis to be that. I brought you here to love you and help you get on your feet" (*TCP* 211). One paragraph later Celie writes:

> 'I sit in the dining room making pants after pants. I got pants now in every color and size under the sun. Since us started making pants down home, I ain't been able to stop [...] then one day I made the perfect pair of pants. For my sugar, naturally' (Walker, *TCP* 211-12).

The Color Purple, Pamela, and a Lesbian Model for Social Reform

Pants making is the perfect metaphor for Celie and Shug's sexual relationship and becomes the symbol of a union that expands into a model for healthy human interactions of all kinds throughout the novel. Celie's sewing challenges the male definition of authority that wearing the pants in the family denotes. In making pants for women, Celie shifts the paradigm so that the women in her world can also wear "the pants," i.e. can define the family. But the analogy does not end there. More important in Walker's metaphor is her implication that merely reversing the hierarchical dyad will not solve the problems with authority that have victimized both Celie and Pamela. Sewing pants involves joining pairs of pattern pieces that are not hierarchically opposed but, rather, are mirror opposites of each other. Like Walker's model of lesbianism, Celie's sewing emphasizes that a

hierarchical social structure based on the opposition of male and
female sexuality in the heterosexual union can be reconceived
according to the model of lesbian sexuality as a mirroring. Once
joined, the mirrored halves dissolve their opposition and the unit
becomes a functional whole—two pant legs can walk and work
together.

The mirroring that organizes Shug and Celie's sexual
relationship extends to redefine non-sexual dyads that appear to be
opposed to one another throughout Celie's story. In fact, Celie's first
encounter with Sofia Butler finds both women intent on denigrating
the other as all that she herself does not want to be. Celie tells Harpo
to beat Sofia because Sofia takes liberties that Celie denies herself"

> 'I like Sophia, but she don't act like me at all. If she talking when
> Harpo and [Albert] come in the room, she keep right on. If they
> ast her where something at, she say she don't know. Keep talking
> [. . .] I think about this when Harpo ast me what he ought to do to
> make her mind [. . .] Beat her. I say' (*TCP* 35-36).

Soon enough it becomes apparent to both women that their
seemingly opposite responses to domination are actually mirrors of
one another. Sophia barges into Abert's house carrying a pair of
curtains that Celie made for her, shoves them into her hand and scoffs,
"Just want you to know I looked to you for help" (*TCP* 39). Ready to
fight Celie for her betrayal, Sofia gets the wind "took" out "of her
jaws" when she realizes that Celie's belief that women ought to be
beaten arises from the same fear that inspired her own refusal to take
abuse. "A girl child ain't safe in a family of men" (Walker, *TCP* 40),
Sophia asserts, and she picks up the curtains she had thrown to the
ground. "Let's make quilt pieces out of these messed up curtains, she
[Sophia] say. And I [Celie] run get my pattern book" (Walker, *TCP*
42).

Like Shug and Celie's sexual union, Sofia and Celie stitch
together a non-sexual union that is based on equivalence and
recognition rather than on opposition. Just as each quilt block in a
pattern mirrors its neighbor, Celie and Sophia mirror each other. After
Sophia is put in prison for striking the mayor's wife, she explains to
Celie how she survived there: "Every time they ast me to do
something, Miss Celie, I act like I'm you. I jump up and do just what
they say" (Walker, *TCP* 88). And when Celie discovers Nettie's
letters in Albert's trunk and feels anger for the first time in her life,
she explains,

'All day long I act just like Sofia. I stutter. I mutter to myself. I
stumble bout the house crazy for Mr. _____ blood.' (*TCP* 120).

Accepting hierarchical opposition that depends on a
benevolent authority is not an option in *The Color Purple* as it is in
Pamela. Once Pamela's "white angel [gets] the better of [Mr. B's]
black one" (Richardson, *Pamela* 283) and he is converted to the
higher principles of Christian charity and love, Pamela is happy to
serve him faithfully. Similarly, Pamela's intense relationships with
Mrs. Jewkes and Mrs. Jervis completely disappear once she is married
to Mr. B. Both women, and even Pamela herself, dissolve into their
roles as functionaries in Mr. B's household. All three women's
relationships with each other exist only as a function of Mr. B's
attempts to control Pamela, and once this catalyst is removed, the
women have little or nothing to do with one another. Female
relationships are formed in *Pamela* only in response to male power.
But *The Color Purple* recognizes that female connection, whether
sexual or not, is an end in itself. Walker makes it clear that hierarchy
of any kind prevents genuine human intimacy and that no one wins
when relationships define either party as prey or as a tool. The
oppressor and the oppressed too easily change roles. Even women's
power is not a solution to the problem as Walker depicts it. Sofia's
attempt to dominate in white society quickly reveals that she will not
find peace until she can envision a community based on connection
rather than opposition and hierarchy.

The Color Purple, Walker's Lesbian Social Model, and Race Relations

The inadequacy of hierarchy is perhaps best depicted in the race relations between the African-Americans and the whites in *The Color Purple.* By striking back rather than accepting Harpo's beatings, Sophia maintains independence from black male domination. However, the autonomy that empowers her in the black community victimizes her in the white southern community that works to control black power. When the mayor slaps Sophia for telling his wife in no uncertain terms that she does not want to be her maid, "Sophia knock the man down" (Walker, *TCP* 85). Unfortunately, the same method of self-defense that convinced Harpo to let her go and live with her sister, Odessa, lands Sofia in prison when she tries to use it on a white man.

In a similar attempt to subvert white authority and rescue Sofia, Albert devises a plan to reverse the hierarchy and get power over the white legal system by using the logic of the African folk myth "Brer Rabbit" to free Sofia from jail. Realizing that Bubber Hodges, the warden of the prison, is the uncle of Mary Agnes, Harpo's girlfriend, Albert persuades her to dress up "like a white woman" and convince Bubber that being Miss Millie's maid would be a much more appropriate punishment for Sofia than prison. But this "ole uncle Tomming" (Walker, *TCP* 94) is not a success. Although Sofia is released into Miss Millie's custody, she finds that life as Miss Millie's maid is anything but liberation. As Alfonso explains later in the novel, if you try to barter with the white man of the racist south, he'll take "Either your money, your land, your woman or your ass" (Walker, *TCP* 182). In this case, Bubber Hodges takes the woman. In exchange for Sofia's so-called freedom, Mary Agnes is sacrificed and comes home "with a limp. Her dress rip. Her hat missing and one of the heels come off her shoe" (Walker, *TCP* 95). Walker makes clear that fighting authority with like authority is no solution, and to further this assertion she offers a subplot to echo it. We cannot forget that both Celie's father's attempt to run a store in competition with a local white businessman and Alfonso's decision to appease that same businessman by giving one-third of all he makes to "the white man" are both ultimately unsuccessful ways of dealing with the white hierarchy. Celie's father is lynched by the whites, and Alfonso is ostracized by the black community for *his* "ole uncle Tomming."

Walker's depiction of the racial struggle in *The Color Purple* never lets us forget that the privileges of women like Pamela ride on the backs of the world's Celies and Sophias. Richardson's novel ignores eighteenth-century British colonialism and the extent to which the thriving British economy and the wealth of families like Mr. B and his wife, Pamela, were dependent on African slavery in the British colonies. Walker, however, reminds us that more than a hundred years after emancipation, Miss Millie's leisure is a remnant of the colonialist racial prejudice that still privileges her white husband to hire black labor more cheaply than white. Ultimately, Pamela never challenges white male authority because she can marry into it and thereby profit from it. Walker keeps us aware throughout *The Color Purple* that a wider definition of *Pamela's* "Everywoman" reveals that not all women have the chance or the desire for this kind of hierarchical power.

By the end of the novel, the women (and men) of *The Color Purple* must abandon their attempts to gain power over others, regardless of their race, gender, or sexual orientation, in order to join a new nurturing community founded on true intimacy and connection. Walker makes it clear that loving relationships based in a system of reciprocal support can regenerate the lives of all who find themselves a part of the web. Whereas Pamela's acceptance of Mr. B's authority, however benevolent, leads to her continued subservience as his wife, Walker's novel suggests that walking away from an oppressive relationship can be as therapeutic for the oppressor as for the oppressed. Albert has envied the nurturing relationship that Shug and Celie share (Walker, *TCP* 271), and when the two of them reject his abuse of Celie and walk out of his house together, they open the door for his reciprocal connection with Harpo. Albert has learned his lesson and lets his son (already domesticated by the exodus of both Sophia and Mary Agnes) nurture him in a healing relationship that helps both Harpo and Albert to give up their power and to attain connection. When Celie returns from Memphis, she observes that "when you talk to" Albert "now he really listen, and one time, out of nowhere in the conversation us was having, he said Celie, I'm satisfied this the first time I ever lived on Earth as a natural man" (Walker, *TCP* 260). Celie and Shug's relationship transforms Albert's entire definition of what it means to be a man, and, consequently, he gives up power for love. "The more I wonder," Albert says, "the more I love." Celie replies, "And people start to love you back" (Walker, *TCP* 283).

The "Everywoman" of *The Color Purple* is a black lesbian, but Walker's Womanism shows us how the union, rather than the polarization, of opposites in all kinds of relationships can lead to a supportive community that ultimately can include everyone. By the end of the novel, Albert has been initiated into the Womanist community and, rather than making a slave of Celie, works side by side with her, sewing shirts to be worn with the pants she designs and creates. The white Eleanor Jane, daughter of Miss Millie, joins the Womanist community by working in Sophia's kitchen, by nurturing Sophia's daughter, Henrietta, and by teaching her own son to respect blacks. Sophia too has learned by the end of the novel that fighting power with power is a dead end. Having found no contentment in fist-fighting with Mary Agnes and Harpo, or in serving in a white man's jail or a white woman's kitchen, Sophia joins the novel's community of nurturers to mother the children of the woman whose teeth she once knocked out in a bar-fight. Rather than fighting with Mary Agnes over who is Harpo's legitimate mate, Sophia joins with her to care for the children they now both regard as their own.

The Color Purple, Pamela, and Religious Authority

The Color Purple offers a vision of society that re-conceives social interaction by rejecting hierarchy at both the familial and social levels. But Walker's criticism goes beyond the boundaries of family and society to what she sees as the root of the problem—a sexist depiction of humankind that permeates both the religious and psychological infrastructures that govern society. Walker reveals that familial and social hierarchy have been justified first by Western male-defined religions and more recently by Western male-defined psychology.

Samuel Richardson's *Pamela* postulates a benevolent familial and social authority that governs according to religious principles, but Walker's *The Color Purple* challenges religious authority by revealing it as just another manifestation of sexist, heterocentric, and racist hierarchy. *Pamela* depicts human authority as a natural and humane system that emanates from religious hierarchy. Pamela teaches Mr. B to exercise a legitimate control endorsed by a Christian God who is Himself depicted as the ultimate authority. As Pamela explains at the end of the novel:

'All that I value myself upon, is, that God has raised me to a
condition to be useful in my generation, to better persons than
myself. This is my pride: And I hope this will be all my pride.
For what was I of myself!—All good I can do, is but a poor third-
hand good; for my dearest master himself is but the second-hand.
God the gracious, the all-good, the all bountiful, the all-mighty,
the all-merciful God, is the first. To him, therefore, be all the
glory!' (Richardson, *Pamela* 528)

Richardson's novel never questions hierarchical rule but
merely adds Christian virtue as a possible means to gaining authority.
Pamela's moral behavior has moved her up the ladder from servant to
wife in Mr. B's home. However, despite his verbal insistence that her
virtue will "confer" upon him "at least as much honour as she will
receive" from his noble birth (Richardson, *Pamela* 328), he is,
nonetheless, the god in their home. Once they marry, Mr. B delivers a
moral lecture from which Pamela derives, not the Ten
Commandments but, rather, forty eight "rules [for the good wife] [...]
to observe," each of which is numbered in the text and begins with
either "I must" or "I must not" (Richardson, *Pamela* 475-79). After
reciting the rules in a letter to her parents, Pamela admits, "you'll see I
have not the easiest task in the world. But I know my own intentions,
that I shall not willfully err" (Richardson, *Pamela* 479). The analogy
is clear: the good wife is to the good husband as the good Christian is
to God.

In *Pamela,* Mr. B's authority is depicted as God-given and,
therefore, inescapable, but Walker's Shug and Celie create their own
paradise separate from the rule of hierarchy and reject definitions of
God that imply authority. Celie repudiates the God that Pamela
embraces and writes:

'I don't write to God no more [...] the God I been praying and
writing to is a man. An act just like all the other mens I know.
Trifling, forgetful and lowdown.' (Walker, *TCP* 192)

Richardson depicts society as a construct of the Christian God, but
Shug and Celie recognize the Christian God as a construct of white,
patriarchal society. In her early conversation with Shug, Celie
punctuates her description of God by adding, "He big and old and tall
and gray bearded and white" (Walker, *TCP* 194).

In *The Color Purple,* Shug helps Celie challenge the white,
patriarchal version of God by positing a feminine spirituality based on

nurturing and connection rather than on oppositional hierarchy. As Shug explains:

> 'one day when I was sitting quiet and feeling like a motherless child, which I was, it come to me: that feeling of being part of everything, not separate at all. I knew that if I cut a tree, my arm would bleed. And I laughed and I cried and I run all around the house. I knew just what it was. In fact, when it happen, you can't miss it. It sort of like you know what, she say, grinning and rubbing high on my thigh.' (Walker, *TCP* 195-96)

In this passage, Shug equates spirituality with lesbian sex and is careful to explain that this union is not a hierarchical dyad. For Shug, union with God entails a connection with all of creation; human beings are "not separate" but are "part of everything." Like the lesbian social model that Shug and Celie live out, connection with God in Shug's spiritual paradigm involves sacrificing the need to control.

Celie, who has been well-schooled in the patriarchal model of religious hierarchy, is uncertain how to imagine a God who eschews authority. When Shug explains that "God love admiration," Celie asks, "You saying God vain?" And when Shug tries to explain that God just wants "to share a good thing," Celie worries, "What it do when it pissed off?" (Walker, *TCP* 196). Shug explains that God is not a masculine controlling power to be obeyed but a feminine living force that wants "to be loved." "People think pleasing God is all God care about. But any fool living in the world can see it always trying to please us back. [...] It always making little surprises and springing them on us when us least expect" (Walker, *TCP* 196). Shug's God advocates reciprocation. It is not God, but "Man," Shug explains, who "corrupt[s] everything" with hierarchy:

> 'He on your box of grits, in your head, and all over the radio. He trying to make you think he everywhere. Soon as you think he everywhere, you think he God. But he ain't. Whenever you trying to pray, and man plop himself on the other end of it, tell him to git lost [...] Conjure up flowers, wind, water, a big rock.' (Walker, *TCP* 197)

Shug's God is a mother, a nurturer who is one with all she creates, but Celie's patriarchal society, like Pamela's, demands a model of God as Father, a symbol of power and control. Even Celie, despite her ability to nurture the women around her, explains that she cannot conceive of Shug's maternal God.

The hierarchy of a male-constructed God over the procreative power of human women is Walker's target in her rewrite of *Pamela*. Richardson's application of Filmer's *Patriarcha* endorses the Old Testament interpretation of woman as created by God to be man's "helpmate." Although *Pamela* challenges the assumption that women must observe all male requests for sex, whether endorsed by God or not, the novel never questions the assumption that a male-defined God has placed "good" men in charge of women's sexuality and has created it for men's purposes. Mr. B learns through the course of the novel how to be a good Christian husband and father in the model of God the Father, and Pamela defines her obedience to Mr. B exactly as she does her obedience to God:

> 'O how shall I merit all these things at his [Mr. B's] hand! I can only do the best I can; and pray to God to reward him; and resolve to love him with a pure heart, and serve him with a sincere obedience.' (Richardson, *Pamela* 358)

Pamela disparages Mr. B at the beginning of the novel for attempting to use her as a sex object but praises him at the end of it for controlling both her sexuality and maternity when he decides to have children. Pamela explains,

> 'He was pleased to take notice of my dress; and spanning my waist with his hands, said, What a sweet shape is here! It would make one regret to lose it: and yet, my beloved Pamela, I shall think nothing but that loss wanting, to complete my happiness.— I put my bold hand before his mouth and said, Hush, hush! O fie, sir!—The freest thing you have ever yet said, since I have been yours!—He kissed my hand, and said, Such an innocent wish, my dearest, may be permitted me, because it is the end of the institution.—But say, Would such a case be unwelcome to my Pamela?—I will say, sir said I, and hid my blushing face on his bosom, that your wishes, in every thing, shall be mine; but, pray, sir, say no more.' (Richardson, *Pamela* 395)

Once they are married, Pamela's duty to Mr. B and God leaves her husband in charge of deciding when they will first initiate a sexual relationship and when they will have children. Despite several hundred pages of Pamela's insistence on her right to decide whether or not to have sex, she is more than willing to acquiesce to Mr. B's sexual control when she reads it as the earthly equivalent of her duty to God the Father.

Walker's revision of *Pamela* calls attention to the fact that women's sexual subjectivity has been forced underground by Richardson's insistence on a patriarchal religious construction of woman as man's sexual servant. Pamela ultimately marries and surrenders the chastity she has guarded for so long to the service of Mr. B's desire for sex and children. Similarly, the novel's lesbians end the novel as Pamela and Mr. B's penitential servants. After the wedding, Mrs. Jervis is returned to her post as housekeeper at the request of Pamela (in one very brief paragraph) but is never heard of again in the novel. And after Pamela successfully confronts the classism in her husband's social circle, Mrs. Jewkes repents her former actions toward Pamela and dissolves into the background as nothing more than an obedient servant. In short, the patriarchal gods of *Pamela* invalidate and submerge all kinds of female sexuality that do not serve men. *The Color Purple,* however, presents the relationship between Celie and Shug as one free of male dominance. Despite Albert's attempts to poison Shug's perception of Celie by berating her in Shug's presence, Shug's love for Celie remains strong. And despite Shug's insistence on triangulating her relationship with Celie by remaining sexually intimate with men (Albert, Grady, and Germaine), Celie remains constant in her love of Shug. God the Father has no place in the paradise of Celie and Shug's love. It remains free of male control.

The Color Purple, Pamela, and Psychological Authority

In her rewrite of *Pamela,* Walker challenges Richardson's hierarchical and heterocentric depiction of God by putting the power of definition into the mouth of one of her own lesbian characters. Shug redefines God as a part of herself and as like herself. "God is inside you [. . .] You come into the world with God. But only them that search for it inside find it" (Walker, *TCP* 195). Furthermore, Shug's God approves of lesbian sex. Rubbing "high" on Celie's thigh, she explains, "God love all them feelings. That's some of the best stuff God did. And when you know God loves 'em you enjoys 'em a lot more" (Walker, *TCP* 196). Celie struggles to comprehend Shug's god:

'Well, us talk and talk bout God, but I'm still adrift. Trying to
chase that old white man out of my head. I been so busy thinking
bout him I never truly notice nothing God make. [...] Now that
my eyes opening, I feels like a fool. Next to any little scrub of a
bush in my yard, Mr. _____'s evil sort of shrink.' (Walker, *TCP*
197)

Celie's spiritual conversion involves learning to trust a female
perspective. "But this hard work," Celie explains; the patriarchal God
has been "on [my] eyeball" for "so long, he don't want to budge. He
threaten lightening, flood, earthquakes. Us fight" (Walker, *TCP* 197).
In this scene, Celie is moving away from dependence on outward
authority and toward self-definition. The result is a subtle shift from a
spiritual to a psychological paradigm. In Richardson's novel, the
feminine ethic of connection and nurturing has been submerged by a
patriarchal hierarchy that has turned female sexual and procreative
powers to the service of heterosexist, hierarchical domination. But in
The Color Purple, Shug articulates a Womanist psychology that
validates female sexuality as an antidote to a hierarchical depiction of
God.

Psychologist Sigmund Freud postulates in *Moses and
Monotheism* that mythology, religious stories of all types, are not
depictions of the divine but, rather, symbolic representations of the
workings of the human psyche. Like Walker's Shug, Freud reads
religion as socially created. A patriarchal society creates a patriarchal
God, not vice versa. Consequently, Walker's criticism of
Richardson's God-centered world in the story of Shug and Celie's
relationship is perhaps more easily understood as a psychological
model rather than a religious one. Freud's psychological theories are
particularly interesting when read in connection with Walker's novel,
because both writers link sexuality with spirituality. Freud sees
Western religion as a construct of repressed human sexuality. The
psychological restrictions that humans must put upon themselves in
order to live together in society are translated into stories with moral
axioms to guide us. Religious myths are symbolic stories that relate
the human struggle to avoid the lure of sexual acts (incest, polygamy,
homosexuality, etc.) that must be made taboo in order to ensure a
functional society.

According to Freud, society is modeled upon human
interaction with a flesh and blood familial father rather than with a
spiritual godly father. In order to become functional individuals,
young men and women must separate from their bonds with the

mothers who raised them and enter into the domain of the father. Aptly named the "father of psychology," Sigmund Freud describes separation from the mother and entrance into the world of the father as the pivotal moment of self-definition for both boys and girls. According to Freud, boys around the age of three wish to possess the mother sexually but fantasize at their first sight of a naked little girl that her penis is missing because she too desired her mother and was castrated by her father for those wishes. Normal sexuality and normal personality, according to Freud, results for the boy when he acknowledges the superior power of his father, relinquishes the connection to his mother, and refocuses desire for her onto other women (155-56).

Daughters, too, Freud claims, must give up their attachments to their mothers. Freud defines the girl's first sexual attraction as homosexual. Just as the little boy focuses his first sexual attraction on his mother, so the little girl focuses her desire on her mother. Castrated already, however, the little girl is not afraid of the power of the father, but, rather, covets it. She breaks from her mother because she "envies" (Freud 158) the penis, the "far superior equipment" (Freud 157) that denotes power in the world of the father, and she seeks a penis substitute through heterosexual relations and motherhood (Freud 159).

Freud's depiction of the male-defined girl's progress toward "normal" female sexuality and personality mirrors Pamela's story in Richardson's novel. As a child, Pamela is nurtured by her mother figure, the "good Mrs. Jervis." Their connection is latently homosexual and, therefore, Pamela must ultimately reject it in order to obtain power through marriage to Mr. B. Her marriage and her eventual role as the mother of Mr. B's children in the father's world give her the status that she lacked in the mother's world she shared with Mrs. Jervis.

Walker re-conceives the maternal homosexual attachment, which must be left behind in *Pamela,* as a loving relationship between Shug and Celie. The relationship exists apart from the world of the father and for its own sake. Thus, Walker reveals the sexism inherent in any system defined by fathers for fathers, whether social, religious, or psychological. Walker's novel seeks to redefine all kinds of human interaction through a psychology of connection rather than of separation and hierarchy.

Walker challenges Freud and Richardson by modeling "normal" human psychology as a continuing relationship between a mother and daughter, not as an exodus from the mother's world. Just as Shug defines a feminine god as part of all she creates, Walker depicts human psychology as a polygamous attachment to the mother that coexists with and serves as a model for all subsequent attachments. In *The Color Purple,* Shug is not simply Celie's good mother and supportive lover. She is also a self-assertive individual who makes sexual connections with a host of other people outside the union she shares with Celie. When Shug leaves home for her "last fling" with a nineteen-year-old boy, Germaine, Celie writes, "My heart broke" (Walker, *TCP* 247).

   In keeping with traditional Freudian theory that equates separation and psychological normalcy, feminist literary critic E. Ellen Barker interprets this scene as Celie's necessary separation from the woman who has nurtured her into independence. Barker explains:

> With any parent/child relationship there comes a time when both must realize that it's time to let go. This time comes when Shug wants the freedom to pursue her last fling with a boy half her age. Shug can part from Celie knowing that, like any good mother, she has done all that she could to provide an environment of love and security so Celie can stand on her own two feet. (63)

Barker's analysis of Shug's maternal sexuality is convincing overall, but her insistence on the importance of Shug's connection with Celie simply as a means to their eventual separation is less believable. The first problem with Barker's argument is that both feminist and traditional psychological theorists make clear that the "good-enough mother" isn't supposed to break the bond between herself and her child in the way that a dog or cat weans its young. Instead, she is supposed to create a facilitating environment that allows the child to develop the independence necessary to break the bond him- or herself. As Object-Relations psychologist D. W. Winnicott explains:

> Some babies are fortunate enough to have a mother whose initial active adaptation to their infant's need was good enough. This enables them to have the illusion of actually finding what was created [i.e. the child can create and believe the necessary fantasy that the world and he are one]. Eventually, after a capacity for relationships has been established, such babies can take the next step towards recognition of the essential aloneness of the human being. (114)

   The second problem with Barker's argument is that the position of separation as a psychological norm hardly seems in keeping with Shug's world view. Shug sees herself (and God) as part of all creation, but for theorists like Winnicott, normal human psychology demands that children "grow up" to accept their isolation from one other.

According to Freudian theory, psychological normalcy necessitates a separation from the mother that leads to heterosexual development. But Object-Relations theorist, Nancy Chodorow, challenges Freud's phallocentric viewpoint. Chodorow responds to Freud's explanation of the Oedipus Complex by explaining that at the time of psychological separation from the mother, boys separate more completely from the mother than girls do, not because of the father's threat of castration but because the boy is simultaneously learning about sex difference. The boy comes to understand the boundary between his own and his mother's bodies as a firm distinction because he recognizes there not only the separation of self and other but also of male and female (Chodorow 166-70).

The girl, Chodorow argues, develops a less distinct sense of boundaries because her first experience of the separation between self and other is complicated by the fact that she and her mother share the same sex. Because the primary caretakers in our society tend to be female, Chodorow argues, relational boundaries are not so firmly formed for women as for men (169).

Alice Walker's depiction of human relationships in *The Color Purple* seems indebted to Chodorow's theory, but Walker defines an even more pronounced notion of connectedness in her novel, one that challenges the primary assumption that individuation of any kind defines healthy relationships and "normal" sexuality. Unlike Freud's and Chodorow's "normal" girls, Celie never really detaches from her mother at all. As she explains,

> 'I don't even look at mens. That's the truth. I look at women, tho, cause I'm not scared of them. Maybe cause my mama cuss me you think I kept mad at her. But I ain't. I felt sorry for mama' (Walker, *TCP* 5)

This model of attachment to her mother continues throughout Celie's relationships with other women in the novel. Even when she is physically separated from Nettie, rebuffed by Sophia, and temporarily abandoned by Shug, Celie's attachment to these women remains un-assailed.

Unlike Freud's little girl who rejects her mother because she lacks a penis and Richardson's Pamela who gives up her bond with

Mrs. Jervis and all the novel's women to become Mr. B's wife, Celie never gives up on the women she loves. Long after Celie believes her sister to be dead, she continues to maintain a connection to her through the letters she writes to God. In one letter Celie writes,

> 'I say, Write.
> She [Nettie] say, Nothing but death can keep me from it.
> She never write.' (Walker, *TCP* 18)

Despite her belief that Nettie is dead, Celie writes to God all that she would have told her sister had she still been alive. For Celie, God is a conduit to her sister, so when she loses faith in Him, Celie writes directly to her dead sister instead: "Dear Nettie, I don't write to God no more. I write to you" (Walker, *TCP* 192).

Celie also remains connected to her absent sister by learning from her example. When Albert's sister, Kate, tries to encourage Celie to assert herself, Celie observes,

> 'I don't say nothing. I think about Nettie, dead. She fight, she run away. What good it do? I don't fight, I stay where I'm told. But I'm alive.' (Walker, *TCP* 21)

In fact, it is not until Celie discovers Nettie's hidden letters and realizes that she is alive and that running and fighting have saved her, that Celie too begins to assert herself.

Similar to Celie's continued attachment to her absent sister, the apparent breach between Celie and Sophia early in the novel reveals itself to be their means of connection. When Celie advises Harpo to beat Sophia because "she [Sophia] don't act like me [Celie]" (Walker, *TCP* 35), the seeming difference between the two women merely clarifies the fact of their connectedness. As Sophia explains to Celie after confronting her for her advice to Harpo, "To tell you the truth, you remind me of my mama" (Walker, *TCP* 41).

In Shug and Celie's lesbian relationship, Walker continues to challenge the psychological theories that define mental health as predicated on separation. Freud holds that failed separation in a girl's development results in the "patholog[y]" (156) of lesbianism (161-62), but Walker depicts Shug and Celie's lesbian relationship as an uninterrupted connection that empowers both women. In Walker's equation of lesbianism and mothering, the primary bond between Celie and Shug is never broken by subsequent bonds; instead, further bonding is seen as arising from this primary connection. As Celie explains,

> 'if [Shug] come back here dragging Germaine [her nineteen-year-old boyfriend], I'd make them both welcome or die trying. Who am I to tell her who to love? My job just to love her good and true myself.' (Walker, *TCP* 269)

When Shug returns home at the end of the novel to a community that includes both Celie and Albert, only the most naïve reader could assume that Shug will suddenly become monogamous and pair with Celie for life like a turtledove. The novel's plotting suggests that neither Shug nor her relationship with Celie will change.

Unlike Pamela's relationship with Mr. B, which demands disconnection from the world of women to obtain entry into the father's domain of wealth and power, Celie and Shug's relationship challenges the system of competition and exclusivity that underlies the Freudian daughter's struggle for power. As a metaphorical daughter, Celie refuses to compete for power in the world of the father. She has no desire to marry into the father's world and sees her children, raised in Africa by Nettie, as links to her own African ancestry and to her sister who is as much their mother as Celie is. Similarly, Celie refuses to compete with Albert, Grady, or Germaine for Shug's affection but accepts that her lesbian relationship with Shug can exist in harmony with, but apart from, the heterosexual connections that govern the father's world.

Conclusion: *The Color Purple, Pamela,* and Walker's Challenge to Authority

In Alice Walker's *The Color Purple,* Celie and Shug's lesbian relationship renders a Womanist psychology that privileges networks of human connections. Instead of perceiving human bonding as a series of competing dyads, Walker offers a lesbian social model that replaces exclusivity and ownership with inclusion and community. In challenging the rule of the father in its familial, social, religious, and psychological contexts, Walker reveals that allegiance to hierarchy is the root of social dysfunction. *The Color Purple* extends the criticism of hierarchy based on social status and gender privilege begun in Samuel Richardson's *Pamela* to include a "different perspective," an analysis of how race and sexual orientation complicate the paradigm. Walker's rewrite of the characters and events in Richardson's novel exposes Pamela's struggle for gender and class equality as a failed attempt that results in her servitude in a society that values women merely as servants to upper-class, white men like Mr. B. Once she is accepted into Mr. B's world, Pamela must sacrifice the self-assertion and the loving relationship with Mrs. Jervis that helped her to survive.

In transforming the submerged images of women's autonomy from men and their community with each other depicted in *Pamela* into the overtly Womanist relationship between Shug and Celie in *The Color Purple*, Walker offers a model of human connection that challenges divisions based on gender, social class, race, and sexual orientation. Celie and Shug form a Womanist bond that radiates outward in the society of the novel. Not only does their commitment to the principles of Womanism lead to their own eventual rejection of all power structures, but their influence also encourages Albert and Harpo to stop dominating the women in their lives, teaches Eleanor Jane to relinquish white supremacy, and allows Sofia to see other black women as sisters rather than competitors. Black, feminist, social critic, bell hooks, criticizes *The Color Purple* for its lack of social realism at the end of the novel. The fairy tale ending, she claims, belies the difficulty of resolving social tensions caused by human difference. But, perhaps, hooks' criticism misses the point, for Walker offers not a depiction of how the world is but of how it might be if society were to repudiate hierarchy and embrace Womanism.

Apryl Denny, Viterbo University

Notes

[1] Although Walker never refers directly to either of Richardson's novels, *Clarissa* or *Pamela,* Walker's essay, "In Search of Our Mothers' Gardens," reveals her debt to nineteenth-century women writing in the English novel tradition. In *Producing a Womanist Text: The Maternal as Signifier in Alice Walker's* The Color Purple, Janet J. Montelaro applies "In Search of Our Mother's Gardens" to read Nettie's story in *The Color Purple* as a revision of Charlotte Bronte's *Jane Eyre*. In a review of Montelaro's book, Mary Margaret Richards points out, "Further studies might build on Montelaro's work to examine Walker's use of other novels—such as Richardson's *Pamela*—in writing *The Color Purple*" (504).

Works Cited

Abbandonato, Linda. "A View from 'Elsewhere': Subversive Sexuality and the Rewriting of the Heroine's Story in *The Color Purple*" *Publications of the Modern Language Association,* 106.4 (1991): 1106-15.

Abend-David, Dror. "The Occupational Hazard: The Loss of Historical Context in Twentieth-Century Feminist Readings, and a New Reading of the Heroine's Story in Alice Walker's *The Color Purple"* in *Critical Essays on Alice Walker.* ed. I. Dieke (Contributions in Afro-American and African Studies 189). Westport, CT: Greenwood, 1999. (13-20)

Armstrong, Nancy. *Desire and Domestic Fiction: A Political History of the Novel.* New York: Oxford, 1987.

Barker, Ellen. "Creating Generations: The Relationship Between Celie and Shug in Alice Walker's *The Color Purple"* in *Critical Essays on Alice Walker.* ed. I. Dieke (Contributions in Afro-American and African Studies 189).Westport, CT: Greenwood, 1999. (55-65)

Buckley, Jerome. *Season of Youth: The Bildungsroman from Dickens to Golding.* Cambridge, MA: Harvard UP, 1974.

Christian, Barbara. "No More Buried Lives: The Theme of Lesbianism in Audre Lorde's *Zami,* Gloria Naylor's *The Women of Brewster Place,* Ntozake Shange's *Sassafrass, Cypress and Indigo,* and Alice Walker's *The Color Purple"* *Black Feminist Criticism.* New York: Pergamon Press, 1985. (187-204)

Chodorow, Nancy. *Feminism and Psychoanalytic Theory.* London: Yale University Press, 1989.

Davidson, Arnold. "Sex and the Emergence of Sexuality" *Critical Inquiry* 14.4 (1987): 16-48.

Doody, Margaret, ed. "Introduction" in *Pamela; Or, Virtue Rewarded,* Samuel Richardson. New York, NY: Penguin, 1985.

Dussinger, John. "Love and Consanguinity in Richardson's Novels" *Studies in English Literature* 24 (1984): 513-26.

Fraile-Marcos, Ana Maria. "'As Purple to Lavender': Alice Walker's Womanist Representation of Lesbianism" in *Literature and Homosexuality,* ed. M. Meyer. Amsterdam: Rodopi, 2000. (111-33)

Freud, Sigmund. "Femininity" in *New Introductory Lectures on Psycho-analysis.* ed. J. Strachey. New York: W. W. Norton, 1965. (138-67)

Fuderer, Sue. *The Female Bildungsroman in English: An Annotated Bibliography.* New York: Modern Language Association, 1991.

McDowell, Deborah. "New Directions for Black Feminist Theory" in *The New Feminist Criticism: Essays on Women, Literature and Theory.* ed. Elaine Showalter. New York: Pantheon Books, 1985. (186-99)

Montelaro, Janet. *The Maternal as Signifier in Alice Walker's The Color Purple* (English Literary Studies Monograph Series 70). Victoria, BC: U Victoria P, 1996. (61-75)

Richards, M., 'Producing a Womanist Text: The Maternal as Signifier in Alice Walker's *The Color Purple*—Book Review.' *African American Review* (Fall 1998): 503-04.

Richardson, Samuel. *Clarissa or The History of a Young Lady.* New York, NY: Penguin, 1986.

—. *Pamela or Virtue Rewarded.* New York, NY: Norton, 1958.

Smith, Barbara. "Toward a Black Feminist Criticism" in *All the Women Are White, All the Blacks Are Men, But Some of Us Are Brave: Black Women's Studies.* eds. T. Hull, P Bell Scott, and B Smith. Old Westbury, NY: Feminist Press, 1982. (157-75)

Walker, Alice. *The Color Purple.* New York, NY: Harcourt, 1982.

—. "In Search of Our Mothers' Gardens" in *In Search of Our Mothers' Gardens.* New York, NY: Harcourt Brace, 1983. (231-43)

—. "Saving the Life That Is Your Own" in *In Search of Our Mothers' Gardens.* New York, NY: Harcourt Brace, 1983. (3-14)

Webster, Jeremy. "Teaching *Pamela* and the History of Sexuality" in *Approaches to Teaching* Pamela. ed. L. Zunshine (Approaches to Teaching Literature 87). New York: Modern Language Association, 2006. (56-62)

Winnicott, D. W. *Human Nature.* New York: Schocken, 1988.

Focalization Theory and the Epistolary Novel: A Narrative Analysis of *The Color Purple*

Ping Zhou

An epistolary novel is a novel written in the form of a series of letters exchanged among the characters of the story. In *The Color Purple*, Alice Walker uses this form, popular in eighteenth century Europe, to create a portrait of an early twentieth century African American girl.

The novel's success can be defended by using the focalization theory developed by French narratologist Gerard Genette. His focalization theory incorporates such narratological elements as limitation, flexibility, alternating and polyphony. Walker skillfully synthesizes these narrative elements. By using Genette's focalization theory to make a narrative analysis, it becomes quite clear that *The Color Purple* belongs to a modern canon of great epistolary novels.

Focalization—also called the point of view, vision or narrative perspective—is an element of narrative study that can be traced back as far as the end of the nineteenth century. Distinguished literary critics, including Henry James, Percy Lubbock, Cleanth Brooks, and Norman Friedman contributed to the theory, defining the term as the choice of the perspective from which the story is told; it is the first question a writer needs to consider for his work. As British critic Percy Lubbock said in his book, *The Craft of Fiction,* "The whole intricate question of method, in the craft of fiction, I take to be governed by the question of the point of view—the question of the relation in which the narrator stands to the story" (251).

French narratologist Gerard Genette made a milestone demarcation between the narrator and the focal character (from whose perspective the narration is made) in his book *Narrative Discourse* in 1972. According to Genette, there is "confusion between the question (of) *who is the character whose point of view orients the narrative perspective?* and the very different question *who is the narrator*? Or, to put it simply, the question *who sees?* and the question *who speaks?"* (186). Focalization answers the former question: From whose perspective is the narration constructed?

Elaborating on earlier theories, Genette proposed his own classification of focalization:

> 1.   Non-focalized narrative is the common mode in a traditional omniscient narration in which the narrator knows more than any other characters, such as Leo Tolstoy's *War and Peace*;
> 2.   Internal focalization is when the focalization comes from one fixed character or variable or multiple characters; they only know what they are able to know as characters, the early examples including Gustave Flaubert's *Madame Bovary*;
> 3.   External focalization "in which the hero performs in front of us without our ever being allowed to know his thoughts or feelings" *Hills Like White Elephants* by Hemingway is a masterpiece of this focalization type (Genette 190).

The genre of epistolary novel of course falls into the second category, the internal focalization. The focal character (the person who sees) and the narrator (the person who speaks) merge into one person. The epistolary novel takes the form of letters written by the character from his perspective and the whole book could consist of one or several characters' letters.

Some argue that the epistolary novels can enhance the sense of reality since they adopt a form that is commonly used in everyday life. Letters from different characters can provide multiple perspectives without the obtrusiveness of an omniscient narrator. In addition, most letters contain the subjective thoughts of the letter writers, which create an effect similar to that provided in psychological novels.

This literary genre, however, also receives much criticism. Some critics question its very credibility, arguing that the time and the motivation of composing letters are the pitfalls of the epistolary novels (Kennedy 413). For example, it may not be possible for the characters to get the opportunity to sit down, pick up a pen and write down what has happened. Thus the sense of reality is completely lost.

Since *The Color Purple* falls into the second category of Genette's theory, it uses the internal focalization. The novel is composed of ninety-two letters, including fifty-five from Celie to God, fifteen from Celie to Nettie and twenty-two from Nettie to Celie.

Without a doubt, Alice Walker is taking a double risk in this novel. She not only chooses such a time-honored, but controversial form, but she also chooses a black woman, who uses black dialect in writing to God, as the main writer of the letters. In addition, she writes about controversial topics such as rape, incest and domestic violence.

Despite these potential drawbacks, the novel received critical acclaim, winning the Pulitzer Prize for Fiction and the National Book Award in 1983. According to Peter S. Prescott, *The Color Purple* is in the category of the great works of literature. He wrote in *Newsweek* on June 21, 1982, that "This is an American novel of permanent importance, that rare sort of book which amounts to a diversion in the fields of dread [...] Love redeems, meanness kills—that *The Color Purple*'s principal theme, the theme of most of the world's great fiction."

In particular, Walker's use of letters, as well as the language, was often praised. Robert Trowers (1982) in *New York Review of Books* stated that Walker has met the challenge of "the conversion, in Celie's letters, of a sub-literate dialect into a medium of remarkable expressiveness, color, and poignancy" (NCTE Online). As such a complicated work with controversy and acclaim, *The Color Purple* provides comprehensive perspectives for readers to approach it. This narratological analysis will defend the novel by examining four elements of focalization used in this work: limitation, flexibility, alternating and polyphony.

The Limitation of Letter Writers

As stated above, letter writing is internal focalization. However, the limitation of the letter writer in an epistolary novel is the first feature of this type of focalization. The use of internal focalization appears simple, but as pointed out by Genette, it actually has limitations. For example, the letter writer can only write what he knows at the moment that he composes the letter. He cannot transcend the exact moment, nor does he know what is going to happen next (Robyn 184). The letter writer does not have the privilege of entering others' minds, nor is he likely to take an overall stand to judge and comment on others. In other words, he is a common person, like a reader, who does not possess the "super power" of an omniscient narrator.

Alice Walker navigates around these limitations. One example occurs when Sofia is put into jail. The family is worried about her life in prison and tries to figure out a way to get her out. Harpo wants to blow up the whole prison, and the prizefighter thinks of smuggling in a gun to her. Celie writes in her letter, "Me and

Squeak don't say nothing. I don't know what she think, but I think bout angels, God coming down by chariot, swinging down real low and carrying ole Sofia home" (90). Celie even imagines how the angels and God look. But what is going on in Squeak's mind? The reader does not know Squeak's mind, because she is not the letter writer, and Celie is not supposed to have access to her thoughts. "I don't know what she think," declares Celie from the limited position of an internal focal character. At the same time, this brings Squeak to the attention of the readers. It appears to be a tactic of Walker's to mention Squeak here, because in the following part of the story, Squeak goes to see the warden of the prison. Walker's navigation of Celie's limitation as the narrator achieves the sense of reality powerfully while at the same time establishing Squeak as a simple-minded and kind-hearted character.

In another example, after Celie gives birth to her first child, Walker writes "He took it. He took it while I was sleeping. Kilt it out there in the woods" (2). At the time when Celie writes this, all she knows is that her "father" took away her newly born child. She has no means to know the baby's fate, so she assumes that the baby is killed. The letter writer is simply human and is therefore limited to the knowledge, assumption, experience and perception he or she possesses at the time of writing.

Usually the letter writer describes an objective event using subjective descriptions and feelings. Every word in the letter is painted with personal and emotional color, like an interior monologue in the written form.

For example from the first two letters from Celie to God, readers can deduce that she is raped by her "father" and is pregnant (2). Yet since she is only fourteen, Celie knows nothing about sex, pregnancy or birth giving. Therefore, as an innocent girl, she uses her own way to describe a horrible event that is happening to her though it is clear she does not know exactly what is happening or why. She writes to God, "Maybe you can give me a sign letting me know what is happening to me" (1). Here lies the credibility and sense of reality of the narration. Since the perspective is strictly limited to that of the letter writer, without any trace of intrusion from the outside, reading such a description from a girl suffering physically and spiritually can enhance the pathos among readers. The protagonist gains the readers' sympathy and empathy from the very beginning of the novel.

Once the author chooses the use of the internal focalization, he must keep in mind the limitation that this kind of narration is subject to throughout the whole work. Only in this way can consistency be maintained and reinforced. The frequent choice is to allow the narrator to be present in all the scenes he narrates as a witness.

In one letter, Celie describes the conflict between Sofia and Miss Eleanor Jane. Miss Eleanor Jane is eager to hear that Sofia loves her baby boy, while Sofia frankly tells her that she has no feeling about a white baby, who might grow up to persecute the blacks. The whole conversation between Sofia and Miss Eleanor Jane goes on for a while. At this moment a careful reader might ask how Celie knows about it. Then, in the middle of the scene this sentence pops up: "All the time me and Henrietta over in the corner playing pitty pat" (264). Next, the scene continues to be shown in the perspective of Celie. This very sentence resolves the readers' doubt and protects the integrity of the whole scene. In addition, Sofia is created as a character full of self-respect, dignity and uprightness in the eyes of Celie.

Obviously, the letter writer needs to be present in every scene in order to provide the necessary information. She must write about the emotions and thoughts of other characters. What will the letter writer do since she is confined to her own perspective and has no way to act like an omniscient narrator? A careful reader of *The Color Purple* will find no lack of the description about other characters' motivations but these motives are tempered with the frequent appearance of conjectural expressions like "maybe, like, look like, seem..." These words function as the legitimate key for Celie, the letter writer, to enter the interior world of other characters.

For example, when Sofia is leaving Harpo with her children, Celie asks Harpo if he is letting her go. Celie realizes how silly Harpo thinks of her asking such a question: "He look like only a fool could ast the question" (67). "Look like" is the obvious signal of the coherent internal focalization. Celie, as a narrator, is an ordinary person who can only guess others' minds, but it is also her status as a narrator that makes her conjectures reasonable and acceptable to readers. By using the phrase "look like," the narrator keeps her limited perspective, but reveals enough information to readers in an inconspicuous and natural way.

It is interesting to note that Celie uses more conjectural words in her letters than Nettie does. Celie's constant use of such words shows her hesitation to make a judgment. And Celie is very uncertain about the validity of the judgment once she is required to make one.

However, as the plotline of the novel develops, Celie becomes more and more confident and her voice changes from tentativeness to decisiveness—a confidence that is evident by the disappearance of the aforementioned conjectural words. Evidence of this is seen when Celie leaves with Shug for Memphis and Mr.___ becomes very angry. Celie puts a curse on him, imprecating evil on everything he touches, on every dream he has (206). Throughout this passage, Celie does not use any conjectural words. More importantly, she now speaks in the manner of a goddess with the omnipotent super power.

More challenging to the internal focal narrator than knowing others' thoughts is describing an event from which he is absent. In order to maintain this limited focalization, he would usually find some other channels to access the scene. One mechanical device is to turn to other sources of information rather than direct witness, such as letters from others or stories retold to him.

At the end of the novel, Shug falls in love with a young man who is only nineteen. How does Celie know how things are going between them? She is able to access this information since Shug writes letters to Celie every week and Celie shows Shug's correspondence in her letter to Nettie, so readers know what happens to Shug. Celie writes: "Dear Celie, she wrote me, Me and Germaine ended up in Tucson, Arizona where one of my children live" (267). It is obvious that this letter-within-letter structure provides double information flexibly and reasonably.

At times in *The Color Purple,* Celie must use re-told information. For example, how does Celie present the scene in which Sofia fights against the white mayor? She is not there herself. Nevertheless, the scene is so important to characterize Sofia that it needs to be shown in vivid details, as if Celie sees it herself. The cleverness lies in the introduction sentence by Celie: "I tell her what one of Sofia sister tell me and Mr.___" (84). The scene then smoothly shifts from the perspective of Celie's to that of Sofia's sister's. Then Celie describes the conflict between Sofia and the mayor as if she actually witnessed it. Using this strategy, another limitation of internal focalization is overcome—an internal focal character can be used as extensively as an omniscient narrator, as long as he or she is monitored gracefully as done by Walker.

The Flexibility of Letter Writers

Flexibility of the letter writer, also called "alteration" by Genette, is the second feature of internal focalization. Two types of alteration are "paralipsis" and "paralepsis." If the narrator gives less information than is necessary, it is called "paralipsis." The opposite situation is when the narrator gives more than he is authorized and is called "paralepsis" (Genette 195).

In paralipsis, the letter writer omits certain actions or thoughts which he should have access to know. The readers get less information than they should have known from a first person internal focalization narrator. This creates suspense. Curiosity and expectation will accompany the following reading until the moment of revelation. The effect of an unexpected event is heightened.

Paralipsis is quite common in a retrospective novel. It occurs every time the narrator refuses to tell the outcome of an episode in advance, every time he allows the perspective of the experiencing self to dominate (Edmiston 741). Some critics think it is too conventional to be called an infraction.

There is paralipsis in *The Color Purple*. For example, one day, Sofia confronts Celie for telling Harpo to beat her. But the letter begins with Celie's description about her insomnia: "For over a month I have trouble sleeping" (39). A little voice murmurs around her, "Something you done wrong. Somebody spirit you sin against" (39). Then Sofia appears and readers can infer that Celie's uneasiness has something to do with her. But Celie still keeps secret from readers the fact that she knows exactly. "I sin against Sofia spirit. I pray she don't find out, but she do" (39). Celie knows what happens at the moment when she writes the letter, but she deliberately delays the reason of her insomnia. It is also the reason why Sofia comes to see her with a blue and red bruise under her eye. At this moment, Celie recalls this incident and gives way to the experiencing Celie who then dominates the scene.

Paralipsis is different from flashbacks. In a paralipsis, the narrator will not come back to narrate what has been omitted. Instead, readers have to obtain the lost information themselves. In the last example, Celie has no flashbacks on how she suggests that Harpo should beat Sofia in order to control her. Readers get the knowledge from Sofia's words "You told Harpo to beat me" (40). This paralipsis produces intense suspense, more overwhelming than a narration of normal order or a flashback. The very letter that began with Celie's

insomnia then ends with "I sleeps like a baby now" (42). It orbits the
circle from her sense of guilt to her relief after the reconciliation with
Sophia. An innocent and honest Celie is portrayed before readers,
even though she does do harm to Sofia. At this point, the choice of
technique deliberately enhances the positive characterization of the
heroine.

Another point of paralipsis in *The Color Purple* requires
reading at least four letters in order to figure out the whole scene. In
one letter, Squeak goes to see the warden of the prison in order to get
Sofia out (93). In the second letter, Squeak gets back from the prison
and the letter ends by Squeak's telling that she was raped, without
mentioning the fate of Sofia at all (96). The fourth one starts with a
conversation between Celie and Sofia. Readers realize that Sofia has
gotten out of the washhouse of the prison and now works as a maid in
the mayor's house (100). After putting all these four letters together,
readers can conclude that the visit of Squeak saves the life of Sofia,
although Squeak suffers bitterly herself as a result of her intervention.
This case of paralipsis creates a transitory suspense, but the effect is
very intense.

Why does Walker use paralipsis in this plot? Why does she
insert the scene that Squeak begins to sing, breaking a continuous plot
about the fate of Sofia? The answer might be Walker's intention to
characterize Squeak with this detail more than to give an ending to
Sofia's story. Squeak becomes the crucial person who is necessary to
save Sofia's life. After the incident, she demands others to call her by
her real name instead of calling her "Squeak." Her decision to sing is
also her way of finding her own voice. Later it becomes her way to
make a living all by herself. The choice of paralipsis here draws
readers' attention from Sofia to Squeak. Although Squeak's
personality is totally different from Sofia, she is as kind as the rest of
the women in this novel. The deliberate omission of certain
information emphasizes other information, creating more layers
within this story.

Similarly, the use of paralepsis, namely, telling more than the
narrator is supposed to tell, can also contribute to the development of
the plot rather than being regarded as the blunder of the writer. There
is more paralepsis than paralipsis in *The Color Purple*.

For example, after Sophia is put into jail, Celie recalls the
dialogue between Mr.__ and the sheriff. In a regular conversation
introduced by "Mr.__ say," or "Sheriff say," the following sentence
appears: Sheriff think bout the women he know, say, Yep, you right

there (86). How could Celie know what is going on in the mind of the sheriff? Walker does not bother to rationalize the availability of this information. The internal focal character breaks through her limited power and enters the mind of other characters like an omniscient narrator. Here, the reader must be willing to suspend disbelief.

If this example could be dismissed as an oversight or carelessness, there are other places in *The Color Purple* where Walker uses this technique deliberately. For example, at the beginning of the novel, before her departure, Nettie promises that she would write to Celie. Immediately after their conversation, Celie says: "She never write" (18). At the moment when Celie composes this letter, it is impossible for her to know that she would never receive a letter from Nettie for many years. This paralepsis diverts readers' attention to the fate of Nettie. They might be eager to know what has happened to her. Could Nettie's voice be heard by her sister? Would Nettie's rebellion and fight against being a miserable black housewife bring her a more promising life? In this case, paralepsis creates as much suspense as paralipsis.

The fate of Celie's two children, Adam and Olivia, can also be regarded as a paralepsis. The babies are taken away shortly after they are born and Celie assumes that her "father" kills them. But one day, she comes across a baby girl and she can immediately tell that girl is her daughter:

> 'I seen my baby girl. I knowed it was her. She look just like me and daddy. Like more us then us is ourself." "I think she mine. My heart say she mine. But I don't know she mine.' (13)

If this paralepsis could be explained as the maternal instinct of a poor mother, then what Nettie believes can only be explained as paralepsis when she said "I wanted to say, 'God' has sent you their sister and aunt, but I didn't. Yes, their children, sent by 'God' are your children, Celie" (133). At that time, Nettie does not know the relationship between Samuel and her "father," so she has no way to assert affirmatively that the children are Celie's. Nettie violates the rules of limitation and arrives at a paralepsis.

Both of these cases of paralepsis make the fate of the two children more confusing. Readers are in suspense until the last moment when Samuel tells where they are from.

Both paralipsis and paralepsis, like the term "alteration," are the dynamics that generate the change and fluctuation, while also serving as the way to break the regularity and monotony of a traditional work.

The Alternating of Different Focal Characters

The aforementioned limitation and flexibility assumes one focal character in the story. But what if the story has more than one focal character? The alternating of different focal characters is the third feature in the combination of the internal focalization and the epistolary novel. It refers to the fact that sometimes there are more than one focalizations from more than one narrator in a story. The alternating of two focalizations often occurs in an autobiographical novel or a memoir novel so that the story can shift flexibly and freely among the past, the present and the future. One focal character might be the narrating self, who is narrating his own past. The other might be the experiencing self, who is experiencing a moment in the past. The overlap, intersection, unity and conflict between these two selves can create the dramatic tension and sharp contrast of characterization.

For example, in *Great Expectations* by Charles Dickens, the narrator Pip recounts his adventures and experiences when he was young, which include his pursuit of love, fame and wealth. The narrating self is the old Pip. He knows the consequence of each event he narrates. He understands the significance of his experiences. Entirely different from him, young Pip is the experiencing self. For most of the time, young Pip appears as the focal character, the person who sees.

Like in autobiographical novels and memoirs, epistolary novels may shift between the past and the present. The past or the present inner world of the letter writer is the common subject of epistolary novels; the letters alternate between past and present focalization. The time distance between the two focalizations is very short. Recent events appear in the focalization of the narrating self. But in autobiographical novels and memoirs, the events narrated by the narrating self usually happened years ago. Epistolary novels, as Ruth Perry writes, turn out to be "a self-conscious and self-perpetuating process of emotional self examination..." (Perry 117).

For instance, some letters of Celie's record what occurred a moment ago or on that particular day. They function more like a journal or a diary, with a time span of several hours. For example, there are two letters of Celie's starting with "Two of his sister come to visit" (19), and "Mr.__ daddy show up this evening" (54). After these introductory sentences, the letter shifts from the narrating perspective to the experiencing one. Celie stops to narrate in a recalling way. Instead, the dialogues show what happens. It seems that the readers are witnessing the scene at the very moment. This technique is occurs often in *The Color Purple*.

The Color Purple has a few elements that are not often used in epistolary novels. For example, a scene might be shown instead of described, and the depiction of that scene relies on the use of dialogues. Throughout Celie's letters, these dialogues have no quotation marks. In addition, her ungrammatical use of language does not suggest any sense of verb tenses or verb conjugation. Some people might regard this as Walker's characterization of Celie as an uneducated woman. However, a narrative analysis can show how this device facilitates a smooth shift of perspectives. "Two of his sister come to visit. They dress all up. Celie, they say. One thing is for sure. You keep a clean house..." (19). This blurring between the two selves overcomes one limitation of the epistolary novel, namely, the lack of immediacy and authenticity. It is also a proof that showing rather than telling a story can also work in the letter writing.

The shifts of focalization can also be found in Nettie's letters. When Nettie and Samuel fall in love with each other, Nettie tells her sister: "You may have guessed that I loved him all along; but I did not know it. Oh, I loved him as a brother and respected him as friend, but Celie, I love him bodily, as a man!" (238). From the verb tenses used, readers can see the smooth shift of perspective of the present Netties and the previous Nettie: "You may have guessed that I loved him all along; but I did not know it." This part is the retrospection of the present Nettie about a previous Nettie who *did not* know that she loved Samuel. "I loved him as a brother and respected him as friend . . ." is the feeling that the experiencing Nettie had toward Samuel before. Then the experiencing self shifts back to the narrating one by writing that "I love him bodily, as a man!" This is the feeling of the present Nettie who is telling her sister about the birth of her love at the exact moment of her writing.

Another alternating within a novel is the shift of perspectives between different characters. This shift is very common in works with multiple internal focalizations. *As I Lay Dying* by William Faulkner is considered a masterpiece of this technique. The whole novel is composed of the different perspectives of fifteen characters, in the form of fifty-nine interior monologues. Some writers even manage to enter the minds of non-humans, such as Ernest Hemingway's presenting a lion's mind in *The Short and Happy Life of Francis Micawber* and William Marxwell's presenting a dog's mind in *So Long, See You Tomorrow*.

In *The Color Purple*, Nettie's letters very often shifts her focalization to other characters, especially Samuel's, by quoting them:

> 'It did not seem hard for Samuel to talk about Corrine while we were in England.
> It wasn't hard for me to listen.
> It all seems so improbable, he said. Here I am, an aging man whose dreams of helping people have been just that, dreams.'
> (235)

After the transitional sentence "It wasn't hard for me to listen," Nettie becomes the listener and gives the role of narrating to Samuel. This back and forth shifting is intermittent in this particular letter, achieving the effect of multiple focalizations in the frame of one letter. Nettie's language is grammatically perfect compared to that of Celie's, but it shares something in common with her sister's: She also does not use any quotation marks when she needs to retell what others say. This enables the shift of focalization to appear more natural and less noticeable.

The Polyphonic Structure in *The Color Purple*

The aforementioned three features, limitation, flexibility and alternating can be found in most works using the internal focalization. Polyphonic structure is more often found in epistolary novels than in other works using internal focalization (i.e., traditional first person narration). The polyphonic structure results from the paralleling focalizations of different letter writers.

Polyphony is a musical term, used in reference to music containing two or more melodies of nearly equivalent importance. The melodies are harmonically connected but still maintain their linear uniqueness. The melodies are slightly different but explore a complementary theme. In literature, the Russian formalist Mikhail Bakhtin proposed the concept of polyphonic novels. According to Bakhtin, a polyphonic novel is characterized by two features. The novel must have two or more plotlines; these plotlines do not possess any cause-effect relationship or subordinate relationship; instead, they develop exclusively without any interference with each other (Jiang 273). The classic examples in the field of world literature include

Dostoevsky's *The Devils* (1872) and Milan Kundera's *Immortality* (1988).

The *Color Purple* has a polyphonic feature as well. The first forty-eight letters are written by Celie to God but there is a turning point in the forty-ninth one. Celie inserts the first letter she gets from Nettie in this letter with the sentence "This the letter I been holding in my hand" (117). Starting with the fifty-second letter, the book begins to include Nettie's letters, but the first five of them all have the introductory sentences from Celie like "Dear Celie, *the first letter say*," (126) "*Next one say*, Dear Celie" (127), etc. These five letters serve as the transitional bridge to shift the novel from Celie's perspective to Nettie's. It can be regarded as the intersection of two parts within a polyphonic structure.

The respective focalizations of Celie and Nettie are not the different perceptions on the same event. Instead, they are the records of their different individual lives. For the most part, the two focalizations develop in a parallel way; sometimes they happen to mention the same characters and events. A two-way monologue and a complementary dialogue supplant the one-way regularity of traditional novels.

The parallel narrations of Celie and Nettie result in not only the development of the plot, but more importantly, in the characterization of these two characters and the broadening of the theme, resulting in a confluence of form and subject. Finding a voice is regarded as the defining feature of Afro-American literature (Hite 115). The characters in an epistolary novel get the opportunity to talk and to be heard. In this way, they find their own identity and their position in the world. The letters in the epistolary novel may be the best means for the letter writer to obtain a voice because of the privacy and convenience that letter writing provides. According to scholar Molly Hite:

> [...]Walker uses the Afro-American motif of 'finding a voice' primarily to decenter patriarchal authority, giving speech to hitherto muted women, who change meanings in the process of articulating and thus appropriating the dominant discourse. (115)

Nettie's perspective focuses on what she sees, hears, feels and thinks during her experience as a missionary—including the foreign lifestyle of the Olinkas; their primitive but resilient mores and ideology; the deteriorating living environment caused by the invasion and exploitation by the whites; the happy family she enjoys with Samuel, Adam and Olivia.

In her first letter, Nettie's focalization is as confined to domestic affairs as Celie's. Nettie has the common topic of Mr.__ in it, and the language is also colloquial and disregards correct grammar. "You know how he do, you sure is looking fine, Miss Nettie, and stuff like that" (126). However, two months later, there is a sharp difference in Nettie's letters. Her broad and serious focalization achieves a formal, profound and objective narration in standard English. The transformation from the colloquialism to the written discourse reflects the growth of Nettie as a character. When she uses colloquialism, her topic is confined to her previous personal affairs before she leaves for Africa. When she adopts Standard English, her concern has been broadened to include the fate of other people.

Besides, readers can detect a positive and confident tone in her letters, which is quite different from that in Celie's early letters. For example, Nettie is determined to make Olivia into a person who has a bright future. She even predicts Olivia's fate:

> 'You will grow up to be a strong Christian woman, I tell her. Someone who helps her people to advance. You will be a teacher or a nurse. You will travel. You will know many people greater than the chief.' (157)

Even when she is making a guess, she sounds very assured and does not use conjectural words as Celie does: "She is still sweet and good–natured. But sometimes I sense her spirit is being tested and that something in her is not at rest" (157).

During the process of writing to her sister, Nettie becomes an educated and mature woman. She finds her own voice and develops her own view of the world. Her focalization is a journey of a modern African American in search of her roots. Moreover, her focalization is the witness of the invasion of the European colonialism in the twentieth century Africa. It reminds readers of the fate of all the black people who were cheated and enslaved centuries ago. According to Marcellus Blount, "Nettie's letters achieve authority through their political relevancy. As well, her focus on African customs informs and reassures; her discussions of African peoples remind us how much Afro-Americans are like the peoples of Africa" (Blount 121).

Correspondingly, Celie, as a housewife, at first can only focus on her family circle and the triviality of everyday life. As the time goes on, however, she and the other female characters begin to blossom, find their voices.

At first, Celie can only write to God. Only God can listen to her voice and make her feel her own humanity. Even though she never hears from God, she does not give up the writing. It is her way of enduring her reality and learning to become a human being instead of a tree. Consequently, her letters become longer and their tone more formal with the development of the plot, focusing more on the concepts of equality, freedom, self-determination and independence. After she succeeds in making her own living by opening a pants business, Celie ends one of her later letters differently from her earlier letters:

> 'Amen,
> Your Sister, Celie
> Folkspants, Unlimited.
> Sugar Avery Drive
> Memphis, Tennessee' (214)

At this moment, Celie is a sister, but more importantly, she has become a woman with an identity. The address is the information for Nettie to continue to write, but it also symbolizes that Celie finally has found her own place in the world. As the novel ends on July 4th, the day of independence, after writing for years, Celie gains her own independence too.

At the same time, along with her own changing, Celie's attitude towards her husband Mr.___ is changing as well. When she leaves for Memphis with Shug, she puts curses on him for all the hardship she suffers in their loveless marriage. During her absence, Mr.___ transforms and realizes what a miserable life he had inflicted on Celie before. When Celie returns, they become friends. He sews for her pants business, he carves a purple frog for her and he even wants to marry her again. Their common love towards Shug makes Mr.___ the only one to understand her feeling (259). She accepts Albert as a friend whom she would not hate any longer. "But I don't hate him, Nettie" (260). Towards the end of the novel, Celie begins to call him Albert instead of Mr.____. "Oh, I say, a little something Albert carve for me"(284). Her own independence enables her to get an equal position in the relationship between her and Albert, and to give an identity to this person rather than regard him as a nameless authority that controls her life.

In most of her letters, Celie uses a rhythmic and vital vernacular that does not conform to Standard English. As scholar Butler-Evans writes:

> The reader decodes this language as a representation of Black folk speech. As such, it delineates Celie's racial and cultural status. The writing-speech signifies marginality and difference, allowing Celie to describe the oppressive conditions under which she lives and inviting the readers to analyze and interpret those descriptions. (164)

Though Celie's language is not always grammatically correct, it never lacks communicative power. It is filled with subtle humor which reflects her perseverant personality. In one episode, Darlene, employed in Celie's pants-making business, tries to teach Celie to talk like white people. Celie thinks it is silly and would rather stick to her own native and authentic black speech. "Look like to me only a fool would want you to talk in a way that feel peculiar to your mind" (216). Her use of the black folk speech is in perfect conformity with her character and makes her one of the most eloquent heroines in African American fiction.

There is a sharp difference between the perspectives of Celie and Nettie, but at the same time, these two perspectives are compatible in the establishment of the whole novel. At the beginning, the two sisters are forced to leave each other without knowing what life will be waiting for them ahead. In the main body of the book, the two sisters live, fight, mature and struggle in their own ways. Yet, despite their experiences, the two sisters reunite and the whole family comes together.

Corresponding to the plot, the form of the epistolary novel indicates that at first the letters in this work are a one-way monologue. Neither Celie nor Nettie gets replies from each other. But with their growth as characters, the letters serve more as their self-conscious examination rather than messages in common letters intended to be sent and answered. Though most of the letters are not exchanged between Celie and Nettie as the regular correspondence is, the readers of the book have the access to every one of them:

> The interpreter (reader) of the epistolary novel must become omniscient, a reader somewhere above the world of the original text, and must simultaneously keep in mind what is being written, how it is being read, and how the reading affects the writer. The reader of the epistolary novel usually knows more than either the writer or reader in the text itself. (Campbell 338)

Due to the polyphonic structure of *The Color Purple*, the reading of the work is similar to listening to dialogues between the two sisters. The dialogues might be trivial, repetitive, fragmented, or even unconventional, but they serve one coherent theme throughout the work. The whole structural thread is assimilated to the principle of the polyphonic musical work. The form of the epistolary novel enables the letter writer, as a first person narrator, to exercise more freedom to shift in space and time than a traditional first person narrator. Furthermore it allows the setting in the novel to change according to the need of the plot and the accomplishment of the theme. *The Color Purple* may not be a polyphonic novel in the strictest sense, because according to Bakhtin, the different plotlines in a real polyphonic novel should not interact with each other. However, *The Color Purple* does follow the basic pattern of a polyphonic novel by using a dialogue of multiple voices.

As a novel with the first person internal focalization, *The Color Purple* demonstrates such aesthetic elements as limitation, flexibility, alternating and polyphony within the traditional epistolary form. Alice Walker adopts the classical epistolary form, creating two classic heroines in the family of African American literature. Their simple but sincere letters contain their love towards stars, trees, sky, people and God, and generate the perfect synthesis of form and meaning.

Ping Zhou, Heilongjiang University of Harbin, China

Works Cited

Primary Texts

Blount, Marcellus. "Review: A Woman Speaks". *Callaloo* 18. (Spring - Summer, 1983), 118-122.

Butler-Evans, Elliott. *Race, Gender, and Desire*. Philadelphia: Temple U P, 1989.

Campbell, Elizabeth. "Re-Visions, Re-Flections, Re-Creations: Epistolarity in Novels by Contemporary Women". *Twentieth Century Literature* 41: 3 (Autumn, 1995), 332-348.

Edmiston, William F. "Focalization and the First-Person Narrator: A Revision of the Theory". *Poetics Today* 10: 4. (Winter, 1989): 729-744.

Genette, Gerard. *Narrative Discourse: an Essay in Method* translated by Jane E. Lewin. Ithaca, New York: Cornell U P, 1972.

Hite, Molly. *The Other Side of the Story*. Ithaca and London: Cornell U P, 1989.

Jiang, Zilong. *Mikhail Bakhtine and the Principle of Dialogue*. Tianjin: Baihua Literature and Art Publishing House, 2001.

Kennedy, Duncan F. "The Epistolary Mode and the First of Ovid's Heroides". *The Classical Quarterly* New Series 34: 2. (1984): 413-422.

Lubbock, Percy. *The Craft of Fiction*. London: Jonathan Cape, 1921.

NCTE Online The National Council of Teachers of English. Online at: http: //www.ncte.com/ (consulted 11. 17. 07).

Perry, Ruth. *Women, Letters, and the Novel*. New York: AMS, 1980.

Robyn R. Warhol. "How Narration Produces Gender: Femininity as Affect and Effect in Alice Walker's *The Color Purple*". *NARRATIVE* 9:2 (May 2001):184.

Walker, Alice. *The Color Purple*. Orlando: Harcourt, 2003.

Secondary Texts

Bakhtin, M. *The Dialogic Imagination*. Austin: U Texas P, 1981.

Bal, M. *Narratology*. Trans. C. van Boheemen. Toronto: U Toronto P, 1985.

Booth, W. C. *The Rhetoric of Fiction*. Chicago: Chicago U P, 1961.

Chatman, S. *Story and Discourse*. Ithaca: Cornell U P, 1978.

Ehrlich, S. *Point of View: A Linguistic Analysis of Literary Style*. London: Routledge, 1990.

O'Brien, John. *Interviews with Black Writers*. New York: Liverwright, 1973.

Rimmon, Kenan, S. *Narrrative Fiction*. London: Methuen, 1983.

Essay Abstracts

Patricia Lynn Andujo, "Rendering the African-American Woman's God Through *The Color Purple*"

This essay covers the development of the African-American female within the African-American literary tradition, while locating religion as a central influence of her strength, character, and dedication to her family and community. This study uses Alice Walker's *The Color Purple* to demonstrate how African-American women have redefined religion to empower themselves beyond their double minority status in America. Religion, specifically Christianity, has traditionally been conceived of, by some, as a sexist and delimiting institution for women. Celie, spends the majority of her life engaging in a peculiar monologue with a male God who renders her neither empowerment nor self-esteem, yet her existence is sustained through one-way conversations with Him.

Walker's novel is explored as commentary on the survival and transformation of religion in the lives of African-American females as they are forced to renegotiate previously established religious discourse. The women must rethink the way they feel about God, gender, and religion if they hope to triumph over their double minority status. This transformation is most evident in the protagonist, Celie. Once she takes individual ownership of God, she becomes empowered through her new understanding of religion. God is no longer sleep as she supposed Him to be earlier in the novel. What results is an awakening of Celie's sexuality, self-esteem, independence, and ultimate liberation.

Turgay Bayindir, "A House of Her Own: Alice Walker's Readjustment of Virginia Woolf's *A Room of One's Own* in *The Color Purple*"

This essay attempts to establish thematic and rhetorical connections between Virginia Woolf's early feminist essay *A Room of One's Own* (1929) and Alice Walker's Pulitzer Prize winning novel *The Color Purple* (1982). Woolf argues that the real reason for women's servility in society is not their natural inferiority to men but their material dependence on men for centuries. She suggests that women need both their own income and a room of their own within the house in order to grow out of the servile mental condition they have been restricted to. Walker's novel, on the other hand, is about the awakening of its African American protagonist Celie into womanhood. Through an analysis of Celie's journey from absolute subjection to patriarchal power to her attainment of agency as a woman, this essay demonstrates that *The Color Purple* is the product of a "womanist" dialogue between Virginia Woolf and Alice Walker.

Tracy L. Bealer, "Making Hurston's Heroine Her Own: Love and Womanist Resistance in *The Color Purple*"

In *The Color Purple* (1982), Alice Walker rewrites Zora Neale Hurston's *Their Eyes Were Watching God* (1937) with a politically significant twist. *The Color Purple* features another African American woman who achieves self-actualization and resists sexist oppression through romantic love, but does so by overcoming a different set of challenges than Janie faces. Celie's dark skin and homosexuality position her as a heroine particularly suited to resonate within Walker's reformulation of the radical feminist politics of the 1980s. Celie's romance with Shug Avery and the manifestation of Celie's biological family at the end of the book reformulates Hurston's portrayal of a woman's quest for subjectivity by revising the terms of love, autonomy and liberty. Walker counter-intuitively suggests that interpersonal connection and communal support, not stoic individualism, makes personal freedom possible and, in so doing, employs a womanist philosophy to offer a radical revision of the paradigmatic solitary American hero.

Apryl Denny, "Alice Walker's Womanist Reading of Samuel Richardson's *Pamela* in *The Color Purple*"

Alice Walker's *The Color Purple* responds to Samuel Richardson's depiction of the male-identified heroine in the first English epistolary novel, *Pamela.* By merging the epistolary and Bildungsroman genres, Walker redefines the heroine of epistolary fiction as a woman who not only challenges gendered hierarchy, as depicted in *Pamela,* but who actually dissolves it. Walker reinvents the male-identified women in *Pamela* (the predatory lesbian, Mrs. Jewkes; the good mother, Mrs. Jervis; and the chaste girl, Pamela) as a network of African-American womanists who transform familial and social hierarchy by practicing a lesbian model of relationships defined by connection and inclusion rather than separation and hierarchy.

Kathryn Edney, "Adapting and Integrating: *The Color Purple* as Broadway Musical"

The essay explores the ways in which the novel *The Color Purple* was tailored to meet the genre requirements of musical theater when it was adapted for the Broadway stage in 2006. Specific attention is paid to how *The Color Purple* was rhetorically "normalized" to align it within the genre conventions of the idealized Broadway integrated musical epitomized by the works of Richard Rodgers and Oscar Hammerstein. This impulse to place *The Color Purple* within a "universal" genre framework both ignored the musical's connections to earlier all-black musicals and, through the use of pop music idioms, robbed the character Celie of her unique voice so prominent in the novel.

Robin E. Field, "Alice Walker's Revisionary Politics of Rape"

This essay argues that Alice Walker fundamentally transforms how rape is represented in American literature through the narrative strategies and revolutionary politics portrayed in *The Color Purple*. This novel places readers *within* the rape victim's consciousness via the use of a first-person narrative voice. Consequently, the rape victim herself gains control of her story, and through her own voice readers learn about her reality of traumatic sexual assault. In addition, Walker breaks the long-standing taboo of speaking about sexual abuse within the black community. In her early fiction, Walker had thoroughly explored the political ramifications of black men committing rape against white women, as well as the problems of black women protecting black men at the expense of their own safety and self-respect. In *The Color Purple*, Walker affirms the black woman's right to bodily integrity and intellectual independence. Already momentous in so many ways, *The Color Purple* must also be recognized for its landmark revision of the portrayal of rape and rape victims.

Courtney George, "'My Man Treats Me Like a Slave': The Triumph of Womanist Blues over Blues Violence in Alice Walker's *The Color Purple*"

In "'My Man Treats Me Like a Slave': The Triumph of Womanist Blues over Blues Violence in Alice Walker's *The Color Purple*," Courtney George argues that, through the characters of Shug, Sofia, Squeak, and Celie, Walker posits a womanist blues that directly confronts the male blues perspective of Albert, Harpo, and Pa. Drawing from cultural and literary critic Adam Gussow's arguments about "intimate" blues violence, this essay suggests that Walker urges readers to understand how the male blues perspective is informed by interaction with the hostile white world. While the novel's male blues records a cultural memory of racism and sexism, Walker's womanist blues revises historical portraits of the southern black community, and, by novel's end, male and female characters celebrate life despite the sexual, religious, and racial barriers implemented by the dominant white world.

Erin Huskey, "Witnessing and Testifying: Transformed Language and Selves in *The Color Purple*"

With *The Color Purple*, Alice Walker demonstrates that social change begins on a very personal level. By telling the stories of these characters through their letters, she offers an intensely personal and individualized engagement with the revitalization of language and form—both literary and bodily—to signal that alternatives for community start with individual growth and commitment to the self. Through the form, language, and content of the novel, she transforms historically oppressive dominant literary forms and asserts voice as represented by the tangible object of the novel. This is an object or text that symbolizes Walker's personal transformation and envisions the possibility of transformation in the reader. This latter transformation is dependent on the internalization of the novel's message: neither Celie nor any other character can help anyone in the community until they first figure out how to help themselves. The novel is a textual act of testifying and witnessing to inspire the reader to transform his/her life and the terms in which he/she thinks about the self.

Raphaël Lambert, "Alice Walker's *The Color Purple*: Womanist Folk Tale and Capitalist Fairy Tale"

Alice Walker's *The Color Purple* draws on both oral folktales and feminist tales to convey a renewed, more positive image of female characters. However, the progressiveness of Walker's story is deceptive as the story also reproduces fairytales' celebration of free-market economy and Calvinist ideals. As a consequence, the feminist, subversive tale grows into a capitalist fantasy.

Marlon Rachquel Moore, "God is (a) Pussy: The Pleasure Principle and Homo-Spirituality in Shug's Blueswoman Theology"

The writer argues that Shug Avery's theological perspectives and her multiple roles in Celie's life construct Shug as a "Blueswoman evangelist." The essay explores how Shug's evangelism facilitates Celie's spiritual growth and how her message hinges upon the acknowledgement of the spiritual aspects of physical pleasure. In order for Celie to truly identify with Shug's testimony, she must conceive of her clitoral orgasm as the gateway to God.

Danielle Russell, "Homeward Bound: Transformative Spaces in *The Color Purple*"

"Homeward Bound: Transformative Spaces in *The Color Purple*," explores the intimate relationship between identity and location. The spaces that the central figure, Celie, occupies shape and reshape her character. Place is a subjective experience in Walker's novel. Identity is not fixed or static; it shifts with shifts in location. Domestic dwellings dominate in the story; home is, initially, a source of pain, and site of struggle for Celie. It will, however, be ameliorated through the influence of Shug Avery, a series of spatial relocations, and Celie's recognition of the value of a genuine home—the actual one she prepares for her displaced family and the most intimate "home": her abused and exploited body.

Uplabdhi Sangwan, "Significance of Sisterhood and Lesbianism in Fiction of Women of Color"

In *The Color Purple* Alice Walker exemplifies the idea that erotic or emotional bonds between women of color can provide them with the strength to counter the experience of marginalization arising out of their sex, race and class. The paper discusses that in *The Color Purple* the protagonist Celie gains strength from the emotional and erotic bonds with Black women. Due to this support Celie evolves to possess a far more authentic identity which is further sustained by economic independence. Celie in order to reach this juncture had to overcome controlling stereotypes of "mule" and occasionally that of the "jezebel" which men who attempted to exploit her sought to impose upon her.

Though *The Color Purple* is not unique in its representation of the woman's search for self, the text has attracted considerable critical attention with regards to the role it accorded to erotic or emotional bonds between women of color. The paper attempts to validate the efficacy of this aspect of Walker's thesis. In order to do so the paper discusses Beatrice Culleton's novel *In Search of April Raintree* (1984) which is located in the Canadian Aboriginal literature. This novel deals with the oppression along race, class and gender that Métis women (i.e., those groups of people in the Canadian history who are part Native Indian and part white) experience in the North American continent. However the search for an identity in this novel is ultimately self-limiting, problematic and difficult. Where the bonds between women enabled Walker to radically assert Black womanhood, absence of support through such bonds implies that Culleton continues to seek emancipation within the domain of patriarchy and/ or white hegemony.

Brenda R. Smith, "We Need a Hero: African American Female *Bildungsromane* and Celie's Journey to Heroic Female Selfhood in Alice Walker's *The Color Purple*"

The Color Purple is Alice Walker's response to the need for representations of heroic females in African American women's literature and in their lives. This essay analyzes Walker's crafting of modern myth, focusing on the ways in which Walker adapts and transforms the archetypal male and female hero quest paradigms, as she writes her female protagonist into "heroic female selfhood." Through her syncretization of realism and fabulation, the reification of her visionary womanist doctrine, and her privileging of unconventional social conventions and narrative strategies, Walker successfully transcends the expected and accepted endings of quest for black women, like her protagonist Celie. The result is the creation of a womanist myth of empowerment for African American women that liberates them from their history of oppression, subordination, silence and passivity and actualizes the potentialities of agency in all areas of their lives—a modern myth for modern times. In creating a hero for African American women, Walker created a hero for others as well.

Ping Zhou, "Focalization Theory and the Epistolary Novel: A Narrative Analysis of *The Color Purple*"

An epistolary novel is a novel written in the form of a series of letters exchanged among the characters of the story. Focalization or point of view is an important concept in narratology, referring to the choice of a perspective from which the story is told . This essay scrutinizes Alice Walker's classic work *The Color Purple* in the light of the focalization theory developed by French narratologist Gerard Genette, who made a milestone demarcation between the narrator and the focal character. It analyzes four features of focalization employed in this work: the limitation of letter writers, the flexibility of letter writers, the alternating of different focal characters, and the polyphonic structure in the work. This essay argues from the narratological perspective that *The Color Purple* belongs to a modern canon of great epistolary novels.

About The Authors

Patricia Lynn Andujo received her Bachelor of Arts degree from Western Illinois University in Macomb, Illinois where she graduated magna cum laude in English in 1992. She continued her study at the University of Illinois at Urbana-Champaign receiving a M.A. in 1995 and a Ph.D. in 2002 in English. Her dissertation study, "Gendering the Pulpit: Religious Discourse and the African-American Female Experience," traces the entry of African-American women into religious discourse and their continuous appropriation of a literary tradition that grants them voice.

Ankujo has established her career in collegiate education. She taught English courses at the University of Illinois for ten years and Language Arts classes at Amelia Earhart Middle School in Riverside, California for three years. She is currently working as an Associate Professor in the English department at Azusa Pacific University in Azusa, California where she teaches a variety of course such as Freshmen Writing Seminar, Introduction to Literature, Children's Literature, and African-American Literature. Her research and teaching interests are in African-American literature, nineteenth and twentieth-century American literature, and religious studies and literature.

Turgay Bayindir is currently a PhD Candidate in Literary Studies at the Department of English, Purdue University. He received his MA degree in 2003 from Bogazici University in Istanbul, Turkey. His major areas of interest are Modernist British and American Literature, Gender Studies, and Queer Theory. He has also earned an official minor degree in Women's Studies at Purdue. He is in the process of writing his dissertation which is tentatively titled, "Queer Politics of Modernist Fiction on World War I." He is expecting to receive his Ph.D. degree in 2009.

Tracy L. Bealer is a Graduate School Fellow at the University of South Carolina, where she specializes in the 20th century American novel. Her dissertation investigates the intersection of love and violence in American racial politics, and focuses on literary representations of the body as a potential site for subverting racist and sexist hierarchies. She has presented papers on William Faulkner, Toni Morrison, and Zora Neale Hurston at national and regional conferences, and has two forthcoming publications in her secondary area of scholarly interest, popular culture and film.

Apryl Denny, Ph.D., is Professor of English Literature and Coordinator of Women's Studies at Viterbo University in La Crosse, WI. She is associate-editor of the final volume in the Cornell Wordsworth series, *Last Poems 1821-1850,* and author of publications on Oscar Wilde, Robert Browning, and Charles Dickens. Professor Denny currently resides with her daughter in La Crosse, WI.

Kathryn Edney is finishing her dissertation, "Gliding Through Our Memories: American Musical Theater Does 'History', 1943-2000s," in the American Studies Program at Michigan State University. She has presented at numerous national and regional conferences, including PMLA, PCA, and ATHE. She has published in *The Journal of Popular Culture* and contributed to the anthology *Brecht, Broadway and United States Theater*.

Robin E. Field is an Assistant Professor of English and the Director of Women's Studies at King's College in Wilkes-Barre, PA. She teaches courses on ethnic American literature, postcolonial fiction, and gender studies. She has published articles and reviews in *MELUS*, *South Asian Review*, *International Fiction Review*, and *Virginia Quarterly Review*. She is currently completing a book on representations of rape in contemporary American fiction.

Courtney George is currently a Ph.D. candidate in English at Louisiana State University, completing her dissertation on southern women writers' employment of blues, gospel, and country music in fiction. To date, her research in women writers and the blues has been published as articles in *Interdisciplinary Humanities* and *Studies in American Culture*, and related work is forthcoming by the *Southern Literary Journal* and *The New Encyclopedia of Southern Culture*. She has presented aspects of this research at several national and regional conferences including the Popular Culture Association, the South Central MLA, South Atlantic MLA, and the Southern American Studies Association.

Dr. Erin Huskey is an Assistant Professor of English and African American Studies at Valdosta State University. Her areas of specialization include African American Women's Literature, Modern and Contemporary American Literature, and Autobiography Theory. Her publications include an essay on Toni Morrison's novels forthcoming in *The Griot*, a pedagogical essay on collaborative writing in *Notes On Teaching English,* and a review of Yolanda Barnes' novel *When It Burned To The Ground* in *Third Coast.* Currently, she is working on an essay on quantum physics in Toni Morrison's novels, and a book-length manuscript that discusses the gospel ideology in the works of Alice Walker, Toni Morrison, and Suzan-Lori Parks.

Kheven LaGrone, Volume Editor. Art curator and writer based in the San Francisco Bay Area, Kheven LaGrone has written articles and essays for *The San Francisco Chronicle, San Francisco Bayview* and *The Journal of African American Men.* In addition, LaGrone has been involved in films about the arts, and his first video, *The Magic of the Ship* (a video presentation about the conversion of a World War I warship into an art space called The Artship) was screened at the Black International Cinema in Berlin, Germany and elsewhere in Europe in 2005.

In 2006, LaGrone created the art show "Black Artists' Expressions of Father," an exhibit which premiered in San Francisco and Richmond, California, and was later expanded in 2007, to become "BABA: Black Artists' Expressions of Father," a featured exhibit at the International Fatherhood Conference in Atlanta, Georgia. The show was eventually brought to New York City the following year. 2007 also marked his creation, along with his 19-year old nephew Jarrel Phillips, of the art show *"ASPIRE!* Black Teen Artists Interpretations of Success" which exhibited in San Francisco and Richmond California. LaGrone served as the curator of the visual arts program for 2008 AfroSolo Arts Festival in San Francisco.

A licensed civil engineer holding a BS in Civil Engineering from California State Polytechnic University, Pomona, and an MA in Mass Communication from Emerson College in Boston, LaGrone has shown his personal artwork in galleries in the San Francisco Bay Area. This is his first attempt at editing a volume of literary criticism.

Raphaël Lambert holds a PhD in English from the University of Wisconsin-Milwaukee. He is an assistant professor at the University of Tsukuba in Japan where he teaches jazz, the blues, slavery, and Hollywood cinema. His current research focuses on the media representations of the transatlantic slave trade. His recent publications and talks include works on Richard Wright's *Native Son*, Olaudah Equiano's *Interesting Narrative*, and Percival Everett's *Erasure*.

Marlon Rachquel Moore, University of Florida in Gainesville. She teaches and does research in 20th-century African American Literature with a focus on Gay & Lesbian epistemologies. Her work has appeared in *African American Review* and *The Journal of Film and Video*. She is currently co-editing an anthology of black southern lesbian writing.

Michael J. Meyer. Series Editor. Adjunct professor of English at DePaul and Northeastern Illinois Universities in Chicago, Meyer is the present bibliographer for Steinbeck studies, having published *The Hayashi Steinbeck Bibliography (1982-1996)* in 1998 (Scarecrow) and a follow-up volume (1996-2006) in 2008. In addition to his bibliographic work, Meyer's essays have appeared in the *The Steinbeck Quarterly, The Steinbeck Review,* and *The Steinbeck Newsletter*, and he has contributed chapters to numerous monographs and books, including serving as editor for *Cain Sign: The Betrayal of Brotherhood in The Works of John Steinbeck* (Mellen, 2000). He presently is the Poetry Editor and Bibliographer for *The Steinbeck Review* and serves on its editorial boar. Other publications include *A John Steinbeck Encyclopedia* (Greenwood 2006) where he served as co-editor with Brian Railsback. Since 1994, Meyer has been an editor for Rodopi Press's series *Perspectives in Modern Literature* where his seven volumes include *Literature and the Grotesque* (1995), *Literature and Music* (2002), and *Literature and The Law* (2003). As senior editor of Rodopi's new series entitled *Dialogues, he has supervised volumes* where classic canonical texts are examined on the basis of controversial issues and are discussed in parallel studies prepared by recent Ph. D's as well as by more experienced scholars. He is presently at work on a book for Scarecrow which will review the critical reception of Steinbeck's *Of Mice and Men* and which will appear in 2009.

Dr. Danielle Russell is an instructor at York University and Glendon College. She has taught courses in 20th Century American Literature, Victorian Literature, and Children's Literature. Recent publications include *Between the Angle and the Curve: Mapping Gender, Race, Space, and Identity in Cather and Morrison* (Routledge, 2006) and "Familiarity Breeds a Following: Transcending the Formulaic in the Snicket Series." *Telling Children's Stories: Narrative Theory and Children's Literature* (University of Nebraska Press, 2008 [Forthcoming]).

Uplabdhi Sangwan teaches undergraduate students at Delhi University in India. She has a Masters in Philosophy (English Literature) from the Department of English, Delhi University and a Master of Arts (English Literature) from Hans Raj College, Delhi University. Her areas of interest include women's studies, especially Indian women writers in English and Dalit women's narratives and writings. Her thesis dealt with three Indian novels in English namely Bama's *Karukku*, Sashi Deshpande's *The Dark Holds No Terrors* and Nayantara Sahgal's *Rich Like Us*. This comparison argued against the homogenizing label of "Third World Woman" and sought to use and create literary theory specifically suited for the complex hierarchy that comprises the Indian society (and not merely imported from West).

Brenda R. Smith (Ph.D., English, Case Western Reserve University, 2003) is Assistant Professor of English at Kent State University, Stark Campus, where she teaches African American Literature, Women's Literature, 19[th-] century and 20th-century American Literature, business writing, and first-year composition courses. Her essay, "Reaping What She Sows: The Evolution of African American Female *Bildung* and the Journey to Self from Zora Neale Hurston's *Their Eyes Were Watching God* to Octavia Butler's *Parable of the Sower*," is scheduled for publication in *New Essays on the African American Novel: From Hurston and Ellison to Morrison and Whitehead* (Palgrave Macmillan, 2008).

Ping Zhou is a professor of the School of Western Studies in Heilongjiang University, in the city of Harbin, China. She received her master degree of English Language and Literature from the

English Department of Heilongjiang University of China in 1999 and became a professor in the same year. She was the exchange scholar in the University of Illinois at Springfield, America from 2006 to 2007. She teaches Chinese English-major students courses such as translation, American Literature, Western Civilization. Her present area of specialization is narratology and eco-criticism of literature.

Index

Subject

Activist 151, 152, 155, 156, 214, 220, 258

Adaptation (of *The Color Purple* to film and to stage) 16, 215, 233, 243, 244, 280

African American Vernacular English 100, 102, 302

American race caste xxiii

American Book Award xiv

Anti-rape movement 151, 159, 156

Atlanta, Georgia ("The Color Purple" musical in) 226-241

Auditor (as an element of gospel ideology) 98-109

Authentic female selfhood 3,7

Bildung/Bildungsroman/ Bildungsromane 3-19, 95, 100, 101, 161, 175, 179, 180, 182

Bildungsroman/Bildungsromane (female) 7, 15, n18, 101, 161, 180

Bildungsroman/Bildungsromane (African American female) 18n

Black musical 227

Black Power Movement 152

Black women writers 3, n18, 38, 104, 151, 211, 218

Blackface (see also minstrelsy) 227, 228, 230, 231

Blues consciousness 78, 81, 84, 85

Blueswomen 77-83, 89

Blues womanist consciousness 141

Body,
disconnection from 206
healing powers 202, 206

Body/spirit binary 85, 89

Bonds between women 5, 9, 164, 175-189, 215, 260, 282

Broadway 226-244

Calvinism/Calvinist doctrine 49, 52-55

Canon (Locating *The Color Purple* in) 2, 26, 95, 173, 174, 209, 210, 251, 287

Capitalism 43-55

Childhood 14, 184, 196, 233

Christianity 12, 61, 62, 68, 74, 81, 85, 96, 127

Clitoral orgasm 86, 87

Collaboration 38, 239

Collective Memory 121-125, 129, 143

Colonialism 12, 179, 181, 187, 272

Colorism 27

Commodity 252-257, 265, 268

Community of choice 205

Controversy xiv, xv, xix, xxiv, 3, n39, n55, 175, 289

Creativity 11, 74, 81, 85, 106, 166, 196, 203, 218

Destiny 43, 45, 51, 166

Divinely inspired resistance 62-64

Domestic abuse 29-31, 65, 120-144, 177, 206, 272

Domestic comfort 196, 197

Domestic space 29, 34, 197, 201, 206

Domesticity as a subversive act 201

Double minority status 61, 62

Economic independence 11, 181-189

Eighteenth-century gendered class system 252

Elect (Calvinist doctrine) 53, 54

English novel, English traditional novel 254, n284